The Pious Sage in Job

The Pious Sage in Job

Eliphaz in the Context of Wisdom Theodicy

Kyle C. Dunham

WIPF & STOCK · Eugene, Oregon

THE PIOUS SAGE IN JOB
Eliphaz in the Context of Wisdom Theodicy

Copyright © 2016 Kyle C. Dunham. All rights reserved. Except for brief quotations in critical publications or reviews, no part of this book may be reproduced in any manner without prior written permission from the publisher. Write: Permissions, Wipf and Stock Publishers, 199 W. 8th Ave., Suite 3, Eugene, OR 97401.

Wipf & Stock
An Imprint of Wipf and Stock Publishers
199 W. 8th Ave., Suite 3
Eugene, OR 97401

www.wipfandstock.com

PAPERBACK ISBN: 978-1-62564-980-5
HARDCOVER ISBN: 978-1-4982-8563-6

Manufactured in the U.S.A.

Unless otherwise indicated, all Scripture quotations are from the ESV® Bible (The Holy Bible, English Standard Version®), copyright © 2001 by Crossway, a publishing ministry of Good News Publishers. Used by permission. All rights reserved.

Scripture quotations marked (NIV) are taken from the Holy Bible, New International Version®, NIV®. Copyright © 1973, 1978, 1984, 2011 by Biblica, Inc.™ Used by permission of Zondervan. All rights reserved worldwide. www.zondervan.com The "NIV" and "New International Version" are trademarks registered in the United States Patent and Trademark Office by Biblica, Inc.™

Scripture quotations marked (NASB) are taken from the New American Standard Bible®, Copyright © 1960, 1962, 1963, 1968, 1971, 1972, 1973, 1975, 1977, 1995 by The Lockman Foundation. Used by permission. (www.Lockman.org)

This book is dedicated to my lovely wife, Judith, who is rightly to be praised as a "helper fit for me" (עזר כנגדי) (Gen 2:18).

Contents

Preface | ix
Abbreviations | xi

1   Interpretive Ambiguity in Eliphaz | 1
2   The Interpretive History of Eliphaz | 15
3   Contemporary Approaches to Eliphaz | 90
4   The Meaning, Origin, and Theological Provenance of Eliphaz | 115
5   Exegesis and Correlation of the Eliphaz Speeches | 175
6   Conclusion | 232

Appendix | 235
Bibliography | 241
Index

Preface

THE BOOK OF JOB is an elusive masterpiece. St. Jerome famously compared the experience of reading it to that of grasping an eel: the more one squeezes it, the sooner it escapes. Particularly troubling is the conundrum the reader faces about what to do with Job's friends? Early on the reader realizes that Job is unimpressed, if not openly hostile, to their counsel. The antagonism only escalates as the interlocutors spar, parrying rhetorical blows with increasing vitriol. The verbal pugilism belies the seeming innocence of the friends' initial approach and calls into question their motivations. In the end God himself must intervene to referee the row, and the reader is left to wonder at the final narrative's surprising outcome and aftermath.

This unresolved tension over how to interpret the friends' purpose and function has resulted in a wide gamut of reactions. Vilified or lionized, the friends rarely have provoked a neutral response. In spite of the interpretive uncertainty, however, relatively few studies have focused on the nature of these fellow-sages, especially the chief interlocutor, Eliphaz, against the backdrop from which they emerge literarily. My purpose in this book is to fill this gap in small measure by exploring the milieu from which Eliphaz materializes. What is the source and nature of his counsel? Why does he speak in the way that he does? What expectations is the author creating for the implied original audience? Is the reader to sympathize with or repudiate his wisdom? In answering these questions the reader gains fuller insight into the rhetorical intention of the book, a better sense of its wisdom trajectory, and an enhanced understanding of its canonical shape and situation.

This book has its origins in my ThD dissertation written under the tutelage of Drs. William Barrick and Michael Grisanti. I am deeply grateful for their impact upon my own understanding of the Old Testament. In particular, Dr. Barrick served as my adviser and mentor, offering numerous suggestions to improve and hone this study along with fresh and insightful ways of thinking about the text. In the end, any shortcomings in the work are my own.

I must also acknowledge with profound gratitude the patience and grace of my wife, Judith, in supporting and encouraging me through many years of study. I could not have completed this task without her, and a simple word of thanks seems insufficient. Her faithfulness and encouragement are a model of steadfast love. This book is dedicated to her.

Kyle C. Dunham
Allen Park, MI

Abbreviations

AB	Anchor Bible
ABD	*The Anchor Bible Dictionary*. 6 vols. Edited by David Noel Freedman. New York: Doubleday, 1992.
ACCS	Ancient Christian Commentary on Scripture
ACEBT	*Amsterdamse Cahiers voor Exegese en bijbelse theologie*
AJSL	*American Journal of Semitic Languages and Literature*
AJT	*Asia Journal of Theology*
ANET	*Ancient Near Eastern Texts Relating to the Old Testament*. 3rd ed. Edited by James E. Pritchard. Princeton: Princeton University Press, 1969.
Ang	*Angelicum*
AOAT	Alter Orient und Altes Testament
AsTJ	*Asbury Theological Journal*
AUSS	*Andrews University Seminary Studies*
BA	*Biblical Archaeologist*
BASOR	*Bulletin of the American Schools of Oriental Research*
BBR	*Bulletin for Biblical Research*
BDB	Francis Brown, S. R. Driver, and Charles A. Briggs. *Hebrew and English Lexicon of the Old Testament*. Oxford: Clarendon, 1907.
BEC	Baker Exegetical Commentary
BHT	Beiträge zur historischen Theologie

Bib	*Biblica*
BibInt	*Biblical Interpretation*
BibS(N)	*Biblische Studien (Neukirchen, 1951–)*
BJRL	*Bulletin of the John Rylands Library*
BJS	Brown Judaic Studies
BKAT	Biblischer Kommentar, Altes Testament
BN	*Biblische Notizen*
BSac	*Bibliotheca Sacra*
BT	*The Bible Translator*
BV	*Biblical Viewpoint*
BZ	*Biblische Zeitschrift*
BZAW	Beihefte zur Zeitschrift für die alttestamentliche Wissenschaft
CAD	*The Assyrian Dictionary of the Oriental Institute of the University of Chicago*. Edited by Marth T. Roth. Chicago: Oriental Institute, 1956–<2006>.
CBQ	*Catholic Biblical Quarterly*
CBQMS	Catholic Biblical Quarterly Monograph Series
ChrCent	*Christian Century*
CJT	*Canadian Journal of Theology*
ConBOT	Coniectanea biblica: Old Testament Series
COut	Commentaar op het Oude Testament
CTJ	*Calvin Theological Journal*
CTQ	*Concordia Theological Quarterly*
CurBS	*Currents in Research: Biblical Studies*
CurTM	*Currents in Theology and Mission*
DBSJ	*Detroit Baptist Seminary Journal*
DCH	*Dictionary of Classical Hebrew*. Edited by D. J. A. Clines. Sheffield, England: Sheffield Academic Press, 1993–<2011>.

EdF	Erträge der Forschung
EncJud	*Encyclopedia Judaica*
EstBib	*Estudios bíblicos*
ESV	English Standard Version
EvQ	*Evangelical Quarterly*
EvT	*Evangelische Theologie*
ExpTim	*Expository Times*
FOTL	Forms of the Old Testament Literature
FRLANT	Forschungen zur Religion und Literatur des Alten und Neuen Testaments
GKC	*Gesenius' Hebrew Grammar*. Edited by E. Kautzsch. Translated by A. E. Cowley. 2d ed. Oxford, 1910.
GTJ	*Grace Theological Journal*
HALOT	Koehler, Ludwig and Walter Baumgartner. *Hebrew and Aramaic Lexicon of the Old Testament*. Revised by Walter Baumgartner and Johann J. Stamm. Translated and edited by M. E. J. Richardson. Leiden: E. J. Brill, 2001.
HAR	*Hebrew Annual Review*
HAT	Handbuch zum Alten Testament
HeyJ	*Heythrop Journal*
HNTC	Harper's New Testament Commentaries
HS	*Hebrew Studies*
HSM	Harvard Semitic Monographs
HTR	*Harvard Theological Review*
HUCA	*Hebrew Union College Annual*
ICC	International Critical Commentary
IDB	*The Interpreter's Dictionary of the Bible*. 4 vols. Edited by G. A. Buttrick. Nashville: Abingdon, 1962.
Int	*Interpretation*

ISBE	*International Standard Bible Encyclopedia*. 4 vols. Edited by G. W. Bromiley. Grand Rapids: Eerdmans, 1979–1988.
JAOS	*Journal of the American Oriental Society*
JATS	*Journal of the Adventist Theological Society*
JBL	*Journal of Biblical Literature*
JBQ	*Jewish Biblical Quarterly*
JETS	*Journal of the Evangelical Theological Society*
JHS	*Journal of the Hebrew Scriptures*
JNES	*Journal of Near Eastern Studies*
JNSL	*Journal of Northwest Semitic Languages*
JPOS	*Journal of the Palestine Oriental Society*
JPS	Jewish Publication Society
JR	*Journal of Religion*
JSOT	*Journal for the Study of the Old Testament*
JSOTSup	Journal for the Study of the Old Testament Supplement Series
JSP	*Journal for the Study of the Pseudepigrapha*
JTS	*Journal of Theological Studies*
KAT	Kommentar zum Alten Testament
KD	*Kerygma und Dogma*
KJV	King James Version
LQ	*Lutheran Quarterly*
LXX	The Septuagint
MT	Masoretic Text
NAC	New American Commentary
NASB	New American Standard Bible
NDBT	*New Dictionary of Biblical Theology*. Edited by T. D. Alexander and B. S. Rosner. Downers Grove, IL: InterVarsity, 2000.
NCB	The New Century Bible

NET	New English Translation
NIB	*The New Interpreter's Bible*. 12 vols. Nashville: Abingdon, 1996.
NIBCNT	New International Biblical Commentary on the New Testament
NIBCOT	New International Biblical Commentary on the Old Testament
NICOT	New International Commentary on the Old Testament
NIDOTTE	*New International Dictionary of Old Testament Theology and Exegesis*. 5 vols. Edited by W. A. VanGemeren. Grand Rapids: Zondervan, 1997.
NIGTC	New International Greek Testament Commentary
NIV	New International Version
NovT	*Novum Testamentum*
NRSV	New Revised Standard Version
OG	Old Greek Version
Or	*Orientalia* (NS)
OTE	Old Testament Essays
OTL	Old Testament Library
OTS	Old Testament Studies
OtSt	*Oudtestamentische Studiën*
PEQ	Palestine Exploration Quarterly
Proof	*Prooftexts: A Journal of Jewish Literary History*
PRSt	Perspectives in Religious Studies
PSB	Princeton Seminary Bulletin
RB	*Revue biblique*
RevExp	*Review and Expositor*
RSR	*Recherches de science religieuse*
RTR	Reformed Theological Review
SBJT	Southern Baptist Journal of Theology

SBLDS	Society of Biblical Literature Dissertation Series
SBLMS	Society of Biblical Literature Monograph Series
SBLSCS	Society of Biblical Literature Septuagint and Cognate Studies
SBT	Studies in Biblical Theology
Sem	Semitica
SJOT	Scandinavian Journal of the Old Testament
SJT	Scottish Journal of Theology
Sound	Soundings
StudBib	Studia Biblica
TBei	Theologische Beiträge
ThTo	Theology Today
TLOT	Theological Lexicon of the Old Testament
TMSJ	The Master's Seminary Journal
TNTC	Tyndale New Testament Commentaries
TOTC	Tyndale Old Testament Commentaries
Transeu	Transeuphratène
TrinJ	Trinity Journal
TynBul	Tyndale Bulletin
UBL	Ugaritisch-biblische Literatur
UF	Ugarit-Forschungen
VT	Vetus Testamentum
WBC	Word Biblical Commentary
WC	Westminster Commentaries
WHJP	World History of the Jewish People
WMANT	Wissenschaftliche Monographien zum Alten und Neuen Testament
ZAW	Zeitschrift für die alttestamentliche Wissenschaft
ZTK	Zeitschrift für Theologie und Kirche

1

Interpretive Ambiguity in Eliphaz

FOR MILLENNIA INTERPRETERS OF the book of Job have struggled to grasp the complexities of this literary masterpiece.[1] For many readers the intricacies of the dialogue in Job exhibit its greatness, and the book commonly garners literary praise.[2] Yet the interpretive difficulties intensify when the reader attempts to assess the role which the author[3] intended for the three companions of Job: Eliphaz, Bildad, and Zophar. The biblical narrative reports unexpectedly and succinctly that the friends, upon hearing of "all this evil" that had befallen Job, "made an appointment together to come to show

---

1. Robert Alter notes that Job is "the very pinnacle of ancient Hebrew poetry" and "the biblical text that is most daring and innovative in its imagination of God and man" (*The Literary Guide to the Bible*, 15), while John A. Baker deems Job to be the "supreme masterpiece of Israel's wisdom tradition" ("The Book of Job," 17). Yet on the occasional interpretive opacity of Job, John C. L. Gibson laments: "Try to pin this book down and it slips like sand through your fingers" (*Job*, 1).

2. Thomas Carlyle (1795–1881) opined that Job is "one of the grandest things ever written with pen" and that "there is nothing written, I think, in the Bible or out of it, of equal literary merit" ("Heroes and Hero-Worship," 12:59).

3. Although it is impossible to identify the author of Job with certainty, I will contend that an eye toward authorial intent is not only methodologically sound but necessary. E. M. Good argues contrarily, for example, that "even if we could identify the author, we would learn nothing useful for understanding the book" because "the ancient world's assumption about authorship, composition and integrity of the book were so different from ours that all our habitual moves in thinking about books are wrong" (*In Turns of Tempest*, 2, 6). This assertion overlooks the significance, however, of precisely the triangulation of author, text, and audience which "offers an intelligible and productive approach to a text, including the book of Job" ("Was Elihu, the Son of Barachel, the Author of the Book of Job?" 150; Weinberg, "Authorship and Author," 157–69).

him sympathy and comfort him" (Job 2:11).[4] The friends' abrupt appearance, not to mention ensuing long-windedness, incites the reader's curiosity to determine who they are, what exactly they are saying, how they are to be perceived as saying it, and the rationale for speaking as they do. Moreover, the unfolding book increasingly teases the reader to comprehend the nature of the purported "sympathy" and "comfort" that the friends intend to deliver to their erstwhile friend.

In any such assessment of the friends, the interpretive ambiguities implicit in the primary interlocutor Eliphaz emerge quickly to the fore.[5] Eliphaz ranks ostensibly as the eldest and most respected of the three companions for he is the first to speak and his speeches are longer than the others'.[6] A number of scholars thus repute him to be the orthodox warden of traditional wisdom theology who, if in any way blameworthy, little more than errs in the application of his theological principles.[7] In addition, Eliphaz has an integral, even paradigmatic, role in the book as the chief counselor among the friends.[8] His speeches touch upon each of the various theodicies put forth by the human speakers in Job. Still, others soundly criticize Eliphaz for the asperity with which he relentlessly upbraids Job, particularly in his later speeches.[9] A few cast him as a villain who wishes

---

4. Unless otherwise noted, all Scriptural citations are from the English Standard Version (Wheaton, IL: Crossway, 2011).

5. James E. Harding concludes in his study of Eliphaz's first speech, for example, that the "elusive, ambiguous Hebrew of the book of Job" leads ineluctably to "interpretive indeterminacy" ("A Spirit of Deception," 165–66).

6. Gordis, *The Book of God and Man*, 77.

7. Gibson, "Eliphaz the Temanite," 259–72. David Atkinson posits that "Eliphaz seems to be the oldest, profoundest, gentlest, and generally nicest of the three friends" (*The Message of Job*, 41). Georg Fohrer emphasizes the careful and tranquil demeanor of Eliphaz: "Er tritt ruhig und freundlich auf und antwortet behutsam, gütig und vorsichtig" ("He appears calm and friendly, and answers cautiously, gently, and carefully") (*Das Buch Hiob*, 134). Arthur S. Peake concurs that "there is no fault to be found with Eliphaz for the tone of his speech. It is very considerate and tender" (*Job*, 77).

8. As Melanie Köhlmoos observes: "Alle drei Eliphasreden sind darüber hinaus inhaltlich programmatisch für den jeweiligen Dialogabschnitt und die folgende Argumentation der Freunde. Daraus läßt sich jedoch weder ein Schluß hinsichtlich der Charakterisierung des Eliphas ziehen noch vermuten, daß die beiden anderen Freunde nach Eliphas' Ausführungen jeweils nicht mehr viel zur Debatte beizutragen hätten" ("All three speeches of Eliphaz are furthermore programmatic in content for the respective dialogue portions and the ensuing argumentation of the friends. From this, however, is permitted neither to draw a conclusion regarding the characteristic of Eliphaz nor to suppose that both of the other friends after Eliphaz's expositions have contributed nothing more in each case to the debate") (*Das Auge Gottes*, 187n1). See also the excellent survey by Nicholson, "The Limits of Theodicy," 71–82.

9. As John Chrysostom states: "Even if the words are right, they do not come from

ruthlessly to destroy Job at once.¹⁰ With more pointed angst, some accuse Eliphaz of turning into a diabolical tool exploited inadvertently to foist the sinister deception of Satan upon the hapless—and helpless—victim Job.¹¹ A cursory reading of the book of Job confirms that it is little wonder such a range of interpretations for Eliphaz has arisen. Eliphaz, on the one hand, ranks among the most eloquent speakers in the book—indeed perhaps all of Scripture¹²—yet Yahweh singles him out for harsh rebuke.¹³ At first blush one struggles to resolve these apparent inconsistencies.

At least as early as the translation of the Septuagint, interpreters of Job have deliberated over the intended role for the three friends.¹⁴ In the earliest Greek rendering of Job, the Septuagint translator(s) appears to soften the harshness of Eliphaz and the other friends, turning them (along with Job) into petty kings¹⁵ and rendering their speeches more urbane and sophisticated

---

a right intention, aimed not at correction, not at advice, not at reform (it is no ignoramus [they] are lecturing), but at *overthrow*" (*Commentary on Job*, 120, emphasis mine). Moses Buttenwieser agrees that "the conciliatory tone which he occasionally uses, and which has been thought to show consideration, is simply prompted by the hypocritical desire to be friendly" (*The Book of Job*, 161).

10. C. J. Ball is unsparing in his criticism: "Eliphaz is reluctant to argue with a sick man but feels bound to remonstrate with unreasonable despair" (*The Book of Job*, 133). Morris Jastrow views Eliphaz as blunt and tactless and characterizes him as unctuously suggesting that Job "ought to be willing to take some of the medicine that he has so frequently poured down the throats of others" (*The Book of Job*, 210).

11. Fyall, *Now My Eyes Have Seen You*, 146.

12 A. B. Davidson remarks that Eliphaz's speech is one of the masterpieces of the book of Job (*The Book of Job*, 41), while Kemper Fullerton acknowledges that "the first speech of Eliphaz is one of the most carefully thought-out and artistic speeches in the book" ("Double Entendre," 326).

13. In Job 42:7 Yahweh rebukes Eliphaz: "After the LORD had spoken these words to Job, the LORD said to Eliphaz the Temanite: 'My anger burns against you and against your two friends, for you have not spoken of me what is right, as my servant Job has.'" This text—along with the interpretive dilemma it creates—was particularly vexing to Calvin (see Schreiner, "'Through a Mirror Dimly,'" 182).

14. As Buttenwieser notes: "As early as the Greek translation of Job, we have, I believe, evidence that a fixed interpretation must have been current" (*The Book of Job*, viii). The nature of LXX Job is complex, and several articles and monographs have devoted attention to it (e.g., see Orlinsky, "Studies in the Septuagint of the Book of Job," (1957), 53–74; (1958), 229–71; (1959), 153–67; (1961), 239–68; Orlinsky, "The Septuagint as Holy Writ," 89–114; Gerleman, *Studies in the Septuagint*; Gard, *Exegetical Method*). As noted below, the LXX version is 15–20% shorter in length of text than the Masoretic text, and the two traditions differ in several notable respects (for a helpful overview, see Vicchio, *The Image of the Biblical Job*, 102–13).

15. LXX Job 2:11 reads with regard to Eliphaz: Ελιφας ὁ Θαιμανων βασιλεύς, "Eliphaz, the *king* of the Temanites." Bildad and Zophar are also kings of their respective regions.

than one might construe from an observant reading of the Hebrew text.[16] In the New Testament the apostle Paul appears to quote authoritatively from the sage, leading to further interpretive uncertainty.[17] Yet this citation would not presage that all would turn out well amongst Eliphaz's literary audience. Although the early church would treat him ambivalently, by the Middle Ages a handful of earnest but narrow interpreters would all but come to blows with him. An interpretive bipolarity would hound Eliphaz following the Reformation and Enlightenment. In the nineteenth and early twentieth centuries, with few exceptions interpreters kept him at arm's length, denouncing his apparent theological excesses. By the middle of the twentieth century Eliphaz would emerge from an "interpretive rehab" to enjoy something of a renaissance among critical scholars which has lasted in some circles to the present day. Into the twenty-first century, a growing number of synchronic and literary studies suggest an emerging minority voice that the author of Job intended Eliphaz's role to remain purposively ambiguous and indeterminate both in semantic meaning and in literary purpose.[18]

Eliphaz as Pernicious Counselor with No Theological Contribution

In its interpretative history the perceived role for Eliphaz and his compeers tended to divide primarily along two lines. On the one hand, the friends were scoundrels who were to be summarily dismissed as the shallow counterpoint to Job, manipulated skillfully by the author (then exposed and contravened) to emphasize by contrast the principal tenets of the book.[19] The friends thus construed merely illustrate more vividly the chief challenge addressed by the book: How must one reconcile the sufferings of the innocent with the righteousness of God? Through this heuristic lens the author makes glib use of the friends in order to scandalize the perspectives they hold to and to assert that such theological criteria could no longer

---

16. Dell, *Job as Sceptical Literature*, 13–16; Gard, *Exegetical Method*, 17–19.

17. Paul cites Job 5:13 in 1 Cor 3:19: "For it is written, 'He catches the wise in their craftiness.'" The use of the scriptural citation formula "it is written" appears to afford scriptural authority to Eliphaz's words. As will be noted below, perhaps Gregory the Great most keenly feels the tension created by the apostle's quotation of such a putatively ruthless character. Gregory's allegorizing hermeneutic absolves him from the dilemma, however.

18. On this see Good, *In Turns of Tempest*; Harding, "A Spirit of Deception," 137–66; Hoffman, *A Blemished Perfection*.

19. James Barr speaks in this way of Job's "faceless friends" ("Job and Its Modern Interpreters," 43).

be sustained.[20] Typically a corollary to this view is the judgment that the speeches of the friends are wooden and static—with little variety of expression and no variety of substance.[21] These perspectives hold in common that the reader must disavow the role and vantage point of the friends both in their intended purpose and approach, as the friends offer no viable contribution to the theodicy or theological outlook of Job.

Eliphaz as Sophisticated Counselor with Substantial Theological Contribution

Recent studies, on the other hand, such as that of Newsom, seek to rehabilitate Job's friends in hopes of perceiving more acutely "the sense of moral dilemma which the dialogue is capable of providing."[22] Newsom observes that "the literary genre of the wisdom dialogue, which serves as the model for the conversation between Job and his friends, suggests that the exchange was probably intended as a more evenly balanced debate."[23] Manfred Oeming likewise contends that the friends have fared badly at the hands of interpreters in spite of clues in the text that the reader ought to perceive them as "true friends and good ministers":

> The friends of Job set out to try numerous ways to provide relief in external and internal adversity as confidants in his contestation by reference to God and his earlier relationship to Him. In the reception history, they have, however—like

---

20. Bruce Zuckerman appropriates this view by arguing that the book of Job is in reality a parody in which the author appropriates the traditional folktale of "Job the patient" to expostulate against its pietistic worldview (*Job the Silent*, 93). He speculates that the three friends are the invention of the Joban poet created to play the foil to Job's "contrapuntal role" as protester against traditional piety. "The Friends have become, as it were, Anti-Friends who oppose the Anti-Job" (48). Cf. Brenner, "Job the Pious?" 37–52.

21. Samuel R. Driver and George B. Gray favor this tack: "So far as the friends are concerned it is of the very essence of the writer's purpose that they should one and all say essentially the same thing: they are not introduced to represent many existing theories; but the three of them, expounding the same theory, represent that as the unchallenged judgment of ancient and still current opinion" (*Job*, 1:lvi).

22. Newsom, "Job and His Friends," 240.

23. Ibid., 239. Newsom complains elsewhere that the friends are "seldom taken seriously as articulating a view of reality that might have its own claims to truth." She concludes that "such an attitude, though nobly motivated, diminishes the intellectual challenge of the book. What is lost when the friends are dismissed is the generic force of the wisdom dialogue as a confrontation between two significant but incommensurable perspectives" (*The Book of Job*, 90–91).

Job's wife—encountered extremely negative reviews. They are considered as insensitive phrasemongers, pitiful comforters who did not perceive the needs of their specific opponent, who rather with only a dogma which protects God, 'gave a whipping.' I regard these negative opinions as not appropriate to the text; it appears to me that the intention of the poem goes along to draw them as genuine friends and good ministers.[24]

Oeming identifies three specific areas in which he argues that the author purposively underscores the friends as effective counselors.[25] First, by their silent presence at the outset of the interchange (a noteworthy feat in itself) they express solidarity and patience with Job. In this way they are set up from the outset as concerned friends and wise counselors. Second, rather than brashly rushing in, they exhibit the kindness of restrained listening as they sit seven interminable days to wait and discover first what the sufferer himself will say. Only after this does Eliphaz begin his dialogue "very sensitively and cautiously." Third, the friends perceive one another in the ensuing dispute not simply as "reflectors" or "repeaters" but rather as participants in the deliberate process of dialogical exchange by which they are working out a mutually satisfying resolution and bringing to bear pastoral care (*Seelsorge*) upon Job in his adversity.[26] They exhibit their thoughtful *Seelsorge* through several sensitive and pertinent means: vivid reminders of the robust theological position which Job himself affirmed during his former good standing, repeated references to the divine promises of relief

---

24. "Die Freunde des in äußerliche und innerliche Not geratenen Hiob versuchen mancherlei, um dem Vertrauten in seiner Anfechtung durch Verweis auf Gott und seine [frühere] Beziehung zu ihm Linderung zu verschaffen. In der Rezeptionsgeschichte haben sie—wie Hiobs Frau—jedoch denkbar schlechte Beurteilungen gefunden. Sie gelten als unsensible Phrasendrescher, als erbarmliche Tröster, die nicht die Bedürfnisse des konkreten Gegenübers wahrnahmen, sondern nur ein Dogma, das Gott schützt, 'durchpeitschten'. Ich halte diese negativen Urteile für nicht textgemäß; mir scheint, dass die Intention der Dichtung dahin geht, sie als echte Freunde und gute Seelsorger zu zeichnen" (Oeming, "Die Dialoge mit Frau und Freunden," 46) (my translation).

25. Ibid., 46–47.

26. In a similar vein Terrien attests that the author does not construe the friends merely as straw men in the argumentative flow of the book. Rather, the author seeks to render the would-be comforters beguilingly attractive to the reader. By doing so, the reader is drawn into the movement of the dialogue and by the end of the book astonished by the progressive disclosure of the fallacies inherent in the friends' theology. Terrien proposes that the author "never opposed the theology of the friends to that of the hero as if the former were false and the latter true. In effect, he clearly conveyed his conviction that the theological position of the friends was closely akin to that of Job, thus rendering the distinction between them the more important because it was the less apparent" (*Job*, 68).

insofar as Job humbles himself before the hallowed counsels of wisdom, a call to remembrance of the "common property of theological wisdom" pertaining particularly to the importance of *Läuterungsleiden* as a palliative for Job's suffering,[27] and a consistent application of the act-outcome connection to provide Job safe harbor in which to confess sins and seek reconciliation with God. These more recent scholars do not view the friends simplistically as farcical caricatures of the ancient sage or as ideological simpletons but as serious-minded, theologically sophisticated counselors and authentic companions seeking to find resolution to Job's agony.[28]

Eliphaz as a Normative ANE Counselor with Substantial (Though Flawed) Theological Contribution

The following study proposes a composite approach to Eliphaz as the chief interlocutor by a careful assessment of the milieu from which he emerges. Neither an insipid straw-man nor a parodied buffoon, he ties together important elements of ancient Near Eastern theodicy to suggest that Job's only viable resolution is *divine appeasement*. Job has sinned, it is true, and now must utilize all the resources at his disposal to bring about renewed favor from God. Eliphaz embodies the most cherished tenets of the ancient Near Eastern views of suffering and divine providence, and he employs all the available authoritative sources to convince Job and the others of the soundness of his principles. Job's failure to acquiesce, however, embarrasses Eliphaz and ushers in the dramatic and stunning outcome of the book. Previous Joban studies have insufficiently undertaken a consistent and thorough comparison and contrast of Eliphaz—especially with respect to his role and speeches in the book of Job—with the ancient Near Eastern backdrop out of which his ideas materialize. In the course of this study, I will conclude that Eliphaz merits a prominent place in the book of Job as the leading proponent of the finest elements of ancient Near Eastern—and, ultimately, of human—wisdom.

---

27. D. Karl Budde coined the term *Läuterungsleiden*, denoting suffering for eudaemonistic ends, in this connection (*Das Buch Hiob*, xxxv).

28. Selms, *Job*, 17.

Opportunities for Advancement in the Approach to Eliphaz

This brief identification of these poles in historical approaches to Eliphaz, as well as the suggestion of the need for a composite approach, highlights several insufficiencies in the progress of scholarship which have impeded a satisfactory understanding of Eliphaz's place and purpose in Job. A brief outline of these shortcomings will provide the reader with a rough outline of the intended contours of the present study. First, prior approaches have exhibited neither a sufficient nor comprehensive understanding of Eliphaz's reception history. Awareness of the diverse ways in which Eliphaz has been read by various interpretative traditions furnishes a broader outlook for the contemporary interpreter, thus freeing him or her from many of the pitfalls to which previous generations of readers have been predictably susceptible. A wider grasp of Eliphaz's reception history provides firmer footing to move forward in exploring fresh ways to understand Eliphaz's theology and purpose in the book.

Second, previous examinations have failed to explore fully the potential implications for Eliphaz's Edomite provenance.[29] The principal characters in Job are likely Edomite: Job is from Uz (Job 1:1), a land most probably to be identified with Edom southeast of Palestine,[30] and Eliphaz is from Teman (Job 2:11), a locality bordering Edom proper and associated both with Edom and with Edomite wisdom.[31] Edom was renowned traditionally for its wisdom, and the bearing that this wisdom tradition has on Eliphaz's theological outlook and role in the book have not been thoroughly explored. Recent studies of the Edomite dialect and Edomite inscriptions shed additional light on the religious and wisdom context from which Eliphaz and the other friends likely emerged.[32] Further, these connections provide insight

---

29. Joseph Blenkinsopp notes how Eliphaz and the other friends draw upon the legendary wisdom of the Edomites and Arabs (*Wisdom and Law in the Old Testament*, 56). Cf. 1 Kgs 4:30.

30. So Terrien, *Job*, 51; Clines, *Job 1–20*, 10. Lamentations 4:21 clearly points in this direction: "Rejoice and be glad, O daughter of Edom, you who dwell in the land of Uz."

31. Thus Fedrizzi, *Giobbe*, 83; Andersen, *Job*, 94; Horst, *Hiob 1–19*, 32; Balentine, *Job*, 66; Selms, *Job*, 5, 14; Diana V. Edelman, "Edom: A Historical Geography," 10. For the frequent Scriptural connections between Teman and Edom, see Jer 49:7, 20; Ezek 25:13; Amos 1:11–12; Obad 9. For the connections especially between Teman and Edomite wisdom, see Jer 49:7; Bar 3:22–23; Obad 8–9.

32. See Dearman, "Edomite Religion," 119–36; Vanderhooft, "The Edomite Dialect and Script," 137–57; Ahituv, "An Edomite Ostracon," 33–37; Dicou, *Edom, Israel's Brother and Antagonist*; Sasson, "An Edomite Joban Text with a Biblical Joban Parallel," 606–15; Emerton, "New Light on Israelite Religion," 2–20.

into the role of the ANE sage-counselor in dispensing pastoral wisdom to the righteous sufferer.[33]

Third, an overly restrictive view of the wisdom sources from which Eliphaz likely constructed his theological response have hampered interpretative approaches to Eliphaz. For example, Joban scholars frequently have cast Eliphaz as a narrow-minded proponent of Deuteronomic retributive theology. Such an anachronistic approach, however, fails to appreciate the multi-faceted sources and perspectives within the wisdom traditions from which Eliphaz likely drew.[34] Closely related to this, only recently have scholars begun to explore the intertextuality Eliphaz shares with several other sapiential and didactic passages scattered throughout the OT.[35] These affinities offer a potential connection for discerning why the translator(s) of the LXX and eventually Christian writers were predisposed to regard Eliphaz favorably.[36]

Fourth, current studies of Eliphaz have not fully developed an understanding of his role against the backdrop of the ANE theodicies in the wider Mesopotamian wisdom tradition. While comparative studies have deliberated at some length upon the book of Job at the macro-level vis-à-vis other ANE parallels,[37] these studies have not undertaken a thorough consideration of wisdom theodicy traditions with respect to the role of the chief interlocutor—the task fulfilled most prominently here by Eliphaz.[38] Correlating these

33. Rainer Albertz touches upon the "pastoral dimension" of the wisdom milieu of Job and the three friends ("The Sage and Pious Wisdom," 250).

34. Again helpful in this connection is Albertz, "The Sage and Pious Wisdom," 251–52. Cf. also Gordis, *Poets, Prophets, and Sages*, 288.

35. On this see the study of Pyeon, *You Have Not Spoken What Is Right*, 111–17.

36. On the possible toning down of offensive elements in Eliphaz (and the other friends) in the LXX, see Gard, *Exegetical Method*, 6–31; Dell, *Job as Sceptical Literature*, 16.

37. See Jastrow, "A Babylonian Parallel to the Story of Job," 135–91; Walton, *Ancient Israelite Literature*, 170–83; Yates, "Understanding the Book of Job," 448–49; Gray, "Job in the Context of Near Eastern Literature," 251–69; Albertson, "Job and Ancient Near Eastern Wisdom Literature," 213–30.

38. Gerald Mattingly, in an insightful essay on the nature of ANE theodicy, identifies the likely link between the perspective of Eliphaz (and the other friends) with the perspective of the customary sapiential counselors in the Mesopotamian tradition: "The Mesopotamian poets agree with the Hebrew sages in their assessment of mankind's sinful nature, and they indicate that such dogmas have the authority of ancient tradition behind them and are not to be taken lightly. Finally, all of these sages agree that the pious sufferer will find a solution to his dilemma by appealing to the Divine, a personal god, Marduk, or Elohim. Divine assistance is necessary because the nature of man will prohibit him from solving this problem alone" ("The Pious Sufferer," 335–36). Cf. also Lévêque on "le juste souffrant" (*Job et Son Dieu*, 42–47).

perspectives will have implications for discerning how readers in the ANE context would have viewed the friends, including expectations they would harbor for Eliphaz as the principal sage. In addition, putting together these perspectives provides insight into the social context of wisdom, namely, how ANE wisdom was applied pastorally in a context such as that in which Job and the friends find themselves.

Finally, drawing together these insights will provide a greater understanding of the book of Job. If Eliphaz and the other friends are expected, in the tradition of ANE wisdom theology, to lead Job into repentance and reconciliation with God and commensurately fail, this underscores a significant purpose for the author of Job. By means of the ineffectiveness of Eliphaz and the other friends, the author of Job is emphasizing the failure of traditional ANE theological perspectives to solve the deepest questions of suffering (several factors of which are still endemic to philosophical approaches today).[39] Thus, although Eliphaz brings forth the expected counsel of the wise, the biblical author of Job demonstrates that the counsel is flawed. The righteous sufferer may not fully resolve the antinomies inherent in the dichotomy between his or her plight vis-à-vis scriptural emphasis on the goodness and sovereignty of God. From this perspective one realizes that the book of Job functions as truly a remarkable counterpoint within the biblical wisdom writings.

Methodology and Scope of the Present Study

Before beginning the analysis of Eliphaz in his ancient Near Eastern context, I will offer several remarks concerning the methodology and scope of the present study. In his presidential address before the Society of Biblical Literature in 1961, Samuel Sandmel focused attention on a burgeoning phenomenon in biblical studies which he termed "parallelomania."[40] He defined *parallelomania* as the "extravagance among scholars which first overdoes the supposed similarity in passages and then proceeds to describe source and derivation as if implying literary connection flowing in an inevitable or predetermined direction."[41] By his own admission Sandmel did not wish to

---

39. This theme points up potential affinities to the *leitmotif*, for example, of Ecclesiastes. See Balentine, "Job's 'Struggle for the Last Truth About God,'" 579; Smith, "Is There a Place for Job's Wisdom," 19; Barr, "Job and Its Modern Interpreters," 44.

40. Although he himself did not coin the term, his focus upon the phenomenon was something of a watershed in comparative biblical studies and in contemporary discussion his name has come to be associated with a cautionary approach to counterbalance potential abuses. See Sandmel, "Parallelomania," 1–13.

41. Ibid., 1.

negate the value of comparative studies but simply to call attention to the illegitimate use of tenuous parallels, especially those used to justify claims about literary dependence or influence.[42] Since Sandmel's lecture a number of works addressing these concerns have led to useful refinements in comparative methodologies.[43]

William Hallo suggests a methodology in comparative studies which he terms the "contextual approach."[44] He describes the contextual approach as a refinement and broadening of the comparative method by wedding it to another approach called the "contrastive approach" in order to create a composite interpretative system (i.e., the "contextual approach"). The contextual approach concerns itself not so much with the sociological context behind the literary material as with "the literary context itself, broadly interpreted as including the entire Near Eastern literary milieu to the extent that it can be argued to have any conceivable impact on the biblical formulation."[45] The aim of the contextual approach is modest, assaying "not to find the key to every biblical phenomenon in some ancient Near Eastern precedent, but rather to silhouette the biblical text against its wider literary and cultural environment and thus to arrive at a proper assessment of the extent to which the biblical evidence reflects the environment or, on the contrary, is distinctive and innovative over against it."[46]

Hallo criticizes what he perceives as a weakness in most previous comparative studies whereby interpreters often sift the biblical text through the so-called objective facts gleaned from the external data of archaeology. He understands this process to be a "confrontation between unequals" in

---

42. As Sandmel states: "The key word in my essay is *extravagance*. I am not denying that literary parallels and literary influence, in the form of source and derivation, exist. I am not seeking to discourage the study of these parallels, but, especially in the case of the Qumran documents, to encourage them. However, I am speaking words of caution about exaggerations about the parallels and about source and derivation" (ibid., 1, emphasis mine). Although Sandmel focused primarily on rabbinic and NT studies, his circumspection was a helpful check to immoderation across the spectrum of biblical studies.

43. See Kitchen, *Ancient Orient and Old Testament*; Evans, Hallo, and White, eds., *Scripture in Context*; Hallo, Moyer, and Perdue, eds., *Scripture in Context II*; Hallo, Jones, and Mattingly, eds., *The Bible in the Light of Cuneiform Literature*; Walton, *Ancient Israelite Literature*; Roberts, *The Bible and the Ancient Near East*; Sparks, *Ancient Texts for the Study of the Hebrew Bible*; Walton, *Ancient Near Eastern Thought*; Oswalt, *The Bible Among Myths*.

44. Hallo credits this terminology as originating with John B. White but going back potentially even farther to K. A. Kitchen who began circulating the phrase in the 1970's ("Biblical History in Its Near Eastern Setting," 18n4).

45. Hallo, "Biblical History in Its Near Eastern Setting," 2.

46. Hallo, "Compare and Contrast," 3.

attempting to equate "two essentially incommensurable quantities."[47] Still, Hallo recognizes an ongoing need for and value in comparative analyses:

> Rather, it invites a reconsideration of the terms of the comparison. The biblical canon should be weighed, *not* against the archival data excavated from a distant corner of the Mitanni empire, but rather, on the one hand, against the occasional scrap of archival evidence recovered from the soil of Palestine itself and, on the other and far more important, against the literary formulations of the surrounding Near East. Only then will one be comparing commensurate quantities, and only then will one be operating with a standard equally applicable to the other cultures of the ancient Near East.[48]

Hallo thus champions an approach which judiciously utilizes by comparison and contrast the literature of the ambient ancient Near East in order to assess potential literary and conceptual import upon the biblical text. Such an approach for Hallo opens up fresh avenues for elucidating the text and understanding robustly the significance of the biblical message.

In his more recent study of the Hebrew Bible in the context of the ancient Near East, John Walton builds upon Hallo's work by offering three areas in which comparative studies may be useful to a contextualized understanding of the biblical text.[49] First, comparative studies are conducive to a critical analysis of the biblical text by advancing the ways in which one understands the history and literature of the biblical milieu. Such critical evaluation offers a helpful challenge to any scholarly or confessional "assured results" which may need refinement through accountability to the realities of the biblical context.[50] Second, comparative studies furnish a

---

47. Hallo, "Biblical History in Its Near Eastern Setting," 11.

48. Ibid., 12, emphasis his. Earlier Kenneth A. Kitchen had expressed similar concerns: "Principles found to be valid in dealing with Ancient Oriental history and literature will in all likelihood prove to be directly applicable to Old Testament history and literature—and conversely . . . methods or principles which are demonstrably false when applied to first-hand Ancient Near Eastern data should not be imposed upon Old Testament data either" (*Ancient Orient and Old Testament*, 28).

49. Walton, *Ancient Near Eastern Thought*, 38–40.

50. Walton's point should be taken with the caveat, however, that comparative studies themselves need to be accountable to the biblical text. In other words, while comparative studies may offer a check and balance to an erroneous interpretative consensus about certain texts, comparative studies also require a healthy check and balance. They are not an end in and of themselves but must be tied back to the propositions of the canonical text in a meaningful and correlative manner, subservient to the sacred text understood correlatively through what systematic theologians term the analogy of faith. We make clear at the outset that this is a presupposition in our study.

productive means to defend the biblical text against erratic and prejudiced use of cultural studies to proffer specious claims regarding the authenticity, reliability, date, or literary dependence of a biblical book. Third, comparative studies help to discern details in the biblical text for the purposes of proper exegesis, especially in areas in which some feature of the text has been improperly understood.

Taking cue from Hallo and Walton, I approach the comparative aspects of this study with a cautionary view. I seek to elucidate viable ways in which the role and purpose of Eliphaz are better understood through the lens of the cultural matrix out of which the text of Job emerges. The danger in such an approach, of course, is to superimpose elements gained from comparative analyses upon the biblical text. By the inapt application of the comparative approach, alleged insights into the context and environment—and therefore meaning—of the biblical passage may hold interpretive sway over the straightforward literary meaning of the text. A safeguard against this risk includes the acknowledgement of one's presuppositions concerning the inspiration and canonicity of Scripture as over against the relative value of data gleaned from comparative studies.[51] Therefore, I work from the text outward, seeking to utilize comparative studies for a sober assessment of the ways in which Eliphaz's role in Job is properly clarified. Chiefly one accomplishes this by a proper understanding of the role of the grief counselor in other ancient Near Eastern literary texts of theodicy. So then, in the following study I will adopt a cautionary comparative methodology or, in Hallo's terminology, a contextual approach to Eliphaz in the book of Job.

As to the scope of the study, I begin with a historical overview of the ways in which interpreters have handled Eliphaz since ancient times. I follow this with an evaluation of the biblical data for the provenance and theological perspective of Eliphaz. As part of this I will offer exegesis of salient portions of the Eliphaz speeches together with an appraisal of exegetical conclusions in the light of similar ANE works which aid in understanding of Eliphaz's role and theological perspective. Following this I will reach larger conclusions regarding a significant purpose for the book of Job deriving from Eliphaz's proposed purpose within the book.

Summary

Although Eliphaz embodies the highest achievement and most profound perspectives of human wisdom in the ANE, his outlook remains, in the end,

---

51. On the various issues related to this perspective, see Childs, *Introduction to the Old Testament as Scripture*, 71–83.

merely human. God's solution, on the other hand, is contrapuntal, and in the book of Job, as in history, God has the last say. Eliphaz, as an advocate of appeasement, is a foremost ancient theological legalist who seeks to attain righteousness before God (in later NT theological terminology *justification*) by humanly—rather than divinely—prescribed means.[52] As a legalist foreshadowing Mosaic law,[53] Eliphaz exhibits religious and theological traits that are endemic to humanity since the fall. Yet as with Adam, with Cain, and with others from the very origins of human history, Eliphaz's improper means of attaining righteousness with the offended God culminates in failure. The book of Job and the events and speeches outlined demonstrate to readers within religious communities significant truths about sin, suffering, righteousness, and divine providence that would provide in the millennia to come not only grist for thoughtful and sustained theological reflection, but also nurturing solace for the despairing believer. Through the book's vigorous characterization and portrayal of God, who directs and sustains creation and, moreover, one comprehends more fully the divine, benevolent providence which directs the details of life for God's people.[54] Before soaring to the lofty grandeurs of divine providence, however, we must first understand how ancient readers viewed Job—and therefore Eliphaz—as literary figures and sages within their tradition.

---

52. Eliphaz uses the standard Hebrew term meaning "to be righteous" (צדק) only three times in his speeches (4:17; 15:14; 22:3) yet the concept is prevalent throughout his discourses as he enjoins divine appeasement as a means for Job to regain favor with the offended deity. Eliphaz's concern is clearly in line with a prominent trajectory of the later wisdom movement itself. A central purpose of wisdom, after all, is this—correlating revelation from God with observations from life in order to attain "righteousness" with God and, in turn, with others (Prov 1:7 "The fear of the Lord is the beginning of knowledge"). Sinclair Ferguson refers to the narrow type of approach to righteousness with God that Eliphaz espouses as the "Elder Brother Syndrome" in his sermon "Christian Service."

53. I argue for a pre-Mosaic composition of Job. On this, see the appendix.

54. As Rowley acknowledges, the message of Job is not intended solely to be an intellectual solution to the problem of suffering but moreover is to undergird the "spiritual miracle of the wresting of profit from the suffering through the enrichment of the fellowship of God" ("Job and Its Meaning," 207).

2

The Reception History of Eliphaz
Ancient and Modern

A HISTORY OF DIVERSE (and often sullied) interpretation has unhappily befallen Eliphaz. The following chapters trace this interpretative lineage from ancient times to modern. As to methodology, I link together nine relevant criteria, where possible, in determining whether the interpreter on the whole sustains a favorable or unfavorable view of Eliphaz:[1]

A. The tone of Eliphaz throughout his speeches and in the frame portions of the book of Job as directly or indirectly presented by the narrator;[2]

  1. Undoubtedly, given the myriad nuances and interpretive shades, there is a measure of subjectivity in assessing whether an interpreter is favorable or unfavorable. I follow the contours of Kemper Fullerton, who noted in his watershed essay of 1930 that commentators had failed to grasp Eliphaz's complexities, particularly with respect to his first speech, due to "little systematic attempt to relate the different parts of the speech ... with their varying moods, to each other, and this in spite of the fact that the artistic nature of the speech is much insisted upon" ("Double Entendre," 340n9). Fullerton categorizes approaches to Eliphaz generically into two main groups: (1) "Those who see in Eliphaz a sincere and well-meaning friend of Job whose consolations, though somewhat irrelevant and given without a sufficiently sympathetic understanding of the situation, are nevertheless honestly meant"; (2) "Those who see in Eliphaz a secret enemy of Job whose consolations are more or less hypocritical" (ibid.). Fullerton's insights are valid but should be expanded to encompass all of Eliphaz's speeches. Much of the labor of harmonization and correlation has been left undone.

  2. I have selected these identifiers on the basis of the most pertinent character aspects relating to Eliphaz. The tone, purpose, and theological provenance of Eliphaz,

B. The larger purpose and role for Eliphaz in his position among the characters of Job;

C. The nature of the theological creed, together with its provenance, underpinning Eliphaz's theodicy;

D. The nature, purpose, and value of Eliphaz's retributive doctrine, especially in Job 4:5–11;[3]

E. The mode, content, and significance of Eliphaz's special revelation in Job 4:12–21;[4]

F. The purpose and content of Eliphaz's theological perspective on remedial suffering in Job 5:17–24;[5]

G. The import of Eliphaz's status as leading interlocutor and elder statesman among the friend-counselors (I use the term *doyen*), including his use of sources of ancient wisdom in Job 15:7–19;[6]

H. The rationale and purpose of Eliphaz's employment of the sin listing in Job 22:2–12;[7] and,

I. The nature and reasons for the rebuke by Yahweh in the prologue at Job 42:7.[8]

---

for example, are debated across the literature, and therefore are apt and necessary to discern in assessing his role. While I attempt to apply these criteria consistently with all interpreters, they are almost without exception more useful in assessing modern treatments of Job due to the more critical and exhaustive methodology which these interpreters employ.

3. Eliphaz's retributive doctrine in 4:5–11 is a touchstone for the two schools of thought which Fullerton outlines ("Double Entendre," 340–41n9).

4. Eliphaz's special revelatory experience in 4:12–21 is key for its uniqueness within the wisdom tradition. Albertz affirms this recited encounter goes beyond "the traditional horizons of understanding" in hortatory sapience ("The Sage and Pious Wisdom," 251).

5. The doctrine of remedial chastening comes at a critical juncture in the book and functions as an integral component of the overall mood and intent of Eliphaz as grief counselor (Habel, *Job*, 134). Steinmann posits on these lines that the graded numerical saying as a literary device serves as a marker to point the reader to crucial seams in the structure of the book ("Graded Numerical Sayings," 289, 297).

6. The role of Eliphaz as intermediary sage and the sources cited in 15:7–19 tie into Eliphaz's overall doctrinal position (so Habel, "Naked I Came . . .," 377).

7. The use of the sin list reveals Eliphaz's appropriation of ritual purging and is therefore, as I will argue, an integral piece of the counsel he proffers.

8. The final point warrants clarification. It is understood that a rebuke, by its very nature, is usually considered unfavorable, especially a rebuke by Yahweh. What I am assessing here is whether in providing the rationale for Yahweh's rebuke the interpreter places heavy censure upon Eliphaz's approach and speech content. The spectrum is wide, of course, and includes many nuanced shades of interpretation. Still, favorable

Throughout the study I reference these concatenated criteria as the touchstone to evaluate the interpreter's assessment of Eliphaz. This assessment begins with an analysis of ancient readings of Eliphaz.

Ancient Interpretation

The most influential interpretation of Job in the ancient world was not a commentary but a translation. Interest in the so-called translation technique of the Septuagint [hereafter, LXX] has heightened in recent scholarship, gaining considerable momentum over the past two decades.[9] The significance of the LXX for studies of reception history involves its role as a hermeneutical watershed which momentously impacted the stream of subsequent interpretation of the Hebrew Scriptures. With respect to Job, this seminal translational/compositional work influenced readings not only of the main character Job but also of Job's leading disputant.

The Septuagint[10]

The Greek version of Job likely reflects two stages of translation: an Old Greek version [hereafter, OG] translated likely around 150 BC and the

---

readings even of Yahweh's rebuke may be found in an interpreter such as Maimonides who contends that Yahweh rebukes Eliphaz not for anything that he explicitly says or does but simply because he has not humbly acknowledged Yahweh by confessing to his "participation" in sinful humanity as Job does in the wake of the theophany (42:1–6). This perspective essentially clears Eliphaz of any real culpability. In the reading of Maimonides, Yahweh affirms and commends the entire trajectory of Eliphaz's theological perspective by proving Eliphaz's point concerning the universal peccability of mankind: all men must confess to Yahweh when he appears if for no other reason than merely because they are human. Thus, the rebuke, rather than humiliating Eliphaz, underscores the very point he is emphasizing.

9. For a survey of recent work and accompanying bibliographies, see Louw, *Transformations in the Septuagint*, 2–23; Louw, "Approaches in Translation Studies," 17–28; Kraus and Wooden, "Contemporary 'Septuagint' Research," 1–13; Jobes and Silva, *Invitation to the Septuagint*, 69–85; Kutz, "Characterization in the Old Greek of Job," 345–55. This momentum coincides with the welcome publication of *A New English Translation of the Septuagint* (NETS), which incorporates a significant share of current LXX research. On this, see "Electronic Edition of NETS" and in print through Oxford University Press. Of interest to readers of German will also be "Septuaginta Deutsch."

10. Given the variegated and potentially ambiguous nature of the term *Septuagint* (on this problem, see Jobes and Silva, *Invitation to the Septuagint*, 30–32), the terminology must be defined precisely. By the term *Septuagint*, I refer throughout this study to the body of original Jewish Greek translational literature, translated from the Hebrew Scriptures and eventually collected around the Old Greek Pentateuch or Septuagint

Greek version affiliated with Theodotion composed early in the first century AD.[11] In the corpus of the Greek translation of the Hebrew Scriptures, the book of Job has garnered sustained interest and is notable from a textual standpoint for several reasons.[12] Foremost among these reasons is that, in comparative textual analysis of LXX Job with the Hebrew text, the OG text is approximately 84% the length of the Masoretic Text [hereafter, MT] due to 390 fewer stichoi.[13] Of interest, secondly, is the observation of so-called anaphoric translation techniques, whereby the translator transfers and incorporates passages from elsewhere in Job or other parts of the LXX in his translation.[14] Third, several notable additions to the Greek text, such as the expanded depiction of Job's wife in 2:9a–d, the longer confession of Job in 42:3, and the identification of Job with the Edomite king Jobab (cf. Gen 36:33–34) in the expanded conclusion of 42:17, have long enticed scholarly curiosity.[15]

---

proper, approaching its canonical shape by the advent of the first century BC (cf. also Boyd-Taylor, "In a Mirror, Dimly—Reading the Septuagint as a Document of Its Times," 15).

11. Heater, *A Septuagint Translation Technique*, 1–2; Reed, "Job as Jobab," 33–34.

12. Harry M. Orlinsky observes: "Perhaps no book in the Hebrew Bible has offered the student such perplexing textual problems as the book of Job" ("Studies in the Septuagint," 53).

13. Orlinsky, "Studies in the Septuagint," 53–54; Marcos, "The Septuagint Reading of the Book of Job," 251.

14. For a comprehensive survey of examples see Heater, *Septuagint Translation Technique*, 11–130.

15. Perhaps one of the most influential effects of the LXX upon subsequent understandings of Job is the appendage at the end of the book in Job 42:17b–e—no textual evidence for which is found in the Hebrew MT—in which Job is identified with the Jobab of Edomite lineage from Gen 36. In view of the significance of this appendage in the history of Joban interpretation, I include it here in its entirety: "γέγραπται δὲ αὐτὸν πάλιν ἀναστήσεσθαι μεθ' ὧν ὁ κύριος ἀνίστησιν. οὗτος ἑρμηνεύεται ἐκ τῆς Συριακῆς βίβλου ἐν μὲν γῇ κατοικῶν τῇ Αυσίτιδι ἐπὶ τοῖς ὁρίοις τῆς Ιδουμαίας καὶ Ἀραβίας, προϋπῆρχεν δὲ αὐτῷ ὄνομα Ιωβαβ. λαβὼν δὲ γυναῖκα Ἀράβισσαν γεννᾷ υἱόν ᾧ ὄνομα Εννων. ἦν δὲ αὐτὸς πατρὸς μὲν Ζαρε τῶν Ησαυ υἱῶν υἱός μητρὸς δὲ Βοσορρας ὥστε εἶναι αὐτὸν πέμπτον ἀπὸ Αβρααμ. καὶ οὗτοι οἱ βασιλεῖς οἱ βασιλεύσαντες ἐν Εδωμ ἧς καὶ αὐτὸς ἦρξεν χώρας. πρῶτος Βαλακ ὁ τοῦ Βεωρ καὶ ὄνομα τῇ πόλει αὐτοῦ Δενναβα. μετὰ δὲ Βαλακ Ιωβαβ ὁ καλούμενος Ιωβ. μετὰ δὲ τοῦτον Ασομ ὁ ὑπάρχων ἡγεμὼν ἐκ τῆς Θαιμανίτιδος χώρας. μετὰ δὲ τοῦτον Αδαδ υἱὸς Βαραδ ὁ ἐκκόψας Μαδιαμ ἐν τῷ πεδίῳ Μωαβ καὶ ὄνομα τῇ πόλει αὐτοῦ Γεθθαιμ. οἱ δὲ ἐλθόντες πρὸς αὐτὸν φίλοι Ελιφας τῶν Ησαυ υἱῶν Θαιμανων βασιλεύς Βαλδαδ ὁ Σαυχαίων τύραννος Σωφαρ ὁ Μιναίων βασιλεύς" ("It is written that he will rise up again with those whom the Lord raises up. He is explained in the Aramaic book as dwelling in the land of Ausitis, on the borders of Idumea and Arabia. He was previously named Jobab. After he took an Arabian wife, he begot a son whose name was Ennon. And he himself was the son of his father Zerah, one of the sons of Esau, also of his mother Bozrah, so that he was the fifth from

The Reception History of Eliphaz

To deduce the reasons for (and in some cases to rectify) the comparable brevity of the ancient Greek text of Job, significant critical focus over the centuries has attached to LXX Job, beginning with Origen in the third century.[16] Opinions have varied as to whether the longer Hebrew MT or the allegedly shorter Hebrew *Vorlage* of the OG is primary.[17] Recent analysis of the OG Job has shifted to favor the longer Hebrew text (for all practical purposes the MT) as the original canonical work.[18] The basis for favoring the longer Hebrew text lies in the premise that the shorter Greek version is the result of several factors at the time of translation, including the translator's technique of free, and at times paraphrastic, translation, as well as the Greek translator's apparent struggles in rendering the notoriously difficult Hebrew of Job.[19] Whatever one surmises about the original form of the

---

Abraham. And these were the kings who reigned in Edom, which country he also ruled over: first, Bela, the son of Beor, and the name of his city was Dinhabah: but after Bela, Jobab, who is called Job, and after him Husham, who was ruler from the land of Teman: and after him Hadad, the son of Berad, who destroyed Midian in the plain of Moab; and the name of his city was Gethaim. And friends who came to him were Eliphaz, of the sons of Esau, king of the Temanites; Bildad, despot over the Sauchaeans; Sophar, king of the Minaeans" (author's translation with names Hebraized). Although reference is made to the "Syriac book," there is evident borrowing from the genealogical delineation of LXX Gen 36:32–35 (cf. Gray, "The Additions in the Ancient Greek Version of Job," 432; Reed, "Job as Jobab," 31–55).

16. Origen redacted Job toward greater textual conformity with the MT, marking the stichoi which he added to his *Hexapla* with an asterisk. In his *Commentary on Matthew*, Origen claimed to derive these additions from "other versions" (15.14)—such as Aquila, Symmachus, or Theodotion—but nowhere defines the exact version(s) used. Eusebius and Jerome attributed the additions as primarily from Theodotion, and the majority of contemporary scholars concur (Reed, "Job as Jobab," 34; Gray, "The Massoretic Text of the Book of Job," 339; Orlinsky, "Studies in the Septuagint," 55; Marcos, "Septuagintal Reading," 252; Gentry, *The Asterisked Materials*, 5–6). This diacritical marking tradition extends to contemporary critical editions of the LXX (see Gentry, *Asterisked Materials*, 1–15).

17. A full analysis of attempts to discover the reasons for the divergent OG and MT texts lies beyond the pale of our present study. For an historical survey of the efforts to discover the reason(s) for the divergence between the Greek and Hebrew texts, read Orlinsky, "Studies in the Setuagint, 53–73. For a summary, see Vicchio, *Image of the Biblical Job*, 1:102–113.

18. As Kutz acknowledges: "Though some of these divergences are due to variant readings in the translator's Vorlage, many attest to unique interpretations of a text identical to the MT. Moreover, the paraphrastic nature of the translator's rendering of the Hebrew often discloses what he, and his religious community, considered implicit in the text—insights that would not be revealed in a more literal translation" ("Characterization in the Old Greek of Job," 345).

19. Claude E. Cox, "Iob," 667. Cox suggests also that the shorter Greek work originates from the repetitious argument of the book or possible doubts by the translators as to the canonicity of Job (ibid.). Other possible factors include translational fatigue or

Hebrew, however, the OG Job is a translation which Claude Cox identifies as singular among the books of the LXX:

> The Old Greek (OG) Iob is a work of good literary quality. Absent are the usual 'Hebraisms' that are the tell-tale signs of translation Greek in much of the Septuagint corpus.... The usual categories of characterizing a translation fail us when we assess Iob. It is not just free or paraphrastic, it is also something of an epitome of the longer and often difficult original. OG Iob is one of a kind in the Septuagint corpus. We can typify it as among the least literal, both in its attitude toward abbreviating the parent text and in the way the translator worked with that portion of the text for which we have a translation.[20]

In the attempt to solve the dilemma of the differing lengths of the Greek and Hebrew texts, several monographs and studies over the second half of the twentieth century focused upon putative changes the LXX translator made to the Hebrew text, along with the alleged reasons for these modifications.[21] Gard, for example, argues that the LXX translator creates several intentional alterations, toning down the theologically offensive ideas in the Hebrew, removing divine anthropomorphisms, and eliminating potentially offensive descriptions of God.[22] Given the influence of LXX Job on the

---

occasional scribal errors in working through the Hebrew text.

20. Ibid., 667. Orlinsky concurs: "It has long been recognized that the Septuagint of our Book is frequently far from being a translation in the strict sense of the term" ("Studies in the Septuagint of the Book of Job," [1958], 229).

21. See chapter 1, n. 14. Gehman, "Theological Approach of the Greek Translator," 231–40; Heater, *Translation Technique*; Cox, "Methodological Issues," 79–89; Cox, "The Historical, Social, and Literary Context"; Gentry, *Asterisked Materials*. For a fuller bibliography, see Gentry, *Asterisked Materials*, 540–59.

22. Gard, *Exegetical Method*, 6–90; cf. also Katharine J. Dell, *Job as Sceptical Literature*, 13–16. Orlinsky is harshly critical of Gard's study, asserting that the author could have saved himself the task of writing a great portion of his monograph had he simply consulted the older literature ("Studies in the Septuagint," 70). Orlinsky contends that "in point of fact, the Job of the LXX is no more different from the Job of the masoretic text than the portrayal of any of the friends or God in the Greek or Hebrew. There is nothing theological or tendentious in the Greek; there is nothing but the usual factors involved in turning the Hebrew into Greek: the honest attempt on the part of the translator to interpret and translate the Hebrew correctly; the possibility of different Hebrew readings in his *Vorlage*; and the temper of the translator in the matter of style" ("Studies in the Septuagint of the Book of Job," [1961], 250). Although I am sensitive to Orlinsky's response to possible oversimplifications on the part of Gard, he goes too far the other way. The Greek translator in point of fact appears to make systematic changes in his translation.

ensuing centuries of Joban readers, including writers of the NT,[23] these alleged changes would prove of tremendous import in the stream of historical interpretation.

For this reason, a brief survey of translation technique in the LXX version of the Eliphaz speeches offers insight into ways in which the ancient translators of Job perceived him. While I will not analyze all the material, observing a few salient components of the translation technique provide clarity into the context of ancient understandings of the chief interlocutor.[24]

Softening of Harsh Expressions by Eliphaz

At times the LXX translator moderates potentially harsh Hebrew expressions to achieve more polite Greek idiom, which has the cumulative effect of refining Eliphaz. In 4:2 the urgent pique of the Hebrew expression וַעְצֹר בְּמִלִּין מִי יוּכָל ("Who is able to refrain from speaking?") is transformed to a rather more tentative query: ἰσχὺν δὲ ῥημάτων σου τίς ὑποίσει ("Who will endure the force of your words?"). Elsewhere the peremptory malediction וָאֶקּוֹב נָוֵהוּ פִתְאֹם ("I cursed his habitation suddenly") changes to more measured commentary: εὐθέως ἐβρώθη αὐτῶν ἡ δίαιτα ("Immediately their habitation was consumed" [5:3]). The possibly sarcastic counsel אוּלָם אֲנִי אֶדְרֹשׁ אֶל־אֵל וְאֶל־אֱלֹהִים אָשִׂים דִּבְרָתִי ("Indeed, I [myself] would seek God, and to God I would present my case" 5:8) is conveyed by a pious intercession: οὐ μὴν δὲ ἀλλὰ ἐγὼ δεηθήσομαι κυρίου κύριον δὲ τὸν πάντων δεσπότην ἐπικαλέσομαι ("Nonetheless, I [myself] will beseech the Lord, and will call upon the Lord who is sovereign over all").[25] In 5:27 the brash assertion

---

23. As discussed below the apostle Paul quotes Eliphaz in 1 Cor 3:19 (preceded by the Scriptural citation formula γέγραπται γάρ ["for it is written"]) and the writer of Hebrews possibly alludes to Job 5:17 in the parenesis of Heb 12:5–11, although this citation is more clearly dependent upon Prov 3:11–12.

24. The text of the LXX utilized is the standard critical text edited by Joseph Ziegler, part of the Göttingen Septuagint project (Ziegler, ed., *Iob*), while the Hebrew text is the representative Leningrad Codex of *Biblica Hebraica Stuttgartensia*. The asterisked materials are included in this survey. For a detailed analysis of the nature and scope of the asterisked material, see Gentry, *The Asterisked Materials in the Greek Job*. The purpose for inclusion of the asterisked material is to glean a firmer understanding of the ways in which Eliphaz was read and portrayed as a whole in the Greek Scripture tradition vis-à-vis the MT tradition. All translations in the following analysis are my own.

25. That this *is* in fact a softening transformation is exhibited in the commentary by Chrysostom (see more below). Chrysostom paraphrases Eliphaz's words in an affirming way: "Since this is the case, and though my trust is not like yours, yet I persevere in my acknowledgement of the Lord. While you bemoan your lot, I persevere in calling upon God and not despairing; after all, he is ever ready to bring about a complete change in things. I am in difficulties, but he is capable of making me enjoy even good

שְׁמָעֶנָּה וְאַתָּה דַע־לָךְ ("Hear it and know for yourself" [or "apply it for your own good" (NET)]) changes to the gentler, though vague, plea: ταῦτα οὕτως ἐξιχνιάσαμεν ταῦτά ἐστιν ἃ ἀκηκόαμεν σὺ δὲ γνῶθι σεαυτῷ εἴ τι ἔπραξας ("These things are what we have heard, but you must know for yourself if you have practiced something [wrong]"). In 22:2 Eliphaz irascibly queries: הַלְאֵל יִסְכָּן־גָּבֶר כִּי־יִסְכֹּן עָלֵימוֹ מַשְׂכִּיל ("Is man of use to God? Indeed is the wise of use to Him?"), while in the LXX he inquires, more in the vein of an urbane psalmist, πότερον οὐχὶ ὁ κύριός ἐστιν ὁ διδάσκων σύνεσιν καὶ ἐπιστήμην ("Is not the Lord He who teaches insight and knowledge?").

Emphasis upon the Eloquence of Eliphaz

The Greek translator employs at least two ways to underscore the eloquence of Eliphaz. First, his eloquence is emphasized by a consistent focus upon *words*. A curious practice of the OG translator is to render references in the speeches of Eliphaz to prior (or future) *deeds* which Job has (or will have) done into actions associated specifically with *speaking*.[26] One may surmise that this conforms to the Greeks' high view of rhetoric as well as the emphasis in Job upon eloquence and oratory skill. Thus in rendering abbreviated versions of the speeches of Job the translator focuses consistently upon the import of the characters' words. For example, in 4:3 the Greek translator uses παρεκάλεσας ("You have exhorted") to render תְּחַזֵּק ("You have strengthened"). In 15:4 the translator turns וְתִגְרַע שִׂיחָה ("You hinder meditation") into συνετελέσω δὲ ῥήματα τοιαῦτα ("You carry out such words"). In the third speech (22:4) the MT הֲמִיִּרְאָתְךָ יֹכִיחֶךָ ("Is it for your fear that he reproves you?") is rendered with ἦ λόγον σου ποιούμενος ἐλέγξει σε ("In *acting on your word* will he reprove you?"). In 22:26 the translator transforms Eliphaz's statement עַל־שַׁדַּי תִּתְעַנָּג ("You will take pleasure in the Almighty") to παρρησιασθήσῃ ἔναντι κυρίου ("You will *speak freely* before the Lord").

Second, the LXX translator often shifts the import of the metaphor or imagery for the purpose of rendering Eliphaz more accessible (and

---

things, bringing me from one state to the other" (*Commentary on Job*, 83–84).

26. This practice is a species of what Louw identifies as "specification," viz., "a transformation in which the TL [target language] lexeme stands in a hyponymical relationship to the 'literal translation' (the standard rendering) of an SL [source language] lexeme" (*Transformations in the Septuagint*, 67). Louw defines a hyponym as the following: "Some lexemes are more specific than others, e.g., 'cow' is more specific than 'animal,' which is a more generic term. Thus 'cow' is a hyponym of 'animal,' 'rose' is hyponym of 'flower,' and so on" (379).

perhaps more appealing or eloquent) to Greek readers.[27] Often in doing so the translator turns the concrete imagery of the Hebrew into the more abstract *effect* of the imagery (with a consistent penchant here toward desert features) or the neutral Hebrew metaphors into categories of righteous vis-à-vis wicked persons. For example, the Hebrew metaphor of 4:21 pictures a tent cord being plucked up הֲלֹא־נִסַּע יִתְרָם בָּם ("Is not their tent cord plucked up within them?"), while the LXX imagery depicts the blustering desert wind: ἐνεφύσησεν γὰρ αὐτοῖς καὶ ἐξηράνθησαν ("For he breathes on them and they wither up").[28] In 15:7 the topographical Hebrew term גְּבָעוֹת ("hills") is modified to θινῶν ("sand dunes"). The metaphorical יְנַקְתּוֹ תְּיַבֵּשׁ שַׁלְהָבֶת ("The flame will dry up his young shoot") in 15:30 is changed to a like meteorological pronouncement: τὸν βλαστὸν αὐτοῦ μαράναι ἄνεμος ("Let wind wither his shoot"), while the last phrase of the verse וְיָסוּר בְּרוּחַ פִּיו ("And he will turn aside by the breath of his mouth") is kept consistent with the previous images: ἐκπέσοι δὲ αὐτοῦ τὸ ἄνθος ("Let his blossom fall off"). Farther afield, though perhaps in keeping with the desert depictment, in 4:10 the phrase וְשִׁנֵּי כְפִירִים נִתָּעוּ ("and the teeth of the young lions are broken") is transformed to γαυρίαμα δὲ δρακόντων ἐσβέσθη ("and the exultant cry of serpents[?] is extinguished"),[29] while in 5:7 the idiom וּבְנֵי־רֶשֶׁף

---

27. Gordis notes that "the Septuagint was prepared for the uneducated masses. It therefore sought to transmit acceptable religious ideas to its readers and to exclude heretical notions" (*The Book of God and Man*, 223). Vicchio adds that "the translators of the Septuagint were very concerned to reshape the text to avoid what they saw as theological improprieties in the Hebrew text. Divine anthropomorphisms, hints of polytheism, and any suggestion, for example, that God is responsible for evil, were eliminated from the Greek text" (*Image of the Biblical Job*, 1:112). Ziegler observes: "Öfters sind Konkreta durch Abstrakta wiedergegeben, namentlich bei Körperteilen" ("Often the concrete are rendered through the abstract, namely with parts of the body") ("Der textkritische Wert," 28).

28. The Greek translator anaphorically brings in the LXX of Isa 40:24b here (ἔπνευσεν ἐπ' αὐτοὺς καὶ ἐξηράνθησαν "he blows upon them and they wither up"). Heater suggests that "it is possible that the translator has taken the metaphor of the removal of a tent cord as a good opportunity to expound further on the sovereignty of God over man's life, and has brought in Isa 40:24b" (*Translation Technique*, 47). I am more inclined to suggest that the translator is merely explaining the metaphor to his Greek readers given his tendency to do so.

29. Although it remains uncertain why the translator transforms the imagery in this way, several observations may be made. First, since δρακόντων is also used to translate כְּפִירִים in Job 38:39, the possibility is lessened that the translator has before him a different Hebrew *Vorlage* in this text. Second, δρακόντων renders the synonym תַּנִּים ("jackals") elsewhere in LXX Jer 9:10 and Mic 1:8, thus raising the possibility that δρακόντων had various lexical nuances in the Greek milieu of the LXX translators, referring possibly to a carnivorous scavenger animal. Perhaps it is the "wildness" of the beasts that is held in common among these terms. One may note conversely that the Hebrew term for lion אַרְיֵה is cognate to the Tigre term for snake (*HALOT*, 87). Third, bearing in

("and sons of Resheph") is transformed to νεοσσοὶ δὲ γυπὸς ("and the young of the vulture").³⁰ Other similar instances are notable in which the imagery of the Hebrew is rendered specifically into the effect of the imagery. In 4:9 the Hebrew נִשְׁמַת ("breath") becomes the more forceful προστάγματος ("command"). The שַׁאֲגַת אַרְיֵה ("roar of the lion") in 4:10 changes to σθένος λέοντος ("strength of the lion"). In 5:18 the divine action יֶחְבָּשׁ ("He binds") becomes the resultant πάλιν ἀποκαθίστησιν ("He restores again").

Sometimes the adaptation of the metaphor personalizes the imagery to identify persons (often enemies of the righteous or of Job in particular) rather than simply the personification of concepts as in the Hebrew. The metaphor in 5:16 עֹלָתָה קָפְצָה פִּיהָ ("Iniquity closes her mouth") is personalized in the Greek rendering ἀδίκου δὲ στόμα ἐμφραχθείη ("And let the mouth of the unjust be stopped"). In 5:22 Eliphaz promises to laugh at שֹׁד וּלְכָפָן ("violence and hunger"), while in Greek his scorn is personalized toward ἀδίκων καὶ ἀνόμων ("the unrighteous and lawless"). An interesting transformation occurs in 22:12, where וּרְאֵה רֹאשׁ כּוֹכָבִים כִּי־רָמּוּ ("And he sees the chief of stars that they are high") is translated with the more personal application τοὺς δὲ ὕβρει φερομένους ἐταπείνωσεν ("And he humbles those who bear arrogance"). At other times the metaphor change involves specification of categories of righteousness and evil. In 5:5 two metaphors are adapted: the רָעֵב ("hungry") becomes the δίκαιοι ("righteous ones"), and the צִנִּים ("thorns") become κακῶν ("evils") in Greek.

Transformations to Acceptable Jewish Terminology

Consistently the translator of the LXX Job strives to make Eliphaz more orthodox by rendering his Hebrew titles for God into more appropriate Jewish epithets in Greek—nearly uniformly adopting the Greek term κύριος. Thus the translator(s) render Eliphaz's divine title אֱלוֹהַּ ("God") (4:17; cf.

---

mind the translator's free methodology at points, perhaps he simply grew tired of the repetitive terms in the text and wanted to variegate the imagery. Fourth, one other possibility is that the translator is keen to render the Hebrew text in what is perceived as a more sophisticated manner. Vicchio provides a few examples of metaphors which are changed by the translator to accomplish "a more scientific reading of nature" (*Image of the Biblical Job*, 1:112), with one example adduced in which Leviathan (Vicchio mistakenly writes "Behemoth") in 40:25 [EVV 41:1] is rendered as "dragon" (ironically the same term δράκων, there as δράκοντα).

30. One explanation for this curious transformation is that Resheph, the Ugaritic god of pestilence, is associated with death, imagery that the translator captures through the concrete word picture of gathering vultures (cf. 15:23). For a more extensive treatment of the potential connection of Resheph to the motifs in Job, see Fyall, *Now My Eyes Have Seen You*, 117–37.

4:9; 15:8), his common epithet אֵל ("God") (5:8; cf. also 15:4, 13; 22:2, 17), and his popular appellation, שַׁדַּי ("the Almighty") (22:3; cf. 22:23), with variations of κύριος. At times different epithets are substituted. In 22:13 אֵל ("God") is translated ὁ ἰσχυρός ("the Mighty One"), while in 22:25 שַׁדַּי ("the Almighty") is translated with the more literal ὁ παντοκράτωρ ("the Almighty"). In 15:25 the phrase ἐναντίον τοῦ κυρίου ("before the Lord") is used twice—once to render אֶל־אֵל ("against God") and another to render אֶל־שַׁדַּי ("against the Almighty"), adding παντοκράτορος with the latter to clarify the nuance. Elsewhere the translator seems to turn Eliphaz from curmudgeonly disputant to sage psalmist, extolling eloquently the glories of God. For instance in 22:28 the translator transforms the straightforward Hebrew expression וְתִגְזַר־אֹמֶר וְיָקָם לָךְ ("You will decide on a matter and it will be confirmed for you") into ἀποκαταστήσει δέ σοι δίαιταν δικαιοσύνης ("Now he will restore to you a righteous way of living").

Conclusions to the Eliphaz speeches in the LXX

Several conclusions may be drawn concerning the nature of the LXX in the Eliphaz speeches of Job. First, the LXX may be characterized as a dynamically equivalent, and at times free, translation of the Eliphaz speeches. Features of literal translation, such as syntactical Hebraisms, contravention of style in the receptor language, and stereotyping are infrequent, although literal translations are not entirely absent. The Greek translation stands on its own as a literary piece in its receptor language, and the translator appears willing to change, add, or delete words or imagery as necessary to achieve this goal. In addition, one may surmise that the Greek translator struggled at times with the difficult Hebrew of the Eliphaz speeches, owing to which a few of the modifications have arisen. Second, the disparities of the Greek translation of Job from the MT in the Eliphaz speeches need not necessitate a different *Vorlage*. Differences are more readily to be attributed to translation technique, scope, and purpose than to significant textual variations. Third, the LXX presents Eliphaz as more orthodox and refined than he appears in the MT. Not only are Eliphaz and the other friends depicted as regional kings, but Eliphaz is transformed throughout his speeches into a more urbane interlocutor. This does not suggest, of course, a completely sanitized portrayal. Too much vituperation is exchanged to whitewash Eliphaz completely. The moderation of Eliphaz, however, appears to set the table for later sympathetic readings in Jewish and Christian interpretation. At minimum, Eliphaz's prestige is heightened and his eloquence enhanced. This shifting made Eliphaz more accessible to Greek readers and intensified the vivid drama of the book, influencing to a degree the ways in which Eliphaz would be read in the early church. In light of the preceding summary, I conclude that the LXX influenced the stream of historical Joban interpretation toward a somewhat positive (though still often mixed) reading of Eliphaz and that the translation technique was based upon exegetical concerns on the part of the translator.[31] In regard to the nine interpretive criteria outlined in this chapter's introduction, the LXX is difficult to assess since it is a translation rather than exposition. Overall, it appears favorable to Eliphaz with respect to tone (A) and theological creed and provenance (C). In addition, its view of Eliphaz's doctrine of retribution is softened (D). Its view, however, of Eliphaz's purpose (B), special revelation (E), view of remedial suffering (F), status of doyen (G), use of sin list (H), and reason for rebuke (I) cannot be determined with certainty from its translation technique.

Ancient Jewish Interpretation

Roughly following the interpretative stream of the LXX, a few Jewish apocryphal works are useful in efforts to grasp the ways in which Eliphaz was read in the ancient world.

Tobit

The Greek version of the Jewish apocryphal book of Tobit is usually dated between 225–175 BC,[32] while the Latin Vulgate version of the book dates to around the mid-390's to 400.[33] The Vulgate translation is of especial interest, as we will see below, for its unique relationship to Job. The story of Tobit is set in the milieu of seventh-century BC Israel, a time when Assyria controlled the region. The account chronicles the anguished lives of two

---

31. On the latter point see also Kutz, "Characterization in the Old Greek of Job," 346.

32. Littman, *Tobit*, xxviii; Moore, *Tobit*, 40–42. This suggestion is based on the presupposition that the Greek version is original. Others such as John Bright argue for an Aramaic original and date Tobit as early as the fourth century BC on the grounds that fragments discovered among the Qumran scrolls are in "good 'Imperial Aramaic'" (*A History of Israel*, 432). Vicchio identifies, however, clues within the text itself that favor a second-century BC Greek provenance: the mention of the *drachma* in 5:14, the allusion to tithing in 1:7, and the use of various Greek names such as *Dystors* in 2:12 (*Image of the Biblical Job*, 1:120). It is possible that the text was originally written in Aramaic and translated into Greek around 200–170 BC.

33. Otzen, *Tobit and Judith*, 60.

exiles from the tribe of Naphtali, Tobit and Sarah.[34] The protagonist Tobit, of particular interest for this study, is himself, similarly to Job, characterized as a righteous man: "I, Tobit, walked in the ways of truth and righteousness all the days of my life. I performed many acts of charity for my kindred and my people" (Tob 1:3, NRSV). In spite of his personal piety, however, Tobit undergoes a series of severe trials which test his faith, including the dramatic imperilment of execution by the king of Assyria, a significant loss of material goods, calumnies from family and friends, and ultimately physical blindness. As the narrative unfolds the reader learns that for fear of reprisal Tobit has dutifully yet secretly buried the bodies of several kinsmen who were slaughtered ruthlessly by Sennacherib, the king of Assyria. Yet for this pious act Tobit is scorned by friends and neighbors who fear that he will bring down on them the wrath of the king. Tobit returns home discouraged and in fatigue collapses against the wall of the courtyard to fall asleep (Tob 2:10). While he sleeps, two swallows defecate in his eyes, producing "white spots" (NJB) which lead to irreversible blindness in spite of the summoned doctors' best efforts to cure him.

Tobit suffers greatly from the blindness for four years during which he continues to be derided not only by neighbors and former friends but moreover by his wife Anna who must support him by working to the point of exhaustion outside the home.[35] Finally Tobit is healed by means of a remedy

34. For a helpful overview, see Portier-Young, "Alleviation of Suffering in the Book of Tobit," 35–54, especially 38–48. The lives of Tobit and Sara become intertwined as Sara eventually marries Tobit's son, Tobias. That portion of the account, which is extensive, lies beyond the scope of the present study.

35. There are vivid similarities here to the extended account of Job's wife in LXX Job 2:9 along with her role in Job's afflictions: χρόνου δὲ πολλοῦ προβεβηκότος εἶπεν αὐτῷ ἡ γυνὴ αὐτοῦ μέχρι τίνος καρτερήσεις λέγων [a] ἰδοὺ ἀναμένω χρόνον ἔτι μικρὸν προσδεχόμενος τὴν ἐλπίδα τῆς σωτηρίας μου [b] ἰδοὺ γὰρ ἠφάνισταί σου τὸ μνημόσυνον ἀπὸ τῆς γῆς υἱοὶ καὶ θυγατέρες ἐμῆς κοιλίας ὠδῖνες καὶ πόνοι οὓς εἰς τὸ κενὸν ἐκοπίασα μετὰ μόχθων [c] σύ τε αὐτὸς ἐν σαπρίᾳ σκωλήκων κάθησαι διανυκτερεύων αἴθριος κἀγὼ πλανῆτις καὶ λάτρις τόπον ἐκ τόπου περιερχομένη καὶ οἰκίαν ἐξ οἰκίας προσδεχομένη τὸν ἥλιον πότε δύσεται ἵνα ἀναπαύσωμαι τῶν μόχθων καὶ τῶν ὀδυνῶν αἵ με νῦν συνέχουσιν [e] ἀλλὰ εἰπόν τι ῥῆμα εἰς κύριον καὶ τελεύτα ("And when much time had passed, his wife said to him, 'How long will you endure, saying, "See, I tarry a little while longer, waiting for the hope of my salvation"? For indeed your memory is destroyed from the earth, your sons and daughters, the birth pangs and pains of my womb which I labored with hardship for nothing. You yourself sit amidst the putrescence of worms passing the night in the open air, while I am going about as a wanderer and hired laborer from place to place and from house to house waiting for the setting of the sun so that I might rest from my toils and griefs which now oppress me. But say some word against the Lord and die" [my translation]). Compare Anna's activities and reproaches in the book of Tobit: καὶ ἡ γυνή μου Αννα ἠριθεύετο ἐν τοῖς γυναικείοις ("And my wife Anna undertook women's work" [2:11]). Later, she likewise assails Tobit: ἡ δὲ ἀποκριθεῖσα εἶπέν μοι ποῦ εἰσιν αἱ ἐλεημοσύναι σου καὶ αἱ δικαιοσύναι σου ἰδοὺ γνωστὰ πάντα μετὰ σοῦ ("And she

provided by the intervention of the angel Raphael and mixed together by his son Tobias (11:15). He is subsequently restored to his former prominence and rejoices with hymnic praise over the goodness of God.

While the Greek version of the book carries no explicit mention of Job, the parallels to the biblical account are striking.[36] A similar narrative plot and in particular the parallelism of afflictions for Tobit as for Job are noteworthy, suggesting conceptual borrowing from Job. While we remain cautious not to read too much into the account, we may recognize in this book, given the growing consensus concerning the validity of these allusive ties to Job,[37] a negative appraisal of Job's friends in the derision Tobit receives from his neighbors who scorn him harshly for his acts of piety. This connection is made much more explicit in the Vulgate version of Job, as will be discussed in greater detail below. In the stream of Jewish apocryphal literature, the book of Tobit contributes at least conceptually by suggesting ways in which the book of Job fired the imagination of readers such as the author of *Tobit*. In addition, it contributes to our understanding of the interpretive history of Eliphaz by suggesting that most likely he was viewed somewhat negatively with respect to his tone (A) and purpose (B) in Job. We gain no clear perspective from Tobit, however, regarding Eliphaz's theological provenance and creed (C), retributive dogma (D), special revelation (E), espousal of remedial suffering (F), status as doyen (G), use of the sin listing (H), or the nature of the divine rebuke (I).

Aristeas's Life of Job

Aristeas's account of Job comes to us third-hand, consisting of about thirty lines of text that Eusebius preserves from Alexander Polyhistor's treatise *Concerning the Jews*.[38] Aristeas himself is known only through this fragment. Since the text clearly shows dependence on the LXX and must precede the period of Alexander Polyhistor (80–35 BC), Aristeas most likely lived sometime around 100 BC.[39] In the text—like the LXX before and other

---

answered and said to me, 'Where are your acts of charity and your righteous deeds? See, you seem to know everything!" [Tob. 2:14] [my translation]).

36. For Tobit's implicit connections to Job, see Nowell, *The Book of Tobit*, 74–75; Dimant, "The Use and Interpretation of Mikra," 417–19; Weitzman, "Allusion, Artifice, and Exile in the Hymn of Tobit," 58–60.

37. Weitzman, "Tobit," 58.

38. See the overview in Vicchio, *Image of the Biblical Job*, 1:130–31; Doran, "Jewish Hellenistic Historians," 251. The text is translated in English in Eusebius, *Preparation for the Gospel*, 461.

39. Charlesworth, "Aristeas the Exegete," 81.

works to follow— Aristeas identifies Job with Jobab the descendant of Esau (Gen 36:33).⁴⁰

Concerning Eliphaz and the other friends, Aristeas records that they are kings who have come to visit Job (borrowing again from the additional material of the LXX). Interestingly, Aristeas takes an impartial view regarding the role of the friends. In his description of their efforts to console Job, Aristeas states: "Comforted, he [Job] said that even without comfort he would be steadfast in reverence, even in such trying circumstances. God, amazed at his courage, freed him from his illness, and made him master of many possessions."⁴¹ It is noteworthy that although the text is brief, its view of the friends is unbiased, leaning rather toward favorable disposition in describing Job as "comforted." The author hints at no explicit criticism of Eliphaz or the other friends. The friends seek rather to exhort Job, and Job responds with steadfast piety. Although the writer records none of the dialogue among the friends, the fact that Aristeas does not present the friends negatively suggests that perhaps the LXX has influenced his work in some measure, leading to a favorable view of the tone (A), purpose (B), and theological provenance and creed (C) of Eliphaz. Although admittedly brief, the text suggests a favorable understanding as well of Eliphaz's retribution dogma (D), special revelation (E), espousal of remedial suffering (F), doyen status (G), and use of the sin list (H). We gain no clear perspective on the reason for Yahweh's rebuke (I).

Testament of Job

The first-century AD pseudepigraphical work *Testament of Job* is a far more extensive writing which expands prolixly, albeit imaginatively, upon the book of Job.⁴² Certain characters such as Satan and Job's wife are given a

40. Eusebius, *Preparation for the Gospel*, 461.

41. Doran, "Jewish Hellenistic Historians," 253n12. Eusebius, *Preparation for the Gospel*, 461.

42. Suggested dates for the origin and provenance of the Testament of Job vary from as early as the first century BC to the first century AD (Evans, *Noncanonical Writings*, 29). As Thornhill contends, the writer certainly knew of and used the canonical LXX version of Job and left clues that the work is Hellenistic ("The Testament of Job," 618–19). Although Thornhill suggests that the writer may have been Christian due to a possible familiarity with certain passages of the NT (ibid., 619), this seems unlikely in that no overt Christian reference is included (as Philonenko warns "On ne risquera guère de se tromper en plaçant la composition de notre écrit aux alentours de l'ère chrétienne" ("We shall hardly risk making the mistake of placing our writing around the Christian era") ["'Le Testament de Job," 42]). More likely is a Jewish provenance as Gabrielle Oberhänsli-Widmer argues: "Als Konsens der heutigen Forschung können

much more prominent role than in the biblical record. The story is told mostly in the first person from Job's perspective, and a few fanciful events are added along the way to pique the reader's curiosity and to sustain interest. I will focus attention on the parts of the work which touch upon Eliphaz and its understanding of his role.

Job, identified also in this account with Jobab, is the son of Esau and a king of Edom (or, Ausitis as in the LXX). Job reveals certain secrets to his ten children through his second wife, Dinah, Jacob's daughter. Before falling into misfortune Job was the consummately wealthy king whose dominion extended even over the land of Egypt.[43] He is afflicted, however, for twenty years when his three companions—also kings—finally hear of his calamities and come to visit him together with their sumptuous entourages (*T. Job* 28:1). When the kings arrive they sit in silence for seven days, not out of patience or concern for their friend, but merely out of shock at Job's deplorable condition. Although he had been renowned as a splendid potentate with the requisite regalia of affluence and power, Job now sits in putrescent squalor on a dung heap outside the city (28:5).

Eliphaz, for his part, is portrayed in the *Testament of Job* as forceful, impetuous, and at times imperious. It is he rather than Job who breaks the silence after seven long days of waiting:

> While they were still in doubt, Eliphaz, the king of the Temanites, turned and said, 'Are you Job, our fellow-king?' [ἀπαξῶς ἔτι ἀμφιβαλλόντων αὐτῶν στραφεὶς Ἐλιφᾶς ὁ τῶν θεμανῶν βασιλεὺς εἶπεν, σὺ εἶ Ἰὼβ ὁ σθμβασιλεὺς ἡμῶν;] And weeping I threw earth on my head, and shaking it I told them, 'I am.' And when they saw me shaking my head, they fell to the ground in a faint, and their troops were hushed at seeing the three kings collapsed on the ground for about three hours as if dead. Then

---

für das *Testament Hiobs* die folgenden groben Eckdaten angegeben werden. Das Hiob zugeschriebene Pseudipigraph ist ein Produkt des jüdischen Hellenismus, von einem jüdischen Verfasser um die Zeitenwende in der Diaspora verfasst" ("As a consensus of current research on the Testament of Job, the following preliminary key data can be indicated. The pseudepigrapha ascribed to Job is the product of Jewish Hellenism, from a Jewish author who writes around the turn of the era in the Diaspora") (*Hiob in Jüdischer Antike und Moderne*, 59). Possible also is M. Philonenko's suggestion that the book originated among an ascetic sect of Jews known to us through the writing of Philo called the "Thérapeutes" ("therapists") and perhaps residing in Egypt ("Le Testament de Job," 41–53).

43. *T. Job* 28:8 reads "Where is Jobab, who is king of all Egypt?" although this may be a copyist's error (*The Apocryphal Old Testament*, 635n2).

they arose and began saying to one another, 'We do not believe this is he!' (*T. Job* 29:3–30:2).⁴⁴

Job undertakes a protracted and heated discourse to convince the others that he is in fact their former friend. Before Job can finish his speech, however, Eliphaz rashly interrupts him:

> Eliphaz became enraged (ὀργισθεὶς) and said to the other friends: 'What has been the use of us thus having been here <with our armies> so that we might console him? And behold this one indicts us! Therefore, let us depart to our own regions. He sits in the humiliation of worms and in a stench and at the critical moment arouses himself against us. Kingdoms are passing away, as are their rulers, he says, but mine shall be forever! And Eliphaz, arising with great consternation, turned aside from them with deep sorrow, saying, 'I shall go. For we came so that we might console him and at the critical moment he put us down in the presence of our troops' (*T. Job* 34:2–5).

The narrative continues with Bildad taking Eliphaz by the hand in an attempt to allay his anger, reminding Eliphaz that he himself had been sick for two days (!). The exchange continues for several chapters until finally Sitidos, Job's wife, emerges to plead with the visiting kings for pity instead of condescension: She asks the chief friend: "Do you remember, Eliphaz, you and your two friends, what sort of person I used to be among you and how I used to be outfitted? But now do you see how I come forth or what I wear?" (*T. Job* 39:2b). Eliphaz, in an abrupt act of compassion, responds by tearing off his purple robe to wrap it around Job's wife.

His benevolence seems to be short-lived, as Eliphaz soon returns to his confrontation with Job: "Eliphaz and the others <with him> sat beside me arguing and delivering a tirade against me, so that after twenty seven days they were about to arise and go to their own countries" (41:1). The appearance of the Lord forestalls their departure, however, as the cantankerous debate is settled by theophany. From there the book takes an interesting, though perhaps far-fetched, plot twist. The Lord raises the curtain to reveal the real villain of the dialogical exchange. All along it has been *Elihu* that is filled with Satan and spewing out arrogant words (41:7).⁴⁵ The Lord pronounces to Eliphaz that, while he and the other friends have sinned, they

---

44. The text used derives from Kraft, ed., *The Testament of Job According to the SV Text*.

45. The author of *The Testament of Job* undoubtedly carried a harsh view of the character of Elihu and would not have been keen on the possibility of his orthodoxy, much less his authorship of Job.

are to seek forgiveness and reconciliation through Job's intercession (42:3). Eliphaz and the others are subsequently reconciled through Job's intercession. When Eliphaz realizes that the Lord has forgiven their sins, although not considering Elihu worthy of forgiveness, he exults with an eloquent hymn of praise (43:2–13). In this largely imprecatory psalm against Elihu, Eliphaz rejoices that although their sins have been forgiven, Elihu has been snuffed out with no memorial among the living. As the hymn concludes, Job describes the ensuing celebration: "And after Eliphaz stopped the hymn, while they were all making response to him and circling about, we arose and entered the city in which we have a house, and we held festivities in the delight of the Lord" (44:1).

The account is of interest in its portrayal of Eliphaz for several reasons. First, the influence of the LXX is evident again in the expanded depiction of Eliphaz and the other friends as royalties. Eliphaz assumes a commanding, authoritative posture, is robed in purple, and is accompanied by troops. He is crafted by the author as a man of high social standing, respect, and power. Second, the narrative bifurcates the role of Eliphaz by adopting alternately positive and negative perspectives. Positively, Eliphaz acts compassionately toward Job's wife and ends the book somewhat heroically with a restored and festive role as the leading spokesman and initiator of celebration. Furthermore, in the aftermath of one of his outbursts he is described as deeply sorrowful, suggesting a measure of discomfiture at Job's condition rather than mere indignation. Negatively, at points in the speeches he is rash and abrasive toward Job, becoming "enraged" with his former peer. He is at times impatient and self-serving in his remonstrances with Job, incensed by the fact that Job has not submitted to the friends' counsel and offended that he has humiliated them in front of their troops. It is sufficient to observe that already in the early explication of Job an interpretative polarity is at work: Eliphaz is at times eloquent and respectable and at times hasty and insolent. Third, *The Testament of Job* distinguishes the *role* of Eliphaz from the *words* of Eliphaz. This interpretive polarity, which is seen in several interpretive schemes in the ensuing overview, downplays Eliphaz's character and role in the narrative while holding to Eliphaz's words as authoritative. In fact, the words of Eliphaz will be appropriated later by Christian theologians polemically or apologetically as possessing scriptural authority. This interpretive tension becomes a significant feature that is part of the historical reading patterns for Eliphaz.

Although further assessment is uncertain, at minimum *The Testament of Job* is alternately positive or negative toward Eliphaz in his tone (A), role in the account (B), and theological creed (C). The author of the *Testament* appears to remain largely favorable towards Eliphaz's retributive dogma (D) and understanding of remedial suffering (F) if one takes at face value the dialogue portions. Little can be ventured as to whether his special revelation (E), ancient sources of wisdom (G), or use of the sin list (H) are viewed positively in the *Testament*. Probably a rather favorable view of Eliphaz's rebuke by Yahweh may be discerned in Eliphaz's full restoration and verbose hymnody at the close of the book (I).

The New Testament and Early Church

A brief survey of the place of Eliphaz in the New Testament and early church reveals a few more interesting insights into how he was perceived in the ancient times of the NT milieu.

Paul

In a pericope within 1 Corinthians 3 denouncing the putative wisdom of self-styled sophists, the apostle Paul quotes from Eliphaz, a leading self-styled sophist of ancient times, to bolster his principal tenet. By discrediting human wisdom as over against divine, Paul warns the Corinthians of the dangers of subtle philosophical seduction:[46]

> Let no one deceive himself. If anyone among you thinks that he is wise in this age, let him become a fool that he may become wise. For the wisdom of this world is folly with God. For it is written, 'He catches the wise in their craftiness,' and again, 'The Lord knows the thoughts of the wise, that they are futile.' So let no one boast in men. For all things are yours, whether Paul or Apollos or Cephas or the world or life or death or the present or the future—all are yours, and you are Christ's, and Christ is God's (1 Cor 3:18–23).

In the larger context of 1 Cor 3 Paul is using two analogies to expose the carnal behavior of the Corinthian congregation. Whereas the Corinthians have been disposed to factionalism as a means of displaying what they perceive to be superior wisdom, Paul unveils the true folly of this (disobedient) conduct.[47] Since it is not merely a human institution, the church belongs

---

46. On the pericope see Conzelmann, *1 Corinthians*, 79; Bruce, *1 Corinthians*, 45; Barrett, *First Epistle to the Corinthians*, 92; Orr and Walther, *1 Corinthians*, 174–75; Soards, *1 Corinthians*, 79; Morris, *1 Corinthians*, 68; Thiselton, *First Epistle to the Corinthians*, 321–29.

47. On the nature of the Corinthian factionalism as ethical lapse rather than theological divergence, see Welborn, "On the Discord in Corinth," 85–111; Grindheim,

to God, and Paul makes this clear with two analogies first by comparing the church to an agricultural field and then to a building. The work of Paul, Apollos, and other human laborers is simply that of planting and watering on the one hand and of building wisely on the other. No sheer human effort can cause the church to grow, and no mere human ingenuity can replace the foundation that is laid already in Christ.

Paul applies these transcendent truths to the Corinthians' immediate situation. If the Corinthian believers wish to be commended in the sphere of the church, they must first realize the foolishness of focusing solely upon human acumen to advance their cause. Partisanship as a means of displaying so-called wisdom had instead demonstrated folly. The church is not a social matrix for the display of one's philosophical cleverness but an organism which belongs to God and is advanced by him. Those who would minister effectively, by analogy planting and watering fruitfully and constructing lastingly, must do so first by paradoxically becoming "fools" who are humbly subservient to the wisdom of God displayed in the cross of Christ.

In the midst of his injunction, Paul cites Job 5:13, "For it is written, 'He catches the wise in their craftiness'" (1 Cor 3:19, ESV). Of note is his use of the scriptural citation formula "For it is written" (γέγραπται γάρ). Paul seems on the surface to be appropriating the words of Eliphaz (bearing scriptural authority) to fortify his parenesis that all merely human wisdom stands in opposition to God. The difficulties with the citation, however, are several. First, identification of the precise *Vorlage* from which Paul is quoting is notoriously elusive. The NT quotes directly from the book of Job only twice, with Paul citing on both occasions (here and a quotation of Job 41:11 in Rom 11:35). In both cases his citation varies significantly from the LXX, which contravenes his customary method of citing the OT.[48] What certainly is of interest, furthermore, is that Paul's term for "catch," δρασσόμενος, from the root δράσσομαι ("to clutch, seize, scoop up") is not a typical Pauline term and is used only here in the NT.[49] The LXX term for

---

"Wisdom for the Perfect," 690–91; Pogoloff, *Logos and Sophia*, 100–4.

48. See Robertson and Plummer, *First Epistle of St. Paul to the Corinthians*, 71. Conzelmann opines that there is a tendency here toward the traditions of Aquila, Theodotion, and Symmachus (*1 Corinthians*, 80n13).

49. The term δράσσομαι is used six times in the LXX. In the cultic texts of Lev 2:2; 5:12; and Num 5:26 the term translates the Hebrew קמץ ("to grasp, pick up") and is used to describe the priests' "taking a handful" of the grain offering to offer upon the altar. In the Messianic context of Ps 2:12 the more idiomatic δράξασθε παιδείας ("lay hold of/embrace correction") translates the difficult Hebrew phrase נַשְּׁקוּ־בַר ("Kiss the son"). In 2 Macc 4:41 the participial form is used to describe scooping up handfuls of ashes to throw at an assailant, and in Sir 26:7 dealing with a "wicked wife" (γυνὴ πονηρά) is compared to "grasping" a scorpion.

"catch" in Job 5:13 (καταλαμβάνω), however, *is* typically Pauline, suggesting that Paul is not merely altering the LXX to conform to his own conventional style. In addition, Paul replaces φρόνησις ("understanding, insight") in LXX Job 5:13 with πανουργία ("craftiness").⁵⁰ Another intriguing factor in the citation is that Paul follows verse 19 with a nearly direct quotation from the LXX version of Ps 93:11 [EVV, Ps 94:11] in verse 20.⁵¹ Some have suggested that Paul has access to another Greek translation which he incorporates in this passage.⁵² More likely, however, Paul offers a Hebraized revision of the LXX or translates directly from the Hebrew, seeking to render the text in a more vivid and emphatic manner.⁵³

A second and perhaps more serious difficulty is determining the way in which Paul uses Eliphaz. The interpretive dilemma arises from Paul's quotation of a sage who appears to embody the very worldly wisdom he is refuting.⁵⁴ For Paul to argue against the folly of human wisdom by quoting a sage that is ultimately rebuked by Yahweh for his apparent folly (Job 42:7) seems contradictory. Lying below the surface, however, is a more satisfying solution gained by a fresh approach to the passage.⁵⁵ The focus of two recent arenas of research within Pauline studies—Paul's rhetorical strategy of Scripture citation and his literary use of irony as a means of championing theological truth in the face of challengers—together promise a useful approach in assessing Paul's use of Job 5:13.

Studies of rhetorical strategies in the Pauline corpus have broken new ground over the last few decades in understanding the apostle's use of scriptural citations.⁵⁶ These approaches seek to comprehend Pauline

---

50. Frederic Godet notes that both modifications from the LXX are advantageous, more vividly capturing the sense of the Hebrew (*Commentary on First Corinthians*, 197).

51. While clearly borrowing from the LXX text, Paul appears to take minor liberties with the quote changing ἀνθρώπων ("men") to σοφῶν ("the wise"), which is more suited to his argument (Robertson and Plummer, *First Corinthians*, 71).

52. Conzelmann, *1 Corinthians*, 80; C. K. Barrett, *First Epistle to the Corinthians*, 94; Orr and Walther, *1 Corinthians*, 170.

53. Ciampa and Rosner, "1 Corinthians," 704; Morris, *1 Corinthians*, 69; Schaller, "Zum Textcharakter der Hiobzitate," 21–26; Koch, *Die Schrift als Zeuge des Evangeliums*, 72. Most convincing is the fact that the Greek in Paul's citation more forcefully captures the essence of the Hebrew than the LXX.

54. Hübner, *Biblische Theologie des Neuen Testaments*, 2:136–37; Williams, *The Wisdom of the Wise*, 301.

55. David E. Garland hints at what I will argue for by pointing out that Paul's quotation proves its point since it is from Eliphaz, whose "wise" counsel is ultimately rejected (*1 Corinthians*, 123).

56. Hays, *Echoes of Scripture*; Stanley, *Arguing with Scripture*.

NT citations not merely in terms of Paul's own apprehension of the quoted text but in terms of the rhetorical purposes for which Paul appropriates the quotation and the ways in which readers and hearers would have responded to the quoted text. Stanley proposes that Paul routinely uses OT scripture rhetorically as a means of persuading and galvanizing the recipients of his letters.[57] In discerning the ways in which the audiences of Paul's epistles would have understood his citations, Stanley begins by sketching a number of erroneous assumptions often used incautiously in Pauline studies which treat his appropriation of OT scripture.[58] While Stanley overreaches in a few of his points and posits assumptions that in reality few scholars would legitimate, he seeks to disabuse his readers of these faulty premises by concluding the following on the basis of these spuriously touted assumptions:

> It seems unlikely that many of the people in Paul's congregations knew the Jewish Scriptures well enough to evaluate his handling of the biblical text. It seems equally implausible that Paul expected them to do so. . . . Paul normally embeds his quotations in an interpretive framework that signals to the audience how he intends the biblical text to be understood. In these cases little or no knowledge of the original context is required; the quotation achieves its rhetorical effect as long as the audience

---

57. As Stanley observes: "Paul's letters show clearly that he regarded direct quotations from the Jewish Scriptures as an effective tool for motivating various first-century Christian audiences to accept his ideas and follow his recommendations" (*Arguing with Scripture*, 38).

58. These errant assumptions are as follows: (1) Paul's audiences acknowledged the authority of the Jewish Scriptures as a source of truth and guide for Christian conduct; (2) Paul and his audiences had relatively free access to the LXX and could study or consult them whenever they wished; (3) Paul's audiences routinely read and studied the Jewish Scriptures for themselves in his absence; (4) Paul's audiences were able to recognize and appreciate all his quotations, allusions, and "echoes" from the Jewish Scriptures; (5) Paul composed his letters with the expectation that the recipients would know and supply the background and context for his many quotations, allusions, and other references to the Jewish Scriptures; (6) Paul himself knew and took into account the original context of his biblical quotations; (7) Paul expected his audiences to evaluate and accept his interpretations of Scripture; (8) Paul expected everyone in his churches to have an equal appreciation of the biblical quotations; and (9) the best way to determine the meaning of a Pauline biblical quotation is to study how Paul interpreted the biblical text (ibid., 40–60). While several of Stanley's points are valid, a few of his posited assumptions are "straw men" if indeed he believes that all these erroneous presuppositions really comprise "questionable assumptions scholars have traditionally made about the way in which Paul and his churches interacted with the biblical text" (ibid., 40). It is doubtful that a majority "tradition" of scholars would agree unequivocally, for example, to points (2), (4), and (8).

acknowledges the authority of the Jewish Scriptures and accepts Paul's reputation as a reliable interpreter of the holy text.[59]

Stanley deduces that Paul has in view a purposive rhetorical strategy toward certain subsets of his audience when he adduces citations from the OT Scriptures. In some cases the more literate or informed members of his audience are targeted; in other cases it is more difficult to discern the intended audience.

Stanley uses this interpretive point of reference to gain firmer ground in identifying three likely subsets among the recipients of Paul's letters:[60] (1) the informed audience: recipients who know the original context of every quotation Paul uses and are willing to engage in critical dialogue with Paul about his handling of the biblical text; (2) the competent audience: recipients who know just enough of the Jewish Scriptures to grasp the point of Paul's quotation and its current rhetorical context; and (3) the minimal audience: recipients who have little specific knowledge of the Jewish Scriptures and thus respect the authority of the quotation but cannot infer additional significance from the source of the citation. Stanley uses these proposed audience units as a foil to analyze the process by which Paul's use of quotations would bring about an intended response among the letter's recipients. He argues that the lion's share of recipients would have fallen into the third category.[61] While Stanley's proposed categories are sound,

---

59. Ibid., 60. Again Stanley overstates his case here especially in his first statement. It is notoriously difficult to achieve any definitive understanding of the level of scriptural knowledge in Paul's audience since we have only one side of the correspondence.

60. Ibid., 68–69.

61. Stanley argues that "careful historical analysis suggests that the majority of Paul's addressees would have been unable to read and study the biblical text for themselves" (ibid., 48–49). For Gentile converts in Paul's churches, he posits that they likely would have possessed no real knowledge of the Jewish Scriptures prior to conversion. Upon entering the church most of these illiterate initiates learned only what came to them through the oral instruction of the few literate and/or Jewish members of the congregation (ibid., 45–46). That Stanley's proposal in all likelihood goes too far, however, is the fact that Paul appears to take for granted a certain level of knowledge of the OT Scriptures amongst his Corinthian audience. In particular Paul references certain truths associated with the creation account in Genesis (1 Cor 11:8–9, 12; 15:44–45; 2 Cor 11:3), the exodus from Egypt (1 Cor 10:1–10; 2 Cor 3:3–12), aspects of Jewish ritual from the Torah (passover regulations in 1 Cor 5:7–8; prohibition of muzzling a working ox in 1 Cor 9:8–9), and common Jewish concepts derived from the OT Scriptures (the day of the Lord [1 Cor 3:13]; circumcision [1 Cor 7:18]; Pentecost [2 Cor 16:8]). Stanley's assessment seems to brush too broad a stroke to be applied universally, failing also to take into account that Paul had instructed the congregation in Corinth for one and one-half years (Acts 18:11) and that in an auditory culture listeners frequently had greater facility for memory of spoken texts. Thus Paul's audience need not be fully literate by modern standards to retain biblical truths and concepts. Stanley Porter and Bryan Dyer

he is overly dismissive in assigning the majority of recipients to the third category. Given the amount of background knowledge of the OT Scriptures that Paul takes for granted in his Corinthian correspondence, the more plausible conclusion is that most of the recipients would have comprised the second category with a fair share in the first category.[62] This assessment will bear upon the interpretation of Paul's citation below.

A second arena of Pauline studies which influence our understanding of Paul's use of Job 5:13 concerns the use of the literary device of irony. Paul's use of this rhetorical device, especially in the Corinthian correspondence, is something of a consensus among scholars.[63] Paul is particularly fond of this technique in 1 Cor 1–4 and 2 Cor 10–13, where he is able to utilize irony as an "ideal rhetorical weapon for attacking [his] opponents" who are influential in the Corinthian congregation.[64] How then is irony to be discerned in the immediate passage?

Linda Hutcheon, in her work on the nature of this literary device, identifies three elements which point to irony as a communicative process in a given text, with the first element serving as the building block upon which the others are built:[65] (1) the relational strategy between author and the readers allows for irony to be utilized as a rhetorical tool; (2) the explicit and disguised meanings must be inclusive, simultaneously implying and touching upon one another; and (3) the disguised meaning must be different from or other than the explicit meaning.[66] Another theoretician of rhetoric, T. L. Carter, lists several other clues which alert the reader to the presence of irony in a considered text: (1) the straightforward mean-

---

argue persuasively that literacy in the ancient world was likely higher and certainly more complicated than the frequently-cited statistic of an 80–95% illiteracy rate ("Oral Texts?" 239–32).

62. See Evans, *Noncanonical*, 190–219. Evans lists 72 Pauline citations from or allusions to wisdom sources (viz., Job, Prov, Eccl, Sir, Wis), several within the Corinthian correspondence.

63. See Reumann, "St. Paul's Use of Irony," 140–45; Spencer, "The Wise Fool (and the Foolish Wise," 349–60; Jónsson, *Humour and Irony in the New Testament*; Holland, "Paul's Use of Irony as a Rhetorical Technique," 234–48. So pervasive, in fact, is Paul's use of this device in 1 Corinthians that Jerome remarked the epistle is "written in gall, not ink" (quoted in Glover, *The Mind of St. Paul*, 14).

64. Carter, "The Irony of Romans 13," 214.

65. Hutcheon, *Irony's Edge*, 57–66.

66. Hutcheon states: "Ironic meaning comes into being as the consequence of a relationship, a dynamic, performative bringing together of different meaning-makers, but also of different meanings, first, to create something new and, then, . . . to endow it with the critical edge of judgment" (ibid., 58). Hutcheon expands upon this concept by contending that irony is determined first by the receptive community, who is the principal partner in creating irony (ibid., 89).

ing of a word or a text is recognizably implausible or unacceptable; (2) the detectable use of over- or understatement; (3) the (purposeful) presence of factual or logical errors; (4) inappropriate use of style; or (5) the grounding of conclusions on overtly specious reasoning.[67]

For several reasons, we suggest that irony is evident in Paul's use of the citation from Eliphaz in 1 Cor 3:19. First, the relational strategy which enables and produces irony is evident throughout the epistle and, more importantly, in the immediate context.[68] Paul knew the Corinthian congregation very well and leveraged this relationship rhetorically in his letters. He is clearly ironical earlier within the immediate pericope when he states that "if anyone among you thinks that he is wise in this age, let him become a fool that he may become wise" (v. 18). In this carefully crafted paradox Paul purposefully implements the ironical juxtaposition of incongruent/

---

67. Carter, "The Irony of Romans 13," 213. Admittedly, some of the indicators he identifies are subjective. For example, it is notoriously difficult for the modern reader to discern accurately where the meaning of an ancient text was "recognizably implausible or unacceptable" to the ancient reader (cf. Stanley, *Arguing with Scripture*, 66). Furthermore, one might add from a theological perspective that by its very nature Scripture is implausible and unacceptable to the natural man (1 Cor 2:14) and contains some things difficult to understand which "ignorant and unstable people twist to their own destruction" (2 Pet 3:16). In averring the use of irony, however, we are referring to the use of a literary device within the literal, grammatical scope of meaning rather than to the theological import of the words. Again Hutcheon is helpful in tracing this implication. "You don't actually have to reject a 'literal' meaning in order to get at what is usually called the 'ironic' or 'real' meaning of the utterance. . . . Some theorists claim that we cannot consistently embrace both the literal and ironic meanings, but I would suggest not only that we can but that, if we do not, then we are not interpreting the utterance *as ironic* at all" (*Irony's Edge*, 60, emphasis hers). In other words, the perception of irony is not (and should not be) a repudiation of literal-grammatical hermeneutics because the literal meaning must be understood if the ironic meaning is to be properly interpreted as ironical at all. When clear elements of irony are present, however, one's understanding of the passage is advanced significantly. An example of this is the recognition of the presence of Corinthian slogans to which Paul is responding, which has proved fruitful in opening new ways of understanding certain passages in 1 Corinthians (see Murphy-O'Connor, "Corinthian Slogans," 391–96; Smith, "The Roots of a 'Libertine' Slogan," 63–95).

68. Hutcheon outlines three elements of context which frame and identify irony in a work: (1) a circumstantial environment in which the "communicative context" allows for statements rendered to be possible and meaningful as irony; (2) a textual environment in which the actual or formal context of the work furnishes signs of irony; and (3) an intertextual environment in which other relevant utterances are brought to bear upon the utterance in question to produce an "inferential process" of interpretation (*Irony's Edge*, 143–44). All three environments are present in 1 Cor 3, as Paul uses his relationship with the Corinthian church to create an environment or occasion for irony, employs hyperbole and incongruity (two formal uses of irony [ibid., 156]) overtly in the epistle, and brings to bear intertextual echoes to corroborate his argument.

contradictory concepts. He does not mean, of course, that one is literally to become foolish by obviating one's rational faculties but rather that one is to become a "fool in Christ," as he previously underscored in 1 Cor 1:18–25. This apparent contradiction means that the Christian believer is one who repudiates the wisdom of this age to embrace the wisdom of God exhibited in the "folly" of the cross of Christ together with all its ethical implications.[69] He follows up this assertion by basing his argument upon another paradox, unequivocally stating that "the wisdom of this world is folly with God" (3:19). Paul moves from setting a relational tone of irony between author and readers immediately to the (ironical) appropriation of citations from the OT. Syntactically he connects the irony of verse 18 with the content of verse 19 through the twin use of the causal conjunction γάρ. As a conjunction γάρ identifies here the basis or ground for Paul's argument.[70] One must become a fool in order to be wise on the basis that (γάρ) the wisdom of this world is folly with God (v. 19a). That the wisdom of the world is folly to God is grounded in (γάρ) the citation: "It is written, 'He catches the wise in their craftiness'" (v. 19b). So then, the recognition of an ongoing relational strategy of irony is suitable to the immediate context. From this angle Paul is perceptive in his citation of the sage who himself was caught in his "worldly wisdom," providing a graphic illustration of the greater assertion he is making about the utter folly and inadequacy of human wisdom.

The second indicator of irony is that the explicit and concealed meanings of the quotation impinge upon one another. Likely Paul's readers would have been familiar with the book of Job.[71] Paul is drawing upon shared meaning and knowledge in his allusion. Thus, Paul's readers likely would have been well-versed with the ending of the book and with Eliphaz's rebuke by the Lord. To use this quote is a subtle but graphic pointer, then, to the limitations of human wisdom. On the surface Paul is saying that God seizes the wise in their craftiness; disguised or embedded in the quotation is the meaning which provides an illustration of this reality: Eliphaz the philo-

---

69. See Grindheim, "Wisdom," 693.

70. On this use of the conjunction, see Wallace, *Beyond the Basics*, 674.

71. Hays notes, *contra* Stanley, that in general the implied readers of Paul's letters appear to be "primarily Gentile Christians with an extensive knowledge of the LXX and an urgent interest in its interpretation" (*Echoes of Scripture*, 29; cf. Stanley, *Arguing with Scripture*, 38). Acts 18:11 reports that Paul remained in Corinth for eighteen months teaching the Word of God, insinuating that Paul systematically instructed from the Old Testament. Furthermore, it appears that the book of Job had a far-reaching audience since its wide circulation had given rise to pseudepigraphical works such as the *Testament of Job*. Although speaking to a primarily Jewish audience, the apostolic church leader James takes for granted that the book was well known to Christians ("You have heard of the steadfastness of Job" Jas 5:11).

sophically sly Babbitt is "apprehended" by Yahweh in an ironical exhibition of his own folly.

Third, the disguised meaning is distinct from the explicit meaning in that the disguised meaning intensifies what the recipient gains from the explicit meaning. In other words, the "cloaked" meaning of the citation is that the speaker Eliphaz is divinely "seized" by means of his own craftiness (i.e., "rebuked by Yahweh") in the unfolding events of Job, while the on-the-surface meaning is that Eliphaz pronounces (the truth) that God catches all the allegedly wise through the plying of their own cunning devices. The citation bolsters Paul's point that the one who professes to be wise cannot escape the judgment of God by worldly cunning or ingenuity no matter how eloquent a sophist he or she claims to be.

As to Carter's criteria for identifying irony, the passage fits at least two of his marshalled traits of irony as well. First, with regard to Carter's first category that the straightforward meaning of a word or a text is recognizably implausible or unacceptable, we find that what might seem to the informed reader of 1 Corinthians (and Job) as an implausible appropriation by Paul is rendered poignant by the perception of irony. Second, in his next category of the use of over- or understatement, the discerning reader observes that Paul is subtly understating the perspective that he is arguing for. That God catches the wise in their craftiness is dramatically presented in the striking conclusion to Job when the eloquent sage himself is apprehended by God.

Our conclusion, then, is that Paul appropriates the citation of Job 5:13 as part of a rhetorical strategy of irony in 1 Cor 3:18–23. He aspires to convince recipients among the informed and biblically literate audience groups who would draw out the implications of the quote and to countervail his detractors who by the illegitimate use of worldly speculation are heedlessly hurtling toward apprehension by God. This perspective provides insight into what otherwise has been construed as a potential interpretive conundrum in Paul's citational purpose. At the same time it aids in understanding that Paul may quote from Eliphaz in a compelling way without necessarily endorsing every aspect of what the sage declares to and about God in the book of Job.[72] Paul's use of Eliphaz is masterful; his assessment of Eliphaz

---

72. I anticipate two objections which the reader may raise. First, one might demur that what I have proposed is illegitimate because Paul does not use irony in the second passage he cites in v. 20, "And again, 'The Lord knows the thoughts of the wise, that they are futile.'" I would suggest, however, that an ironical meaning is likely also present here, although a lengthy development of this is beyond the scope of this section. As noted previously, Paul modifies the LXX ἀνθρώπων ("men") to σοφῶν ("the wise") in 3:20. In doing so Paul seems to be adding another ironical twist to his point. Instead of merely citing that the Lord knows the thoughts of men, he uses the quote rhetorically to declare that the Lord knows the thoughts of "all men-who-think-themselves-to-be-wise,"

in the light of our interpretation of the passage is ambivalent as to Eliphaz's tone (A), purpose (B), theological provenance (C), retributive doctrine (D), special revelation (E), doctrine of remedial suffering (F), use of ancient sources (G), and status as doyen (H). He is likely negative toward Eliphaz's rebuke by Yahweh (I).

Clement of Rome

Early church father Clement of Rome (*ca.* AD 30–100) makes several allusions to Job in his first epistle to the Corinthians, written most likely around AD 95 or 96.[73] The letter was commissioned by a group of presbyters from the church in Rome and composed to resolve dissensions in the Corinthian church because of which certain elders had been forcibly removed from office and (illegitimately) replaced by others.[74] The letter was written originally in Greek and comes down to us in the form of two Greek manuscripts, the eleventh-century Codex Hierosolymitanus and the fifth-century Codex Alexandrinus, together with Latin and Syriac versions.[75] Although most of

---

namely the worldly wise he has confronted earlier (those who think themselves *wise* in their own eyes is a valid description for all unregenerate humanity according to Paul's theological perspective elsewhere [Rom 1:22]; cf. also Hans Hübner: "In seinen Augen ist das aber keine sachliche Modifikation, da für ihn die Weisen dieser Welt nichts anderes sind als—Menschen!" ("The modification, however non-material, is in his eyes that for him the wise of this world are nothing else than—men!") (*Biblische Theologie des Neuen Testaments*, 2:137). Second, one may argue that straightforward irony is one thing, a rhetorical strategy of citing texts for the purpose of irony is another thing altogether. It appears that Paul does this very thing elsewhere, however, in Tit 1:12–13 as he quotes from the Cretan poet: "One of the Cretans, a prophet of their own, said, 'Cretans are always liars, evil beasts, lazy gluttons.' This testimony is true." Paul does not mean that all Cretans are actually always liars, and so forth, [e.g., this would make Titus's task of appointing overseers who were above reproach [1:7] an impossibility!]. Paul uses hyperbole [i.e., one of the most commonly agreed-upon signs of irony (Hutcheon, *Irony's Edge*, 156)] to prove his point that Titus must directly confront the Cretans' besetting sins. In a similar way I contend that Paul is quoting Eliphaz somewhat tongue-in-cheek in this passage to prove his point that human wisdom never rivals the unsurpassed insight of the Lord.

73. As Otto Bardenhewer proposes the letter was probably written toward the end of the reign of Domitian (81–96) or the beginning of the reign of Nerva (96–98) (*Patrology*, 27). Donald A. Hagner notes that Clement's epistle is the earliest extant Christian writing that is not part of the NT canon (*Old and New Testaments in Clement*, 1).

74. Evans, *Noncanonical Writings*, 156; Ehrman, *Lost Scriptures*, 167–68. For an overview of the conflict which occasioned the epistle, see Peterlin, "Clement's Answer to the Corinthian Conflict," 57–69; Peterlin, "The Corinthian Church," 49–57; Welborn, "On the Date of First Clement," 35–54; Welborn, "Clement, First Epistle of," 1:1055–60.

75. Bardenhewer, *Patrology*, 26–27.

Clement's remarks concerning Job focus upon his exemplary character (e.g., *1 Clem.* 17:3), noteworthy for our purposes is the thirty-ninth chapter of the epistle. Clement is here admonishing the church against self-conceit, known also from Paul's epistles of 1 and 2 Corinthians to be a problem plaguing the congregation. Clement writes: "Foolish and inconsiderate men, who have neither wisdom nor instruction, mock and deride us, being eager to exalt themselves in their own conceits. For what can a mortal man do? Or what strength is there in one made out of the dust?" (*1 Clem.* 39:1–2). Clement goes on in the chapter to argue polemically against the hubris of his opponents by quoting four passages from Eliphaz: Job 4:16–18; 4:19–21; 5:1–5; and 15:15.[76] Clement uses the scriptural citation formula γέγραπται γάρ to introduce the quotations. In chapter 56 Clement quotes Eliphaz at length again, citing nearly verbatim LXX Job 5:17–26 in an exhortation to pray for and admonish those who have fallen into sin so that they might humbly and graciously submit to the will of God.[77] Eliphaz's eloquent assertions regarding the material blessings and longevity that accompany the chastening of the Lord are well-suited to Clement's own exhortations to the Corinthians to remove the sin in their midst.

In summary, a few observations merit mention. Clement is obviously influenced by the LXX and its interpretive trajectory. In view of the previous suggestion that the LXX softened Eliphaz and removed objectionable elements in his dialogues, the LXX precipitated warm reception and appropriation of Eliphaz's speeches in the later writings of church fathers such as Clement. Thus without making explicit reference to Eliphaz or his character, Clement quotes generously from Eliphaz's speeches, implicitly presupposing the scriptural authority of his words. On the positive side of this previously observed interpretive polarity, Clement adopts Eliphaz's speeches as with the full weight of divine revelation. Thus, by appropriating Eliphaz's insights Clement appears favorable toward his theological sources (C), special revelation (E), doctrine of remedial suffering (F), and use of ancient sources (G). His understanding of Eliphaz's tone (A), purpose (B), retributive doctrine (C), use of sin list (H), and the purpose of Yahweh's rebuke (I) are uncertain.

---

76. Hagner observes that there is little departure here from the LXX aside from slight rearrangement of material by inserting a quotation from LXX Job 15:15 towards the beginning of the citation (*Clement*, 57).

77. On the character of the quotation, see Hagner, *Clement*, 41.

Methodius

Methodius of Olympius (d. 311) is a mostly obscure early church father who is identified principally from his inclusion in Jerome's anthology *Lives of Illustrious Men*[78] and from his extant writings entitled *Symposium* and *Fragments on Job*.[79] Little is known of Methodius other than that he was bishop of Olympus in Lycia, becoming a martyr there toward the end of the Diocletian persecution in AD 311 Also noteworthy was his virulent opposition to Origen.[80]

In his exposition of the chapter extolling the excellences of wisdom in Job 28, Methodius proposes that Job has recited the discourse as the antipode to the three friends who "imagined that they understood the reason why he suffered."[81] Job contends in his poem that the wisdom of the divine Judge is incomprehensible and unattainable to every man, even more so by the exertion of human effort. The earthly sphere is, moreover, not a fitting place for understanding the divine counsels. Although Methodius is brief in his reference to the friends of Job, he offers a clear perspective on their wisdom. Methodius argues the wisdom of Eliphaz and the others is spurious—laying claim to insight that is by mere human exertion unobtainable. Thus, where the tone of Eliphaz (A), purpose (B), theological provenance and creed (C), and likely retributive dogma (D) are in view, Methodius is disparaging. His perspective on Eliphaz's special revelation (E), understanding of remedial suffering (F), status as doyen (G), use of the sin list (H), and rebuke by Yahweh (I) is inconclusive.

Chrysostom

The renowned fourth-century church father John Chrysostom (347–407), the "golden-mouthed" expositor of Scripture, is among the most revered early leaders of the Greek church.[82] His unrivalled eloquence garnered him high esteem in Constantinople, where he was archbishop, and throughout the ancient world.[83] As part of the Antiochene school of interpretation,

---

78. Jerome, *Lives of Illustrious Men*, 3:378–79.

79. Methodius, *Fragments on Job*, 6:401.

80. Krüger, *History of Early Christian Literature*, 235–37.

81. Methodius, *Fragments on Job*, 6:401.

82. Philip Schaff, *History of the Christian Church*, 9:933–34.

83. Henri Sorlin writes of his rhetorical eloquence: "Chrysostome est un apôtre, mais il ne néglige pas pour autant les moyens que lui fournit la rhétorique pour entraîner l'adhésion de ses auditeurs. L'orateur n'est jamais seul. Sans cesse, il interpelle des assistants réels ou fictifs. Son style est donc éminemment oratoire" ("Chrysostom is an

The Reception History of Eliphaz

which staunchly opposed the Alexandrian allegorical method, Chrysostom was sensitive to communicate consistently the historical, grammatical sense of the biblical text.[84] His commentary on Job was an influential piece which likely coalesced from exegetical digests that Chrysostom prepared for preaching through Job.[85] The textual basis for the commentary is LXX Job, exhibiting particular affinities to the Antiochene or Lucianic recension.[86] The commentary comes to us in the form of two tenth-century manuscripts, the Mosquensis edition and Laurentianus edition which together comprise the complete commentary.[87] Given Chrysostom's stature as a communicator of biblical truth, his commentary will provide insight into perceptions toward Eliphaz in the fourth century Antiochene school and Greek-speaking milieu.

Chrysostom begins his treatment of the friends with an explanation of their controvertible appearance in the narrative of Job: "Just as, from the quarter he expected to find some excellent consolation and encouragement, he found ruin from his wife, so too from the friends. While they come to give consolation, they do the opposite, and before their words sight alone

---

apostle, yet he does not disregard for all that the means which provide him the rhetoric for carrying the support of his listeners. The speaker is never alone. Without ceasing he calls out to assistants, real or fictitious. His style is thus eminently oratorical.") ("Introduction," 1:61). As an eloquent preacher "not unaccustomed to being given standing ovations even in church," Chrysostom was highly revered in and out of the church for this oratorical skill (Hill, "Introduction," 10) (Schaff notes—amusingly—that "this Greek custom of applauding the preacher by clapping the hands and stamping the feet [called κρότος, from κρούω] was a sign of the secularization of the church after its union with the state. It is characteristic of his age that a powerful sermon of Chrysostom against this abuse was most enthusiastically applauded by his hearers!" [*History of the Christian Church*, 9:938n3]).

84. Kepple, "Analysis of Antiochene Exegesis," 240.

85. Hill makes the point that Chrysostom's comments on Job are much more concise than, for example, his homilies on Genesis, suggesting that the commentary is not commensurable to the full homiletical manuscripts which Chrysostom would have usually preached from ("Introduction," 3–4).

86. Fernández, *The Septuagint in Context*, 228; Hill, "Introduction," 6.

87. Sorlin, "Introduction," 1:12–14. The only possible exception being the complete omission of commentary on chapter 41, which Sorlin attributes to the fact that Chrysostom grew tired (as incidentally likely did also the translator of LXX Job) as the book wore on: "Plus on avançait dans le livre de Job, plus commentaire était court," owing to the fact that the author "progressivement se lasser au cours des chapitres." ("The more we advance in the book of Job, the more the comment is short" because the author "gradually grows tired through the course of the chapters.") Moreover, this was not his intended scope: "Il n'a pas cherché à présenter un exposé développé et exhaustif de tout le Livre de Job" ("He did not try to present a developed and exhaustive presentation of all the book of Job") ("Introduction," 44–45, 46).

is sufficient to make the righteous man downcast."[88] Indeed the friends are inconsistent, outwardly unctuous but inwardly conjuring spite against Job: "Friendly indeed was their appearance, but not friendly their exhortation and advice" (Φιλικὴ μέν ἡ παρουσία, οὐ φιλικὴ δὲ ἡ παραίνεσις καὶ ἡ σθμβουλή) (my translation).[89] Still, Chrysostom is occasionally ambivalent, acknowledging that the companions exhibit a few traits of genuine friendship, while realizing that in the course of the debate they do not show themselves friendly: "All these were noble gestures worthy of friends who were sympathetic [lit. "who were sympathizing (by) proofs"], but what came later was not, instead being quite contrary to it and lacking what was needed."[90]

Chrysostom sustains this interpretive tension regarding the figure of Eliphaz. In his vanity Eliphaz is acerbic in tone and harmful in the ways he inaptly and ineffectually applies truth to Job. He and the others from the outset "intend to trample him down and rush against (him) while he is down" (ἐβούλοντο αὐτῷ ἐπεμβαίνειν καὶ ἐνάλλεσθαι κειμένῳ) (my translation).[91] Because of this, Chrysostom has scorn for the way Eliphaz mistreats Job:

---

88. Ὥσπερ, ὅθεν προσεδόκησε παραμθθίαν τινὰ καὶ παραίνεσιν ἀρίστην εὑρήσεῖν, ἐντεῦθεν εὗρεν ὄλεθρον ἀπὸ τῆς γθναικός, οὕτω καὶ ἀπὸ τῶν φίλων. Παραγίνονται μὲν ὡς παραμυθησόμενοι, τὸ δὲ ἐναντίον ποιοῦσι, καὶ πρὸ τῶν ῥημάτων δὲ αὐτῶν, ἱκανὴ μόνη ἡ ὄψις τὸν δίκαιον καταβαλεῖν. The Greek text is taken from Sorlin's edition (*Commentaire sur Job*, 1:192). For the translation we borrow from Hill, *Commentaries on the Sages*, 61–62.

89. Reading Chrysostom in Greek gives one an appreciation for his oratorical skill exhibited in the assonance and cadence of his words. Hill's translation is rather clunky: "While their presence was a gesture of friendship, their recommendations and advice were not friendly" (*Commentaries on the Sages*, 63). Sorlin's translation is better: "Amicale, en effet, était leur présence, inamicaux, par contre, leurs conseils et leurs exhortations" ("Friendly, in effect, was their presence; unfriendly, on the other hand, [were] their advice and their exhortations") (*Commentaire sur Job*, 1:195).

90. Ταῦτα πάντα καλὰ καὶ φίλων ἄξια καὶ συμπαθούντων τεκμήρια, ἀλλὰ τὰ μετὰ ταῦτα οὐκέτι τοιαῦτα, ἀλλὰ πολλῶν ἐναντία καὶ ἀποδέοντα. Hill, *Commentaries on the Sages*, 63; *Commentaire sur Job*, 1:196. The last phrase "lacking what was needed" I prefer to render "falling short" (so Liddell and Scott). One might read Chrysostom here as overtly negative against the friends. I would argue, however, that Chrysostom is suggesting Eliphaz and the other companions were in fact genuine friends but that their growing ire against Job would eventually get the best of them. Chrysostom maintains skillfully the tension between the friends' shortcoming in their censorious approach to Job and their facility in sustaining an eloquent and profound dialogue. His argument here is that while Eliphaz and the others held on to the customary tokens of genuine friendship, they could not in reality deliver upon this friendship as their dogma prohibited them from acknowledging Job as an exception to the stringent rules which governed their outlook.

91. *Commentaire sur Job*, 1:218.

They were therefore well named 'surgeons of trouble' [lit. 'physicians of evils'—I prefer 'doctors of disaster' while Sorlin renders 'médecins de malheur'] for aggravating the complaint and doing so out of envy. What awful malice would one be guilty of amid such a tempest to show envy and be jealous of a person laid low, and to invest him with countless disasters when he deserves pity? I mean, observe how the words coming from them are not only devoid of comfort, but even instill deep depression and develop lengthy accusations.⁹²

Eliphaz's harassment of Job is at times to the point of diabolical: "The most terrible of all is this, that under the pretense of godly words and arrangement of consolation, the devil armed them to wound him. Notice how surgingly they assail by discourse, mocking him for his folly."⁹³

Part of Eliphaz's shortcoming is the infelicitous application of his rigid rules regarding divine providence. For Eliphaz the divine governance is established to operate inflexibly according to fixed patterns or norms:⁹⁴

> See what he is saying: just as natural events would happen in no other way than by an arrangement in keeping with nature, so too here (he is saying) in regard to evil people's perishing and good people's enjoying prosperity. . . . Notice: he cites natural events, that is to say, nothing happens that is strange or unexpected; rather, everything is organized by certain laws, nothing changes.⁹⁵

---

92. Καλῶς οὖν <ἰατροὶ κακῶν> ἐκλήθησαν, ἐπιτρίβοντες τὸ τραῦμα, πάσχουσι δὲ αὐτὸ ἀπὸ βασκανίας· Πόσης δὲ πονηρίας ἂν εἴη, ἐν τοσούτῳ βασκαίνειν χειμῶνι καὶ κειμένῳ φθονεῖν, καὶ τὸν ἄξιον ἐλεεῖσθαι τοῦτον μυρίοις περιβάλλειν δεινοῖς; Ὅρα γὰρ πῶς οὐ μόνον παραμυθίας ἀπέχει τὰ ῥήματα τὰ παρ' αὐτῶν, ἀλλὰ καὶ πολλὴν τὴν ἀθυμίαν ἐντίθησι καὶ κατηγορίας μακροὺς ἀποτείνει λόγους. (Hill, *Commentaries on the Sages*, 72; *Commentaire sur Job*, 1:218).

93. Τὸ πάντων δεινότατον τοῦτ' ἔστιν, ὅτι ἐν προσχήματι λόγων εὐσεβῶν καὶ τάξει πραμυθίας ὥπλισεν αὐτοὺς ὁ διάβολος τιτρώσκειν αὐτόν· καὶ ὅρα πῶς καταφορικῶς κέχρηνται τῷ λόγῳ, εἰς ἄνοιαν αὐτὸν σκώπτοντες· (my translation). (Hill's translation is somewhat imprecise: "The worst feature of all is that under the guise of pious words and the pretext of giving comfort the devil equipped them to wound him. Notice how volubly they assail him, jeering at his folly" [*Commentaries on the Sages*, 126]). The Greek text is from *Commentaire sur Job*, 2:10.

94. See Hill, *Commentaries on the Sages*, 216, nn. 5, 7.

95. Ὅρα τί φησιν· Ὥσπερ τὰ κατὰ φύσιν πράγματα οὐκ ἂν ἑτέρως γένοιτο, ἀλλ' ἢ ὡς κατὰ φύσιν τέτακται, οὕτω, φησί, καὶ ἐνταῦθα, οἷον δήτω τοὺς μὲν πονηροὺς ἀπολέσθαι, τοὺς δὲ ἀγαθοὺς ἐν εὐθηνίᾳ εἶναι. . . . Καὶ ὅρα· φυσικὰ πράγματα λαμβάνει, τοῦτ' ἔστιν· οὐδὲν καινὸν οὐδὲ ξένον γίνεται, ἀλλὰ νόμοις τισὶ πάντα τέτακται, καὶ οὐδὲν ἐνήλλακται· *Commentary on Job*, 75–76; *Commentaire sur Job*, 1:227–28.

That is, Eliphaz propounds that it is in keeping with the irrevocable laws of nature that prosperity is the lot of the righteous and calamity the lot of the evildoers—with the obvious implication that Job falls into the latter category.[96]

Chrysostom has subtle esteem, nonetheless, for segments of Eliphaz's speeches, particularly his remarks in chapter 5, where the leading interlocutor is at his high water mark. In addition, I would suggest that Chrysostom has inconspicuous sympathy for certain aspects of Eliphaz's view of retributive providence. Chrysostom hints that Eliphaz here and there shows flashes of brilliance as a purveyor of key tenets of biblical wisdom. For example, in commenting on 4:17 Chrysostom shows concord with Eliphaz's perspective, citing two passages from the Psalms to undergird the truth (it is "not a matter of opinion") of Eliphaz's declaration:

> Let us not take this as a matter of opinion, dearly beloved; [Eliphaz] did well to add *before the Lord*, as the prophet says, 'Surely no living thing will be found righteous before you?' and again, 'If you took note of sins, Lord, who would stand?' You see, just as our goodness is wickedness compared with his goodness, so too in other respects. (Μὴ δὴ ταῦτα εἰς δόγματα δεξώμεθα, ἀγαπητοί· καὶ καλῶς προσέθηκεν <Ἔναντι Κυρίου> καθὼς ὁ Προφήτης φησί· <Μὴ δικαιωθήσεται ἐνώπιόν σου πᾶς ζῶν;> Καθάπερ γὰρ ἡμῶν ἡ ἀγαθότης πονηρία ἐστὶν πρὸς τὴν ἐκείνου ἀγαυότητα σθγρινομένη, οὕτω καὶ τὰ λοιπά.)[97]

In chapter 5 Eliphaz, in speaking eloquently of God's transcendence, communicates realities that Job had not been able to perceive due to the limitations of his human perspective: "Since Job probably examined his situation on the basis of his own reasoning, you see, note what he says, 'Do not say this to me; God is great, he does many things of which we are unaware. Our lowliness is profound; we are at a great distance from him.'"[98] In his ensuing comments on chapter 5, Chrysostom notes a few places in which other authors of Scripture agree with Eliphaz, hinting at the conclusion that Eliphaz has useful and authentic sapience to contribute at these junctures.[99] Yet in

---

96. *Commentary on Job*, 74.

97. *Commentary on Job*, 79; *Commentaire sur Job*, 1:234. Chrysostom quotes from LXX Pss 143:2 and 130:3.

98. Ἐπειδὴ γὰρ εἰκὸς ἦν ἀπὸ οἰκείων λογισμῶν ἐξετάζειν τὰ καθ' ἑαυτὸν τὸν Ἰώβ, ὅρα τί φησι· Μή μοι τοῦτο εἴπῃς· μέγας ἐστὶν ὁ θεός, πολλὰ ποιεῖ ὧν οὐκ ἴσμεν· Πολὺ τὸ ταπεινὸν τὸ ἡμέτερον· ἀτοκείμεθά που πόρρω. *Commentary on Job*, 81; *Commentaire sur Job*, 1:242.

99. Chrysostom quotes Ps 90:10 and Gen 47:9 as agreeing with Eliphaz in his statements at 5:6 (*Commentary on Job*, 83) and Prov 2:12 as agreeing with Eliphaz at

the end Eliphaz lamentably "overturns altogether the benefit of what was spoken and deals a painful blow" (ὠφέλειαν τῶν εἰρημένων κατέστρεψεν ἅπασαν, καὶ χαλεπὴν ἔδωκεν τὴν πληγὴν) (my translation).[100] By the insensitive application of his censure, Eliphaz mitigates much of the insight he had provided.

For Chrysostom Eliphaz is an interpretative conundrum. Eliphaz's tone (A), purpose (B), use of the sin list (H), and rebuke by Yahweh (I) are viewed unfavorably. Yet Chrysostom has affinities at times for Eliphaz's theological provenance and creed (C), retributive teaching (D), special revelation (E), view of remedial suffering (F), and status as elder statesman (G). Eliphaz's theological matrix aligns with commendable truths from the biblical wisdom of the Psalms and Proverbs. Therefore, Chrysostom embodies the ambivalent (although at times favorable) reading of Eliphaz which would characterize much of the interpretive history down to the contemporary era. We turn next from the Greek-speaking church to the tradition of rabbinic interpretation which has its own way of dealing with Eliphaz.

Rabbinic Interpretation

Rabbinic interpretation of Eliphaz, as with most readings of the biblical text, is diffuse. The rabbinic authorities identify Eliphaz as one of seven Gentiles who will testify of Israel at the end of the age that she was faithful to the whole Torah.[101] He is also one of seven Gentile prophets who prophesied to the heathen, distinguished from genuine Israelite prophets who address themselves primarily to the nation of Israel.[102] In an imaginative suggestion by Rabbi Judah, Eliphaz and the other friends were kings who knew of Job's afflictions because each wore a crown with the figure of the others on it. When one of the kings was in trouble his visage on the others' crown would become distorted to alert them of his need.[103]

As to elucidations of Eliphaz's character and role in Job, one may again observe a distinction between perceptions of his purpose in the book and the use of his speech-dialogues as authoritative scriptural text. As to the former, rabbinic law taught that if a man is visited by suffering, is afflicted with disease, or has buried his children, one is not permitted to speak to

---

5:21 (ibid., 86).

100. *Commentaire sur Job*, 1:256.
101. 'Abod. Zar. 3a.
102. B. Bat. 15b.
103. B. Bat. 16b

him as Eliphaz does in Job 4:6.[104] Elsewhere, Rabbi Johanan on the authority of Rabbi José ben Zimra insinuates in his remarks upon Genesis 22:1 a very negative view of Eliphaz ("After these 'words' [Heb. הַדְּבָרִים הָאֵלֶּה] God tested Abraham").[105] The phrase "these words" (הַדְּבָרִים הָאֵלֶּה) refers, according to the rabbi, to the words of Satan who appears before God to accuse Abraham of self-interested piety. The ensuing account in Genesis 22 is the means by which God proves Abraham's devotion. The rabbi claims that when Abraham is on his way to offer up Isaac, Satan comes to him and quotes insidiously from the words of Eliphaz in Job 4:6 ("Is not your fear of God your confidence, and the integrity of your ways your hope?"), mingled with other excerpts from Eliphaz's first speech.[106] This vignette, although fanciful eisegesis, provides insight into the rabbi's view of the role of Eliphaz in Job. As inferable by the fact that Eliphaz's words are put in Satan's mouth, one may surmise that the rabbis conversely view Eliphaz as Satan's mouthpiece to tempt and harass Job.

The eloquent pronouncements of Eliphaz are used frequently by the rabbis, however, to prove an abstruse point or to add weight at times to obscurantist argumentation. An important observation on this score is that every authoritative quotation of Eliphaz in rabbinic interpretation derives from Eliphaz's first speech in Job, by far his most eloquent and psalmic (Job 4–5), a trend that is noticeable in the majority of interpreters. For example, the rabbis argue on the basis of Eliphaz's words in Job 5:24 ("You shall know that your tent is at peace, and you shall inspect your fold and miss nothing") that he who loves his wife as himself and honors her more than himself and who leads his children in the right path and marries them off just before they attain puberty lives in peace and does not sin.[107] Eliphaz's words in Job 5:10 ("He gives rain on the earth [אָרֶץ] and sends waters on the fields [חוּצוֹת]") are interpreted by some rabbis to mean that Palestine is watered by rain and the rest of the world only by its residue.[108] Rabbi Isaac takes as authoritative Eliphaz's words in Job 5:7 ("the sons of Resheph soar aloft" [בְּנֵי־רֶשֶׁף יַגְבִּיהוּ עוּף] [my translation]) as proving that demons flee when one recites the Torah.[109] Rabbi Nathan argues on the basis of Job 5:13 that God

---

104. B. Meṣiʿa 58b

105. In consulting over 20 English and German versions, I found no version that translates the Hebrew term הַדְּבָרִים as "words," using uniformly the glosses "things," "Dingen," or "Geschichten." The LXX, however, uses ῥήματα, which evidently has colored rabbinical discussion.

106. Sanh. 89b

107. Sanh. 76b

108. Taʿan. 9b

109. Ber. 5a

metes out justice to everyone, including Abraham. Attributing the book of Job to Solomon, he contends: "King Solomon saw how he [Abraham] was caught in a trap, for it says, He taketh the wise in their own craftiness (Job v, 13)."[110] In addition, according to another rabbi, Moses appropriates the words of Eliphaz from Job 5:13 when weighing whether to heed the people or to heed God in the wilderness, deciding not to heed the crafty counsel of the people.[111] Other examples may be adduced to illustrate that Eliphaz's speeches were often appropriated as authoritative Scripture.[112] Thus an interpretive distinction is again made by the rabbinic use of Eliphaz's words as Scripture while rejecting his role in the book of Job. Rabbinic exegesis of Eliphaz is negative generally toward his tone (A), purpose (B), and retributive doctrine (D). More positive is its assessment of Eliphaz's doctrine of remedial suffering (F), and special revelation (as a Gentile prophet) (E). The rabbis fluctuate concerning his theological provenance and creed (C): sometimes he is the mouthpiece of Satan and other times his words carry full scriptural authority. The evaluation of other salient features, his status as doyen (G), use of the sin list (H), and rebuke by Yahweh (I) are inconclusive.

Medieval and Protestant Interpretation

The course of interpretation for the book of Job in the Middle Ages and into the Protestant Reformation is set by a few leading figures who were heavily influential upon later interpreters.

Jerome and the Latin Vulgate

With the standardization in the fifth century of his Latin translation of the Bible known as the Vulgate, Jerome (346–420) would become highly influential upon the early medieval church.[113] Jerome actually made two translations of Job, the first from the LXX between 389 and 392 and the second from Hebrew sometime in the mid 390's.[114] The latter translation would become the standard version, however, and is the version commonly referred to as Vulgate Job. In this latter translation Jerome claimed to have

---

110. *Exod. Rab.* 30.16.

111. *Num. Rab.* 19.9.

112. Job 4:12 in *Ned.* 90a; Job 5:9–10 in *Ta'an.* 2a.

113. For an overview of Jerome's life and thought, see Kelly, *His Life, Writings, and Controversies*; Sigüenza, *The Life of St. Jerome*; Steinman, *Saint Jerome and His Times*. For his influence upon the Middle Ages, see Rice, *Saint Jerome in the Renaissance*.

114. See Vicchio, *Image of the Biblical Job*, 2:5.

"rescued Job from the dunghill" by reproducing faithfully the words and meaning from "the original Hebrew, Arabic, and occasionally the Syriac" into Latin.[115] He was quick to point out to his critics, who charged him with corrupting the LXX Greek version of Job, that reaching back from the LXX no translation of the book, including the revered versions/recensions of Aquila, Symmachus, Theodotion, and Origen, had been free from textual missteps, and that no version constituted a complete and thorough translation of the entire Hebrew text as his did.[116]

Although Jerome's Latin translation of Job does not reveal much of his opinion of Eliphaz, quite relevant for our study is what Jerome translated in the Jewish apocryphal work of Tobit. According to Otzen, Jerome only half-heartedly agreed to translate the apocryphal books at the behest of the church synods in North Africa in the 390's.[117] Of Tobit, he claimed to have translated the book in one day by having a Jew translate the Aramaic original into Hebrew.[118] It appears evident, however, that Jerome also had by his side an old Latin version of the book and probably recourse to a Greek version as well.[119] As to the character of the Vulgate translation, it is mostly uneven, including several additions, abridgements, and periphrases.

The portion of the account which is salient for the present study is Tob 2:12–18. Here the Latin Vulgate has an extended portion which does not correspond to any other ancient textual witnesses of Tobit.[120] Of particular note is verse 15 which reads "nam sicut beato Iob insultabant reges ita isti parentes et cognati eius et invidebant vitam eius" ("For as the kings insulted holy Job, so his relatives and kinsmen mocked at his life").[121] Whether Jerome obtained this reading from his *Vorlage* or added it himself cannot be determined with any certainty.

---

115. Jerome, "Preface to Job," 6:491.

116. Ibid.

117. Vicchio, *Image of the Biblical Job*, 2:64.

118. Jerome, "Preface to Tobit and Judith," 6:494.

119. Moore argues that Jerome most likely added portions himself to his translation rather than deriving them from the Aramaic version he was allegedly consulting (*Tobit*, 132). The source of these additions is not easily deciphered, however, given the complex textual history of Tobit. Although Jerome claims to have used an Aramaic original, his translation exhibits certain affinities to the LXX version (e.g., Job's friends are kings) and does not closely match the Aramaic version discovered among the Qumran scrolls. In addition, the LXX produced two versions of Tobit, both of which demonstrate noticeable differences from the apparent *Vorlage* that Jerome used (for more on this, see Vicchio, *Image of the Biblical Job*, 1:122).

120. See Skemp, *The Vulgate of Tobit*, 86.

121. See Moore, *Tobit*, 132.

Although the excerpt is quite brief, at least two observations are significant for the present study. First, the Latin Vulgate translation clearly follows the interpretive stream of the LXX in identifying the friends of Job as "kings" (*reges*; cf. LXX Job 2:11 βασιλεύς). This rendering confirms the wide influence of the LXX and is evidence that the friends were accepted as men of high (royal) standing for several centuries of interpretation. Second, Eliphaz and the others putatively "insult holy Job." This brief allusion reveals a negative view of the tone (A) and purpose (B) of Eliphaz and the other friends vis-à-vis the pious Job. Its assessment of Eliphaz's theological provenance and creed (C), retributive dogma (D), special revelation (E), view of remedial suffering (F), elder statesman status (G), use of the sin list (H), and rebuke by Yahweh (I) are inconclusive based on what may be gleaned from the terse excerpt.

Gregory the Great

The figure most influential upon Joban interpretation in the Middle Ages was undoubtedly Gregory the Great (*ca.* 540–604)[122] by means of his widely disseminated commentary entitled *Moralia in Iob*.[123] In this extensive tract[124] Gregory expounds upon the book of Job according to its historical or literal, its allegorical, and its moral meaning.[125] Gregory seeks first to ascertain the

122. For an overview of Gregory's life and thought, see Barmby, *Gregory the Great*; Dudden, *Gregory the Great*; Howorth, *Saint Gregory the Great*; Wasselynck, "L'Influence des Moralia"; Evans, *The Thought of Gregory the Great*; Bethancourt, *The Pastoral Vision of Gregory the Great*.

123. As Wilken notes: "No exegetical work from the early church was more admired, studied, excerpted, and cited than Gregory the Great's large commentary on the book of Job, the *Moralia* ("The *Moralia* of Gregory the Great," 213). Wasselynck highlights its pedagogical value: "Le livre de Job fournit la seule unité de cette vaste encyclopédie théologique par laquelle S. Grégorie léguait à la postérité non seulement un enseignement moral mais une solide méthode exégétique qui devait être adoptée par tous les théologiens médiévaux. Cette méthode restait fort souple, n'ayant qu'un seul but: éduquer. Une fois admis le principe des trois sens bibliques, elle laissait à l'exégète une grande liberté de dévelopement" ("The book of Job provided the sole unity of this vast theological encyclopedia by which Saint Gregory bequeathed to posterity not only a moral teaching but a solid exegetical method that was adopted by all medieval theologians. This method remained quite flexible, having only one goal: to educate. Once the principle of three biblical senses was accepted, it allowed the exegete a great liberty of development") (*L'Influence des* Moralia, 1:55).

124. The potential obstacle that Gregory knew neither Hebrew nor Greek was no bar to his prolixity, as the tome encompasses thirty-five books (Schaff, *History of the Christian Church*, 4:226–27). The English translation spans three volumes (*Morals on Job*).

125. The fanciful allegorizations, while taken for granted by Gregory, are distasteful

literal significance of the text, which he claims to be of essential importance.[126] As to their literal significance, Eliphaz and the other friends, according to Gregory, are clearly heretics:

> [Job's] friends, who, while acting as his counsellors, at the same time inveigh against him, are an express image of heretics, who under shew of giving counsel, are busied in leading astray; and hence they address the blessed Job as though in behalf of the Lord, but yet the Lord does not command them, that is, because all heretics, while they try to defend, only offend God.[127]

Gregory points out in addition that the significance of Eliphaz's name is indicative of his character: "Eliphas is called in the Latin tongue, 'contempt of the Lord,' and what else do heretics, than in entertaining false notions of God contemn him by their proud conceits?"[128] In their insolence the friends rebel against divine providence.[129] Therefore, Eliphaz and the other friends "begin with the reverence of a gentle address, but they burst forth even to launching the darts of the bitterest invectives; for the roots of thorns themselves are soft, yet from that very softness of their own they put forth that whereby they pierce."[130]

Yet not all the words of Eliphaz are to be repudiated. Beyond the literal import of his words lies a greater, allegorical sense which Gregory alternately identifies as the typical or mystical sense.[131] The typical sense

---

to the modern reader as arbitrary and superficial. For example, Gregory teaches that Job represents Christ, Job's wife symbolizes the carnal nature, his seven sons (as seven is the number of perfection) are the apostles and derivatively the clergy, Job's three daughters represent the three classes of laity who are to worship the Trinity, Job's friends symbolize church heretics, and the seven thousand sheep symbolize perfected Christians (see Schaff, *History of the Christian Church*, 4:227).

126. As Wasselynck discusses of Gregory's exegetical method: "S. Gregory accorde une importance primordiale au sens littéral du texte sacré." Thus, "le sens littéral est le fondement nécessaire des autres sens bibliques" ("L'Influence des *Moralia*," 1:9–10).

127. Ibid., 1:27.

128. Ibid.

129. Gregory insists that Eliphaz and the other friends "misinterpret God's actions and rebel imperiously against them" (Straw, *Gregory the Great*, 186).

130. Gregory, *Morals*, 1:263.

131. Gregory argues that "forasmuch as we have said that the friends of blessed Job contain a figure of Heretics, there is a pressing necessity to show how these same words of Eliphaz are to be understood in a typical sense likewise" (*Morals*, 1:272). Methodologically the allegorical approach or "mystical mode of interpretation" is a necessary tool to biblical exposition since "it is plain to all who are acquainted with the truth, that Holy Writ takes care to hold out in promise the Redeemer of the world *in all its statements*" (ibid., 1:312, emphasis mine). Only the allegorical approach leads the interpreter to this truth which is hidden from those who do not have eyes to see.

The Reception History of Eliphaz

is necessary when we must go, guided by faith, beyond the literal sense where it is "obscure and ineffectual."[132] In one example of such exegesis, Gregory unfolds Eliphaz's allusion to the "strong lion" (לַיִשׁ) in Job 4:11 (μυρμηκολέων) ["lion ant"] in the LXX;[133] *tigris* ["tigress"] in the Vulgate). On the literal level Eliphaz intends his statement to be an insult against Job in that he, although once powerful like the lion, will perish for lack of prey. In other words, he is suffering destruction because of his evil deeds. Yet on the mystical level Eliphaz is revealing truth for believers concerning the devil. The devil is represented in the figure of the strong lion, while Babylon is present in the figure of the lioness.[134] Satan is marked for destruction just as the lion which lacks prey, and Satan will thus by no means prevail against the church. In this way Eliphaz's intended insults to Job in reality carry a far more profound "treasure" of truth for the church.

While Gregory is not the first to use this interpretive scheme, he appears to be the first in a major commentary to use these interpretive categories purposively as a means of circumventing the customary tension between the apparent *character* (and *role*) of Eliphaz as malevolent and the *words* of Eliphaz as constituting holy Scripture. The nature of this tension was nonetheless keenly felt by Gregory. That the apostle Paul in 1 Corinthians makes use of Eliphaz, even though the latter was representative of church heretics and was rebuked directly by the Lord, actualized a serious interpretive thorn for Gregory:

> But I see that we must enquire, wherefore Paul makes use of their sentiments with so much weight of authority, if these sentiments of theirs be nullified by the Lord's rebuke? For they are the words of Eliphaz which he brought before the Corinthians, saying, 'For it is written, "He taketh the wise in their own craftiness."' How then do we reject as evil what Paul establishes by authority? Or how shall we account that to be right by testimony of Paul, which the Lord by his own lips determined not to be right? It is because many of the things they say are admirable if they were not so spoken against the afflicted Job. Thus a great statement is taken by Paul for its own intrinsic excellence.[135]

---

132. See Wasselynck, "L'Influence des *Moralia*," 1:11.

133. The term occurs only here in the LXX (Lust, Eynikel, and Hauspie, *Greek-English Lexicon of the Septuagint*, 410).

134. Gregory, *Morals*, 1:273.

135. Ibid., 1:261. This is more or less also the solution of Williams, who contends that although much of Eliphaz's counsel is incorrect, he is correct in Job 5:13 (*The Wisdom of the Wise*, 304). This view leaves unresolved the tension, however, of how the reader is to pick and choose which parts of Eliphaz's speech—a unit intended to remain

Thus Eliphaz is largely to blame, not for and in spite of the eloquence of his speeches, but rather for the context in which they coalesce and more specifically for the vitriol with which they are wrongly applied to Job. Gregory's multi-level interpretive scheme extricates him adroitly from interpretive conundrums and frees him to discover details in the text that no one before (or since) would see. By unfolding the mystical sense Gregory contends that he is ministering to the spiritual understanding of believers. He remains in this way free to condemn the friends while still wielding their statements authoritatively.[136] Through diverse levels of meaning Gregory resolves interpretive tensions in the text and largely evades the hermeneutical difficulties in Eliphaz. In the evaluation of Gregory's view of Eliphaz, on the literal level of meaning he harshly criticizes Eliphaz's tone (A), purpose (B), theological provenance and creed (C), doctrine of retribution (D), special revelation (E), use of remedial suffering (F), position as doyen (G), use of the sin list (H), and rebuke by Yahweh (I). Categories C, D, F, and G remain latently positive, however, if one perceives Eliphaz through the allegorical or mystical sense of his remonstrances. These pronouncements thus are taken to contain profound truth for insightful Christians such as Gregory, although the reader must repudiate them on the literal interpretive level.

Maimonides

Maimonides (1135–1204), a brilliant and highly revered medieval Jewish philosopher and physician, was born in Cordoba, Spain, to a seventh-generation rabbinic family.[137] Soon evicted from their homeland by the threat of invading Muslim jihadists, Maimonides and his family fled by wandering through Europe, North Africa, and the Middle East for a time. At the age of 28 he finally settled, along with his relatives, in Egypt. There Maimonides became the leader of exiled Jews and composed some of his greatest literary masterpieces. He completed his expansive *Commentary on the Mishnah* by the age of 30. Next he undertook a fourteen-volume work entitled *Mishneh Torah*, a compendium of legal code which encompassed

---

intact—are good and which parts are bad.

136. "Now the friends of blessed Job, who, we have said, bear the likeness of heretics, we by no means condemn for their words throughout; for whereas it is delivered against them by the sentence from above, 'For ye have not spoken before Me the thing that is right,' it is thereupon added, 'Like my servant Job'; it is plainly manifest that it is not altogether set at naught, which is only disapproved by comparison with what is better" (ibid., 1:313).

137. For an overview of Maimonides life and thought, see Friedländer, "The Life of Moses Maimonides"; Blant, "The Moses of Cairo," 82–88; Kraemer, *Maimonides*.

and built upon all Jewish oral law, soon heralded as "the greatest Jewish work since the Talmud."[138] Maimonides's crowning achievement, however, was his philosophical and metaphysical tract, *The Guide for the Perplexed*, which he completed at the age of 53. The work was written in Arabic with Hebrew characters and was intended to correlate Aristotelian philosophy with religious thought to establish the centrality of the intellect for all spiritual life. Maimonides saw the perfection of the intellect as the goal of being (true righteousness) and the highest end toward which humans strive.

In the third part of his *Guide* (chapters 22–23) in a section dealing with divine providence, Maimonides interacts with the book of Job philosophically to elucidate its teaching. Prior to handling and fully grasping Maimonides's interpretation of Job, however, one must first grapple with his view of divine providence as outlined in the *Guide*. Maimonides contends that only five views of divine providence have existed throughout human history as legitimate means of understanding God's governance of the world:[139] (1) the Epicurean view that there is no providence whatsoever but that everything happens by chance; (2) the Aristotelian view that divine providence governs certain aspects of the cosmos while leaving others to chance (i.e., governs universals rather than particulars); (3) the view of the Ash'ariyya, an Islamic sect, that among both universals and particulars nothing occurs from sheer chance but that everything comes about through divine will, purpose, and governance though no purpose may be discerned in it; (4) the view of Islamic and Jewish rational philosophers, the Mu'tazila, that God governs by all things by His wisdom and that no injustice may be ascribed to Him so that all things which come to pass occur for the good of the particulars involved whether in the present life or in the life to come; and (5) the view of the Torah which operates according to strict retribution, viz., that man is endowed with absolute determinative capacity to act, that God is free in every way from injustice, and that whatsoever comes to pass is in accordance with the just deserts by which the individual is equitably either punished or rewarded, commensurate with his conduct. The last view is championed by Maimonides, although he incorporates elements of the Aristotelian view in his limiting of divine providence to human affairs rather than to the particulars of creation, such as animals or plants, which are subject to pure contingency.[140]

---

138. Blant, "Moses of Cairo," 84.
139. Maimonides, *The Guide of the Perplexed*, 464–70.
140. Ibid., 471.

Given the ensuing popularity and influence of the *Guide* and Maimonides's persuasive and erudite philosophical approach,[141] one must in his or her analysis understand Maimonides's view of Eliphaz and the other friends. In his introduction Maimonides makes clear that while he is uncertain whether Job and the other characters were fictional or actually existed,[142] he is nevertheless certain that in the interchange between Job and his four friends lies the interpretive key to the book as they individually purport fundamentally distinct views of divine providence.[143] In principle the five interlocutors agree generally that everything which had occurred to Job was known to God and that God had caused the misfortunes to befall him.[144] In addition, they are agreed that with no injustice or wrongdoing God is thereby to be inculpated.

As a scriptural interpreter Maimonides provides several helpful insights which in large measure anticipate modern discussions of the book. First, he argues that although the discourses of the friends may seem to overlap and repeat one another that this is owing rather to the ideological commonality to which they hold and not to a defect of the dialogues. It is not at all the purpose of the friends merely to be repetitive, but rather each seeks to develop by way of dialectic his unique view of providence. Second, the basic intent and purpose of the friends is viewed positively. They provide Job with "exhortations to patience, words of consolation, appeals to him to be amicable, and advice that he ought to be silent and not give rein to his speech like an individual quarreling another individual; he should rather submit to God's judgments and be silent."[145] Maimonides's benign view extends especially to Eliphaz, who of all the human characters in the book, defends most ably and ardently the truth of the Torah. Third, the friends are all agreed to one degree or another as to the retributive principle. This principle ensures the following:

---

141. Blant writes, "The treatise marks the highest achievement of Jewish thought. It has been translated more than any other medieval Jewish work. Readers like Albertus Magnus, Thomas Aquinas, and Meister Eckhart made admiring references to 'Moses Aegyptius.' Aquinas borrowed from the *Guide* his arguments for the existence of God. (Closer to the present day, after Egyptian President Anwar Sadat signed a peace treaty with Israel in 1979, Israel's President Yitzhak Navon presented him with a copy of the *Guide* in the original Arabic)" ("Moses of Cairo," 86).

142. While Maimonides terms the book of Job a "parable," he appears non-committal concerning the historical verity of the account (*Guide*, 486).

143. Maimonides, *Guide of the Perplexed*, 486.

144. Ibid., 490.

145. Ibid., 491.

Everyone who does good obtains a reward and that everyone who does evil is punished; and that if you see a disobedient man who is fortunate, in the end this state of affairs will be transformed into its contrary, for he will perish and misfortunes will befall him, his sons, and his offspring. If, however, you see an obedient man who is in misery, his fracture will certainly be remedied.[146]

Fourth, Maimonides suggests that Yahweh's rebuke of Eliphaz in Job 42:7 does *not* pertain to the content of the preceding speech dialogues. It is rather Job's *confession* and penitence before the Lord in Job 42:5–6 that constitutes speaking rightly. When Job repents of his verbal recriminations against Yahweh and is restored, the Lord charges Eliphaz and the others with likewise needing to "speak rightly." Their previously lofty words need to be balanced with humble submission to Yahweh out of existential reverence toward God.[147]

As for Eliphaz, Maimonides believes him to be a strict proponent of the retribution principle: "[Eliphaz] believes that everything that befalls a man is deserved, but that the deficiencies for which we deserve punishment and the way in which we deserve to be punished because of them are hidden from our perception."[148] Eliphaz is convinced that Job's sins have precipitated his misfortunes, and he adheres to this notion throughout the speeches. Eliphaz's assessment of Job's condition is not in error, however, because his view of providence is essentially that of the Torah.[149] Thus Eliphaz is the able proponent of the Torah who is to be commended for what he says to Job and not at all censured for the content of his speeches. If Eliphaz is lacking in any area, it is simply in his need to attain to an existential knowledge of God—not merely through the Law—as Job does through the humbling experience of the theophany. Thus, Maimonides insightfully puts forth an overwhelmingly positive assessment of Eliphaz in his tone (A), purpose (B), theological provenance and creed (C), doctrine of retribution (D), special revelation (E), doctrine of remedial suffering (F), position as doyen (G), use of the retributive sin list (H), and even rebuke by Yahweh (I). Several of these nuances would become the starting point for similar approaches to Eliphaz in the modern era as we shall see in the next chapter.

146. Ibid.
147. Ibid., 492–93.
148. Ibid., 493.
149. According to Maimonides, Job's view of providence is in keeping with the opinion of Aristotle, Eliphaz's view is in accordance with the Torah, Bildad's view is in keeping with the Mu☒tazila, and Zophar's view is in keeping with the doctrine of the Ash☒ariyya (ibid., 494).

Thomas Aquinas

A commentary on Job is one of only two full commentaries that the renowned medieval philosopher and Dominican church leader Thomas Aquinas (*ca*. 1225–1274) completed from his thirteenth-century Latin Vulgate text.[150] Thomas's commentary was a major advance, constituting "the first major literal commentary on Job"[151] as over against the lesser homilies and commentaries that preceded it, including the largely allegorical exposition of Gregory. Unfortunately, however, Thomas's exegesis was to be dependent upon the Latin rather than Hebrew text.

Relying heavily on Aristotelian thought, Thomas seeks to correlate reason, gleaned above all in the philosophy of his leading philosophical guide,[152] with revelation delivered to the church through the Old and New Testaments and in keeping with the insights of the church fathers.[153] By "literal" Thomas seeks to distinguish the basic historical sense of the text from the "spiritual."[154] While the literal sense must precede the other senses, the spiritual sense goes beyond the surface meaning of the individual words to the deeper significance intended by the divine author.[155] Under the rubric

---

150. Yaffe, "Intrepetative Essay," 8. Although Aquinas left behind manuscript evidence of expositions on John, 1 Corinthians, and Hebrews in the form of lecture notes, only his expositions of Job and Romans take the form of a finished, line-by-line commentary on the text. On the importance of Aquinas's commentary among others on Job, Marcos F. Manzanedo writes: "Probablemente el comentario de Santo Tomás es el más completo y profundo entre los comentarious antiguos. Aunque superado en el plano lingüístico, en el histórico, y en el de las ciencias naturales, conserva todavía un profundo valor doctrinal en los campos de la filosofía y de la teología" ("Probably the commentary of St. Thomas is the most complete and profound of the ancient commentaries. Even though superseded on the linguistic level, on the historical, and on that of the natural sciences, it still maintains a profound doctrinal value in the fields of philosophy and theology") ("La antropología filosófica," 419).

151. Schreiner, "Through a Mirror Dimly," 178.

152. As Yaffe notes, one must familiarize oneself with Aristotelian terminology to make sense of Thomas's exposition, particularly the former's philosophical dialecticisms such as "potency"/"act," "imperfect"/"perfect," and "corruptible"/"incorruptible" ("Interpretative Essay," 2). For specific treatment of Thomas's thinking in some of these key areas, see the categories such as "el hombre y la inmortalidad" ("man and immortality"), "la felicidad humana" ("human happiness"), "el conocimiento humano" ("human knowledge"), or "la voluntad y las pasiones" ("the will and the passions") in Manzanedo, "La antropología filosófica," 429–50.

153. Yaffe, "Interpretative Essay," 1–2;

154. For Aquinas the literal sense is the historical sense of a text or the aggregate meaning of the words themselves (Aquinas, *Summa Theologiae*, 1:37–39).

155. Aquinas writes: "In every branch of knowledge words have meaning, but what is special here is that the things meant by the words are also themselves mean something. That first meaning whereby the words signify things belongs to the sense

of "spiritual" are three other categories of meaning, including the allegorical, moral, and anagogical. The allegorical sense describes those things unfolded in the OT which anticipate truths of the NT beyond their immediate context. The moral sense encompasses those things in the Bible explicitly ascribed or referred to Christ and that are furthermore signs of what believers are themselves to do. The anagogical sense goes beyond these other meanings to signify to that which pertains to God's eternal glory. While the literal sense is the necessary starting point for any interpretative endeavor, the other senses flow naturally out of it and necessarily supplement it.

Likely taking his cue from Maimonides's work, with which he was familiar,[156] Thomas interprets Job as a treatise on the role of divine providence in human affairs, although he disagrees with Maimonides concerning the compass of divine providence as taught by the book of Job.[157] The nature of divine providence is viewed especially through the lens of the affliction of righteous Job.[158] Although Eliphaz has commendable things to say about divine providence,[159] Thomas concludes that Eliphaz's grounds for rebuking Job are mistaken. Eliphaz fails to grasp the spirit of what Job is saying and moreover errs in attributing despair to Job on the basis of Job's alleged claims of hatred for the present life, his impatience as evident in his bitter

---

first-mentioned, namely the historical or literal. That meaning, however, whereby the things signified by the words in their turn also signify other things is called the spiritual sense; it is based on and presupposes the literal sense" (*Summa Theologiae*, 1:37). As David C. Steinmetz more fully explains, "Thomas argued that while words are the signs of things, things designated by words can themselves be the signs of other things. In all merely human sciences, words alone have a sign-character. But in Holy Scripture the things designated by words can themselves have the character of a sign. The literal sense of Scripture has to do with the sign-character of words; the spiritual sense of Scripture has to do with the sign-character of things. By arguing this way, Thomas was able to show that the spiritual sense of Scripture is always based on the literal sense and derived from it" ("The Superiority of Pre-Critical Exegesis," 31).

156. Ibid., 4.

157. Schreiner contends that Thomas disagrees with Maimonides concerning divine providence in three respects ("Through a Mirror Dimly," 178–79). First, Maimonides asserts that providence does not extend to singulars, rather only to those endowed with perfection of intellect. Thomas, on the other hand, stresses that providence extends to particulars, not simply perfected intellects. Second, Maimonides maintains that if Job is suffering for his sin then Eliphaz is right, whereas Thomas asserts that Job is not suffering for his sin. Third, Maimonides argues that the book of Job proves that divine providence is inaccessible to human understanding. Thomas contends rather that the singular purpose of the book is precisely to explicate divine providence to mankind.

158. Aquinas, *Literal Exposition*, 72.

159. Especially in the latter portion of Eliphaz's first speech to Job (Job 5) (see ibid., 132–33).

words, and his presumptive and ill-founded protestations of innocence.[160] In his first reply Eliphaz is hasty and ireful: "He portrays the usual behavior of a very impatient and angry man who cannot bear to hear the words to the end but is provoked immediately at the very beginning." Heedlessly Eliphaz displays his own "impatience and foolishness."[161] Furthermore, Eliphaz is regrettably a staunch advocate of the retribution principle:

> It was the opinion of Eliphaz and of the other two friends that the adversities of this world do not come to anyone except as punishment for sin, and conversely, prosperity does not come except as a reward for justice. Hence, in his opinion, it seemed unfitting that anyone who was straightforward, that is, just on the score of virtue, should be destroyed through the loss of temporal glory, which he believed to be the reward of justice.[162]

As the speeches progress Eliphaz worsens by his neglect of the deeper import of Job's words. In the second speech Eliphaz begins to remonstrate cunningly with Job by confronting only the superficial meaning of Job's words rather than the fuller significance.[163] By the third speech Eliphaz has completely misinterpreted Job's replies and has imputed to Job a thoroughgoing denial of divine providence.[164] From this denial of providence Eliphaz fancies Job to be a mere step from the next debilitating stage of outright vice which would be to brazenly repudiate all fear of God.[165] With this step surely would come swift and absolute destruction, a certain expectation for Job if he continues with such intransigence.

When Eliphaz is singled out for rebuke from Yahweh in 42:7, Thomas proposes that the censure originates from Eliphaz's pertinacity in holding to perverse dogmas.[166] Job had sinned out of levity and Elihu out of inexperience, but both held in the main to correct doctrine. Eliphaz, on the other hand, had "invented the lie that Job had led an iniquitous life." He concocted this lie, later in tandem with the others, because of a failure to know and worship the true God: "They were in error concerning the faith with which God is worshipped, believing that in this life only was made the retribution of merits and punishments. Therefore, [Job] adds 'and worshippers of perverse dogmas,' for whoever deviates from the true knowledge of God

---

160. Ibid., 113.
161. Ibid.
162. Ibid., 115.
163. Ibid., 233.
164. Ibid., 293.
165. Ibid., 295.
166. Ibid., 471.

worships not God but his own false dogmas."¹⁶⁷ Thus for Thomas, Eliphaz has fashioned and worshiped an idol of his own dogma, is at times a rash and haughty liar, and exhibits frequently the traits of an impatient fool. He follows the contours of Gregory's harsh approach with an equally negative assessment of Eliphaz's tone (A), purpose (B), theological provenance and creed (C), retributive doctrine (D), special revelation (E), doctrine of remedial suffering (F), status as doyen of the counselors (G), use of the sin list (H), and rebuke by Yahweh (I). This negative view of his character will continue with several subsequent interpreters.

John Calvin

Little background needs to be provided for the well-known French Reformer John Calvin (1509–1564), one of the most influential theologians and ecclesiastical principals in church history. Although he did not write a commentary on Job, Calvin preached in Geneva a series of over 150 daily and weekly sermons on Job from 1554 to 1555 in which he exposited the text verse by verse.¹⁶⁸ Calvin's literal exposition of the book was in keeping with the rigors of his customary exegetical and hermeneutical methodology.¹⁶⁹

The most important commentaries to which Calvin would have had access in his study of Job were those of Gregory and Thomas Aquinas; Calvin stands in the Thomistic tradition in his view of the book as a treatise on divine providence.¹⁷⁰ In departure from several of his predecessors, however, Calvin is largely favorable in his assessment of the friends. T. M. Moore notes that Calvin "heartily concurred in the theology which serves as the basis of the advice of Job's friends," adding that "he labeled their teaching 'good doctrine'; received their advice as 'authentic summons' from God; embraced their counsel as good and a very useful warning to sinners; and declared that the Holy Spirit himself was speaking through the mouths of Eliphaz, Bildad, and Zophar."¹⁷¹

Calvin identifies Eliphaz and the other friends as "exquisite persons" who were "skillful and wise to comfort."¹⁷² Further, "these are none of the

---

167. Ibid., 214.

168. Thomas, *Calvin's Teaching on Job*, 7; Schreiner, "Through a Mirror Dimly," 175.

169. On John Calvin's exegetical method, see Nixon, *John Calvin, Expository Preacher*.

170. Schreiner, "Through a Mirror," 177–79.

171. Moore, "When Orthodoxy Is Not Enough," 13.

172. Calvin, *Sermons on Job*, 44. Citations from this source have been updated to reflect modern spelling.

common and ordinary sort of men (as I have declared already) they be no dullards: but they be great personages, and well advised in all points, accordingly as they show themselves to be."[173] Their initial purpose toward Job was entirely benevolent and Platonic. "They brought no malicious purpose nor wicked intent with them: but they had a right and hearty goodwill and love towards him."[174] In fact, Eliphaz and the other friends are an example of the love and compassion one is to bestow upon a friend bearing providential hardship. "We must follow the fashion that is set down here: namely to be pitiful and tenderhearted after such a sort when we see any man endure adversity, as we always have our hands at liberty to succour him after the ability that God hath given us."[175]

The friends are to be blamed only for maintaining a "*mauvaise cause*" but not for the malevolent content of their speeches: "We have also to note that in all the dispute Job supports a good case while his contrary party supports a wrong case. Yet what is more, that Job supports a good case which he deduces badly, while the others support a wrong case which they deduce well."[176] Calvin expands this premise to argue that although this "wrong case" is advanced by the friends in their misapplication to Job of certain theological principles, much of the content of their speeches is sound, even commendable:

> But on the contrary, they that take up the wrong case—that God always punishes men according to the measure of their sins—have lovely and holy sentences, and there is nothing in their discourse that would not necessitate us to receive it as if the Holy Spirit had uttered it, for it is plain truth. These are the foundations of religion. They treat of God's providence, they treat of his justice, they treat of human sins. Thus we see a doctrine which we must receive without contradicting.[177]

---

173. Ibid.

174. Ibid.

175. Calvin, *Sermons on Job*, 45.

176. "Lais cependant nous avons aussi a noter, qu'en toute la dispute Iob maintient une bonne cause, et son adverse partie en maintient une mauvaise. Or il y a plue, que Iob maintenant une bonne cause la deduit mal, et les autres menans une mauvaise cause la deduisent bien" (Calvin, *Sermons sur le Livre de Iob*, 23) (my translation).

177. "Or au contraire ceux qui soutiennent cete mauvaise cause, que Dieu punit tousiours les hommes selon la mesure de leurs pechez, ont de belles sentences, et sainctes, il n'y a rien en leurs propos qu'il ne nous faille recevoir, comme si le Sainct Esprit l'avoit prononcé: car c'est pure verité, ce sont les fondemens de la religion, ils traittent de la Providence de Dieu, ils traittent de sa iustice, ils traittent des peschez des hommes. Voila donc une doctrine, laquelle nous avons à recevoir sans contradict" (ibid., 24) (my translation). Cf. the (partial) translation of Susan E. Schreiner: "Those who maintain

Thus, Eliphaz and the other friends in many places speak the very truth of God, although some blame may be found in their overly rigid understanding of divine retribution.

Dealing with Eliphaz in particular, Calvin finds much to commend. Eliphaz perceives hypocrisy in Job due to his failure to receive divine correction properly. Although Eliphaz says a few things that are "utterly false," he corroborates his perspective by adducing many "good and holy reasons, whereout of we may we also may gather good and profitable doctrine."[178] Calvin freely admits of such where in speaking of passages such as Job 4:17 ("Can mortal man be in the right before God? Can a man be pure before his Maker?") and 15:14 ("What is man, that he can be pure?"), he argues that the leading sage has provided much "useful doctrine."[179] In his doctrine of retribution Eliphaz undertakes profitable and holy sentences but still upholds the ill-advised case of asserting that God must uniformly punish evildoers strictly in proportion to their sin. His and the other friends' error lies not in their theological outlook but in their failure to realize that not every aspect of God's providence and justice are discernible in the present life. Thus they teach good doctrine wrongly by misapplying to Job universals which cannot be connected to him in this particular case.[180] Yet not all of Eliphaz's retributive doctrine is to be repudiated. In treating 4:7 Calvin contends that "surely the principles that are set down here are drawn out of God's pure truth by reason whereof it is as much as if the Holy Ghost had pronounced this saying that never any righteous man had yet perished, and that never any right-dealing man had been destroyed. Neither could any such thing happen."[181] As to Eliphaz's revelatory experience, Calvin asserts that it "is a matter of certainty" that God inspired the sage as the content of the revelation is true and the mode of revelation is not altogether uncommon.[182] Regarding the

---

the poor case ... speak beautiful and holy sentences; there is nothing in their propositions that we ought not receive as if the Holy Spirit had not pronounced it, for it is pure truth. These are the foundations of religion; they discuss the Providence of God, they discuss his justice, they discuss the sins of men. Here, then, is a doctrine which we have to receive without contradiction. . . ." (*Where Shall Wisdom Be Found?*, 99–100).

178. Calvin, *Sermons on Job*, 62.

179. Schreiner observes that Calvin accepts most of what Eliphaz and the other friends say. He agrees with them "that an omnipotent God controls history and exercises judgment over the wicked. Human sinfulness is total and a just cause for suffering. When afflicted, we can only examine ourselves and confess our sins. We cannot be righteous before God, after all. Moreover, whatever God wills is, by definition, just" ("Through a Mirror," 182).

180. Ibid., 182–83.

181. Calvin, *Sermons on Job*, 66.

182. Ibid., 70.

doctrine of divine chastisement Eliphaz teaches of God's loving disposition toward his own children "especially that when he chastiseth us, he never uses such sharpness towards us but that he will make us feel his goodness and mercy therewithal to the intent that we should approach unto him and not be dismayed like those that are afraid to be confounded."[183] Again the doctrine of the sage here is by the authority of the Holy Spirit and aligns with apostolic doctrine.[184]

As to his status as doyen, Calvin sees that Eliphaz in his second speech solicits truth from "his own experience, and afterward he addeth that the same doctrine was received and held after the same manner among the wise men to whom God had given the grace not only to be able to rule well themselves but also to have the government of realms and countries."[185] Here Calvin legitimates Eliphaz's counsel, validated by his appeal to tradition. In the third speech Eliphaz continues to speak "very well" but misapplies truth to Job, although Calvin agrees with most of the doctrine Eliphaz proclaims.[186] In his exegesis of Job 42:7–8, Calvin argues that Eliphaz and the other friends are rebuked because the grounds of their case were not applicable to Job (although they adduced many good and profitable reasons) and because they purported some "false and untoward doctrine" that God must always punish men in this world in keeping with their deserts.[187]

In summary Calvin is mostly positive in his appraisal of Eliphaz's tone (A) and (intended) purpose in Job (B), theological provenance and creed (C), retributive doctrine (D), doctrine of remedial suffering (E), status as doyen (F), and use of the sin list (G). Eliphaz is viewed negatively, however, in the application of his doctrine—thus some of his purpose in Job is unwittingly errant (B)—and in his rebuke by Yahweh for the misapplication and mishandling of doctrine (I). Many of the features of Eliphaz's overall trajectory Calvin finds appealing nonetheless, such as aspects of the retribution of evildoing and of the transcendence of God.

Modern Interpretations

I turn now to modern readings of Eliphaz and the other friends, beginning in the seventeenth century and reaching to more recent scholarship. A few

---

183. Ibid., 94.
184. Ibid., 97.
185. Ibid., 275.
186. Ibid., 389.
187. Ibid., 743.

examples of representative and pertinent interpretations will be considered in each era.

Seventeenth- to Eighteenth-Century Scholarship

Two examples of post-Reformation approaches to Job are treated in the following, one by a Puritan author who composed a running homiletical paraphrase of Job and the other by a Spanish Augustinian monk who wrote a more detailed exegetical commentary on Job.

George Abbott

Although not an official clergyman, George Abbott (1603–1648) was a Puritan writer, theologian, and critical scholar of some ability. Born into an aristocratic family in East Yorkshire, Abbott was a member of Parliament in 1640 and 1645.[188] As a writer Abbott is known principally from three works which he authored, *The Whole Booke of Iob Paraphrased, or, Made Easie for Any to Understand* (1640), a rather concise running interpretation of the book of Job intended for laypersons; *Vindiciae Sabbathi* (1641), dealing at length with the Sabbatarian controversy of the day; and *Brief Notes Upon the Whole Book of Psalms* (1651), as the title suggests an exposition (published posthumously) on the Psalms.

Abbott's work on Job provides insight into seventeenth-century understandings of Eliphaz and lies in the train of Thomistic and Calvinist interpretation of the book as concerned with the accessibility of divine providence to the human mind. Although Abbott alludes to the companions as "godly men,"[189] he repudiates their retributive view of divine providence as being "ignorantly prejudiced of God, that he afflicted not but in proportionable punishment to sin committed, and consequently were opinionated of Job, that for all his faire shew, he must needs be but a hollow-hearted hypocrite." Eliphaz and the others "pressed these sore upon [Job] as infallible maximes" and "laboured to loose his hold on God."[190] At times Eliphaz comes close to a role as purveyor of credible advice, for his nocturnal experience in 4:12–21, arising from the supernatural visit of a spirit while meditating upon Job's case, seems to convey genuine revelation from God.[191]

---

188. "Abbot, George," 1:2.
189. Abbot, *The Whole Booke of Iob Paraphrased*, 14.
190. Ibid., x.
191. Ibid., 27.

In his second speech, nonetheless, Eliphaz comes across as an imperious and strident lecturer to Job, and by his final peroration Eliphaz finally spills out what he has surmised of Job all along: he is "an evildoer in the ways of injury and violence."[192]

In the end Eliphaz is singled out for rebuke by Yahweh in 42:7 because he is the eldest and had first committed the error of which the other two friends were guilty, viz., preaching false doctrine about God. Eliphaz was too bold to limit divine sovereignty by "chalking out" God's ways and to prescribe to God rules of justice in the execution of His will and dispensation of providence.[193] Abbott is critical of Eliphaz's tone (A), purpose (B), theological provenance and creed (C), doctrine of retribution (D), dogma of remedial suffering (F), status as doyen (G), use of the sin list (H), and rebuke by Yahweh (I). He is ambivalent toward Eliphaz's special revelation (E). On the whole he maintains a negative outlook in his appraisal of Eliphaz.

Luis de León

Luis de León (1528–1591) was born into the cultural milieu of sixteenth-century Spanish Judaism, which had notable influence on his later orientation toward exegetical and textual methodology, although he himself would profess the Roman Catholic faith.[194] In 1542 León entered the Augustinian monastery of Salamanca, Spain. Beginning in the monastic community under the tutelage of Juan de Guevara and continuing at the University of Salamanca under the renowned dominican scholar Melchor Cano,[195] León's education was steeped in the classics and in scholastic theology with a firm

---

192. Ibid., 141.

193. Ibid., 267.

194. Although "la cultura hispanosemita" would be influential on León from his mother's side, Javier San José Lera is careful not to overdo its significance upon his overall formation ("Estudio Histórico-Literario," 9). Lera sees several factors at work in forging León's outlook toward scholastic humanism: "La Orden de San Agustín y las universidades de Salamanca y Alcalá son las tres fases formativas esenciales que van a convertir a fray Luis de León en el humanisto ejemplar: el eclecticismo, la síntesis de corrientes comienzan a fundirse en su personalidad desde sus inicios. Fray Luis es la abeja que liba de múltiples flores" ("The order of St. Augustine and the universities of Salamanca and Alcalá are the three essential formative phases that are going to convert friar Luis de León into the humanist exemplar: the eclecticism, the synthesis of currents begin to found themselves into his personality from the time of his initiation. Friar Luis de León is the bee which sips at multiple flowers") (ibid., 10).

195. Lera notes of Cano that in him "la escolástica tradicional se revivifica, por la aplicación de fuentes científicas auxiliares, (como la crítica textual o el conocimiento de tres lenguas bíblicas), o la recuperación de la antigua literatura teológica" ("Estudio Histórico-Literario," 13).

grasp of the humanism which would coalesce eventually into the era of the Enlightenment. This approach would at times set León at odds with the Roman Catholic Inquisition as he sought to make accessible the Bible in the vernacular *Castellano* of the Spanish people.[196] In 1579 he was appointed chair of Bible at the University of Salamanca. Here his greatest exegetical labors would take place.[197]

The exact compositional history of León's commentary on Job remains something of a mystery, but the work was likely begun around 1579 and finished just months prior to his death in 1591.[198] In his exposition León works from the Latin Vulgate and Hebrew text to produce a faithful exposition of the book in *Castellano* based on the "sense" of the Latin and the "air" of the Hebrew.[199] He labors additionally to render the text in suitable meter in order to provide for the reader's benefit a greater knowledge and interest in the sacred Scriptures.[200] Although the work had an influential circulation prior to its formal imprint, due to several mitigating factors it was not officially published until 1779 when another Augustinian monk slightly reworked

---

196. For a period León was imprisoned by the Roman Catholic authorities because his translation of Canticles into the Spanish vernacular created conflict for him with the Inquisition authorities (Cabrera, *Voces en el Silencio*, 95). The incarceration was not a deterrent, however, to his later exegetical labors in Job.

197. Lera, "Estudio Histórico-Literario," 24. León published works on Canticles, Psalms, Galatians, and 2 Thessalonians. His exposition of Job would not be imprinted until after his death.

198. So Lera, "Estudio Histórico-Literario," 44–45. Lera outlines the contours of the larger debate as to the precise dating of the work but marshals convincing evidence for his proposal.

199. In addition to these sources which León identifies, he evidently consulted the LXX. He notes that the friends of Job "eran ricos y principales hombres, porque la Escrittura en otra parte los llama reyes" ("were rich and principal men, because the Scripture in another part calls them kings") (*Job*, 181), a view which he undoubtedly gleaned from Greek Job. Given some of the excesses of his era (and that of his predecessors), his exposition is for the most part a commendably accurate handling of the text. All translations from León's commentary in the following are my own.

200. León outlines three specific purposes for his work: "Una, traslado el texto del libro por sus palabras, conservando quanto es posible en ellas el sentido latino y el ayre hebreo, que t[ien]e cierta magestad. Otra, declaro en cada capítulo más estendidamente lo que se dize. La tercera, póngole en verso, imittando muchos sanctos y antiguos que en otros libros sagrados lo hizieron, y pretendiendo por esta manera afficionar algunos al conocimiento de la Sagrada Esc[ritura], en que mucha parte de nuestro bien consiste, [a lo que] yo juzgo" ("First, I translate the text of the book word-for-word, preserving as much as possible in them the Latin sense and Hebrew air, which has a certain majesty. Second, I declare in each chapter more extensively what is said. Third, I set it into verse, imitating many of the holy and ancient men who did so in other sacred books and seeking in this way to fix in some the knowledge of the sacred Scripture, in which a great part of our good consists, as I judge") (*Job*, 144).

the material and the church's imprimatur was finally obtained to publish the commentary.²⁰¹

With regard to Eliphaz and the friends, León adopts a mostly positive view. He recognizes that they are important figures in the ancient context and that they have come to employ their official duty as friends, yet he sees their action toward Job as inadvertently turned on its head by the devil: "They fulfilled the function of friends in attending to the work, even though the devil, as the enemy, converted their visit into new torment for Job."²⁰² Eliphaz respects Job enough to keep quiet until Job has broken the silence. But when Eliphaz begins to apply his counsel, he gets it all wrong. Instead of providing consolation, he dishes out torment. "Although by name friends and by function comforters, now that they speak, they should speak by consoling him but they do it all backwards, either by their blindness or by the order of God, in order that this might be the last test of who Job was."²⁰³ Eliphaz and the other friends are convinced that Job has sinned greatly and therefore suffers greatly. More than this, Job has exhibited an impatient tendency to assign blame to God. For Eliphaz and the others this amounts to divine condemnation, and it is a blasphemous affair. Yet by the end of the first speech Eliphaz speaks rightly, although his counsel is general and common: "Although it is true that Eliphaz speaks here now appropriately to Job, it is also certain that he claims to teach us everything in Job, and that on this particular occasion, his doctrine is general and common."²⁰⁴

In his night-time encounter Eliphaz experiences a genuine brush with the divine as demonstrated by the supernatural ambience with which Eliphaz receives the revelation.²⁰⁵ By the middle of his second speech, how-

---

201. For the outline of the historical events leading to publication, see Lera, "Estudio Histórico-Literario," 73–81. Because of the book's publication in the eighteenth century and the fact that it was updated at that time by another friar, Diego González, I have included it in this section (Cabrera, *Voces*, 95).

202. "Hizieron officio de amigos en acudir al trabajo, aunque el demonio, como enemigo, le convirtió a Job la visita destos [sic] en nuevo tormento" (*Job*, 181).

203. "Aunque al nombre de amigos y al officio de consoladores, ya que hablavan, convenía hablar consolándole, hiziéronlo al revés, o por su ceguedad o por orden de Dios, para que fuesse ésta la última prueva de quién era Job" (*Job*, 214).

204. "Aunque es verdad que Eliphaz habla agora aquí propriamente con Job, también es cierto que pretende en Job enseñarnos a todos, y que de ocasión particular, esta su doctrina es general y común" (*Job*, 252).

205. León comments: "Porque las cosas grandes y que exceden lo natural de los hombres , quando Dios se las dize, óyenlas conforme a su pequeña disposición, y ansí les parece que a malas penas las oyen, tanto ansí por la mucha brevedad con que se les dize . . . quanto porque se las dize en lo muy hondo y secreto del alma, alexadíssimo de todo lo que es potencia y sentido" ("Because great things and things that exceed what is natural to men, when God himself says them, they hear them in accordance with

ever, Eliphaz has lost the moral high ground and fully unloads his "venom" ("ponçoña") on Job as Job by his false pretenses has injured the cause of God.²⁰⁶ León thus sustains a vacillating view of Eliphaz through most of the first speech but sours on him as the book progresses. In his overall assessment, León is harsh toward Eliphaz as to his tone (A), purpose (B), doctrine of retribution (D), position as doyen (G), and use of the sin list (H). He is favorable toward him in his theological provenance and creed (C), experience of special revelation (E) and doctrine of remedial suffering (F). His view of Yahweh's rebuke remains uncertain (I). León has discovered in Eliphaz a counselor who speaks eloquently and assays to console Job but ultimately who fails because of his blind insistence that Job must have sinned.

Nineteenth- and Early Twentieth-Century Continental Scholarship

A survey of nineteenth-century scholarship begins, of course, with critical German scholarship, which turned its sights to apply its customary methodology to the book of Job.

Heinrich Ewald

Heinrich Ewald (1803–1875) has been called "without doubt, the greatest Old Testament scholar of the [nineteenth] century."²⁰⁷ Born into a family of linen-weavers in Göttingen, Ewald would remain there to study under Johann Eichorn at the University of Göttingen, specializing in oriental languages. He eventually would become professor of philosophy and lecturer in OT exegesis at the same university, where he would instruct well-known higher-critical scholars such as Julius Wellhausen and Christian Dillman.²⁰⁸ Ewald published a commentary on Job in 1854 entitled *Das Buch Ijob* in which he casts a mostly critical view of Eliphaz.²⁰⁹ For Ewald, Eliphaz is a

---

their limited disposition, and so it appears to them that with great difficulty they hear them, so much so for the brevity with which it is said to them . . . as much because they are said in the very depth and secret of the soul, greatly remote from all that which is faculty and sense" [*Job*, 223]).

206. *Job*, 426.

207. Davies, *Heinrich Ewald*, 1.

208. Wellhausen dedicated the first edition of his *History of Israel* to Ewald, his "unforgotten master."

209. Ewald, *Das Buch Ijob*. The commentary was translated into English as *Commentary on the Book of Job*.

composite, fictitious figure pieced together from several legends.[210] Yet of the friends he is the most dignified and weighty in appearance and counsel. The theological perspective that Eliphaz represents is an early and antiquated faith which "has already become a delusion and superstition," and the purpose of the author is to paint its deficiencies in contrast with Job, who as a solitary figure must wage the conflict to usher in a fresh way of understanding divine providence.[211]

Ewald begins, however, with an auspicious assessment of the way in which the leading interlocutor approaches Job in his prominent role as an acknowledged friend and teacher. Although Eliphaz is convinced of Job's guilt from the outset, he "speaks to Job with considerable caution and care in order to say what is necessary as carefully and mildly as possible."[212] Eliphaz has only polite intentions as he directs his eloquence to Job. "The first speech is manifestly comprehensive, calmly exhaustive, laid out with uncommon artfulness and most likely executed so that one perceives the alacrity of the deliberate elder statesman to snuff out with well-meaning though serious and strict method the smoldering fire of contempt for God and to point to the necessity of repentance."[213] Yet the first peroration is mingled with vehemence, as he grows bold to lay out forcefully his doctrine of retribution, that only the wicked irreparably perish as they are overtaken by God's wrath. As Eliphaz touches upon this cherished tenet of the certain ruination of the wicked, he becomes the most energetic to terrify and persuade Job that perhaps he belongs to this class of the wicked. By the end of the first speech Eliphaz has returned to sweet appeals for Job to find a happy end through penitence toward God.

As to his special revelation, Eliphaz has likely simply imagined the revelatory experience due to his constant mulling over certain dogmas during the night-time hours.[214] In his second speech Eliphaz continues his dogma of retribution, modestly referring to himself as "the old man" to garner the esteem of his audience.[215] Yet his tone becomes sharper in order to pierce Job more deeply to recognize his certain and clear culpability. By the third speech Eliphaz is exasperated by his lack of success in convincing Job and utters reproaches against Job with no restraint for "certain definite

---

210. Ewald, *Job*, 37.
211. Ibid., 36.
212. Ewald, *Ijob*, 88 (Citations from the German are my translation).
213. Ibid.
214. Ewald, *Job*, 107.
215. Ibid., 180.

and particular sins of great magnitude."²¹⁶ In his rebuke in 42:7 Eliphaz is humiliated because he along with the others had calmly and deliberately denied the divine truth that suffering does not always indicate guilt or divine punishment.²¹⁷

In assessing Ewald's interpretation of Eliphaz, he is sympathetic toward Eliphaz's initial intention and design in offering his counsel to Job, worthy of respect as the eldest member (G), and in his view of the beneficial aspects of suffering (F). Yet in everything else Eliphaz is completely wrong and to be discredited entirely, including his tone (A), his purpose in the book (B), his theological provenance and creed (C), his dogma of retribution (D), his revelatory experience (E), his use of the sin list (H), and rebuke by Yahweh (I). Ewald's analysis of Eliphaz is mostly negative.

Franz Delitzsch

Renowned Hebraist Franz Delitzsch (1813–1890) was born of Jewish parentage in Leipzig, Germany. Early on Delitzsch trained in rabbinics and Hebrew, but after his conversion to Lutheranism became a staunch proponent for evangelization of the Jewish people.²¹⁸ Delitzsch held professorships in Rostock, Erlangen, and Leipzig, and was heralded as a conservative scholar who largely disavowed the principles of higher criticism (although some of these commitments eroded later in his career, blossoming into the full-fledged higher criticism of his son, Friedrich).²¹⁹ While professor at Erlangen in 1864 he published a commentary on Job entitled *Das Buch Iob*, as part of the series of OT commentaries he co-authored with Karl Keil.²²⁰

In this commentary Delitzsch takes up a mostly favorable view of Eliphaz, who is the advocate of truth failing only in the manner of application to Job. "All that Eliphaz says, considered in itself, is blameless" and "the counsel

---

216. Ibid., 227.

217. Ibid., 314.

218. As Raymond Surburg notes, probably no one did as much during his lifetime to use OT studies to confront contemporary Judaism as did Delitzsch. This included the founding of the "Institus Judaicus," the publication of several apologetical tracts and larger works (*Wissenschaft, Kunst, Judentum* in 1838 and *Anekdota zur Geschichte der mittelalterlichen Scholastik unter Juden und Moslemen* in 1841), and the translation of the NT into Hebrew which sold over 70,000 copies before his death ("The Influence of the Two Delitzsches," 226).

219. Ibid., 229.

220. Delitzsch, *Das Buch Iob*,. The work was translated into English as *Biblical Commentary on the Book of Job*.

of Eliphaz is right counsel."[221] He enjoys the "the self-confident pathos of age and the air of one of the prophets" ("selbstzuversichtlichen Pathos des Alters und der Miene eines Propheten").[222] Eliphaz is not only orthodox in his speeches but expounds truth of God that accords with other Scripture: "He says that the destroying judgment of God never touches the innocent, but certainly the wicked; and at the same time expresses the same truth as that placed as a motto to the Psalter in Ps. i and which is even brilliantly confirmed in the issue of the history of Job."[223] So then, although Delitzsch admits that Eliphaz does not represent the entire truth of Scripture, still "there is no doctrinal error to be discovered in the speech of Eliphaz."[224] Moreover, "Job ought to humble himself under this; but since he does not, we must side with Eliphaz."[225]

Eliphaz is in his demeanor, nevertheless, heartless, haughty, stiff, and cold in spite of his eloquence.[226] In the application of divine truth to Job he fails to take into account the entire scope of Job's situation: "Instead of considering that Job's despair and murmuring against God is really of a different kind from that of the godless, he classes them together, and instead of gently correcting him, presents to Job the accursed end of the fool, who also murmurs against God, as he himself has seen it."[227] So Delitzsch is careful somewhat to temper an otherwise complimentary assessment of the chief friend. He is critical of Eliphaz in his tone (A) and rebuke by Yahweh (I), but favorable in his assessment of Eliphaz's purpose (B), theological provenance and creed (C), view of divine retribution (D), special revelatory experience (E), view of remedial suffering (F), his status as doyen (G), and use of the sin list (H).

Karl Budde

Karl Budde (1850–1935) was a renowned professor of OT at the University of Marburg, where he taught for over thirty-five years.[228] The author

---

221. Delitzsch, *Biblical Commentary on the Book of Job*, 104.
222. *Iob*, 58.
223. Delitzsch, *Biblical Commentary*, 104.
224. Ibid., 105.
225. Ibid.
226. Ibid., 108.
227. Ibid., 109.
228. He was described at his death as a man of "an astonishingly acute mind, sound judgment, and great power of concentration with solid, accurate learning and painstaking care" (Cadbury, "Proceedings," iii).

of several commentaries on OT writings, he published a commentary on Job at the close of the nineteenth century.[229] While Budde follows in the train of his German predecessors by adopting a mostly favorable view of Eliphaz, he places somewhat more emphasis on the ruthless outworking of Eliphaz's rigid dogmatism. "The friends have been so deeply permeated by the righteousness of Job, yet they are not after all in his shoes and can renounce this tenuous single feature as opposed to their steadfast doctrine, the basis of their worldview. So they see in Job's sufferings certain evidence that in secret he has incurred heavy guilt."[230] For Eliphaz and the other friends the theological postulate of an innocent sufferer cannot be sustained; therefore, "their obligation as friends can only in this consist, that they bring Job to confession and expiation of his guilt, perhaps that God then may still have pity."[231]

As to Eliphaz's approach, Budde summarizes: "Only timidly Eliphaz tries to rebuke Job." Meanwhile, the content of his reprimand is sound, having been received by direct divine revelation: "Eliphaz, however, knows through revelation that no angel, much less a man, is without error and guilt. No mere irritation comforts against self-inflicted evil; he ought to invoke God, who is able to bring the sole remedy. Then the punishment itself will redound for him into blessing and the rest of his life will pass in peace and fortune."[232] As the debate ensues and tension mounts, Eliphaz grows more confrontational, accusing Job that "you are no sage, otherwise you would not have spoken such useless chatter."[233] Budde argues that Eliphaz's second speech is "nothing but a sermon aimed at Job, with appeal to the testimony of the fathers."[234] By the end of the dialogue "Eliphaz observes that with theoretical discussion nothing is done, so he now pronounces ruthlessly the view of the friends which Job had sensed anyway. Job had earned his calamity through heinous behavior and a godless disposition. Still, he promises in the event of conversion a good end (vv. 21ff.)."[235] Although Eliphaz grows irascible in his discourses, he pronounces truth that Job would do well to heed. Thus Budde is favorable to Eliphaz's purpose (B), theological provenance and creed (C), doctrine of retribution (D), revelatory experience (E), doctrine of remedial suffering (F), status as doyen (G),

---

229. Budde, *Das Buch Hiob*.
230. Ibid., xxiii. Citations from the German are my translation.
231. Ibid., xxiv.
232. Ibid., 17.
233. Ibid., 77.
234. Ibid.
235. Ibid., 123.

and use of sin list (H). He is critical at times, however, of Eliphaz's tone (A) and of his rebuke by Yahweh (I).

Nineteenth- and Early Twentieth-Century English-Speaking Scholarship

Nineteenth-century English-speaking scholarship was certainly less prolific in its handling of Job than were the scholars on the European continent. The most notable examples of English scholarship on Job are similar to their German contemporaries in positing a positive appraisal of Eliphaz.

William Henry Green

William Henry Green (1825–1900) taught at Princeton Theological Seminary for more than a half-century and disseminated widely an approach to the OT known as the "reverent and conservative school of higher criticism."[236] Both prodigious in his literary output and popular as a teacher, Green was recognized warmly as one of the foremost OT scholars at the close of the nineteenth century.[237] While Green devoted much of his labors to the Pentateuch and to wisdom books such as Proverbs and Ecclesiastes,[238] he wished also to encourage the study of the book of Job and to this end authored a volume intended "to set forth its general drift, to exhibit its plan and structure, and trace the course of thought from first to last."[239]

Green took a sober view of the three friends of Job, recognizing that, although they sustained an integral role in the unfolding events of the book, they were unwitting emissaries of Satan artfully used to drive Job toward remonstrance with Yahweh.[240] The tone of Eliphaz and the others toward Job was baneful. Job is "wounded by their harshness, stung by their censures, exasperated by their reproaches, and driven into antagonism by their arguments."[241] They served, in fact, as a further temptation to Job to reject God, exacerbated by their professed advocacy of the divine cause. Yet at the same time the three sages, as "cherished and familiar friends of Job," must

---

236. Taylor, "Working with Wisdom Literature," 45.

237. *Celebration*, 12. This volume is a testament to Green's popularity, encompassing nearly 200 pages filled with accolades for his long tenure and commendable service to the seminary community and church at large.

238. On this see Taylor, "Working with Wisdom Literature," 45–46.

239. Green, *The Argument of Job Unfolded*, 1.

240. Green, *Job*, 144.

241. Ibid., 113.

be understood as "eminent men, wise men, and good men."[242] Eliphaz in particular proves a venerable sage, full of age and experience.[243] He hails from a region "proverbial for the sagacity of its inhabitants," pointing to the likelihood that he and the others are "men of superior ability, of intellectual acumen, and of extensive requirements."[244] Moreover, he and the others were benevolent companions who possessed a genuine affection for Job.[245] Yet for all this, Eliphaz grows increasingly irate at Job's obduracy and must rebuke him. Unfortunately, however, Eliphaz is mistaken in his theological trajectory, assuming that all suffering comes about as the consequence of sin itself and is thus deservedly wrought upon the sinner:

> The special significance of suffering, therefore, remains unexplained. Its importance as a test of character, its value as a means of discipline and training, and the far more exceeding reward by which it shall be abundantly compensated, are not once suspected. Eliphaz alleges that man suffers because he is a sinner; he knew not that a man may likewise suffer because he is a saint; that he may thus exhibit more distinctly his saintly character; that he may be ripened still more in holiness; and that his final recompense may be proportionably increased. Suffering, to Eliphaz, was ever and only a punishment, a judgment for sin, an infliction of the divine pleasure. He knew not that it might also be a token of love, a means of grace, a blessing in disguise.[246]

By this failure Eliphaz is short-sighted and a further affliction to Job in his suffering. His counsel is flawed and his prescribed remedy falls short. Green's portrayal of Eliphaz is thus somewhat mixed. He is favorable toward Eliphaz in his understanding of the latter's intentions and basic character and in this way his status as doyen (G). In the analysis of Eliphaz's speech content and theological matrix, however, Green is critical of Eliphaz's tone (A), purpose (B), theological provenance and creed (C), doctrine of retribution (D), and rebuke by Yahweh (I). Green does not treat Eliphaz's revelatory experience (E), doctrine of remedial suffering (F), or use of the sin list (H).

242. Ibid., 117.
243. Green posits Eliphaz as the eldest of the friends and therefore at a minimum age of 75 or 80, as compared with Job who is likely 55 or 60 (ibid., 118).
244. Ibid., 119.
245. Ibid., 121.
246. Ibid., 132. Green's comments here appear at odds, however, with a few of Eliphaz's exhortations to Job: "Behold, blessed is the one whom God reproves; therefore despise not the discipline of the Almighty. For he wounds, but he binds up; he shatters, but his hands heal" (Job 5:17–18) or "If you return to the Almighty you will be built up" (22:23).

A. B. Davidson

Although in the nineteenth century most critical commentaries on the book of Job originated from continental European scholarship, especially amidst the German higher critical schools, one notable exception was the commentary published in 1889 by the celebrated British Hebraist A. B. Davidson.[247] Much in line with Ewald's analysis studied earlier, Davidson views Eliphaz and the others as flat characters whose purpose is to provide counterpoint to Job. Job, rather than the friends, is the author's mouthpiece for the principal tenets expressed in the book, although even in this role Job has nothing positive to contribute other than to refute the outdated views of providence espoused by the friends.[248] "When the three friends, the representatives of former theories of providence, are reduced to silence and driven off the ground by Job (ch. xxi, xxiii, xxiv), we may assume that it was the author's purpose to discredit the ideas which they support."[249]

Davidson has warm words regarding Eliphaz's approach, notwithstanding. He is "the most dignified, the calmest, and most considerate, and perhaps oldest of Job's friends."[250] Eliphaz has no ill feelings toward Job nor mordancy in his tone. "We must beware of supposing that there is any flavour of sarcasm in the words of Eliphaz." Rather, "such a things is wholly foreign to the mood of Eliphaz at starting, who, though he does find something to blame in Job's state of mind, is perfectly sincere and friendly."[251] His first speech is eloquent, one of the masterpieces of the book. Further, Eliphaz enjoys a place in the prophetic rank as one who speaks with the composure, authority and clear eye of the seer, to whom revelations from heaven have been granted through nocturnal visions.

Yet Davidson sees two flaws in Eliphaz's approach. First, as the speeches continue Eliphaz becomes cold and uncompassionate. Second, his theory of suffering is ultimately flawed, however true it may be generally as a principle of God's moral governance of the cosmos.[252] The shortcoming is that it does not apply to Job's case and is therefore incorrectly applied to Job's angst. On the whole, Davidson is mostly favorable to Eliphaz in his tone (A), his reception of special revelation (E), his view of remedial suffering (F), and his position as the eldest spokesman (G). He is unfavorable, however, in his

---

247. Davidson, *The Book of Job*.
248. Ibid., 25.
249. Davidson, *Job*, xxiv. Cf. also p. 25.
250. Ibid.
251. Ibid., 29.
252. Ibid., 41.

view of Eliphaz's purpose in the book of Job (B), his theological provenance and creed (C), his doctrine of retribution (D), correlative use of the sin list (H), and rebuke by Yahweh (I).

Arthur Samuel Peake

Arthur S. Peake (1865–1929) was a Methodist biblical scholar and Hebrew professor at the University of Manchester. He became a popularizer of higher criticism in England through a work which he authored in 1922 to reassure the faithful that the *en vogue* higher critical approaches posed no threat to the Christian faith. With this salvo Peake is credited as having spared the British isle from the fundamentalist-modernist controversy that swept through America in the early twentieth century.[253] In 1904 Peake published a critical commentary on Job in the New Century Bible series.[254] He undertakes a favorable view of Eliphaz and the other friends with respect to their tone and approach.

From the beginning Eliphaz, along with the other friends, assumes Job's fundamental integrity as a pious and godly man. Eliphaz underscores God's transcendent purity, and although he strays little beyond this principle, he is sophisticated enough to realize that there is in Job's suffering more than simply punishment for sins. Job is being chastened, which Eliphaz is eager to show will surely result in blessing. As to Eliphaz's tone in his first speech, Peake is complimentary: "There is no fault to be found with Eliphaz for the tone of his speech. It is very considerate and tender, but his theology has misled his diagnosis."[255] In his explication of the doctrine of retribution in 4:8–11, Eliphaz does not mean to include Job amongst the sinners whom he excoriates but instead to provide an example of what invariably occurs to the wicked.[256] Eliphaz is commendable also in his experience of the special revelatory experience: "Eliphaz is a seer who is privileged to see night visions."[257] By the end of the first speech Eliphaz outlines with "beautiful and glowing" eloquence the blessing that results from chastening such as Job has experienced.[258]

---

253. See Sell, "The Rise and Reception of Modern Biblical Criticism," 146. The work was entitled *The Nature of Scripture*.

254. Peake, *Job*.

255. Ibid., 77.

256. Ibid., 79.

257. Ibid., 80.

258. Ibid., 89.

By the second speech Eliphaz and the other friends are alienated from Job. Deeply shocked by Job's blasphemous attacks on God, Eliphaz must respond in kind with ever growing protestations that God's ways are above reproach.[259] Eliphaz's reference to his aged wisdom perspective rings hollow in light of Job's traumatic experience and is therefore not effective.[260] By the third speech Eliphaz has turned God into a "cold, passionless ruler, who has no vital concern in man's conduct, and adjusts retribution to behaviour with the inhuman precision of a machine."[261] With regard to the rebuke by Yahweh, Peake is surprised, insofar that "Yahweh's harsh judgment seems to correspond ill with the pious tone in which the friends speak."[262] The solution is to be found, nonetheless, in the author's purpose for the book. The author has taken the original prose portions of the prologue and epilogue and added to them the poetic dialogue leaving in some inherent incongruities. Although Yahweh's rebuke in 42:7 appears overly austere in the light of the tone and purpose of the friends in the dialogue, the author sees fit to retain this portion because he sides with Job and wishes for the verdict by Yahweh to substantiate this perspective. Peake is quite favorable toward Eliphaz in nearly every regard, including his tone (A), purpose (B), theological provenance and creed (C), doctrine of retribution (D), visionary experience (E), doctrine of remedial suffering (F), and rebuke by Yahweh (as overly harsh and contradictory to the dialogue speeches) (I). The only slightly critical assessments of Eliphaz relate to his appeal to his aged wisdom perspective (G) and the use of the sin listing (H).

J. T. Marshall

J. T. Marshall, professor at Manchester Baptist College, also published a commentary on Job in 1904. In this work Marshall takes a decidedly favorable view of Eliphaz, profuse from the outset in his praise of the sage: "[Eliphaz] is a venerable philosopher, a pious Edomite, familiar with the sayings of the wise of past ages, but claiming also direct communication with heaven, for he derived part of his creed—the doctrine of universal peccability—from special revelation."[263] Eliphaz is, moreover, anxious to avoid wounding Job's feelings and to keep in the background the notion of retributive divine providence as having any part in Job's case. Eliphaz's re-

259. Ibid., 151.
260. Ibid., 154–55.
261. Ibid., 212.
262. Ibid., 344.
263. Marshall, *The Book of Job*, 31.

velatory experience is sublime and its description is of considerable value to the history of revelation.[264] Eliphaz expounds on his view of remedial suffering in hopes that Job, if he is submissive, will receive even greater blessing than before.[265] By his second speech Eliphaz discerns sly deceit on the part of Job to mask certain sins, and he confronts him for it.[266] By the third speech Eliphaz's dogma has grown to one of a God of "merely impassive justice" whose "moral government [is] a mere machine for weighing man's actions."[267]

When Eliphaz is rebuked by Yahweh in the epilogue, Marshall offers several reasons: (1) in some passages Eliphaz and the others lack an inner truthfulness; (2) Eliphaz and the others persistently insist that Job was a wicked man in spite of his protestations to the contrary; (3) the friends equally adhered tenaciously to a dogma that falsified facts; and, (4) in their personal prosperity Eliphaz and the others deemed themselves to be righteous and thus eschewed humility or penitence.[268] Eliphaz's particular difficulty was an over-zealousness to come to a resolution when one was not forthcoming. In his eagerness he imprudently joined together realities that were properly left antinomies, thereby discrediting Job. Marshall takes a high view of Eliphaz in regard to his tone (A), purpose in the dialogue (B), mode and content of special revelation (E), views on remedial suffering (F), and status as doyen (G). Where he is less favorable, although not harshly critical, is upon Eliphaz's theological provenance and creed (C), his views on retribution (D), his use of the sin list (H), and the nature of his rebuke by Yahweh (I). While willing to point out a few deficiencies in Eliphaz's approach, Marshall nevertheless sustains a propitious view of the sage.

Mid Twentieth-Century Scholarship

As the twentieth century ensued a few interpretive trends evidenced a continued softening toward Eliphaz. Yet perhaps as a reaction toward this increasing moderation or as a product of scholarship birthed principally in the German universities of the late nineteenth century, harshly critical readings of Eliphaz were also published, most notably in the work of Moses Buttenwieser and to a lesser extent Morris Jastrow. Probably no one is more to be credited, however, with turning the tide in studies of Eliphaz as Kemper

264. Ibid., 32.
265. Ibid., 35.
266. Ibid., 61.
267. Ibid., 80.
268. Ibid., 130.

Fullerton, whose article on Eliphaz was a watershed in interpretive efforts, becoming a *locus classicus* in the ensuing *Forschungsgeschichte*.

Morris Jastrow

Morris Jastrow, Jr. (1861–1921) was born in Poland but immigrated to the United States as a youth.[269] Upon graduating from the University of Pennsylvania in 1881, he took up graduate studies in France and Germany, earning a PhD from Leipzig in 1884. From 1893 he returned to teach at the University of Pennsylvania and was recognized at the time of his death as one of the foremost Semitic scholars in the world.

Jastrow's commentary on Job, published in 1920 just a year before his death,[270] bears marks of the German higher criticism and Enlightenment rationalism, which he imbibed during his doctoral studies.[271] Eliphaz and the other friends begin with genuine sympathy for Job as evident by the overtures they exhibit in the authentic prologue narrative.[272] Yet although mildly restrained, once Eliphaz begins to speak his sympathy turns harsh with growing umbrage. His role is to accuse Job of being a wicked sinner whose punishment is deserved—and more so—because of his failure to repent.[273]

Although Eliphaz in his opening speech begins with an apology for hurting Job's feelings, he soon bluntly and tactlessly avers that Job must be a terrible sinner because no one righteous has ever perished.[274] Eliphaz grows more and more outlandish, as he assumes the "ridiculous position" of asseverating that his nocturnal vision is divine intuition.[275] In his peroration on remedial suffering, Eliphaz pronounces sayings which perhaps originate from a collection of ancient adages and are in the wisdom current of the biblical maxims found in Prov 3:11; 6:16; and 19:3.[276] Eliphaz in his second

---

269. Jastrow's biographical facts are taken from the notice n.a., "Dr. Morris Jastrow," 14.

270. Jastrow, *The Book of Job*.

271. The reality of this assertion is evident, for example, in Jastrow's remarkable comment that "it is no exaggeration to say that barring the two introductory chapters, which tell the story of Job in prose form, and the prose epilogue at the end of the book, there are not ten consecutive verses in the Symposium between Job and his friends or in the speeches of Elihu or in the magnificent closing chapters placed as speeches in the mouth of Yahweh, the text of which can be regarded as correct" (ibid., 9).

272. Ibid., 41–42.

273. Ibid., 43.

274. Ibid., 210.

275. Ibid., 212.

276. Ibid., 214–15.

speech appeals to traditional wisdom from a previous age when the population was not yet diluted with foreigners as lamentably it is in their day. In his third speech Eliphaz borrows from the Mosaic covenant (Exod 22:25-26) and Deuteronomic code (Deut 24:12-13) to impugn Job.[277] At the conclusion Eliphaz and the other friends are rebuked by Yahweh because, in contrast to Job as the mouthpiece of the unorthodox writer, they have not rightly reproached against the abuse and inequity of God's governance over the world.[278]

Jastrow is largely ambivalent towards Eliphaz. He is negative toward Eliphaz's purpose in the book (B), which is flat simply as an accuser of Job, toward his retributive doctrine (D), and revelatory experience (E). He is rather more positive with respect to the sage's theological provenance and creed (C), as his views of remedial suffering (F) share affinities with the wisdom of Proverbs and his use of the sin list (H) borrows from the Mosaic code. He also sees him as laying claim to ancient traditions which would have been respected in that context (G). Yet Jastrow is unclear toward Eliphaz in his tone (A), contending that he begins sympathetically but grows increasingly ireful, and in the rebuke by Yahweh (I) over which he has little comment.

Moses Buttenwieser

Moses Buttenwieser (1862–1939) was a German Jewish scholar, educated at the universities of Würzburg, Leipzig, and Heidelberg. He taught as Professor of Biblical Exegesis at Hebrew Union College from 1897 until his death. He was highly influential not only for his erudition but as a teacher and mentor to a generation of biblical Hebrew students.[279] Although he published a commentary on Job in 1922—well into the twentieth century—his work also shows the lingering impact of concepts inculcated from his German critical scholarly upbringing.[280]

---

277. Ibid., 275.

278. Ibid., 365.

279. Buttenwieser's obituary in the 1939 proceedings of the Society of Biblical Literature laments that "one cannot think of Dr. Moses Buttenwieser without mental exhilaration and spiritual pleasure. There was always much good humored charm and wholesome love for one's fellowmen about this beloved teacher while he was among the living" (Flight, "Proceedings," ii). He dedicated his commentary on Job "to the boys who have been my pupils at The Hebrew Union College in affection and esteem" (*The Book of Job*, v).

280. Perhaps this is most evident in his extensive efforts to reconstruct the allegedly correct order of the speeches.

The purpose for the book of Job, according to Buttenwieser, is to explore the reality of whether disinterested piety or virtue can exist within a righteous man for its own sake.[281] Eliphaz and the other friends are static figures whose only purpose is to offer up the antiquated conventions concerning divine providence which Job is meant to refute: "They are the exponents of the religious views of their age, upholders of tradition, and as such, all three, without appreciable difference, tenaciously defend the doctrine of retributive justice."[282] The friends view Job's outbursts with coldhearted suspicion and growing wrath, and Eliphaz takes his part in rejoining to Job with "wild charges" and acerbic contumelies.[283] Although Buttenwieser observed a trend in his day of growing sympathy toward Eliphaz and the others, he would have none of it: "It has become almost a rule with interpreters of Job to apologize for the friends, and to paint them in a quite friendly light, whereas the writer of Job was intent on portraying them as fanatics pure and simple."[284] Buttenwieser feels he is faithful to the writer's intent by recognizing the frenzied intolerance and blind resentment seething under the surface in every of the friends' reprimands.

In his first speech Eliphaz is incensed with Job from the outset, consummately unmoved by his erstwhile friend's sad plight and completely insincere as to the perception of any feigned sympathy as he remonstrates with Job.[285] In disseminating the insights disclosed in the nocturnal vision, Eliphaz is slyly leveraging divine revelation in order to seek to add divine authority to his perspective.[286] In the more eloquent latter section of the first speech, rather than graciously offering hope to Job Eliphaz is simply acrimoniously adding to his scolding of Job to accept his counsel as the only means for relief.[287] By the second speech Eliphaz turns up the heat, convinced that Job's blasphemous words spring from true guilt. "Relying complacently on his advanced age and superior wisdom," Eliphaz has nothing new to contribute and only becomes increasingly rigid and dogmatic in adhering to his original tenets.[288] By the third speech Eliphaz resorts to

---

281. Buttenwieser, *Job*, 29–30.

282. Ibid., 41.

283. "After the manner of fanatics they, Eliphaz like the others, heap upon him the most heartless taunts and accusations" (ibid., 47; cf. also 54).

284. Ibid., 201.

285. Ibid., 161.

286. Ibid., 48.

287. Ibid., 168–69.

288. Ibid., 201.

fabricating lies about Job, giving unbridled reign to his fanaticism.[289] Yahweh rebukes Eliphaz and the other friends in 42:7 for their intellectual dishonesty as their defense of retributive justice has been really a defense of falsehood on behalf of God. Buttenwieser is, to my knowledge, the most consistently harsh reviewer of Eliphaz in the history of Joban interpretation. He is reproachful toward the sage in every identified interpretive category: his tone (A), purpose in Job (B), theological provenance and creed (C), doctrine of retributive justice (D), special revelation (E), doctrine of remedial suffering (F), status as elder (G), use of the sin list (H), and rebuke by Yahweh for intellectual dishonesty (I).

Kemper Fullerton

Students of Job would do well to pay heed to the contribution made by Kemper Fullerton (1865–1941), whose essay published in 1930 on the first speech of Eliphaz seemed remarkably ahead of its time and set a course for later interpretive efforts.[290] Fullerton was a renowned Hebraist who taught at Lane Theological Seminary (1893–1904) and at the Graduate School of Theology at Oberlin College (1904–1934).[291] He studied at Princeton University and Union Theological Seminary and would contribute to OT studies through the publication of several tomes in including *Studies in the Psalter* and *Prophecy and Authority*.[292] His several essays on Job formed the nucleus of what he hoped would one day become a full-fledged commentary.[293]

Fullerton recognized throughout the book of Job "the very effective use of *double entendre*" employed by the author subtly so that "the orthodox reader could peruse them with approval, whereas the more attentive reader would find in them an indirect but none the less real criticism of the orthodox position."[294] Eliphaz's speeches are among the most creative and carefully deliberated in the book. The attention devoted to these speeches springs from the author's desire that at first the friends, rather than Job,

---

289. Ibid., 54.

290. Fullerton, "Double Entendre," 320–74.

291. Flight, "Proceedings," *JBL* 61, no. 1 (1942): viii; Oberlin College Archives, "RG 11 – Graduate School of Theology (1833–1966)."

292. Flight, "Proceedings," viii. See *Studies in the Psalter*; *Prophecy and Authority*; *Essays and Sketches*. The commentary never materialized.

293. See Fullerton, "The Original Conclusion to the Book of Job," 116–35; Fullerton, "Double Entrende," 320–74; Fullerton, "On Job, Chapters 9 and 10," 321–49. On Fullerton's aspirations for a commentary on Job, see "Double Entendre," 321.

294. Fullerton, "Double Entendre," 320, emphasis his.

would be perceived as incontrovertible. This insight allows Fullerton to take a sanguine appraisal of Eliphaz as a figure to be warmly received by the reader: "The affirmations of Eliphaz, doctrinally so sound and steadying, bring a welcome relief. Further, the dignity, sobriety, and beauty with which Eliphaz enforces his views contrast with the vehement, almost ungovernable outbursts of Job, to the great initial disadvantage of the latter."[295] Eliphaz has flaws, to be sure, but these blemishes are covered up skillfully by the author at the start "in order that the Friends may seem gloriously in the right as against Job."[296]

Eliphaz is solicitous toward Job from the outset. Although he must mildly rebuke his friend, he does so with utmost care and concern in spite of Job's fervid outcries.[297] Above all Eliphaz is perplexed over Job's dismay, for it was common knowledge—and here the reader must side with Eliphaz—that the innocent do not perish (4:7). Still, a more disconcerting but necessary warning has to be issued: "As I have seen, those who plow iniquity and sow trouble reap the same" (4:8). Even in this Eliphaz does not design to indict Job so much as to put into his remembrance that habitual sinners are those who reap trouble—and Job is not to be included among this lot—thus Job must not confound himself regarding the outcome of his predicament: this distress will of certainty turn out for his good.

Even in his gentle admonition Eliphaz intends to encourage Job, and he follows this reproof with the most didactic portion of his first speech in 4:12–21. In this part Eliphaz reminds Job of general truths regarding sin and suffering to provide some clarity to Job in the crucible of his anguish. Fullerton is lavish in his assessment of Eliphaz here, and it is helpful to quote him in full:

> Eliphaz seems to show the greatest considerateness for Job. He implicates him in sin, it is true, but in the gentlest possible way. He does not accuse him of any specific transgressions which might account for his sufferings. He refers only to the general sinfulness of man which is inherent in man's creatureliness. Job, it is implied, must expect to suffer, not because he was a sinner above all others,

---

295. Ibid., 326.

296. Fullerton adds insightfully: "The subtle skill with which all this is done is proved, as Delitzsch long ago pointed out, by the difficulty which the Expositors have always experienced in detecting just what was false in the speech" (ibid., 327).

297. Fullerton notes that "Eliphaz, who, as is generally recognized, is an elderly man, has managed, under the greatest provocation, to control his feelings quite admirably. As he supposed, he was doing the very best he could by his friend. What more could be expected of him? In all this there is no indication of any insincerity or unkindness, and doctrinally he was true to the deepest convictions of the pious of his day" (ibid., 329).

> but because he was a man.... In this passage [4:12–21], as in the concluding one, the nobility of the language, the impressive way in which the oracle is described, and the truth of the oracle itself, which few people in antiquity would refuse to accept—all these admirable qualities strongly recommend the position of Eliphaz to the reader. They show the assured calm and the profound reverence of this friend of Job to advantage as contrasted with Job's fury that verges on blasphemy.[298]

Eliphaz's receipt of divine revelation is impressive and true, and he is contending for truths meant to condole with Job. Job's present condition is connected to no personal fault but attributable solely to his common humanity. All men are sinners; therefore, by implication, Job is a sinner. Furthermore, all sinners suffer; therefore, Job also suffers as a sinner though in a general and not specific way.[299]

In the longest and culminating portion of his first speech (Job 5:8–27) Eliphaz is solidly consolatory. Here Eliphaz is at his best with an eloquent piece elaborating on the "kindlier doctrine of suffering as chastisement" in place of the harder line of retribution expounded upon earlier. These are certainly not the words of a hypocrite but nothing less than those of a true friend.[300] If any fault is to be found in Eliphaz's first speech it is Eliphaz's failure to discern with foresight the effect of his words upon Job. The unfortunate result is that Job interprets his words as a personal attack even though Eliphaz in no way intends them to be so.[301] Eliphaz is merely insensitive and at times clumsy, certainly dogmatic in his orthodoxy, but not to be reprehended by the reader:

> We are to see in Eliphaz an aged, dignified, well-meaning man, dominated by the current doctrine of retribution, who wishes to spare Job's feelings and comfort him, but is able to do neither the one nor the other because he is a doctrinaire, unable to sense the tragic realities of life. He is not a malignant person. He is not hiding his real feelings toward Job under a mantle of hypocritical sympathy while indulging in bitter asides at his expense. He is simply a rather stupid good person, blundering into words that would cut Job to the quick because he did not have a

---

298. Ibid., 328.
299. Ibid., 330.
300. Ibid.
301. Ibid., 337.

sufficiently sympathetic imagination to realize what impression he was likely to make by them.[302]

Although Fullerton does not treat at length Eliphaz's status as doyen in the second speech (G), his use of the sin listing in the third speech (H), or the rebuke by Yahweh in the prologue (I), he is overwhelmingly positive in his overall assessment of the leading interlocutor as to his tone (A), purpose in the book (B), theological provenance and creed (C), perspective on retribution (D), special revelation (E), and teaching on remedial suffering (F). Fullerton is perhaps the most favorable interpreter of Eliphaz in the history of Joban interpretation, interestingly coming only a few years after the harshest critique of Buttenwieser.

Summary

The foregoing sketch has outlined the contours of an extensive interpretive history for Job's leading interlocutor Eliphaz. At this point, a few conclusions and implications are in order. Beginning with the LXX, readers of Eliphaz have diverged generally into two streams. The first line of reception history understands Eliphaz positively as contributing a meaningful theological perspective to the book. For these interpreters, Eliphaz is an experienced sage who provides significant means to aid Job in his suffering. This interpretative approach bears influence from LXX Job, as evident in several subsequent works based in part on this translation, such as *Testament of Job*, Aristeas's *Life of Job*, Clement of Rome's first epistle to the Corinthians, and Chrysostom's sermons on Job. In addition, ancient Jewish readings of Eliphaz were mostly positive, culminating eventually in Maimonides's high praise for Eliphaz in the Middle Ages. Intermittent Christian interpreters, such as Gregory the Great (on the allegorical level), Luis de León, and John Calvin, were also rather positive, apparently persuaded toward a more favorable view by the apostle Paul's citation of Eliphaz in 1 Corinthians 3. By the modern era, a growing number of Jewish and Christian interpreters, including Franz Delitzsch, A. B. Davidson, Morris Jastrow, Karl Budde, Arthur Peake, J. T. Marshall, and Kemper Fullerton, were championing a more sympathetic view of Eliphaz in an attempt to moderate the harshly critical readings which had dominated Joban scholarship.

The other stream of reception history, however, vilified Eliphaz from the outset as fomenting an evil ideological assault against the righteous Job who, for his part, clings tenaciously to the truth. This interpretative strain

---

302. Ibid., 339–40.

is evident already in some ancient Jewish rabbinical sources as well as in *Tobit*. Early Christian interpreters most consistently took this tack, however, including such luminaries as Jerome, Gregory the Great, and Thomas Aquinas, as well as Methodius and the Puritan divine, George Abbott. In spite of trends toward a more congenial understanding of Eliphaz, a number of modern Jewish and Christian interpreters also remained harshly critical, including Heinrich Ewald, Moses Buttenwieser, and William Henry Green. From this detailed overview of Eliphaz's more distant reception history, we must turn now to the ways in which these interpretive streams diffused in the later twentieth century through a growing spate of Joban studies.

3

Contemporary Approaches to Eliphaz

IN THE PREVIOUS DECADE F. L. Downing observed that the final quarter of the twentieth century had witnessed a literary explosion of reinvigorated biblical studies and innovative approaches to the text, including a significant share of attention devoted to Job.[1] This flurry of scholarly activity produced a growing number of significant analyses of the role of Eliphaz in the book of Job.

Leo Perdue: Eliphaz as Cocksure Fundamentalist

Over several decades of research and writing, Leo Perdue distinguished himself as a formidable scholar in the field of wisdom literature.[2] Having completed his graduate and postgraduate work at Vanderbilt University,[3] Perdue is the former Dean, President, and Professor of Hebrew Bible at the Brite Divinity School in Fort Worth, Texas.

Analysis

In his monograph *Wisdom in Revolt*, Leo Perdue argues for a fresh approach to discerning the nature of wisdom literature in general and the book of

---

1. "Voices from the Whirlwind," 389–92.
2. See, e.g., Perdue, *The Sword and the Stylus*; Perdue, ed., *Scribes, Sages, and Seers*; Perdue, *Wisdom Literature*; Perdue, *Proverbs*; Perdue, ed., *In Search of Wisdom*; Perdue, *Wisdom in Revolt*.
3. See Perdue, "Wisdom and Cult."

Job in particular. Traditionally, studies of wisdom literature have identified four disparate organizing principles which form the lens through which to read and interpret wisdom literature: anthropology, theodicy, world-order (also *Maat*), and the dialectic of anthropology and cosmology.[4] Suggesting these models are inadequate, Perdue attempts to enhance and refine the cosmology-anthropology dialectic model in order to forge a more lucid paradigm through which to interpret the wisdom corpus.

Specifically, Perdue proposes the recognition of metaphor as a powerful tool to recognize the significance of religious language in the sapiential literature: "Religious language is metaphorical" and such language "constructs models which are extended metaphors."[5] In particular, four metaphors were the common stock of ancient near Eastern cultures, including Israel: fertility, artistry, word, and struggle (*Chaoskampf*).[6] These "mythic metaphors" became the modes of expression for the culture's conceptions of reality and the common ground from which to articulate the culture's theological formulations.

Turning to Job, Perdue asserts that two mythic traditions, which balance the cosmology-anthropology dialectic, serve as the source and backdrop for the theological formulations of the book.[7] The first is the anthropological mythic tradition of humanity as slave to the gods, played out through the cycle of creation and consignment to slavery, ensuing slavery and toil, revolt against the tyranny of the gods, fall and threatened destruction, and, finally, judgment and redemption. The second is the cosmological mythic tradition of *Chaoskampf* between creator and the monster of chaos, which proceeds through the following cycle: battle, victory over chaos, kingship, judgment, and creation. In Job these two mythic traditions form a tensive nexus in which the creator's cosmological conflict with the chaos monster is superimposed upon Job's anthropological struggle with the creator, resulting in "all-out revolt."[8] The conflict between the characters of the book of Job materializes the struggle over the proper appropriation of these mythic traditions, as Perdue summarizes:

---

4. Ibid., 13. Perdue identifies the leading proponent of each of the organizing principles as the following: Walther Zimmerli for anthropology, James L. Crenshaw for theodicy, Hartmut Gese for world-order, and Gerhard von Rad for the dialectic of anthropology and cosmology (see ibid., 13–17, for bibliographic sources).

5. Ibid., 22, 27.

6. Ibid., 29.

7. Ibid., 30.

8. Ibid., 31.

> As with any theological tradition, wisdom struggled with the problems of the domestication of its language and the potential idolatry of its theological formulations. Its metaphors did not die, but they suffered the threats of abuse by those less perceptive and occasionally dogmatic tradents whose efforts almost led to the extinction of the tradition. The threat to wisdom came not from the clash of metaphors which led to heated and invigorating theological exchanges, but from the destructive misuse of religious language.[9]

Perdue here adumbrates the role he perceives for Eliphaz in the book of Job: Eliphaz is a ruthless, dogmatic tradent who idolizes and abuses religious language and thereby inadvertently threatens the very tradition that undergirds him.[10] Through his inflexible and domineering construction of retributive cosmology and slave anthropology, Eliphaz empties these mythic metaphors of their real significance and power.

In his first speech Eliphaz emerges as a doctrinaire defender of the power, wisdom, justice, and sovereignty of God, who upholds the equilibrium of the created order and metes out punishment to the wicked and reward to the righteous in accordance with the canons of the Deuteronomic doctrine of retribution.[11] Eliphaz corroborates his argument not only by the traditional dictums of wisdom—experience, analogy from nature, and first-hand assessment of human nature—but also by means of prophetic revelation (4:12–21) and the poetic distillation of doxological praise for the Creator (5:8–16). But throughout his theological harangue, Eliphaz runs roughshod over the customary question and disputation approach of wisdom, choosing to level at Job instead the iron fist of theological orthodoxy:

> The 'fear of God' in the faith of Eliphaz has become cocksure fundamentalism, unyielding in its claims to absolute truth and intolerance of critical questioning and contrary expressions. It is this rigidity of attitude that is incapable of engaging existence

---

9. Ibid.

10. For views similar to Perdue's harshly negative understanding of Eliphaz, cf. Buttenwieser, *Job*, 161; Girard, "'The Ancient Trail Trodden by the Wicked,'" 22, 25; Ball, *Job*, 133; Bullinger, *Job*, 13–14. Heinrich Ewald sees Eliphaz as fully convinced of Job's guilt before beginning to speak: "Zwar schon vollkommen von Ijobs Schuld überzeugt und mit höherer Zuversicht wie ein anerkannt vielerfahrner Freunde und Lehrer zu ihm als Irrendem redend" ("Indeed he is already fully confident of Job's guilt and with higher confidence as a recognized and experienced friend and teacher is speaking to him as to an errant one") (*Das Buch Ijob*, 88). Habel, however, calls such an understanding "gratuitous" (*Job*, 121).

11. Ibid., 111; cf. also Scott, *Way of Wisdom*, 136; Rankin, *Israel's Wisdom Literature*, 91; Parsons, "Guidelines," 403.

in torment, whether that of the righteous Job or the nation decimated by holocaust. The sacred canopy of Eliphaz' construction strains under the enormity of evil present in Job's and the human experience, the weight of theological expression which gives rightful place to questioning of divine action, and unyielding rigidity which disallowed openness to change and new insights.[12]

Thus, according to Perdue, Eliphaz misuses the metaphor of creation through an unbending literalism, which threatens to vitiate its very significance: "Metaphor has been reshaped into hardened, idolatrous dogma which distorts the power of language to build new worlds of faith. Uncontested, Eliphaz' fundamentalism misdirects faith's search for understanding towards a blind avowal of its own simplistic propositions."[13] In the end, Eliphaz is censured by Yahweh, along with the other friends, for his dogmatic misuse of religious metaphor: "In finding for Job over against the friends, what God does is vindicate Job's stringent questioning of divine justice and deconstruction of the friends' false theology of retribution and unquestionable sovereignty."[14] Eliphaz is thus an insidious, cocksure fundamentalist, abusive of religious metaphor and noxious of the tradition from which he has sprung.

Strengths and Weaknesses

Perdue has written an intriguing analysis of Job against the backdrop of its ANE cultural milieu. Although commendably sensitive to the ANE correlations found in Job, there are a few shortcomings in his approach. First, he allows the concept of metaphor to obscure elements of Job that may not be intended by the author to be metaphorical. Indeed, one may challenge on epistemological grounds his assertion that all religious language is metaphorical. Second, Perdue places undue interpretive weight upon the two anthropology-cosmology mythic traditions, which he argues form the theological basis for Job. It seems tenuous upon careful reading of the book to argue as he does that Job perceives his agonies as simply the playing out of the anthropological mythic metaphor concerning humanity as slave to the gods. Further, Job and Eliphaz appear to be doing more than simply sparring about which is the proper mythic tradition to apply. Third, Perdue views Eliphaz too narrowly as merely a tradent who espouses dogmatically the Deuteronomic principle of retribution. Such an approach

12. Ibid., 111–12.
13. Ibid., 112.
14. Ibid., 239.

is an oversimplification and fails to appreciate the textured characterization evident in the author's portrayal of Eliphaz. Perdue is thoroughly negative toward Eliphaz regarding his tone (A), purpose (B), theological provenance and creed (C), retributive perspective (D), special revelation (E), doctrine of remedial suffering (F), status as doyen (G), use of the sin list (H), and rebuke by Yahweh (I).

John C. L. Gibson: Eliphaz as Urbane Yet Curmudgeonly Sage

Long-time professor of Hebrew and Semitics at the University of Edinburgh from 1962 until his retirement in 1994, John C. L. Gibson (1930–2008) was well respected as a linguistic scholar, gifted writer, and staunch Scottish churchman.[15] In 1985 he authored a concise and popularly written Daily Study Bible Series commentary on the book of Job. Job would remain his favorite biblical book, as he perceived it to be full of "incomparable glories."[16] In addition to his commentary, Gibson penned a focused essay treating in more detail Eliphaz's role and purpose in the ancient book.[17]

Analysis

Gibson characterizes Eliphaz broadly as an "urbane and far-seeing exponent of orthodox Wisdom who is well aware of its weaknesses" and who "seems, too, to have a genuine sympathy for his old friend's tragic plight."[18] Beyond this, Eliphaz is the most-developed character of the three friends, as the other would-be comforters resort to stereotyped expressions while Eliphaz develops instead as a complex and cultured, opinionated and skeptical old scholar.[19]

Gibson proposes that Eliphaz begins gently with Job, acknowledging kindly Job's previous piety and altruism.[20] Yet though his approach seems heartfelt, cracks in Eliphaz's benevolent façade begin to show before he

---

15. Auld, "John C. L. Gibson," Internet.

16. Quoted in ibid.

17. *Job*; "Eliphaz the Temanite," 259–72; "Job and the Cure of Souls," 303–317.

18. *Job*, 37. Cf. "Eliphaz the Temanite," 267. For broadly similar views cf. Pope, *Job*, 36; Ellison, *A Study of Job*, 34, 77; Ward, *Out of the Whirlwind*, 43; Davies, *The Book of Job I–XIV*, 129–30; Paterson, *The Wisdom of Israel*, 29; Kelley, "Speeches," 483; Vischer, "God's Truth and Man's Lie," 133; Peake, *Job*, 77.

19. "Eliphaz the Temanite," 263.

20. *Job*, 37.

has ventured far into his first speech. He expounds more on the fate of the wicked than on the rewards of the righteous (4:8–11), and he alludes insouciantly to the oppressive desert şirocco as analogous to the fate of the wicked (4:9), the same gale that had snuffed out Job's children (1:18–19).[21] Eliphaz comes close to tipping his hand; as Gibson suggests, "by his maladroitness Eliphaz destroys right at the start the possibility of rapport with a man with whom intellectually he has much in common."[22]

The turning point comes midway through Eliphaz's first speech. He has reported vividly the details of an eerie nocturnal vision he received (4:12–21), an uncommon though not unprecedented source for sapiential theology. Yet despite its mysterious delivery of the banal truism that all men are sinful before God, the visionary experience tells us more about Eliphaz and about his frame of mind than does it disclose fresh insight into the plight of Job. Gibson argues that here Eliphaz "presents us with a picture of a Wisdom teacher who has lost his nerve" in so far as "the old distinctions between good and bad men have not ceased to be relevant for him, but they have become blurred by a new appreciation of God's holiness and hiddenness, and of men's frailty and corruption and ignorance."[23] Eliphaz resolves now to call Job to account. He suggests that God may no longer heed Job's prayers (5:1), and he all but labels Job a "fool" about to be slain by his inept "vexation" (5:2).[24] As his invective gains momentum, Eliphaz appears to turn increasingly cruel, tactless, and insensitive.[25]

Yet Gibson holds that Eliphaz remains throughout his first speech a sincere, albeit indelicate, counselor in his attempt to snatch Job from the brink of blasphemy.[26] Eliphaz is wholly convinced of Job's goodness and admonishes the latter to take comfort in the fact that his suffering is the common lot of sinful humanity. By the end of his first oration Eliphaz has compassionately afforded Job the benefit of the doubt and has delivered an eloquent and theologically sophisticated entreaty to his old friend to make amends with the Almighty.[27]

Gibson observes that by his second speech, however, Eliphaz has become aggrieved at Job's petulance. Rather than heeding Eliphaz's advice,

21. Ibid., 38.
22. "Eliphaz the Temanite," 268.
23. *Job*, 41.
24. Ibid., 44.
25. Ibid., 45.
26. Ibid., 48. Gibson muses, "It is nothing less than amazing that so talented and urbane a theologian should be at the same time so thoughtless and insensitive a counselor" (ibid.).
27. Ibid., 53.

Job is trenchant in his refusal to beseech God. For Eliphaz "the man whom he had once been pleased to count as his colleague, and who did seem to him to be getting more than his fair share of mankind's misery had, to his chagrin, turned out to be a rebel at heart."[28] So Eliphaz reluctantly prepares to peel off the gloves.[29] With mounting asperity and intolerance he rebukes Job.[30] In the shift from concerned friend in the first discourse to malicious recriminator in the second, Eliphaz teeters perilously close to hypocrisy.[31] Yet still there are positive features in Eliphaz's censure. He forcefully lands a handful of valid strikes against Job's mutinous language (15:2–14) and echoes with eloquence the reader's certain shock at Job's belligerence. Further, Gibson suggests, Eliphaz's cynical queries proceed not far afield of the similarly sarcastic questions posed by Yahweh himself in chapter 38.[32]

By his final harangue in chapter 22, Eliphaz's invective has turned more acerbic. "The well tried and tested precepts and procedures of Israel's 'wise men' have failed in the face of a man in Job's extreme position."[33] Though he argues again with eloquence, regrettably "his speech is the speech of a devout man turned hunter of heretics."[34] By the conclusion of his final bombast, all that is left for Eliphaz is to admit of the ideological impasse and to attempt one last appeal for Job to humble himself before God. This he does movingly, but the genuine touches and affection of the previous Eliphaz are absent in the tirade. Although he began so promisingly with sincere affection and genuine warmth, he has ended with malevolence toward his erstwhile friend.[35] Thus the urbane gentleman and the sophisticated scholar ends on a sour note as the curmudgeonly calumniator. Yet despite Eliphaz's lapses into angry rebuke, Gibson on the whole keeps a favorable reading of Eliphaz. He affords Eliphaz the benefit of the doubt and on more

---

28. Ibid., 126.

29. Gibson writes: "Eliphaz is, when the crunch comes, too timid for Prometheus's role and forces himself back on to the consolations of an orthodox faith" ("Eliphaz the Temanite," 272).

30. *Job*, 126–27.

31. Ibid., 131.

32. Ibid., 127.

33. Ibid., 173.

34. Ibid.

35. Ibid., 175.

than one occasion sides with Eliphaz against Job.³⁶ With reluctance Gibson calls Eliphaz to task for the brazen recriminations of his final peroration.³⁷

Strengths and Weaknesses

Gibson is a lucid and appealing writer. He possesses a firm grasp of Hebrew, and his commentary is on the whole insightful. He enlarges upon several important features of Eliphaz, such as the proximity of Eliphaz's view with Job's at the outset of the debate and his recognition of Eliphaz's prominence in the book through the author's development of him. Still, in a few ways his treatment of Eliphaz falls short. First, Gibson's portrayal of Eliphaz is somewhat uneven. In his favorable view of the Temanite counselor, Gibson tends to gloss over some of Eliphaz's inconsistencies and alternates equivocally between a favorable and doubtful opinion of the character. Second, Gibson fails to correlate the ANE wisdom background to the role Eliphaz and the other friends have in Job. This oversight leaves out potentially important connections that aid one's understanding of the role for the counselor in the ANE context of Job. With the exception of Eliphaz's tone (A) and use of the sin list (H), Gibson offers a positive portrayal of the leading counselor in each of the other categories of assessment: purpose (B), theological provenance and creed (C), retributive doctrine (D), special revelation (E), understanding of remedial suffering (F), status as doyen (G), and rebuke by Yahweh (I) (the latter reprimand due to *how* things are said by Eliphaz, not due to *which* things are said).

Lael Caesar: Eliphaz as Devious, Implausible Belligerent

Lael Caesar, Research Professor of Hebrew Bible at Andrews University, is not so kind to Eliphaz. Having done extensive research on the characterization of Eliphaz and the other friends in Job, both in doctoral studies and later writings, Caesar has authored several influential assessments of the lead counselor.³⁸ In his provocative article in *Vetus Testamentum*, Caesar explores specifically the contribution Eliphaz's visionary experience makes to the book as a whole by highlighting the issue of human integrity, which

---

36. Ibid., 56, 60, 62–63. He argues that Job is "unforgivably malicious" towards Eliphaz and the other friends and that "his vindictiveness toward his friends is deeply reprehensible" (62, 63).

37. Gibson argues that Eliphaz and the friends are later indicted by Yahweh not for *what* they say but simply for how they say it ("Job and the Cure of Souls," 308).

38. "Character in Job"; "Job"; "Job as a Paradigm for the Eschaton," 148–62.

he perceives to be a neglected *Leitmotif* within the work. Caesar builds upon this correlation to offer fresh insight into understanding Eliphaz.

Analysis

Caesar argues that the fundamental axiom pervading Eliphaz's thinking derives from the truism whispered to him in the nocturnal vision: הַאֱנוֹשׁ מֵאֱלוֹהַּ יִצְדָּק אִם מֵעֹשֵׂהוּ יִטְהַר־גָּבֶר ("Can mortal man be in the right before God? Can a man be pure before his Maker?" [Job 4:17]). This mystical encounter becomes determinative for the entirety of the ensuing interchange.[39] Furthermore, the visionary episode provides the reader intuition into the constitution of Eliphaz whom Caesar casts as a maverick, and at times narcissistic, sage who prefers to center authority in his own opinions rather than in the wisdom of the ancients:

> More than a third of the 47 verses, and 39 of the 97 cola of his first speech are devoted to directing audience attention to himself (iv 8-21; v 3-5, 8). He is subject in all of the 8 verses and 14 cola of his first speech, which he punctuates with his explicit self reference [sic] (once each in iv 8; v 27; twice in iv 12, 14, 15; v 3, 8; thrice in iv 16). Twice he emphasizes these proofs of self-centered assurance with use of *'ny,* (v 3, 8), and then concludes with a triumphant 'we' (v 27).[40]

Caesar compares Eliphaz's predilection for first person pronouns with Qohelet's catalogue of firsthand observations, interpreted by the latter sage as a reliable locus for normative wisdom. Caesar concludes that Eliphaz and Qohelet differ significantly with respect to the object of their observations and to the tone of their discourses.[41] The effect of this discrepancy underscores the irregularity of Eliphaz's wisdom orientation and calls into question his credibility.[42] Given the incongruities, Caesar concludes that Eliphaz has likely fabricated his visionary-dream experience as a ploy to gain the

---

39. "Job," 436.
40. Ibid., 437.
41. Ibid., 437–39. Eliphaz differs from Qohelet chiefly in the fervor of his dogmatism and in the mysteriousness of his firsthand observation (439).
42. Specifically, the following elements cast doubt on the reliability of Eliphaz's account: the ambiguity of his revelatory experience—whether dream or vision, the uncommon language used to denote reception of revelation (lit. "a word was stolen" [יְגֻנָּב Pual imperfect of גנב]), and the overall infrequency of appeal to revelatory dreams within the wisdom tradition (ibid., 440–41).

argumentative upper hand over Job at any cost.[43] "Eliphaz, in his rage for vindication, will make a case for rightness against all the evidence."[44]

Eliphaz, the champion of orthodoxy, will not relent until Job acquiesces to his cherished tenets. But to achieve this unsavory outcome, Eliphaz sells out and undermines the very principles he upholds. "Eliphaz [is] the questionable disputant, who invents divine testimonials in pursuit of vindication of old theology. Eliphaz never concedes error. He only earns a dubious victory when the frustrated Bildad attempts in the end to authenticate his farce. Job bends his knees in honest acknowledgement. Eliphaz will not bow, till an angry God so commands him."[45] Thus for Caesar Eliphaz is a devious debater, draconian in his criticism of Job and disingenuous in his appeal to a sham visionary experience in order to subvert Job at all costs.

Strengths and Weaknesses

Caesar has elucidated a few insightful points regarding Eliphaz, including Eliphaz's fascination with his own opinions proved out by the use of first person pronouns and, in addition, the pivotal place of Eliphaz's night vision in the flow of the dialogues. Still, Caesar's reading of Eliphaz falls short in several ways. First, he fails to prove convincingly that Eliphaz has merely fabricated his visionary experience. This view can only be conjecture, and, occupying such a key place in the dialogues, the vision appears to be accepted at face value by each of the characters, as several references are made to the experience later in the dialogues (7:14; 18:11; 27:20).[46] Second, Caesar does not wholly take into account Eliphaz's apparent esteem for the wisdom of the ancients, as Eliphaz clearly resorts to it later in the dialogues ("What I have seen, I will declare, what wise men have told, without hiding it from their fathers" [15:17b–18]). Caesar's construal of Eliphaz overdoes the alleged self-absorption, neglecting Eliphaz's clear appeal to the ANE wisdom context of which he is product. Third, although Caesar himself questions

---

43. Given the sweep of his argumentation, Caesar is surprisingly tentative on this point. He speaks vaguely of Eliphaz's "apparent falsehood" (ibid., 441) and that the author "apparently intended" for readers to disbelieve the visionary experience (442). Gary V. Smith on the other hand suggests instead that Eliphaz has not experienced the nocturnal encounter at all but rather that Job has. Eliphaz simply is quoting Job's earlier description of the vision in order to call into question its source and with it to question *Job's* credibility ("Job IV 12–21," 456).

44. Ibid., 444.

45. Ibid., 446.

46. John E. Course demonstrates that the speeches of Job and the friends are interrelated more than often thought (*Speech and Response*).

the credibility of Eliphaz, he falls short of proving that the ancient author or readers would have doubted the reliability of Eliphaz.[47] Fourth, Caesar's entirely negative view of Eliphaz fails to correlate some of the apparently commendable aspects of Eliphaz's approach to Job, features which many scholars have recognized. To classify Caesar in keeping with our interpretive benchmarks, he is negative toward the sage in every area of assessment: tone (A), purpose (B), theological provenance and creed (C), retributive doctrine (D), special revelation (E), remedial suffering (F), status as doyen (G), use of sin list (H), and rebuke by Yahweh (I).

Robert Fyall: Eliphaz as Demonic Instrument

Robert Fyall is the Senior Tutor in Ministry for the Cornhill Training Course in Scotland.[48] Prior to this post, he served as minister of a parish church in Scotland and as Director of the Rutherford House in Edinburgh (2003–2007). Fyall has produced a fascinating monograph on the imagery of creation and evil in the book of Job.[49]

Analysis

With respect to the imagery of evil, Fyall focuses upon the figures of Behemoth and Leviathan, which he argues are the mythical representative of Mot, the ANE god of death, and of Satan respectively. Fyall traces the characteristics of the Resheph/Mot god of Death in ANE comparative literature to draw out comparisons with the depiction of Behemoth in Job.[50] He concludes, in view of the creature's appearance, habitat, and invincibility, that "contextual, linguistic, and structural considerations make the identification of Behemoth with Mot, the god of death, a very strong probability."[51] Next, he explores the depiction of Leviathan in Job, pointing up the overwhelming fear Leviathan produces, the supernatural elements he possesses, the unrivaled power he exhibits in the created order, as well as the habitat in which he dwells. Fyall concludes that the mythic

---

47. Kemper Fullerton insightfully argues that the ancient readers readily would have sided with Eliphaz at the outset of the book ("Double Entendre," 326, 340).
48. "Teaching Staff," Internet.
49. Fyall, *Now My Eyes Have Seen You*.
50. Ibid., 117–37.
51. Ibid., 137.

depiction of the creature suggests identification with Satan himself, the terrifying personification of evil.[52]

In drawing out the connection between Leviathan and Satan, Fyall analyzes a portion of Job's first reply to Eliphaz in which Job remonstrates against God concerning the agony he is enduring (Job 6–7). Job accuses God of perpetrating horrors against him in the night: "You scare me with dreams and terrify me with visions" (7:14). Seeing similar imagery earlier in the book, Fyall observes here an explicit reference to Eliphaz's nocturnal visionary experience of 4:12–17.[53] Eliciting this comparison furnishes Fyall opportunity to develop his interpretation of Eliphaz's role in Job and to argue that in his visionary experience Eliphaz has encountered Satan, who exploits Eliphaz to harass Job toward repudiation of Yahweh.

Fyall admits that certain elements of the visionary experience might lead one to conclude that Eliphaz has received authentic divine revelation: the dread (פַּחַד) which he senses (cf. the Isaianic "Woe to me!" [Isa 6:5] and the Danielic psychosomatic paralysis [Dan 10:8] upon receipt of vision), the "deep sleep" falling on men (cf. with Elihu [Job 33:15–18] and Abraham [Gen 15:1–2]), and the impartation of a theological message.[54] Fyall points out other considerations, however, which suggest Satanic presence. The dread felt by Eliphaz adumbrates the dismay which is portentous of Leviathan in 41:14 (Eng. 41:22). Significant in this connection is the psychological effect the dread has upon Eliphaz and by extension upon the others:

> The fear and trembling that come on the true prophets of the Lord at once convince them of God's greatness and their own unworthiness and give them a specific message. But here Eliphaz (like Bildad later in chapter 25) legalistically condemns the whole human race and slams shut the door of hope. In other words, unlike a genuine prophetic message, which does indeed condemn human sinfulness but also calls attention to the remedy and provides the strength to carry it out, this 'Message' induces paralysing fear and subtly exploits Job's growing alienation from God whom he had regarded as a friend.[55]

---

52. Ibid., 139–68. He posits that "the evidence, then, identifies Leviathan with Satan, the culmination of various guises in which he has appeared, for example: Leviathan (3:8); Yam and Tannin (7:12); Sea (9:8 and 38:8–11); Rahab (9:13 and 26:12); the gliding serpent (26:13)" (168).

53. Ibid., 146.

54. Ibid.

55. Ibid., 147.

Fyall proposes that throughout the poetic dialogues Satan is exploiting the friends as his instruments to torment Job and to evoke terrifying imagery of the baleful powers that are attacking him.[56] The error of the naïve Eliphaz, however, is his "bland ignorance of the cosmic forces behind the situation."[57] Therein lies his mistake, and the reproof of Yahweh (42:7) bears this out: Job has been aware consistently of the cosmic and supernatural dimensions to his agonies while Eliphaz and the other friends have not. Consequently, Eliphaz is proved to be simply an unwitting demonic instrument manipulated by Satan to taunt Job and to alienate him from Yahweh.

Strengths and Weaknesses

With persuasive argumentation Fyall points up several connections Job enjoys with the ANE wisdom context with which it shares affinities. Further, Fyall identifies a potentially fascinating connection between Eliphaz's nocturnal vision and Satan's lingering sway in the book following his appearance in the prologue. The minor weaknesses in Fyall's treatment for our purposes, however, are the following. First, although he is careful to draw out implications that the ANE context has on the imagery of creation and evil in Job, he does not correlate the implications of this context for the role Eliphaz and the other friends have in the book.[58] Second, to highlight only the potentially demonic origin of the revelatory vision leaves the reader with a partial understanding of the larger role Eliphaz plays in the book. Eliphaz appeals as well to other traditional wisdom sources as his argumentation develops. For a holistic view of Eliphaz, these other features of Eliphaz's theological trajectory must be connected and the ANE context of his wisdom orientation must be more fully advanced. In assessment of Fyall's interpretation of Eliphaz, he perceives the sage unfavorably in tone (A), theological provenance and creed (C), retributive doctrine (D), special revelation (E), remedial suffering (F), status as doyen (G), use of the sin list (H), and rebuke by Yahweh (I). If anything positive can be gleaned, it lies in Eliphaz's purpose (B), as the sage is unwittingly exploited by Satan.

---

56. Cf. McKechnie, *Job*, 52. Larry J. Waters argues for a less explicit promulgation simply of the retributive doctrine of Satan ("Reflections," 442).

57. Fyall, *Now My Eyes Have Seen You*, 148.

58. To be fair, this is not Fyall's central concern, and his analysis of Eliphaz is an ancillary aspect of his treatment of Job. However, for the purposes of the present discussion, it is important to point out the lacunae in his advancement of Eliphaz.

William Whedbee: Eliphaz as Comic Relief

William Whedbee (1938–2004) was the Nancy M. Lyon Professor of Biblical History and Literature and of Religious Studies at Pomona College from 1966 until his death in 2004. In 1977 William Whedbee wrote a lengthy and influential essay on the nature of the book of Job as comedy, a theme which would continue to blossom in his later studies of the OT.[59] In this essay Whedbee sets forth an important interpretation of the role of Eliphaz and the other friends in Job.

Analysis

In his treatment Whedbee argues that the book of Job is a parody lampooning the folly of traditional piety.[60] Part of the comedic setup is the ludicrous part played by Eliphaz and the other friends, whom the poet uses to create a "magnificent caricature of the wise counselor."[61] Though not privy to the proceedings of the divine council, Eliphaz, Whedbee argues, is fairly spot on in his initial assessment of Job's situation.[62] Eliphaz is motivated apparently by a genuine concern for Job and seems convinced that Job is what he seems to be, as an innocent sufferer. Job is implicated only because he is a member of the human race, not because of any particular sin he has committed; he need only hold on to his integrity and be confident in his piety before God. If he turns to God, he will receive restoration in full.

Whedbee suggests that Eliphaz's speech may be viewed from another angle, however, which offers a negative slant to his initial peroration.[63] Eliphaz relies heavily on the accumulation of proverbial wisdom gained from traditional teachings and his own personal observations. Thus, he, along with the other friends, attempts to strike the pose of exemplary sage. Eliphaz goes beyond the typical role of the exemplary sage, when, to authenticate his wise counsel, he delineates the terrifying night vision he has witnessed. Viewing his speech from this angle, "Eliphaz comes across as a rather

---

59. Whedbee, "The Comedy of Job," 1–39. Cf. Exum and Whedbee, "Isaac, Samson, and Saul," 5–40; Whedbee, *The Bible and the Comic Vision*.

60. This interpretive line has been taken up by other scholars to the extent that Katherine J. Dell speaks of the consensus amongst modern scholars that the book of Job is skeptical (*Job as Sceptical Literature*, 1–2; cf. Zuckerman, *Job the Silent*; Brenner, "Job the Pious?" 37–52; Tsoi, "The Vision of Eliphaz," 155–82).

61. Whedbee, "The Comedy of Job," 10.

62. Ibid.

63. Ibid., 11.

pompous, pretentious counselor, who must in the end resort to general maxims which simply fail to apply in this situation."[64]

By his second and third speeches Eliphaz has opted for long, lurid portrayals of the grim destiny of the wicked. In doing so he becomes increasingly absurd and farcical. With growing uneasiness the reader becomes aware of the utter incongruity between Eliphaz's speeches and Job's actual situation. "The friends become cruelly and grotesquely comic as they strive with increasing dogmatism to apply their faulty solutions to the wrong problem—and the wrong person."[65] Eliphaz and the other friends play farcical foil to Job and are used by the author to point up the preposterousness of traditional religiosity.[66] Whedbee summarizes: "In conclusion, the poet has created a brilliant caricature of the friends in their role as wise counselors, who indeed say some 'right things about God' but who become ridiculous in their approach to Job because of the irrelevance of their counsel. The would-be wise men become fools, the mockers become a mockery. The friends represent the classic figure of the alazon—the impostor, the offender, and finally the enemy of God (cf. 42:7)."[67] Thus for Whedbee Eliphaz is an ancient buffoon whose ludicrous demagoguery is comic relief to the agonies of Job and is a ploy used by the author to excoriate with biting irony his societal nemeses.

Strengths and Weaknesses

Whedbee convinced a growing number of scholars that the book of Job is irony and that the three friends play a comedic set-up role to deliver the point with flourish. Whedbee's understanding of the role of Job and of Eliphaz falls short in several ways, however. First, the weightiness of the book of Job as a consideration of the problems of theodicy is on the whole emptied of its force if the book is solely satire[68] (particularly so if an obscure satire not read correctly until the twentieth century!). To interpret Eliphaz and the other friends as mere parody diminishes their role as upholders of a traditional wisdom approach that in fact had been the stock of ANE cultures for

64. Ibid.

65. Ibid., 12.

66. Zuckerman suggests similarly that the three friends are the invention of the Joban poet and that their sole purpose is to play the foil to Job's "contrapuntal role" as protester against traditional piety. "The Friends have become, as it were, Anti-Friends who oppose the Anti-Job" (*Job the Silent*, 48).

67. Ibid., 13.

68. See Carson, "Job," 40; Fox, "Job the Pious," 363–64; Cooper, "Reading and Misreading," 74.

millennia.[69] In addition, it robs Job of its intellectual viability as a canonical treatise dealing with the motif of the suffering righteous.

Second, although correct to point out the mounting incongruity between Eliphaz's understanding and the actual situation of Job as the speeches develop, Whedbee fails to convince that the ancient author and readers would have interpreted this disparity as indicative of poetic parody. In fact, his approach fails to deal adequately with the ANE cultural matrix from which the unfolding drama emerges and upon which the wisdom perspective of Eliphaz and the other friends is constructed. Third, Whedbee's view has implications for the intertextuality of Job and the NT.[70] As Paul and (perhaps) the writer of Hebrews cite from Eliphaz's first speech, it is doubtful that they read Eliphaz as a caricatured buffoon who is simply playing the part of a comedic set-up man.[71] In terms of the assessment of Whedbee's analysis, he takes up a negative view of the leading counselor in his tone (A), purpose (B), theological provenance and creed (C), retributive doctrine (D), special revelatory experience (E), doctrine of remedial suffering (F), status as doyen (G), use of the sin list (H), and rebuke by Yahweh (I).

Carol Newsom: Eliphaz as Reputable Ancient Sage

Having written two commentaries, a monograph, and several essays on the book of Job, Carol Newsom has distinguished herself as a leading scholar in Joban studies.[72] With a specialization in Qumran scrolls during her postgraduate studies at Harvard University, Newsom is currently the Charles Howard Candler Professor of Old Testament at the Candler School of Theology, Emory University.[73] Newsom's monograph on the book of Job provides extensive discussion regarding her interpretation of Eliphaz and the other friends in Job.

---

69. See Mattingly, "The Pious Sufferer," 333.

70. For a helpful study of intertextuality and the book of Job, see Pyeon, *You Have Not Spoken What Is Right About Me*.

71. See Selms, *Job*, 17.

72. *The Book of Job*; "The Book of Job"; "Job"; "Job and His Friends," 239–53; "Reconsidering Job," 155–82; "The Moral Sense of Nature," 9–27; "The Book of Job as Polyphonic Text," 87–108.

73. "Dr. Carol A. Newsom," Internet.

Analysis

In her consideration of the poetic dialogues, Newsom admittedly sets out in pursuit of a "self-conscious rehabilitation of the friends."[74] She delineates this interpretive starting point:

> Frequently, the friends are interpreted as religiously narrow, mean-spirited hypocrites. Even when given credit for sincerity and initial compassion, they are seldom taken seriously as articulating a view of reality that might have its own claims to truth. Such reactions toward the friends, whether hostile or merely condescending, seem motivated, at least in part, by a sense that to take their arguments seriously is somehow to join in a vicious blaming of the victim, a further act of violence against Job. Such an attitude, though nobly motivated, diminishes the intellectual challenge of the book. What is lost when the friends are dismissed is the generic force of the wisdom dialogue as a confrontation between two significant but incommensurable perspectives.[75]

Newsom lays the ground work for her analysis of Eliphaz's role in Job by considering Job's lament in chapter 3 against the backdrop of the comparative ANE work, the Babylonian *Theodicy*. Like the sufferer in the Babylonian Theodicy, Job utilizes a key term to underscore the *Leitmotif* of his lament: *turmoil* (3:26, רֹגֶז [*rōgez*]).[76] Having aimed his outburst at no one in particular, Job does not intend at first to interact with the friends in dialogical give-and-take. Eliphaz, nonetheless, perceives the lament as an opportunity for counsel and initiates the interchange. In doing so, Eliphaz leads the other friends in bringing to bear the refined cultural resources available to them to counteract effectively Job's professed *rōgez* and to resist its encroachment.

Newsom identifies three ways in which Eliphaz and the others play the role of esteemed sages to confront Job's *rōgez*.[77] First, Eliphaz resists *rōgez*

---

74. Newsom, *Book of Job*, 90.

75. Ibid., 90–91.

76. Ibid., 92. The Hebrew term רֹגֶז is used five times in Job (Job 3:17, 26; 14:1; 37:2; 39:24) and twice outside of Job (Isa 14:3; Hab 3:2) with a semantical range of "go wild, nervousness, agitation, anger" (*HALAT*, 1104). The LXX translator of Job uses the Greek term ὀργή ("wrath, anger, rage" *Greek-English Lexicon of the Septuagint*, 444]) to translate every instance of the word in Job.

77. Ibid., 96. Although Newsom develops the role each of the friends plays in this effort, the lion's share of her analysis deals wih Eliphaz, which will be the focus for our present study.

by attempting to construe Job's experience in terms of narrative structures that integrate and ultimately transcend his present experience of turmoil (chaps. 4–5; cf. chap. 8). Newsom elaborates upon this as Eliphaz's effort to restore to Job "a sense of the narratability of his life,"[78] that is, to provide a narrative structure in which Job may be reminded transcendentally of his true role and place. Eliphaz does this by recounting Job's previous acts of piety: "Behold, you have instructed many, and you have strengthened the weak hands. Your words have upheld him who was stumbling, and you have made firm the feeble knees" (4:3–4). These altruistic deeds are metaphors for Job's larger life-narrative:

> The references to weak hands, stumbling, and knees giving way all bear a metaphorical resonance. These are transparent images of the human capacity for directed action: hands that grasp and manipulate objects, knees that move the body forward. Metonymically, these body parts represent the whole person as an intentional being. Thus, Eliphaz's metaphor casts the psychic paralysis of a traumatized individual as a physical weakness of hands and knees.[79]

Eliphaz is aiding Job in the fundamental task of recognizing a plot line which will create the entry point for his return to equilibrium. In his opening speech Eliphaz sketches four additional narratives (4:6–7; 4:8–9; 5:17–18; 5:19–26) in an effort to offer story patterns which favor endings that allow Job to move beyond the scope of his present calamity.[80]

Second, Eliphaz advocates vigorously the religious practice of prayer. Through its symbolic forms, words, and bodily gestures, ritualistic prayer has the "therapeutic capacity" to enact normative order and to neutralize the encroaching *rōgez* (chaps. 5, 22; cf. chaps. 8, 11). Eliphaz pointedly begins and ends his orations with eloquent appeals to seek God, the rites and postures of which direct Job to "an important resource that he may appropriate for himself, and by doing so gain some control over his experience of turmoil."[81]

Third, Eliphaz and the other friends offer Job iconic narratives (i.e., the "fate of the wicked" poems) that combine narrative frameworks with a set of generative metaphors that reaffirm the moral order of the world and thus deny *rōgez* an ontological status (chap. 15; cf. chaps. 18, 21). With this Eliphaz is responding to Job's Promethean assertions about the illegitimacy

78. Ibid., 101.
79. Ibid.
80. Ibid., 105.
81. Ibid., 109.

of God's moral governance of the world (e.g., chap. 12), misgivings which for Eliphaz and the others undermine reality itself.[82] Newsom argues on this basis that rather than thinly veiled accusations against Job, these vivid accounts are to be taken as generic arguments about the nature of the world. Rather than arguing naively about what "*should be* the case in a moral world . . . the friends are making a claim for the *truth* of their narratives (15:17–19; 20:4; cf. 5:27; 8:8–10)."[83] When Job fails to respond to these accounts, Eliphaz concretizes evil as acts committed by Job himself (chap. 22), although whether or not he actually believes this is doubtful. The point is that "from Eliphaz's perspective Job has committed the moral equivalent of those actions by denying that the moral order has a grounding in transcendent reality."[84] Job has become the blameworthy bogeyman, reprehensible for his failure to see beyond the ash heap and to respond as he ought to the resources Eliphaz and the other friends have introduced.[85] Although Eliphaz, along with the others, has applied effectively the gamut of cultural resources available to nullify and eradicate the alien *rōgez* from its grip on Job, he has failed ultimately to mend and restore Job.

Strengths and Weaknesses

Newsom is to be commended in having resisted the pull to join other contemporary scholars of Job who view the book on the one hand as thoroughgoing satire or on the other as entirely ambiguous and bereft of univocal import. She exhibits care in a measure of sensitivity to the ANE cultural matrix of Job, even though much of her analysis of Job proceeds from a literary rather than exegetical or textual starting point. As nearly a lone voice in the wilderness, she has exerted worthy effort to restore to current interpreters of Job a sense for the ideological tension between the incongruous perspectives of Eliphaz and Job, a tension that undoubtedly

---

82. Ibid., 116.

83. Ibid., 117, emphasis hers.

84. Ibid., 125. Newsom argues further: "If all is *rōgez*, then the foundation that makes it meaningful to distinguish between the goodness of protecting the orphan and the abhorrence of denying food to the hungry is swept away. What is at stake is in the argument over the iconic narratives of the fate of the wicked is Eliphaz's belief that one cannot have a stable and coherent moral society in the absence of a belief that the cosmic order is itself ultimately a moral one" (ibid.).

85. Newsom describes this as the application of the friends' "moral technique," which she quantifies as their effort to contain and manage evil through the directed application of their wisdom insight. Job, however, goes rogue and will not be tamed, leading to ideological impasse (ibid., 128–29).

was meant to be felt by readers. Still, in other ways her analysis does not convince or go far enough. First, she places undue weight, from my perspective, on the Hebrew term *rōgez*, which Job uses first to depict the activity of the wicked (as that which ceases in the grave, 3:17) and is simply one of several different terms Job uses in his attempt to articulate his agony (e.g., cognates of the term חשׁד are used more frequently in Job's lament in chapter 3). That the prominence of this term should form the basis for her entire analysis of the friends is questionable. Second, Newsom fails to convince that Eliphaz is benign both in his efforts to lead Job into therapeutic prayer and in his attempts to deny Job's turmoil an ontological status by concocting (potentially) a laundry list of his evil deeds. Though hers is a creative approach to these passages, it runs counter to what is more likely thinly disguised sarcasm on the part of Eliphaz. Newsom commends Eliphaz in every interpretive area previously discussed, including tone (A), purpose (B), theological provenance and creed (C), retributive doctrine (D), special revelation (E), view of remedial suffering (F), status as doyen (G), use of the sin list (H), and Yahweh's rebuke (I).

David Cotter: Eliphaz as Ambiguous, Elusive Counselor

In his analysis of Hebrew poetry in the context of Job 4–5, David Cotter argues that ambiguity is a governing element—both in Hebrew poetry in general and in Eliphaz's initial address in particular.[86] Cotter is a monk at St. John's Abbey and an editor at The Liturgical Press in Collegeville, MN.

Analysis

Building upon the work of Hoffman, Cotter proposes that from the very outset of his oration, Eliphaz may be construed by the reader in multiple ways.[87] Perhaps he is praising and encouraging Job by aiding him to realize that sufferers in any situation may be helped. Alternatively, Eliphaz may be blaming Job for hypocrisy: though he has chastened others beset by troubles, now he blasphemes God when trouble has overtaken him. "This ambiguity, placed right at the beginning, determines the nature of the entire exhortation, and dominates the reader's reaction to it. The author intended

---

86. *A Study of Job 4–5*, 109. Concerning purposeful ambiguity in the first speech of Eliphaz, cf. also Hoffman, "Use of Equivocal Words," 114–19; Harding, "A Spirit of Deception in Job 4:15?" 137–66; Dailey, "The Wisdom of Irreverence," 276–89.

87. Ibid., 157.

both meanings to be read, to keep the reader a little off balance, a little unsure as to whether Eliphaz is still a friend to Job or become foe."[88]

Cotter seeks to prove this alleged ambiguity by his inductive analysis of the ostensibly elusive words of Eliphaz in Job 4–5. In one example, Eliphaz asks Job in 4:6, "Is not your fear of God your *confidence*?" The Hebrew term כִּסְלָה may be read positively, according to Cotter, as "confidence" (so cognates in Job 8:14; 31:24; Ps 78:7) or negatively as "folly, stupidity" (so cognates in Qoh 7:25; Ps 49:11, 14), depending entirely on which direction the reader wishes to go.[89] Thus Eliphaz again is heartening Job with hope or is lashing out at him for his presumed wrongdoing. In 4:10–11 Eliphaz expounds on the ravenous lion and its whelps, using five different Hebrew terms to depict the animal; here again Cotter observes ambiguity in Eliphaz's metaphor. Possibly Eliphaz is referring by allusion to the gruesome fate of Job and by implication his children: "Job is guilty of sin against the poor [and] the symbol of the lion is an apt one."[90] Job, like the rapacious lion, through his evil misdeeds has destroyed others and indeed has slain his own children.

From start to finish Cotter perceives in the figure of Eliphaz purposeful ambiguity, a ploy used by the author to tease the reader:

> In trying to understand who this character of Eliphaz is, whether or not we are intended to find him a sympathetic figure, whether or not we are to find ourselves agreeing with him despite ourselves, and all the other decisions that a reader must make in building a character, the author uses ambiguity to trip us up. Lexical, semantic, stylistic ambiguities make it difficult for us to get a clear picture of who Eliphaz is. Is he still a friend or has he turned nasty, not to say even a little antagonistic? Does he feel Job to have been a good God-fearing man or a craven whiner? Is he one who speaks with God or a slightly silly buffoon? The author, having created all sorts of ambiguities, refuses to resolve them for us, refuses to tell us how we are to react to Eliphaz.[91]

For Cotter Eliphaz is a riddle, an ambiguous interlocutor who refuses to be read definitively in any single direction.

---

88. Ibid.
89. Ibid., 162–63.
90. Ibid., 174.
91. Ibid., 236.

Strengths and Weaknesses

Cotter has advanced elements of the study of Eliphaz through his detailed literary analysis of Job 4–5, bringing together helpful connections in the text.[92] His methodology and the tenor of his conclusions, however, are problematic for a few reasons. First, to argue that an extended biblical text is purposefully ambiguous contravenes a traditional approach to the canon by undermining the doctrines of the perspicuity and sufficiency of Scripture.[93] Second, although Cotter's approach is sensitive to the interpretive tensions many have observed in the book of Job, his argument overreaches. To suggest that the whole of Eliphaz's speeches are intentionally ambiguous falls short hermeneutically. His proposal contravenes the univocal nature of Scripture and fails to apply consistently the standards of grammatical-historical interpretation.[94] Third, Cotter approaches the text from a literary perspective but neglects to bring together adequately the ANE cultural resources which clarify the purpose for Eliphaz and the other friends in Job. Cotter is ambiguous in his reading of Eliphaz in most of the interpretive categories so far discussed, including tone (A), purpose (B), theological provenance and creed (C), retributive doctrine (D), special revelation (E), and view of remedial suffering (F). Eliphaz's status as doyen (G), use of the sin list (H), and rebuke by Yahweh (I) are not discussed at length in the treatise.

Summary and Conclusions

In the spectrum of current opinions, Eliphaz is read and interpreted from many angles. In fact, an earmark of contemporary opinion regarding Eliphaz includes its wide disparity and marked polarity, along with, on the other hand, a growing reticence to posit univocal meaning to anything Eliphaz utters. Recent studies have taken to interpretive extremes. Eliphaz becomes a strident fundamentalist so dogmatic in his assertions that he undermines their potency and vitiates his own theological reference point. Or, he remains a sophisticated sage whose biggest mistake is, understandably, that he has lost his temper. Others view Eliphaz as a narcissistic, implausible

---

92. Cotter is quite helpful, for example, in his structural analysis of Job 4–5, which considers extensively semantic parallelism in the passage (ibid., 117–52).

93. Though a full appraisal of this danger lies beyond the pale of the present study, see generally, e.g., the Westminster Confession of Faith, I/vi–vii; Erickson, *Christian Theology*, 246–88; Grudem, *Systematic Theology*, 105–111, 127–40; Young, *Thy Word Is Truth*; Stonehouse and Woolley, *The Infallible Word*.

94. See Thomas, *Evangelical Hermeneutics*, 141–64.

disputant who has fabricated a visionary experience to leverage himself against the hapless victim. A few claim him a naïve, ineffectual counselor whom Satan dupes and exploits to harass Job. Others understand him as an unwitting farce, the caricature of the wise counselor and the ideological buffoon who serves as welcome comic relief to the anguish of Job. A handful see in him an admirable sage who utilizes the gamut of cultural and traditional resources to shepherd Job toward reconciliation with God. To a growing number of interpreters, however, who come down along predictably postmodern lines,[95] Eliphaz is an intentionally ambiguous and elusive figure whom the author uses playfully to tease the reader with multiple realms of interpretive possibilities.

Based upon the observations and categorizations of interpreters in the preceding chapters, we are now finally in a position to draw several key conclusions regarding the interpretive history of Eliphaz. First, although multiple shades of nuance are ubiquitously present and no interpreter fits neatly in every detail into one or the other category, the integral component to the way in which an interpreter reads Eliphaz—whether principally in the positive or negative current—comes down invariably to how he or she understands Eliphaz's doctrine of retribution. More specifically, one's perception of the minatory side of the doctrine expressed by Eliphaz in Job 4:8–11 is crucial:[96]

> As I have seen, those who plow iniquity
> and sow trouble reap the same.
> By the breath of God they perish,
> and by the blast of his anger they are consumed.
> The roar of the lion, the voice of the fierce lion,
> the teeth of the young lions are broken.
> The strong lion perishes for lack of prey,
> and the cubs of the lioness are scattered.

This exhortation determines largely into which interpretive stream the reader falls. Either Eliphaz refers here to Job's sorry state as proof of his wicked life or he offers a well-meant (though perhaps indelicately stated) path to restoration through acknowledgement that the wicked alone suffer divine judgment. The first group mostly read 4:8–11 in light of 4:17–21 and 5:1–7 as a hypocritical reproach insinuating that Job is to be counted among the despicable sinners who merit God's just wrath. The second group, on the

---

95. On a postmodern approach to the OT, see Brueggemann, *Theology of the Old Testament*, 707–720.

96. See also Fullerton, "Double Entendre," 340–41, n. 9.

other hand, typically read 4:8–11 in light of 4:1–7 and 5:8–26 as a benign, albeit ill-worded, admonition offered in hopes of ultimate restoration for Job. The first group see Eliphaz as suspicious of Job from the outset and as launching with alacrity into this stern warning because of an inflexible connection to his intransigent doctrine. They perceive in Eliphaz little regard for the effect of his speeches upon Job. The second group perceive Eliphaz as gentle and kind in the opening of his address and as growing disillusioned with his former friend only after Job's conspicuous inattention to his advice. In this way, if 4:8–11 is interpreted negatively as harsh remonstrance, Eliphaz is hypocritical, wicked, and ill-advised. If 4:8–11 is considered positively as well-meaning, kindly intentioned counsel, Eliphaz is a significant, at times profound, and benign friend whose only fault is heightening irascibility as the speeches progress.

Second, as a general pattern Jewish interpreters—noticeably more so than Christian interpreters—have tended to look favorably upon Eliphaz. This predisposition toward Eliphaz began with the LXX and continued with Aristeas, *The Testament of Job*, numerous rabbinical interpreters, and Maimonides. In light of the preceding point, we would suggest that this propensity originates from favorable predilection for Eliphaz's doctrine of retribution, a teaching which also is clearly delineated in other biblical passages such as Proverbs 3 and in the *lex talionis* portions of the Mosaic Law. Beyond this, the inclination may originate from the distinctively Jewish tendency to approach the scriptural text, and therefore its characters, as open-ended and polyphonic, resistant to the tidy closure that is perhaps more commensurate to Western, Christian interpretation.[97]

Third, critical scholars, particularly those of the nineteenth century, who presupposed a naturalistic view of religion and a theologically liberal understanding of the inherent goodness of mankind—especially correlated to the Enlightenment tenet of exalted reason as supremely determinate in one's epistemology and empiricism—tended more staunchly to oppose Eliphaz on the grounds that his doctrine of retribution promoted ancient superstition. The difficulty with Eliphaz's core doctrine appears to correlate closely with these critical scholars' own latitudinarian views on religion and morality along with a tendency toward viewing man as autonomously uncorrupted in his intellectual faculties vis-à-vis the Reformer's emphasis on

---

97. On this approach as distinctively Jewish, see Brueggemann's comments on the "Jewishness" and dialectical quality of the text and this reading community (*Theology of the Old Testament*, 80–86) as well as Blumenthal's suggestion that a *seriatim* reading of the Hebrew Bible is preferable as more consistent with the nature of life itself (*Facing the Abusing God*, 1993], 47–48, 239). Cf. Brueggemann, "Texts That Linger," 21–41; Levenson, *Creation and the Persistence of Evil*.

the noetic effects of total depravity. Often for this reason the views of Eliphaz were summarily dismissed in the interpretive efforts of these scholars.

Fourth, contemporary scholars are reluctant to classify Eliphaz as univocally signifying a single meaning. It is *en vogue*, in keeping with reader response theories and preference for synchronic and literary studies of the Bible, for current students of Eliphaz to shy away from seeking any transcendent meaning in the text and to promote rather an intentional authorial indeterminacy. This approach is largely due to a preference for postmodern approaches to the text.[98] In both this and the preceding observation, it is a useful check to realize that interpreters are often more influenced by their cultural and religious ambience than they might suppose.

Fifth, the fact that Jewish interpreters tended to view the book more favorably advances somewhat the argument that the events in the book unfold in such a way as to suggest that the author intended original readers to be predisposed toward Eliphaz. Jewish interpreters, who were in all probability, the original recipients and intended audience of the work, largely saw Eliphaz auspiciously as a defender of truth. At minimum in his first speech, Eliphaz is likely to be perceived by the audience as an eloquent, pious counselor who contributes much to the theological outlook of the book. This set-up conforms to other ANE attitudes and norms for the counselor of the pious sufferer. In the Babylonian *Theodicy*, the grief counselor is expected to bring the sufferer back to restoration with the offended deity. Thus the counselor advises the sufferer: "Seek the kindly wind of the god, what you have lost over a year you will make up in a moment."[99] The piece ends with the sufferer following this advice by seeking the kindness of the offended god and goddess and by an appeal to "the shepherd Šamaš [who] guides the peoples like a god."[100] The role of Eliphaz in Job was to be viewed in a similar way—Eliphaz is to bring Job back to restoration with the offended deity, in this case Yahweh. So now, having examined the long interpretive history of Eliphaz, we must turn to get better acquainted with the man himself. From clues within the book of Job itself, we will seek to reconstruct Eliphaz's theological provenance and creed as the eminent and pious sage from Edom.

---

98. One can see this approach, for instance in the work of David Clines, who in his commentary on Job offers feminist, vegetarian, materialist, and Christian readings of Job (*Job 1–20*, xlviii–lvi).

99. "Babylonian *Theodicy*," lines 241–42 (*Babylonian Wisdom Literature* [hereafter *BWL*], 85).

100. Ibid., line 297 (*BWL*, 89).

4

The Meaning, Origin, and Theological Provenance of Eliphaz

THE PRINCIPAL CHARACTERS IN Job are likely Edomite: Job is from Uz (Job 1:1), a land most probably to be identified with Edom southeast of Palestine,[1] and Eliphaz originates from Teman (Job 2:11), a locality bordering Edom proper and associated both with Edom and with Edomite wisdom. Edom was renowned traditionally for its wisdom, and the implications that this wisdom tradition have on Eliphaz's theological trajectory and role in the book have not been fully realized. To lend further support to these assertions we begin in the narrative prologue of Job, Eliphaz the Temanite is identified first among the friends of Job who arrive to console him.

The Meaning of *Eliphaz*

The name *Eliphaz* appears fifteen times in the Hebrew Bible and sixteen times in the LXX. Of these occurrences, nine are found in the Edomite genealogical lists of Gen 36 (vv. 4, 10, 11, 12 [2x], 15, 16) and 1 Chron 1 (vv. 35, 36), while six occurrences appear in the Hebrew text of Job (2:11; 4:1; 15:1; 22:1; 42:7, 9) compared to seven in LXX Job (2:11; 4:1; 15:1; 22:1; 42:7, 9, 17). Genesis 36 records that Esau selects several Canaanite wives, one of whom is Adah, a daughter of Elon the Hittite.[2] Adah bears a son named

---

1. So Terrien, *Job*, 51; Clines, *Job 1–20*, 10. Lamentations 4:21 clearly points in this direction: "Rejoice and be glad, O daughter of Edom, you who dwell in the land of Uz."

2. Although most of his conclusions are sociologically based rather than exegetically, for lexical and cultural background to the Gen 36 genealogies see Tebes, "'You

Eliphaz to Esau (Gen 36:4), additionally identified as Esau's firstborn (36:15). This Eliphaz in turn fathers seven sons who come to be distinguished as "chieftains of Eliphaz in the land of Edom" (v. 16): Teman, Omar, Zepho, Kenaz, Korah, Gatam, and Amalek (vv. 15–16). Of these, special mention is made of Amalek, whom Timna, Eliphaz's concubine, bears (36:12).[3] In the book of Job, the name *Eliphaz* occurs each time with the toponymical description "the Temanite." No further information is provided regarding his lineage or background, although LXX Job identifies him as βασιλεύς ("king") of the Temanites.

Various suggestions have been offered for the lexical significance of the name *Eliphaz*, including "(My) God is fine gold,"[4] "God is agile/nimble" ("Gott behend ist")[5] and the rather improbable "contempt of the Lord."[6] Others have proposed a Hurrian provenance and etymology.[7] Currently the favored etymological meaning among scholars is "God conquers" or "God is victorious," correlative to the Old South Arabic *fawwâz* "to conquer, triumph."[8] I will propose a different etymological source, however, which corresponds fittingly to Eliphaz's theological bent in the book of Job.

A. A. Macintosh, in his persuasive essay on the relationship and significance of the Hebrew roots פדה and פדד in Exod 8, posits a connection between these roots and the biblical Hebrew lexemes מוּפָז and פַּז through a previously undesignated cognate פדד/פזז. According to Macintosh, the Hebrew root פדד/פזז is cognate to the Arabic root verb *fzz* with a gloss meaning

---

Shall Not Abhor an Edomite," 6, 14–16.

3. One can imagine that Amalek receives special mention, among other reasons, in view of the battle that Moses and the Israelites must wage against the Amalekites at Rephidim as depicted in Exod 17:8–16. The conflict sequence ends with Moses' taunt to these enemies: "A hand upon the throne of the LORD! The LORD will have war with Amalek from generation to generation" (Exod 17:16; cf. the oracle of Balaam in Num 24:20).

4. BDB, 45. Walter Michel suggests the rendering "My God is pure gold" based upon an Eblaite toponym (*Job in the Light of Northwest Semitic*, 35).

5. Meyer, *Die Israeliten und ihre Nachbarstämme*, 347.

6. Gregory the Great, *Moralia in Iob*, 1:27. Gregory bases his definition for *Eliphaz* on the meaning of the Latin term *Elifas*.

7. Harold L. Ginsberg and Benjamin Maislerargue argue for a Hurrian ending in the form *-izzi* ("Semitised Hurrians in Syria and Palestine," 258–59). Although Eliphaz's concubine Timna is said to be a Horite (36:12, 22), it is more likely that the Horites of Edom had nothing to do with the Horites who are Hurrians (Horwitz, "Were There Twelve Horite Tribes?" 69; Speiser, "Horites," 2: 645).

8. This interpretation harks back to Moritz, "Edomitischen Genealogien," 83–91; cf. also Ginsberg, "Eliphaz," 6:663; Clines, *Job 1–20*, 58.

"to remove"[9] and signifies "to be alone, be separate."[10] The interchange of the letters ז and ד represents a Hebrew dialectal nuance similar to the one found, for example, in the root נדר/נזר ("to withdraw from customary practices, consecrate oneself to the deity").[11] Developing this connection further the cognates מוּפָז and פַּז, which are used often in parallel to זהב ("gold") and customarily translated as "pure/refined gold" (e.g., Pss 19:11; 119:127; Job 28:17), signified at their inception a semantic field of "that which is set apart, unique, holy." Macintosh suggests that "the semantic development from *separation* to *unalloyed/pure (gold)* is a natural one" and is a legitimate explication for the linguistic evolvement of the terms over time.[12] Macintosh's suggested lexical interrelationship—although he makes no explicit mention of its import on the name *Eliphaz*—is significant to the present etymological study of the name.

First, since I contend for an early date for the events taking place in Job and for the composition of the book (on this, see Appendix 1), it is not unlikely that פַּז in the name *Eliphaz* reflects the early linguistic denotation of פזז/פדד as "be separate, alone, set apart." Second, if פזז/פדד is a legitimate Hebrew cognate, the form פַּז in the latter portion of *Eliphaz* is to be conjugated either as the Qal masculine singular active participle ("[he/it] who/that is alone/separate") or, more likely, as the Qal perfect 3ms ("[he/it] is alone/separate).[13] This form, coupled with the preceding syntagma אֱלִי (the monosyllabic i-stem אֵל with the vestigial genitive case ending identifying "God"),[14] together designates אֵל + פַּז = "God is separate, alone, unique" or "God separates/makes alone."[15] The verbal form פַּז deriving from the

---

9. On this root see Zammit, *A Comparative Lexical Study*, 321. Zammit compares the Arabic *fzz* to the Hebrew *pāzaz*, meaning "to be agile, supple."

10. Macintosh, "Exodus VIII 19," 552.

11. Macintosh identifies this as a Hebrew dialectal variation, occurring also in Aramaic (ibid.). Thus as the Arabic and Ugaritic consonant *ḏ* frequently interchanges with the Akkadian and Hebrew *z* in cognate terms as, e.g., in the Hebrew term זְרוֹעַ ("arm") corresponding to the Ugaritic *ḏrʿ* and the Arabic *ḏirāḏ*. See *HAL*, 269.

12. Ibid. Macintosh's thesis is corroborated by 1 Kgs 10:18, which describes Solomon's commissioning of an exquisite throne: וַיַּעַשׂ הַמֶּלֶךְ כִּסֵּא־שֵׁן גָּדוֹל וַיְצַפֵּהוּ זָהָב מוּפָז ("The king built a great ivory throne and overlaid it with choice gold" [author's translation]). Here זָהָב is modified by מוּפָז, a redundancy if the terms are synonyms. I would suggest, rather, following Macintosh's postulate, that מוּפָז in this context denotes gold that is separate, holy, and therefore "choice" (cf. ESV, JPS, and NRSV). In this way the term came to be used figuratively over time to connote the fine gold itself which was dedicated for special use.

13. On the morphology of geminate verbs, see Merwe, Naudé, and Kroeze, *A Biblical Hebrew Reference Grammar*, 128–33.

14. For this form see ibid., 220–21.

15. The etymology is analogous, for example, to the appellative פלל + אֵל < אֱלִיפַל =

geminate פזז may reflect grammatically, as indicated, an active or stative sense. As the pointing of the form may indicate either sense,[16] one cannot surmise with complete certainty which sense is more likely. I have selected the stative nuance in that it reflects accurately the early linguistic denotation of the verb as noted above. Third, the proposed etymology corresponds well to the theme of divine transcendence so prevalent in Eliphaz's speeches.[17] Eliphaz serves a completely transcendent God ("Is not God high in the heavens?" [22:12]), who in his divine holiness is distant and removed from the corrupt created order ("Can a mortal man be in the right before God? Can a man be pure before his Maker? Even in his servants he puts no trust, and his angels he charges with error" [4:17–18]), and who in the execution of his mighty works is incomprehensible to mankind ("who does great things and unsearchable, marvelous things without number" [5:9]). I would suggest, then, that Eliphaz in his very name identifies a God who is remote from creation, transcendent, and unfathomable. This theological tenet forms a core principle in Eliphaz's counsel to Job to submit to the transcendent God who must be appeased through abject acquiescence.

In summary, Eliphaz's name points to two factors which will be significant in the successive dialogue and have import to the following interpretation of the leading interlocutor. First, this view places him within the parameters of Edomite lineage and provenance.[18] One may surmise that in the extended ending to LXX Job—which identifies Job with Jobab of Genesis 36—the translators who composed or appropriated this additional material also likely identified Eliphaz in Job with the Eliphaz of Genesis 36 (corroborated in the extended ending by the mention there that Eliphaz is one of the "sons of Esau").[19] So then, at least as early as the LXX a credible tradition tied Eliphaz to the Edomite ancestry spelled out in Genesis as a

---

"God has judged" (*HAL*, p. 54).

16. See Merwe, Naudé, and Kroeze, *Biblical Hebrew Reference Grammar*, 131. The authors include an analysis of the active vis-à-vis stative geminate forms. They demonstrate that in the *active* Qal perf 3ms, 3fs, and 3cp forms the identical second and third consonants may be visibly repeated (e.g., סָבְבָה < סבב or סָבְבָה ["she/it surrounded"]), indicated by means of a *dagesh* (e.g., סַבָּה) or omitted altogether (e.g., סַב). In the *stative* Qal perf 3ms the third consonant always drops off (e.g., קַל < קָלַל ["he/it is swift"]).

17. This is not to suggest, however, that Eliphaz is fictitious, that the author is using a pseudonym, or that his name is contrived. I am proposing, rather, that the meaning of his name as the Edomite sage is integral to the theological storyline of Job, as, for example, the meanings of Abraham, Isaac, and Jacob are integral to the storyline of Genesis.

18. On this, see also Pope, *Job*, 23; Fedrizzi, *Giobbe*, 83; Andersen, *Job*, 94; Horst, *Hiob 1–19*, 32; Balentine, *Job*, 66; Selms, *Job*, 5, 14.

19. For extensive treatment of this topic, see Reed, "Job as Jobab," 31–55.

The Meaning, Origin, and Theological Provenance of Eliphaz 119

direct descendant of Esau.[20] Viewed as Edomite, Eliphaz would be understood by the early readers of Job naturally to be a proponent of "Edomite wisdom theology." Identifying this correlation factors in consequentially to my later, more fully developed understanding of Eliphaz's theological wisdom perspective, specifically as to whether it was intended to be viewed favorably or critically as divinely inspired or humanly motivated. Second, the name *Eliphaz* is quite likely a clue to this posited "Edomite wisdom theology." Incorporating the significance of the name there is an adumbration of the substance of this theology which delineates a transcendent deity who in his divine holiness is set apart uniquely from the created order. But what of the ubiquitous toponymical designation "Temanite" in Job? Does one find here further significance for revealing the identity of Eliphaz?

The Meaning of *Temanite*

The Hebrew term *Teman* (תֵּימָן) denotes at its lexical root "south" or "territory in the south," used also of the "south wind."[21] In this usage the term usually points as a sweeping geographical label to anything located in the south or southward from the speaker, connoting for example the southern border of Judah at the wilderness of Zin (e.g., Josh 15:1) or God's eschatological redemptive work in summoning His people from the south (Isa 43:6).[22] The term has two additional imports which are pertinent to this study. The eponym תֵּימָן is used for one of the descendants of Esau who is the tribal chieftain (אַלּוּף) of his clan (Gen 36:15, 42; 1 Chron 1:53).[23] The individual named Teman is identified more precisely in the biblical taxonomy as a grandson of Esau and son of Eliphaz, Esau's firstborn (Gen 36:11; 1 Chron 1:36).[24] It is apparent that the names of the Edomite chieftains in

---

20. This is presuming, as Reed points out, that the addition originated in the OG Job and was appropriated by Theodotion in his translation rather than vice-versa (ibid., 40). Elie Assis argues that the corollary genealogical passage in 1 Chron 1 is an anti-Edomite polemic ("From Adam to Esau," 287–302).

21. *HALOT*, 1725. The term occurs most frequently with the meaning "south" or "south wind," approximately twenty times in the OT: Exod 26:18, 35; 27:9; 38:9; Num 2:10; 3:29; 10:6; Deut 3:27; Josh 12:3; 13:4; 15:1; Ps 78:26; Cant 4:16; Ezek 47:19; 48:28; Isa 43:6; Job 9:9; 39:26; Zech 6:6; 9:14. The term derives from the lexeme ימן "right hand, right side" with the ת preformative (Gilchrist, "2:383 ",ימן). From an orientation facing east, "that which is to the right hand" is south geographically.

22. Rogers, "תֵּימָן."

23. Ibid., 1726. The name תֵּימָן is used five times in Gen 36:11, 15, 42; 1 Chron 1:36, 53.

24. The lineage from Esau places Teman prominently in the ancestry of the Edomites, as Moses underscores in Gen 36:8b–9, עֵשָׂו הוּא אֱדוֹם וְאֵלֶּה תֹּלְדוֹת עֵשָׂו אֲבִי

time came to be associated with the regional precincts of the Edomite territory.²⁵ Husham is identified as king over the land of the Temanites in Gen 36:34-35, succeeding Jobab the Zerahite as king.²⁶

As a toponym Teman denotes a territory which was "perhaps originally . . . an area of land in the south in Edom, and lying in the south because of etymological connection with תֵּימָן."²⁷ Nelson Glueck initially identified Teman with Tawilân, a site northeast of Elji and roughly halfway between the Dead Sea and Elath,²⁸ but later changed his mind.²⁹ The toponym is most likely to be associated simply with the southern region of Edom, as Roland de Vaux convincingly pointed out.³⁰ As the two most prominent territories of Edom, Teman is paired in biblical prophecy with Bozrah, identifying the region of Teman most likely with the southern district of Edom and linking Bozrah with the northern district.³¹ Thus Amos proph-

---

אֱדוֹם בְּהַר שֵׂעִיר ("Esau is Edom. These are the generations of Esau, the father of Edom, in the hill country of Seir" [author's translation]).

25. Knauf, "Teman," 6:347-48. Knauf posits that no certainty may be gained as to whether Eliphaz hails from Teman as a region of Edom or from Tema, a city in northern Arabia (cf. Knauf, "Tema" 6:346-47). Eliphaz's link with the Edomite genealogical lists mentioned above makes a strong case, however, that the former rather than the latter is intended.

26. Knauf identifies "Temanites" here as denoting Tema in Arabia ("Teman," 6:348), but this is not certain.

27. Ibid., 1726; Vaux, "Téman," 379-85; Emerton, "New Light on Israelite Religion," 9. The toponym תֵּימָן is found six times in the OT including Jer 49:7, 20; Ezek 25:13; Amos 1:12; Obad 9; and Hab 3:3.

28. Glueck, *The Other Side of the Jordan*, 26. Aharoni and Avi-Yonah perpetuate this identification (see *The Macmillan Bible Atlas*, 48, map 52).

29. Glueck, *The Other Side of the Jordan*, 32. Crystal-M. Bennett adduces several reasons for not equating Tawilān with Teman, including the fact that the earliest settlement of Tawilân would have been the eighth century BC which is too late for identification with Teman and the fact that Tawilân was apparently unfortified, a highly unlikely feature for Teman given its prominence as a city of Edom in, e.g., Amos 1:13 and 2:2 ("Archaeological Survey," 41-43).

30. Roland de Vaux summarizes, "La conclusion est que nulle part dans la Bible Téman n'est employé, pour désigner une ville. Originairement le nom désigne une région d'Édom, le pays des Témanites de Gen. XXXVI, 34; d'après l'étymologie du mot, il s'agit du sud d' Édom" ("The conclusion is that nowhere in the Bible is Teman employed to designate a city. Originally the name designated a region of Edom, the country of the Temanites of Gen 36:34; according to the etymology of the word, it appears to be south of Edom") ("Ville ou Région," 385). Vaux points out further that all the prophets use the term as a poetic reference to the nation of Edom itself.

31. Diana Edelman, on the other hand, posits that Teman originally designated the northern portion of the Edomite plateau and the region surrounding Bozrah. "After the state emerged at Bozrah, this local term came to be synonymous with the core territory of the state, so that Jer 49:7, 20 and Obad 9 could use Teman as a synonym for Edom"

esies concerning Yahweh's verdict, "I will send a fire upon Teman, and it shall devour the strongholds of Bozrah" (Amos 1:12). Ezekiel 25:13 links Teman with Dedan, another region of Edom: "Thus says the Lord GOD, I will stretch out my hand against Edom and cut off from it man and beast. And I will make it desolate; from Teman even to Dedan they shall fall by the sword." God emerges from Teman in Hab 3:3 ("God came from Teman, and the Holy One from Mount Paran"), most likely a reference to his powerful theophanic work in the exodus, codification of the Law, and conquest.[32] Also of interest in this connection is the inscription discovered at Kuntillet 'Ajrud which reads *yhwh Tmn* ("Yahweh from Teman").[33] The inscription points likely to a syncretistic form of Yahweh worship practiced through a fertility cult in the Negev.[34]

In several passages Teman comes to be identified with Edom itself, particularly in its association with a renown for wisdom. In Jer 49:7, 20 the prophet Jeremiah foretells doom for the celebrated wise men of Teman, a region which has come to refer by synecdoche to all of Edom: "Concerning

---

("Edom," 10).

32. Mount Paran is associated elsewhere in the Hebrew Bible with Seir (Gen 14:6), shown above to be a mountainous district linked to Edom (Gen 36:8-9). It denotes a range of peaks west and south of Edom and northeast of Sinai (see Patterson, "The Psalm of Habakkuk," 166). Other texts point up the significance of these geographical regions with reference to the exodus, provision of the Law, and conquest of Canaan. In Deut 33:2 Moses recalls in his blessing upon the Israelites before his death that "the LORD came from Sinai and dawned from Seir upon us; he shone forth from Mount Paran; he came from the ten thousands of holy ones, with flaming fire at his right hand." Deborah and Barak likewise sing praise to Yahweh in Judg 5:4-5, "LORD, when you went out from Seir, when you marched from the region of Edom, the earth trembled and the heavens dropped, yes, the clouds dropped water. The mountains quaked before the LORD, even Sinai before the LORD, the God of Israel."

33. The inscription dates from between the middle of the ninth to the middle of the eighth century BC See Emerton, "New Light on Israelite Religion," 2; Meshel, "Kuntillet 'Ajrud," 4:103-9. In the inscription Yahweh of Teman is paired with "his Asherah" and mention also is made of "Yahweh of Samaria" and his Asherah, pointing perhaps to a cult center for Yahweh worship (Dicou, *Edom, Israel's Brother and Antagonist*, 179). Meshel proposes it was a "wayside shrine" operated by cultic officials from the northern kingdom of Israel ("Kuntillet 'Ajrud," 4:108). Alleged Yahweh worship here would likely have been syncretistic at best, as the allusions to Asherah suggest (see Dever, "Asherah," 21-37).

34. Some scholars conjecture beyond the data, however, suggesting a primitive Yahwism in the region of Sinai/southern Judah which preceded Israel's emergence as a nation (see Dearman, "Edomite Religion," 127). Gösta W. Ahlström develops this further to argue that Yahweh worship originated among the Edomites and was later adopted by the Israelites (*Who Were the Israelites?*, 58). The evidence for this, however, is tenuous, based on a superficial understanding of passages which speak of Yahweh coming from Teman and a single inscription from Kuntillet 'Ajrud.

Edom. Thus says the LORD of hosts: 'Is wisdom no more in Teman? Has counsel perished from the prudent? Has their wisdom vanished?'" He pronounces Edom's utter demise: "Therefore hear the plan that the LORD has made against Edom and the purposes that he has formed against the inhabitants of Teman: Even the little ones of the flock shall be dragged away. Surely their fold shall be appalled at their fate" (49:20). Obadiah has the harshest words for Edom, likewise decreeing the ruinous fate of these arrogant cliff-dwellers (v. 3) for their complicities in sacking Jerusalem (v. 13) and for their aid to Babylon in rounding up the Israelite deportees (v. 14): "Will I not on that day, declares the LORD, destroy the wise men out of Edom, and understanding out of Mount Esau? And your mighty men shall be dismayed, O Teman, so that every man from Mount Esau will be cut off by slaughter" (Obad 8–9).

Furthermore, the Jewish apocryphal work Baruch (*ca.* 200–50 BC) clearly links Teman with Edom and its reputation for the pursuit of wisdom.[35] Deliberating at length on the motif of wisdom against the background of Israel's failure to attain divine wisdom in light of its chastening through the exile, the author of Baruch admonishes his audience to tenaciously pursue true sapience which originates only in the God of Israel (3:1, 4, 6): "Learn where there is wisdom, where there is strength, where there is understanding, so that you may at the same time discern where there is length of days, and life, where there is light for the eyes, and peace" (μάθε ποῦ ἐστιν φρόνησις ποῦ ἐστιν ἰσχύς ποῦ ἐστιν σύνεσις τοῦ γνῶναι ἅμα ποῦ ἐστιν μακροβίωσις καὶ ζωή ποῦ ἐστιν φῶς ὀφθαλμῶν καὶ εἰρήνη [3:14, NRSV]). He offers contrapuntal examples of those who have fruitlessly pursued human wisdom, consequently to come to nothing, including the erstwhile sages of Canaan and Edom. "She [wisdom] has not been heard of in Canaan, or seen in Teman; the descendants of Hagar, who seek for understanding on the earth, the merchants of Merran and Teman, the story-tellers and the seekers for understanding, have not learned the way to wisdom, or given thought to her paths" (οὐδὲ ἠκούσθη ἐν Χανααν οὐδὲ ὤφθη ἐν Θαιμαν. οὔτε υἱοὶ Αγαρ οἱ ἐκζητοῦντες τὴν σύνεσιν ἐπὶ τῆς γῆς οἱ ἔμποροι τῆς Μερραν καὶ Θαιμαν οἱ μυθολόγοι καὶ οἱ ἐκζητηταὶ τῆς συνέσεως ὁδὸν τῆς σοφίας οὐκ ἔγνωσαν οὐδὲ ἐμνήσθησαν τὰς τρίβους αὐτῆς [Bar 3:22–23, NRSV]). Teman is here also

---

35. On the date and background to Baruch (1 Baruch), see Harrington, *Invitation to the Apocrypha*, 92–102; DeSilva, *Introducing the Apocrypha*, 198–213; Moore, *Daniel, Esther, and Jeremiah*, 255–61; Metzger, *Introduction to the Apocrypha*, 89–94. Harrington argues that Baruch was initially composed in Hebrew and originated in Palestine from 200–50 BC likely during the national revival of Israel in the Maccabbean period (*Invitation to the Apocrypha*, 94). DeSilva takes a more critical approach to the redactive history of the work, dating its final version to the late second century or early first century BC (*Introducing the Apocrypha*, 205).

The Meaning, Origin, and Theological Provenance of Eliphaz

clearly connected with the celebrated wisdom tradition of an Edomite and Arabian provenance which, the sixth-century prophets foretold, had come to naught.

Given the biblical record several conclusions may be drawn regarding the significance of Teman in our understanding of Eliphaz. First, Eliphaz by his toponymical/genealogical epithet "the Temanite," as by the association of his name with the genealogical taxonomy of Genesis 36, is again clearly linked to an Edomite ancestry and provenance. To develop this connection further, I refer the reader to the Appendix, which outlines a proposed genealogical collocation for Eliphaz and the events of the book of Job. Second, in that Eliphaz originates out of this milieu which was acclaimed traditionally with ancient wisdom, he appears to emerge in the book of Job as a proponent of this distinguished "normative" wisdom theology.[36] As a Temanite Eliphaz should be part of this great wisdom tradition, and moreover is expected to champion the renowned wisdom of the ANE for which Teman came to be celebrated. Third, to develop further upon this point, Eliphaz is quite conceivably to be understood—although this conclusion is offered with caution—as an epic sage in the Edomite wisdom tradition. Given his status as a revered sage from Teman and given the theological motifs of his speeches, which I will trace in greater detail below, I will argue that Eliphaz is himself in many ways constitutive of Edomite sapience and to be viewed as a fountainhead of this wisdom perspective. To draw out these implications I turn now to a fuller development of Eliphaz's place in traditional Edomite wisdom theology. I will begin with a brief survey of the likely political structure of Edom, which may have nurtured the type of wisdom Eliphaz embodied, followed by a more detailed analysis of his collocation in that wisdom tradition.

Eliphaz, Edom, and Edomite Wisdom

Regarding Edom's early culture and political organization, much remains a mystery. Archaeologists often have remained reluctant to lend credence to biblical accounts of the Edomites in major part due to the lack of artifacts or inscriptions which would substantiate conclusively the existence of a vibrant ancient Edomite society, particularly one with a sufficiently developed political structure to coincide with biblical descriptions of Edom's resistance

---

36. As Joseph Blenkinsopp acknowledges, one should view Eliphaz and the other friends as drawing upon the legendary wisdom of the Edomites and Arabs (*Wisdom and Law in the Old Testament*, 56; cf. 1 Kgs 4:30).

to the Israelite exodus and conquest.[37] The correlation of archaeological data with the biblical narratives, as Roland Harrison cautions, however, is many times subjective and fraught with challenges, often leading to a wide divergence of opinion.[38] For this reason one must exercise prudence to avoid extenuating the value of archaeology by drawing hard and fast implications from sketchy data which contravene the straightforward record of the Hebrew Scriptures. Rather, in keeping with the methodology stated at the outset, the merits of the biblical record are to be given pride of place as the starting point for our understanding of ancient Edom, with extra-biblical finds appropriated judiciously to fill in and round out the picture.

Edom's Contact with Other Nations of the ANE

According to the biblical record, Edom had an established monarchy prior to the advent of the Saulite kingdom of Israel (Gen 36:31; 1 Chron 1:43),[39] suggesting that early in its history Edom had sufficient political organization and societal cohesion to support in some degree the origin and dissemination of wisdom materials which were common stock of the ANE.[40] Examples of Edom's interaction with leading nations and figures of the ancient world are helpful in supporting this conclusion. The Egyptian Pharaoh Ramses II (*ca.* 1290–1224 BC), for example, appears to have catalogued the theophoric names of Edomite chiefs or clans in his topographical lists at the temple of Karnak.[41] In addition, William F. Albright identifies several clues which point to an established semi-political organization for the Edomites early in their history. Two obelisks discovered at Tanis dating from the end

---

37. For example, Num 20:14–21 speaks of Edom's refusal to permit entry to Israel in order to pass through their land, confronting the Israelites with a sizeable military force.

38. Harrison, *Old Testament Times*, 133.

39. Genesis 36:31 reads "These are the kings who reigned in the land of Edom, before any king reigned over the Israelites." Although it is possible that the author writes proleptically, commentators often see here a later editorial comment (Ross, *Creation and Blessing*, 587).

40. Nelson Glueck disputed this claim, as he alleged that archaeological finds proved no sedentary population existed in the regions of Moab and Edom from the time of Abraham until the thirteenth century (*The Other Side of the Jordan*, 125). William F. Albright admitted, however, that based on further evidence some modifications would need to be made in Glueck's approach as the gap in the sedentary population between 1900 and 1300 BC was not so clear as he had argued ("Archaeology of Palestine," 4; cf. Harrison, *Old Testament Times*, 133).

41. Oded, "Egyptian References," 47–50; Knauf, "Qaus," 93–95. Dearman is somewhat skeptical, however ("Edomite Religion," 123).

The Meaning, Origin, and Theological Provenance of Eliphaz

of the fourteenth century BC imply an organized, if not somewhat formidable, Edomite culture.[42] Of the two obelisks, which stood opposite one another, the southern stele proclaims victory over the Libyans and Nubians, while the northern stele pronounces the following: "Fierce raging lion, who has laid waste the land of the Asiatic nomads, who has plundered Mount Seir with his valiant arm."[43] As Albright notes, "About 1300, then, Mount Seir was already sufficiently threatening to be raided by an Egyptian army."[44] This conclusion finds further corroboration from the Anastasi Papyri which reads "We have finished passing the Asiatic nomad tribes of Edom by the fortress of Marniptah which is (in) Succoth, in order to keep them and their flocks alive. . . ."[45] This record, which dates from the reign of Sethos II (ca. 1219-1213 BC), indicates that the Edomites were partly sedentary (Edom is described as a "foreign land" rather than "foreign people"), although still sufficiently nomadic to seek refuge in Egypt during an extreme drought. In addition, a reference from the Papyrus Harris, dating from the reign of Ramses III (1195-1164 BC), mentions the nomadic Seirites: "I brought about the destruction of Seir among the tribes of the Asiatic nomads. I laid waste their tents, with their people, their belongings and likewise their cattle, without number. They were bound and brought as spoil, as tribute of Egypt. I gave them to the divine Ennead as slaves of their temples. . . ."[46] Regarding this inscription, Albright summarizes the following:

> This passage proves that the Egyptians regarded the peoples of Seir as still essentially nomadic; the shift to sedentary life was only partial and had by no means affected the majority of the Edomites as yet. It is clear that the Edomites must have become a serious menace to the Egyptian caravan routes to Sinai and Palestine, since a difficult and expensive raid would scarcely have been undertaken merely for slaves and cattle. It is perhaps safe to infer that the nomads occupying the regions between Egypt and Palestine took advantage of the fact that Egypt was busy repelling invasion during the early part of the reign of Ramesses III, and organized their forays more elaborately and boldly than they had in the past.[47]

---

42. Montet excavated Tanis from 1929-1956, although much of the material from his finds remains unpublished (Ritner, review of Philippe Brissaud, *Cahiers de Tanis*, 1, 132).

43. Albright, "Oracles of Balaam," 228.

44. Ibid.

45. Ibid., 229.

46. Ibid.

47. Ibid., 229-30.

Assyrian records from the eighth and seventh centuries identify the existence of a well-established Edomite kingdom, but it appears that from the eighth century onward the kingdom was disintegrating.[48] Cumulatively these evidences offer a solid case for the early political organization and societal structure which would have supported in some measure the context of ancient wisdom for which Edom gained its reputation.

Edom's Prime Location in the Commercial Avenues of the ANE

Situated along the King's Highway (cf. Num 20:17), Edom was central in the flow of traffic and commerce in the ancient world.[49] The King's Highway was secondarily the most valuable major international trade route of the ancient world, passing through the Edomite hill-country of Transjordan and providing a direct link from Egypt to Damascus and beyond to Mesopotamia, passing through the regions of Assyria all the way to Babylon.[50] Edom's major importance along this trade route was its position as the gateway to Arabian commerce centers geographically further southeast on the Arabian peninsula. Babylon indeed had much to gain from trade with these regions, as it frequently commissioned wood from as far away as Egypt during the Cassite period (*ca.* 2000–1500 BC).[51] The ancient cultures of Ebla, Babylonia, Assyria, Egypt, and Arabia exchanged a number of other goods and luxury items, including gold, silver, copper, ivory, tin, lapis lazuli, timber, tree oils, wine, slaves, agricultural produce, and textile fabrics during the Old Babylonian period.[52]

Of special interest for the Mesopotamians, however, were these luxury items to be obtained from Arabia.[53] As Gonzalo Rubio points out:

---

48. Bartlett, "Rise and Fall," 32.

49. See, for example, Byrne, "Early Assyrian Contacts," 11; Glueck, *The Other Side of the Jordan*, 32.

50. Aharoni and Avi-Yonah, *Macmillan Bible Atlas*, 16.

51. Rubio, "From Sumer to Babylonia," 22. The Babylonian Cassites preferred the African blackwood as a building material.

52. Leemans, *Foreign Trade*, 120–31. Leemans notes that "in general, evidence of trade during a certain period may only be supposed to be a symptom of trade over a prolonged period, if this trade was a natural one, as was the export of Syrian articles to Babylonia" (ibid., 136). Evidence of such patterns of trade behavior extends down to the Cassite period (ibid., 137).

53. Marc van de Mieroop points out that such luxury items were imported not due to a scarcity of materials in Mesopotamia but rather due to ameliorating economic conditions which sustained the import of opulent goods for the wealthy class. He identifies specifically three concurrent factors: (1) the availability of luxury articles, (2) contacts with other cultures at the periphery, and (3) the rise of a social elite ("Foreign Contacts,"

The Meaning, Origin, and Theological Provenance of Eliphaz 127

"Throughout Mesopotamian history, there are three regions that are abundantly mentioned in texts and which eventually became part of a mental map, frequently inhabited by the collective dreams of faraway lands from which all sorts of wealth came: Dilmun, Magan, and Meluhha."[54] Of these several exotic places with which Mesopotamia desired to trade, two regions—Dilmun and Magan—were located on the Arabian peninsula. Dilmun, most likely to be identified with modern-day Bahrain, was sought after for its wood, precious stones, and metals, especially copper. Exports from Ur to Dilmun included textile fabrics during the Third Dynasty.[55] Lagash exported textiles, finished garments, wool, cedar oil, barley, flour, and silver to Dilmun in exchange for copper.[56] From the region of Magan, associated with modern-day Oman, Mesopotamia sought wood, copper, and diorite, while exporting textiles.[57] Yet more than mere business transactions took place between the regions. Cultural exchanges were commonplace as well, as evident from a Mesopotamian Ur III inscriptional tablet uncovered on the island of Bahrain and conversely from the inclusion of gods from the Dilmunite pantheon in Akkadian and Sumerian ritualistic purgation spells. The commercial transactions between Arabia and Mesopotamia—and beyond these including Egypt—were so significant that at least as early as 1385 BC Mesopotamia apparently was asserting itself militarily in the Levant. The Mesopotamian King Cushan-rishathaim subjugated Israel during the early period of the Judges (Judg 3:8),[58] perhaps with the intent ultimately of annexing Egypt.[59] Several centuries later Nabonidus would intervene militarily in the Arabian peninsula to protect Mesopotamia's interests in the frankincense trade.[60]

Edom's prominent position along the Transjordanian portion of the King's Highway as the gateway to the key aforementioned business centers

---

130). Mieroop continues: "The growth of a wealthy class led to a desire for luxury items which enabled members of that class to distinguish themselves from the mass of the population. Conspicuous display of wealth was part of Mesopotamian economic behavior, just as it was in ancient Egypt" (ibid.).

54. Rubio, "From Sumer to Babylonia," 20–21, 22.

55. Leemans, *Foreign Trade*, 136; Good, "Textiles as a Medium of Exchange," 201.

56. Leemans, *Foreign Trade*, 116; Good, "Textiles as a Medium of Exchange," 201.

57. Good, "Textiles as a Medium of Exchange," 200–1.

58. Although some question persists as to his exact provenance, for the connection of Cushan-rishathaim with the general region of Mesopotamia, see Malamat, "The Egyptian Decline," 3:25–26; Block, *Judges, Ruth*, 152–53; Moore, *Judges*, 87; Wood, *Distressing Days of the Judges*, 92–96 [Wood is tentative]; Walton, *Chronological and Background Charts*, 26.

59. So argues Malamat, "Egyptian Decline," 3:25–26.

60. Ibid., 43–44.

as well as other Arabian nexuses of commerce undoubtedly afforded exposure to Edom with the variegated cultures and societies of its day. In fact, the rivalry between Israel and Edom would in time grow bitter in part over the struggle to control these Arabian trade routes to which Edom by its location had natural access.[61] It is important to note also in arguing for these early international contacts that written materials of theological and cultic importance were quite likely part of the interaction among these various peoples, more than simply the exchange of records of commercial transactions. This is apparent, in addition to the examples provided earlier of the inclusion of the Arabian pantheon in Mesopotamian ritualistic texts, in that fragments of the *Gilgamesh Epic* dating back to at least the fourteenth century BC have been discovered in several locations a considerable distance from Mesopotamia, including Emar in upper Syria and Megiddo in Canaan.[62] These discoveries have led one scholar to posit that by the Late Bronze Age "Gilgamesh's adventures had come into full vogue in the Near East."[63] Furthermore, the discovery of a cache of inscribed seals of the Kassite variety (ca. 1595–1157 BC) at Thebes in Greece suggests that the interchange of cultures and their native articles (especially from Babylonia westward) was far-reaching.[64] Job, in fact, in his response to Zophar in Job 21:29—to substantiate his assertion concerning the inconsistency of divine retributive justice—asks rhetorically if no one has paid attention to the well-known stories of travelers: "Have you not asked those who travel the roads, and do you not accept their testimony?" This reference suggests at the very least access to commercial roads and contact with other peoples and cultures who would be travelling these trade routes on way to further regions—travelers with stories to tell. Thus, both oral and written traditions had coin in the region in tandem with the ongoing flow of commerce. It is reasonable to posit that a number of written materials of theological and cultural significance were exchanged through the ancient world, including materials relevant to our discussion of Job.

Archaeological Traces of Edomite Wisdom

In light of the preceding discussion, the plaguing question lingers nonetheless of why so few tangible, written evidences of this renowned Edomite

---

61. Finkelstein, "Edom in Iron I," 164.
62. Tigay, *Evolution of the Gilgamesh Epic*, 123.
63. Sasson, "Gilgamesh Epic," 2:1025.
64. Grayson, "Mesopotamia, History of (Babylonia)," 4:762.

wisdom have been discovered.⁶⁵ There are several possible reasons, a few of which point in the direction of a more satisfying resolution. First, one possibility is, as Robert Pfeiffer suggests, that several of the most noteworthy exemplars of Edomite wisdom actually found their way into the Hebrew canon in the writings, for example, of Ethan the Ezrahite (Ps 89), Heman the Ezrahite (Ps 88), Agur (Prov 30), and Lemuel (Prov 31).⁶⁶ The difficulty with this proposal, however, is its somewhat theologically careless placement of inscripturated revelation as originating outside the boundaries of God's special covenant people, the nation of Israel.⁶⁷ Second, taking seriously the prophetic oracles which pronounced the utter decimation of Edom (e.g., Jer 49; Obadiah), it is possible that no inscriptional evidences were left in the wake of Edom's destruction. Third, it is rather likely that given the persistent semi-nomadic state of Edomite society and culture that no significant library of Edomite materials ever was amassed like that for which Ashurbanipal, for example, is renowned. Most Edomite inscriptions have been found on ostracons, and perhaps given the nature of the Edomite societal organization as a semi-nomadic people, such inscriptions were the most sensible means of encapsulating the folk wisdom which seems the most common form of wisdom embodied in Edom.⁶⁸ It may be that in this area

65. The scarcity of inscriptional evidence has led to the recent suggestion to abandon altogether the postulation of an Edomite wisdom tradition (Crowell, "A Reevaluation," 404–16).

66. Pfeiffer, "Edomitic Wisdom," 14–15.

67. Pfeiffer's suggestion runs into two theological difficulties. First, the NT specifies that the Jews were recipients of God's special revelation inscripturated in the Hebrew canon: "Then what advantage has the Jew? Or what is the value of circumcision? Much in every way. To begin with, the Jews were entrusted with the oracles of God" (Rom 3:1–2) That this refers most probably to the entirety of OT inscripturated revelation with special reference, perhaps, to the promises for Israel, see Moo, *Romans*, 182–83. Second, the theological implications of Israel's founding as a nation and special place as mediatory people, both as a kingdom of priests and a holy nation (Exod 19:6), suggest that especially by means of the Mosaic covenant and later canonical writings God's inscripturated revelation is in many ways itself constitutive of the nation of Israel, thus leading to the conclusion that God revealed himself in a particular way to Israel through the inspired Word of the Hebrew canon (see Merrill, *Everlasting Dominion*, 325–45). The proposition that these (likely) Edomite wise men were authors of Scripture appears to run up against this understanding of Israel's uniqueness as the recipient of divine inscripturated revelation. Although I am arguing that the book of Job precedes the formulation of the Mosaic covenant, I contend that it was written by a Jew, Elihu, for the Jewish people and thus was appropriated by the Jews. For more on this, see the Appendix.

68. Piotr Bienkowski notes of the finds at Tawilân that the material culture of Edomite society well into the Persian period (one inscription dates to 423 BC) was overwhelmingly agricultural and domestic, with about half of the non-ceramic objects excavated being associated with food preparation, one quarter with textile manufacturing

modern scholars' hopes of discovering a wealth of Edomite written materials are simply overzealous aspirations greater than what actually existed in the ancient context. Fourth, in light of the well-known similarities to be found among several cognate South Canaanite dialects, including Edomite, Moabite, Ammonite, epigraphic Hebrew, and Phoenician,[69] another possibility is that early Edomite inscriptions have been simply misidentified as belonging to other dialects or cognate languages.[70] A comparison of Edomite and Ammonite epigraphy, for example, exhibits several striking similarities with the letters ב, ל, מ, among others.[71] Additionally, the feature of epigraphic discoveries used most often to invoke Edomite provenance for an inscription is reference to Qos, usually by means of a theophoric name.[72] Depending on the chronology and scope of Qos worship among the Edomites, however, this criterion may not be equally applicable to all early Edomite inscriptions.[73] Although there are telling difficulties with Pfeiffer's suggestion that portions of the Hebrew Scriptures such as Proverbs 30–31 originate from an Edomite provenance, one merit of his proposal lies in the fact that he acknowledges the plausibility of an Edomite dialect being written in ancient Hebrew script.[74] Of the suggestions listed, most likely a combination of these factors took place. The fact that Edom's complete and utter demise was foretold in the OT scriptures casts a shadow over the prospects of discovering a wealth of Edomite written materials. It is likely, moreover, that Edomite inscriptions were confined in the main to pottery or other useful implements—due to the lingering semi-nomadic nature of Edomite society—and were written potentially in an epigraphic Hebrew or

and one-fifth with items of personal adornment or connected with the preparation of personal cosmetics ("The Archaeological Evidence," 59).

69. Waltke and O'Connor, *Biblical Hebrew Syntax*, 8.

70. Sasson argues, for example, that an inscription from Horvat Uzza was initially misidentified as Hebrew but is in reality an Edomite dialect (see below). Lawrence T. Geraty also identifies an Edomite inscription from Khirbet el-Kôm written in Aramaic script ("Khirbet el-Kôm Bilingual Ostracon," 55–61). If these observations are correct, this holds out the likelihood of the practice of writing the Edomite dialect in Hebrew or another Canaanite script. Although later Edomite inscriptions have a distinct writing style, it is quite possible that some Edomite writings, especially early writings, were written in another Canaanite script. On the peculiarities of the later Edomite script, see Beit-Arieh, "The Edomites in Cisjordan," 34.

71. I am comparing here the Tell el-Kheleifeh Edomite inscriptions from Elath with the Tell Siran Ammonite bottle inscriptions (Ahituv, הכתב והמכתב, 334–37 [Hebrew]).

72. See, e.g., Ahituv, "An Edomite Ostracon," 33–37.

73. As we argue below, for example, evidence from Kuntillet 'Ajrud points to a form of syncretistic Yahweh worship practiced in the Negev, perhaps consisting of a fertility cult imported from northern Israel.

74. Pfeiffer, "Edomitic Wisdom," 15.

other South Canaanite script. The hopes of discovering a library of Edomite materials to rival that of Ashurbanipal in all likelihood is simply unrealistic. Having considered briefly the tenability of the Edomite wisdom tradition, we move now to consider more fully what evidences may be adduced for a clearer understanding of the constitutive features of this reputed Edomite wisdom.

The Theological Contours of Edomite Wisdom

Identifying the main tenets of Edomite wisdom, in spite of its acclaimed status in the ancient world as a repository of sapience, is notoriously difficult in light of the paucity of confirmed written Edomite materials. Yet the fact that the Hebrew Bible refers repeatedly to Edomite wisdom, and that it does so in spite of the persistent hostility between the peoples of Israel and Edom,[75] advises against facile dismissal of the validity of the Edomite wisdom tradition.[76] Our purpose in the following is to outline the contours of Edomite wisdom and to offer tangible connections in which Eliphaz may be viewed as a champion of these wisdom perspectives.

Probably no one has put forth more effort among modern scholars to trace the background of Edomite wisdom, particularly as it pertains to an ostensible backdrop to Job, as Robert H. Pfeiffer.[77] In his 1926 essay "Edomitic Wisdom," Pfeiffer suggests that Job was originally an Edomite wisdom composition embodying literarily the pinnacle of the Edomite wisdom perspective.[78] While not all his claims are equally tenable, Pfeiffer argues at length that ancient Edom was a repository of Near Eastern wisdom in light of several factors. First, biblical emphasis on the legendary wisdom of Edom in exilic passages such as Jer 49:7, 20 and Obadiah solidify the prominence of Edomite wisdom. This prominence is remarkable in light of the fact that Edom's demise was predicted in biblical prophecy

75. Esau came over time to be symbolic for Israel of foreign nations and more specifically of Israel's antagonists and adversaries (Torrey, "The Edomites in Southern Judah," 20; Dicou, *Edom, Israel's Brother and Antagonist*, 13–15, 17, 26). On the enmity between Israel and Edom, see Glueck, "The Civilization of the Edomites," 77–84; Woudstra, "Edom and Israel in Ezekiel," 21–35; Gosse, "Detournement de la vengeance du Seigneur," 105–110; idem, "Le châtiment d'Edom," 396–404.

76. Sasson, "An Edomite Joban Text," 614.

77. Pfeiffer, *Introduction to the Old Testament*, 681–82.

78. "Edomitic Wisdom," 113–25. Few scholars have followed Pfeiffer's approach. One methodological weakness of Pfeiffer is that in seeking to prove the Edomite provenance of Job he begs the question as he essentially presumes that Job is the foremost example of Edomite wisdom and then uses the book of Job to outline the contours of Edomite wisdom.

and that pious Jews would later exult over its ruin. The very fact that this tradition was preserved by pious Israelites is telling for Pfeiffer insofar as a staunch refusal to commend their bitter rivals would have been more natural. Second, Solomon is said to be wiser than all the sons of the east (1 Kgs 5:10 [EVV, 4:30]), which Pfeiffer takes as an overt reference to the Edomites inasmuch as the Edomite Job was the greatest of the sons of the east (Job 1:3) and the other sages to whom Solomon is compared—Ethan and Heman the Ezrahites in particular—are most likely Edomite.[79] Pfeiffer conjectures that in Solomon's day Egypt and Edom were renowned as the foremost seats of wisdom. Third, Pfeiffer postulates that select exemplars of Edomite wisdom found their way into the Hebrew Scriptures.[80] He contends that several OT passages betray an Edomite provenance, including Ps 88 (Heman the Ezrahite), Ps 89 (Ethan the Ezrahite), Prov 30 (Agur), Prov 31 (Lemuel), and, most notably, the book of Job. Furthermore, Pfeiffer suggests that a number of other OT passages likely originated from an Egyptian provenance and were appropriated and reworked by Edomite redactors who polished these wisdom pieces for inclusion in the OT. Pfeiffer offers Ps 104 and Prov 22:17–23:14 as examples of Edomite redaction.[81] Fourth, Pfeiffer adds to his hypothesis by seeking to contrast sharply the "Jewish" theology of portions of Psalms and Proverbs with the "Edomite" theology of the Edomite passages, especially Job and Prov 30–31.[82] Pfeiffer contends that Edomite wisdom was pessimistic and agnostic. It viewed the human lot as one of toil with no hope of retributive reward or punishment. God was considered remote and unconcerned with human affairs, absolutely sovereign in his being and power, and unconnected in any tangible way to the praxis of religious ethics. Divine transcendence was most notably exhibited in the utter remoteness of the divine essence and standards vis-à-vis the human.

---

79. Although 1 Chron 2:6 places Ethan and Heman in the line of Judah through their father Zerah, Pfeiffer argues that Gen 36 points rather to an Edomite origin for Zerah and thus for Ethan and Heman (Gen 36:13, 17, 33) (with the epithet "Ezrahite" deriving from the transposition of "Zerah[ite]" ["Edomitic Wisdom," 14]).

80. As Pfeiffer argues, "There must have been in Edom a wisdom literature of decided value, and, if so, some of its productions unquestionably found readers in Judah, if not in North Israel. If such was the case, at least some fragments of Edomitic wisdom books may have found their way into the Hebrew Scriptures" ("Edomitic Wisdom," 14).

81. These observations are clear indicators of the methodology and environment in which Pfeiffer conducted his OT studies. Thus not only the Hebrews but the Edomites too were avid redactors of Scripture!

82. What Pfeiffer fails to develop satisfactorily, however, is the fact that Job is not monolithic in its wisdom perspective. To seek to develop a holistic Edomite wisdom from the multiple perspectives of the book leaves the reader asking "Which Edomite wisdom?"

The Meaning, Origin, and Theological Provenance of Eliphaz

Based upon these observations Pfeiffer concluded that the outlook of the book of Job was "without parallel in the OT" and commensurately the most extensive delineation of Edomitic wisdom which has survived to the present day.[83] Although Pfeiffer appears to be correct in a few of his observations, he overstates several of his conclusions and unfortunately begs the question when he both presumes Job to be an example of Edomite wisdom and in turn uses Job to identify the contours of Edomite wisdom. These cautions notwithstanding, some benefit may be derived from Pfeiffer's study, and this study will now identify and develop a few of the stronger threads in Pfeiffer's arguments in order to trace potential affinities to the *Weltanschauung* of this elusive Edomite wisdom which Eliphaz appears to champion.

A God Who Induces Fear

Pfeiffer asserts that "the god of the Edomites was a force of nature,"[84] and "a God [sic] mysterious in his being and almighty in power."[85] Contemplating the imminence of God was unthinkable to the Edomites, according to Pfeiffer, as they were "terrified by [conception of the] the nearness of the almighty."[86] If Eliphaz is in fact a proponent of Edomite wisdom theology, we need to draw out the implications of his view of God as over against Pfeiffer's suggested emphases to ascertain if the latter's understanding holds validity on this point. Doing so within the larger context of what is known about Edomite religion and theology, however, is no easy task. Certainty in the study of Edomite religion seems nearly out of reach, as the nature of it is a complex one,[87] and attempts to trace the religious history of a conjectured Edomite pantheon have led to mixed and unsatisfactory results.[88] Furthermore, any putative ties between Edomite religion and Edomite wisdom must be based upon meager sources. I shall attempt to outline the possible correlation, nonetheless, in the following.

---

83. "Edomitic Wisdom," 20–21.

84. Ibid., 23.

85. Ibid., 22.

86. Ibid., 24. Samuel Terrien speaks also in Barthian terms of the "wholly otherness" of Eliphaz's god (*Job*, 75).

87. See Dearman, "Edomite Religion," 119–23.

88. Although Theodore Vriezen made reference to an Edomite pantheon ("The Edomitic Deity Qaus," 332), Dearman demurs that there is no evidence of a state-endorsed pantheon as the concept is normally understood in the context of the ANE ("Edomite Religion," 128). The biblical record of 2 Chron 25:14, 20 mentioned below points to the existence of an Edomite pantheon, although no divine names are listed.

References to the Edomite god Qos (alternately Kos or Qaus) are found potentially as early as the thirteenth century BC in the inscriptions of Ramses II.[89] Other scholars are not convinced there is concrete evidence until Tiglath Pileser III in the eighth–seventh century BC within Neo-Assyrian texts which mention Qos in the context of theophoric names.[90] What is more assured is that from the eighth century on the increasing proliferation of theophoric names bearing Qos imply an increasingly established religion of the Edomite royal line and a national Edomite cult of Qos.[91] It is certain, in fact, that over time Qos came to be regarded as the patron deity of the Edomites/Idumeans.[92] The OT, on the other hand, does not overtly identify Qos as the god of the Edomites outside an occurrence of the post-exilic theophoric name Bar-Qos (בַּרְקוֹס) in Ezra 2:53 and Neh 7:55. Even though it does not mention Qos or other deities by name, a strange allusion in 2 Chron 25:14, 20 points also to Amaziah's worship of Edomite deities after slaughtering a vast number of Edomites. The Chronicler records that Amaziah "brought the gods of the men of Seir and set them up as his gods and worshiped them, making offerings to them" (v. 14). For this act of perfidy God exacts wrath upon Amaziah, and Amaziah subsequently fails militarily (v. 20).

Some scholars have suggested, based upon the paucity of references to Qos in early inscriptions, that Edom and Israel in essence worshiped the same deity from the outset and that this religious unanimity lies behind the enjoined compassion toward the Edomites in the Deuteronomic code ("You shall not abhor an Edomite, for he is your brother"; Deut 23:7).[93] Dicou and Bartlett have adduced a number of elements for this affiliation. First, Dicou suggests that the etymologies of both deities originate potentially from Arabic roots, with Qos denoting the weaponry of "bow" and Yahweh deriving from a northwest Arabic term meaning "he blows." In this way both divine names could possibly serve as constructions of the Syrian-Arabic weather deities with attributes in their divine function pertaining to the bow as well as the storm.[94] Second, in the OT Yahweh is frequently associated with the southern regions of Seir and Edom (Judg 5:4–5; Deut 33:2; Isa 63:1; Hab

---

89. Knauf, "Qaus in Ägypten," 33–36.

90. Bartlett, *Edom and the Edomites*, 204; Dearman, "Edomite Religion," 123. Bartlett cites the first reference to Qos in the theophoric name Kaush-malaku of Edom in the annals of Tiglath-Pileser III (744–727 BC) For the text, see Pritchard, *Ancient Near Eastern Texts*, 228.

91. Dearman, "Edomite Religion," 121.

92. Rose, "Yahweh in Israel—Qaus in Edom?" 28.

93. Dicou, *Edom*, 177–79; Bartlett, "The Brotherhood of Edom," 6.

94. Dicou, *Edom*, 177.

3:3).⁹⁵ This connection is claimed to identify the original provenance of Yahweh as the God who originates from the southern Negev. Third, topographical references in the Egyptian lists at Soleb in Nubia and Amara West identify the "land of the *šaśw yhwʼ*" (shasu of Yhwh) and the "land of the *šaśw sʻrr*" (shasu of Seir [?]), signifying perhaps a firmer connection.⁹⁶ Fourth, possible references to Doeg, an Edomite, worshiping Yahweh (1 Sam 21:7) and Amaziah, an Israelite, worshiping Qos (2 Chron 25:14 [n.b. this is an inference on their part as no explicit mention is made of Qos]) suggest that the two divine names might have been affiliated conceptually as pertaining to one deity and were therefore from a cultic perspective interchangeable.⁹⁷ Fifth, allegedly the religion of Edom is never explicitly censured in Deut 23 as are the religions of Ammon and Moab.⁹⁸ That the Moabites and Ammonites clearly worshipped false gods and are imprecated accordingly is clear; Edom apparently receives no such indictment. Finally, inscriptions at Kuntillet ʻAjrud which mention "Yahweh of Teman" as over against "Yahweh of Samaria" imply for Dicou a cult center of Yahweh worship in Edom as late as the eighth century BC.⁹⁹

While these scholars have delineated a number of arguments in favor of an alleged co-religion of the Israelites and Edomites, their hypothesis fails to integrate all of the biblical data. Although it is true that Edom was considered in the Deuteronomic code to be a brother to Israel, nowhere is this association clearly demonstrated to be grounded in worship of the same deity. The evidence for co-religion remains tenuous and theoretical at best, as there is simply scant evidence by which to affirm or deny the claim. The only assured references to the rudiments of Edom's religion appear much later in the biblical record when the likely features of its syncretistic polytheism are condemned in the account of Amaziah's seeking after the gods of Edom (2 Chron 25:20). In addition, later inscriptional evidence points to a syncretism in which Edom worshiped Yahweh along with other gods and goddesses as the aforementioned inscription at Kuntillet ʻAjrud makes mention of "Yahweh of Teman" and his Asherah. These references suggest more likely the aberration of a northern Israel fertility cult imported into

---

95. Bartlett, "Brotherhood," 6.

96. Ibid.

97. Ibid., 7. This proposal runs into the difficulty, however, that Amaziah is censured and punished for worshiping Edomite gods and that Doeg the Edomite is cast in a villainous light through the accession narrative rather than as a pious devotee of Yahweh (1 Sam 22:9, 18, 22; cf. Ps 52:1–9).

98. Dicou, *Edom*, 178.

99. Ibid., 179.

the Negev in the mid-ninth to eighth century,[100] a sure sign that polytheism was an accepted practice at least several centuries later. Other inscriptional evidence discovered from Horvat Uzza may also point in the direction of syncretism, at least in the acknowledgement of Yahweh as over against the already attested worship of Qos from at least the eighth century BC. Victor Sasson has more recently alleged this with respect to an inscription from a seventh-century ostracon discovered in excavations at Horvat Uzza from 1982–1988 and published in 1993. Although identified initially as Hebrew script, Sasson argues that the inscription in reality reflects an Edomite dialect.[101] He postulates that the text derives from an Edomite poetic composition originating in Edom's didactic scribal wisdom circles, propounding Edomite wisdom traditions prevalent in the era. Of special interest is that the ostracon admonishes the reader to achieve success by following the way of wisdom found in the worship of Yahweh. The prescribed path to wisdom will result in blessing "to live to old age and to give glory to Yah,"[102] suggesting—if Sasson's hypothesis is accepted—that some form of Yahweh worship in Edomite region held sway as late as the seventh century BC The exact nature of this Yahweh worship and whether or not it incorporated some form of syncretism is unclear.

A more promising correlation between the patron deity of Edom and Edom's theological orientation may be found in the connection made by Lawrence Zalcman.[103] He proposes a fresh etymology for Qos which affords greater insight into how the deity may have been understood and worshiped in the ancient Edomite context. Zalcman contends that traditional studies which have argued for an Arabic etymology of the term קוֹס have been misguided in their approach:

> That the Edomites, the most intellectually advanced of all the ancient peoples inhabiting the Jordan basin, a nation whose wisdom had become proverbial, should have relied on Arab influence in a matter of such significance as the name of their chief deity seems nothing short of incredible. . . . Much more likely, any influence occurred in the opposite direction, possibly through Nabatean meditation. Accordingly, the source of the name, if it is to be found, must be sought in the West

---

100. Dever, "Asherah," 21–37.

101. Sasson, "An Edomite Joban Text," 606–15. Although the text is not clear in all of its lines, it is identified by Sasson as pertaining to some of the peculiar features of Edomite provenance.

102. Ibid., 602.

103. Zalcman, "Shield of Abraham," 405–10.

The Meaning, Origin, and Theological Provenance of Eliphaz

Semitic language spoken by the Edomites and their closely related neighbor peoples.[104]

Zalcman argues that the etymological root for קוֹס is to be found instead in relation to the Hebrew cognate קוּץ, which he translates "feel a sickening dread." The interchange of sibilants צ and ס in allomorphs such as עלץ and עלס ("to exult, rejoice") is well attested, along with the occasional interchange of other sibilants.[105] The term קוּץ is used three times in the Hebrew Bible with the significance of perceived "dread" one person/people inflicts upon another.[106] Exodus 1:12 reports that the Egyptians "were in *dread* of the people of Israel" (וַיָּקֻצוּ מִפְּנֵי בְּנֵי יִשְׂרָאֵל), while Numbers 22:3 declares that "Moab was *overcome with dread* of the people of Israel" (וַיָּקָץ מוֹאָב מִפְּנֵי בְּנֵי יִשְׂרָאֵל). By the sign of the עַלְמָה ("virgin, young woman") who will conceive (Isa 7:14), the prophet Isaiah foretells to Ahaz that before the child knows the difference between good and evil "the land whose two kings you *dread* will be deserted" (תֵּעָזֵב הָאֲדָמָה אֲשֶׁר אַתָּה קָץ מִפְּנֵי שְׁנֵי מְלָכֶיהָ [v16]). In a related use, the Hiphil stem in Isaiah 7:6 denotes "to frighten, horrify" as in the plot of the Arameans against Ahaz and the land of Judah: "Let's go up against Judah and *terrorize* it" (נַעֲלֶה בִיהוּדָה וּנְקִיצֶנָּה).

Zalcman compares the significance of his proposed etymology of קוֹס to the conceptually and syntactically similar epithet "Fear of Isaac" (פַּחַד יִצְחָק) found in Genesis 31:42 to describe Yahweh. Later in the passage Yahweh is described simply as "Fear" when Jacob swears "by 'Fear' of his father Isaac." He concludes that "פחד is to be taken as a noun in its own right and not as an inseparable component of a single name."[107] Zalcman infers on this basis that קוֹץ/קוֹס is the stand-alone component of the original god of the Edomites known initially as the "Dread of Esau" (קוֹץ עֵשָׂו) and later simply as קוֹץ/קוֹס.

If Zalcman's proposal is correct, the etymology of קוֹס has implications for the wisdom theology of Eliphaz, who also subscribes to a deity who induces dread. In Job 4:12–21 Eliphaz vividly describes a visionary experience which overtakes him during the darkness of night.[108] Eliphaz

---

104. Ibid., 407.

105. See Waltke and O'Connor, *Biblical Hebrew Syntax*, 94. On the interchange of other sibilants, see Halton, "Samson's Last Laugh," 61–64.

106. *HALAT*, 1018.

107. Zalcman, "Shield of Abraham," 407.

108. Although interpretations of the visionary experience differ, based on the ensuing dialogues it is apparent that Eliphaz intends for his visionary experience to be accepted as special revelation from God. See Harding, "A Spirit of Deception in Job 4:15?" 146; Tsoi, "The Vision of Eliphaz," 160–61; Caesar, "Job as Paradigm for the Eschaton," 160; Albertz, "The Sage and Pious Wisdom," 252; Buttenwieser, *The Book of Job*, 48.

outlines in graphic terms the dread induced by a mysterious spirit being (רוּחַ) that passes before him.¹⁰⁹ His portrayal is particularly striking in verses 14–15: "Dread (פַּחַד) came upon me, and trembling, which made all my bones shake (הִפְחִיד). A spirit glided past my face; the hair of my flesh stood up." Eliphaz uses the term פחד as a noun and as a Hiphil-stem verb to describe the terror which the deity induces, along with the concretized synonym רְעָדָה ("trembling") to depict his psychosomatic response. In fact, throughout his speeches Eliphaz exhibits a marked preference for the term פחד to describe religious experiences which impinge upon the divine, particularly associated with divine revelation or punishment. The terminology is especially helpful as Eliphaz delineates his retributive doctrine that the wicked assuredly experience the dismaying presence of God in judgment. In his second speech Eliphaz uses the term to note that the wicked person is visited by divine retribution as indicated when "sounds of dread / terror are in his ears" (קוֹל־פְּחָדִים בְּאָזְנָיו [15:21]). In his third speech Eliphaz describes again the dread and terror that has specifically overtaken Job as an evildoer: "Therefore snares are all around you, and sudden terror (פַּחַד פִּתְאֹם) overwhelms you" (22:10), anxieties which result from the heavy hand of God. Eliphaz's God is a God who induces terror and dread. Possible later links with the divine name קוֹס are particularly intriguing.

A God Who Is Transcendent

One of the most distinguishing characteristics of the Edomite perception of God, according to Pfeiffer, is his transcendence from the created order. As Pfeiffer reports, from the Edomite perspective "God does not concern himself with human affairs and is unknown to mortals."¹¹⁰ Such an outlook is clearly consonant with Eliphaz, observable from several key statements. In the content of Eliphaz's dream-vision the spirit relays that the vast chasm between God and man allows for no mortal—much less any constituent element of the created order—to attain righteousness with God: "Can mortal man be in the right before God? Can a man be pure before his Maker? Even in his servants he puts no trust, and his angels he charges with error" (4:17–18). The divine transcendence is so great that not even the celestial angels are free from perversion. In his second speech Eliphaz reiterates

---

109. It is most likely that רוּחַ refers here to a spirit rather than merely a "breeze" or "wind," especially in the light of v. 16 where רוּחַ appears syntactically to be the subject of יַעֲמֹד ("stood [still]"), a feat which wind cannot do (Harding, "A Spirit of Deception in Job 4:15?" 148).

110. "Edomitic Wisdom," 22.

The Meaning, Origin, and Theological Provenance of Eliphaz 139

the content of that dream-vision concerning the reprehensibility of mortal man. Because of God's absolute separation from the created order, mankind is loathsome to him: "What is man, that he can be pure? Or he who is born of a woman, that he can be righteous? Behold, God puts no trust in his holy ones, and the heavens are not pure in his sight; how much less one who is abominable and corrupt, a man who drinks injustice like water!" (15:14–16).

Divine transcendence touches upon commensurate divine incomprehensibility. In the latter half of his first speech Eliphaz portrays God as largely undiscernible to mankind, a God who "does great things and unsearchable, marvelous things without number" (5:9). This strain in Eliphaz's theological perspective grows more pronounced by his third speech. Since God has no concern for the affairs of humanity, human efforts are of no value to him. "Can a man be of benefit to God? Can even a wise man benefit him? What pleasure would it give the Almighty if you were righteous? What would he gain if your ways were blameless?" (Job 22:2–3, NIV). This lack of concern for human affairs proceeds from his utter divine remoteness. "Is not God high in the heavens? See the highest stars, how lofty they are!" (22:12). For Eliphaz God is far removed from the material universe. God remains absolutely transcendent and largely unconcerned with human affairs. Even more, he is thus unknowable to mortal and depraved mankind.

A God Who Is Capriciously Retributive

Eliphaz posits a deity who is capriciously retributive. Although at times inconsistent in the application of these principles, Eliphaz in the main pontificates upon God as a cosmic justice-meter who rewards man according to his own divine whims principally in keeping with the deeds of man defined by his submission to the deity. This doctrine is a core tenet to Eliphaz's entire belief system and breaks forth at several key junctures. At the keystone of his retributive doctrine in 4:7–9, Eliphaz portrays the evildoer as one who is destroyed by the breath of God and consumed "by the blast of his anger" (4:9). God is the all-powerful arbiter in human affairs, who arbitrarily metes out punishment or blessing at the dictates of his will. "He wounds, but he binds up; he shatters, but his hands heal" (5:18). God's material blessing or destructive punishment issue forth not from divine character so much as from whether or not God takes umbrage at man's person and conduct. The evildoer is punished simply "because he has stretched out his hand against God and defies the Almighty" (15:25). Nowhere is this punishment integrally linked to divine moral character; rather it is an act of brute will. In the third speech Eliphaz propounds that the wicked are punished because "they said to God, 'Depart from us,' and 'What can the Almighty do to us?'" (22:17). In this way submission to the sheer power of God is the highest good, while defiance and opposition to the divine will is rank evil. For Eliphaz, God is indeed a retributive God but the retribution does not issue from divine moral character.

Having assessed Eliphaz's Edomite provenance and the potential implications of placing the sage within the parameters of Edomite wisdom, we turn now to examine the applied setting the Edomite sage would enjoy. As the proponent of Edomite wisdom tenets, how did Eliphaz anticipate application of these tenets to Job? What is the more precise milieu from which Eliphaz counsels Job? These questions pertain to a fuller study of the social wisdom context of Eliphaz in Job.

Eliphaz and Social Wisdom

A quarter century ago consensus was emerging among studies of Job that a noticeable gap in contemporary approaches included lack of focus upon the social milieu lying behind the composition.[111] This neglect had left unanswered significant questions relating to the context from which the book materialized. Rainer Albertz was among the first to remark in his comparative study of Job that "the issue of the social-historical background of the book of Job has hardly been put forth up to now."[112] R. Norman Whybray observed likewise in a later essay on the social ambience of biblical wisdom writers that "very few attempts have been made, despite the immense quantity of literature on the Book of Job, to study its social setting."[113] He concluded that "the social background of the Book of Job continues to be an enigma."[114]

---

111. For example, Hans-Peter Müller remarked in his study of Job that "a thorough investigation of the socio-cultural background of the book of Job belongs to the tasks of the future" ("eine gründliche Untersuchung des soziokulturellen Hintergrundes des Buches Hiob noch zu den Aufgaben der Zukunft gehört") (*Das Hiobproblem*, 128). Müller's first edition, published in 1978, includes this observation.

112. Albretz, "Der sozialgeschichtliche Hintergrund," 349.

113. Whybray, "The Social World," 238.

114. Ibid., 242. Carol Newsom also noted in her analysis of current research trends in Job: "Nothing is more strikingly absent from recent commentaries than a consideration of the social location of the book of Job." ("Considering Job," 95). More recently, Leon Roper has reiterated this shortfall and lack of consensus ("The Social Context of the Book of Job," 756).

The Meaning, Origin, and Theological Provenance of Eliphaz

Obstacles to a Social-Wisdom[115] Analysis of Job

Yet, while advancing the need for such study, proponents promptly acknowledged factors that would render its undertaking difficult. First, redactional criticism, in its attempts to synthesize the variety of genres in the book, had offered little promise of solving satisfactorily the questions of origin.[116] Earlier efforts at reconstruction of the composition process were in fact increasingly set aside in favor of literary approaches to the canonical text.[117] Second, while scholars often claimed that a social crisis of some sort had triggered composition of the book, pinpointing the precise situation for this social upheaval was notoriously elusive.[118] What is more, attempts to

---

115. Although various terms such as socio-historical, socio-cultural, and sociological, are used interchangeably in the literature to designate the social background of the book, I prefer and will use throughout this study the terminology of *social-wisdom*, as I intend to convey analysis precisely of the social milieu of the wisdom disseminated in Job.

116. Albertz, "Der sozialgeschichtliche Hintergrund," 350; Whybray, "The Social World," 242. Single authorship of Job frequently has been dismissed due to alleged incongruities between the prologue-epilogue (Job 1–2 and 42:7–17) and the dialogue (3:1–42:6) (see, e.g., Driver and Gray, *Job*, xxxviii; Pfeiffer, *Introduction to the Old Testament*, 667–75; Eissfeldt, *Einleitung in das Alte Testament*, 560–7, and Fohrer, *Introduction to the Old Testament*, 324–30). A major putative distinction includes perceived dissonance between the pious Job of the frame narrative and the contentious Job of the dialogue (see Yates, "Understanding the Book of Job," 445; Illman, "Theodicy in Job," 311–13). Such apparent inconsistencies are often overdrawn, however, and are at odds with other factors which suggest unity of authorship (see Sawyer, "Authorship and Structure," 253–57; Hoffman, "The Relation Between the Prologue and the Speech-Cycles," 165–68). As Elmer B. Smick observes: "There is as much reason to believe that the book, substantially as we have it, was the work of a single literary and theological genius as to assume it is the product of numerous hands often with contrary purposes" ("Job," 4:847).

117. Biblical studies have continued to move away from the preoccupation with redactional criticism of recent centuries. For example, one may compare space devoted to redactional study in the mid twentieth-century OT introductions of Pfeiffer, Eissfeldt, and Fohrer (see previous footnote) to Brevard Childs's shifted emphasis upon the "canonical shape" of the book and its "normative function" (*Introduction to the Old Testament as Scripture*, 533; cf. also Barr, "The Book of Job and Its Modern Interpreters," 29). Newsom observed the shift taking place in commentaries of the 80's and 90's, with the studies of de Wilde, Sicre-Diaz, and Hartley showing concern for redactional history, as compared with the studies of Habel, Clines, and Good emphasizing literary interpretation of the final canonical form ("Considering Job," 88). The latter emphasis is evident in the more recent literary studies of David Cotter, John Course, or Yohan Pyeon (Cotter, *A Study of Job 4–5*; Course, *Speech and Response*; Pyeon, *You Have Not Spoken*). A useful alternative to these approaches is the exegetical, canonical, and thematic perspective suggested by Bruce Waltke (*An Old Testament Theology*, 9–10).

118. Johannes C. de Moor rightly notes that clues within the work are insufficient to suppose a national crisis as precipitating its composition ("Ugarit and the Origin of

do so typically exposed what Whybray calls elsewhere the "danger of over-interpretation."[119] In one such example, Rainer Albertz attempts to identify the compositional *Sitz im Leben* by constructing an elaborate scenario in which the book of Job, as well as Proverbs 1–9, emerge out of tensions created between upper and lower classes caused by shifting socio-economic conditions in post-exilic Judah during the Persian period (500–300 BC).[120] Notwithstanding the intricate and carefully nuanced reconstruction by Albertz, to argue as he does for one particular social milieu as an inimitable crisis uniquely capable of producing wisdom masterpieces remains tenuous.[121] To make matters worse, the methodology required for this tack is

---

Job," 227).

119. Whybray, "Social World," 244. This admonition was levelled regarding Qoheleth, but the adage applies equally here. With respect to Job Whybray wisely warns that "it is clearly important to be on one's guard against the temptation to allow one's own interests—for example, a view of history as a struggle between the classes—to dictate one's interpretation of an ancient text" ("Social World," 241–42).

120. According to Albertz, the growing economic gap between the upper and lower classes, in tandem with the ruthless victimization of the lower classes by the elite for the sake of retaining power (cf. Neh 5:1–5), precipitated a reactionary crisis of personal piety among the more scrupulous members of the wealthy. As a consequence these pious aristocrats "theologized" wisdom. The literary result was the book of Job and Prov 1–9, compositions functioning primarily as a means to moralize personal piety and to embody a more robust theology of wisdom by which to govern one's private life (*A History of Israelite Religion*, 2:508–513). With respect to Job, Albertz remarks: "The book of Job as a whole bears witness that this personal theology of the upper class underwent a serious crisis. The reason for this is not its 'hardening into dogma,' as is constantly asserted, but the severity of the crisis which shook the community of Judah in the second half of the fifth century" (2:514). Perdue argues for much the same conditions with respect to the origin of biblical wisdom literature in the Persian period, only he proposes the opposing parties to be Zadokite priests who wielded power on the one hand and apocalypticists who were the marginalized exiles returning from Babylon on the other hand. Traditional sages comprised the centrist Zadokite party and authored Prov 1–9 as a means to retain power in training younger intellectuals. Critical sages constituted the latter visionary group and composed Job and Qoheleth as a reaction against the powerful hierocrats ("Wisdom Theology and Social History," 82–85). While Albertz's and Perdue's scenarios make for fascinating reading, one wonders if they have any basis in reality.

121. A caution is suggested by Karel van der Toorn who, while on the whole amenable to Albertz's analysis of the milieu of the Babylonian *Theodicy*, realizes that other epochs also engendered societal transformations of such a scale as to warrant heightened focus upon community theodicy ("Theodicy in Akkadian Literature," 86). Concerning ancient Israel and its context, even a superficial reading of the OT might suggest several periods of significant societal upheaval which may well have elicited a so-called crisis of theology, culminating in but by no means exclusive to the fall of Jerusalem, which undoubtedly was a greater calamity to Judah than the economic instability of post-exilic Palestine. Furthermore, it is not clear at all that a "social crisis" lies behind composition of the book, as this is a rather naïve use of historical method.

The Meaning, Origin, and Theological Provenance of Eliphaz

inherently flawed.[122] Third, the unique genre of the poetic dialogues compares too few other OT writings to obtain a standard for evaluation.[123] As a result the interpreter has little on which to base an analysis of potential social backgrounds to the composition of the book.

A Proposed Social-Wisdom Analysis of Eliphaz in Job

To develop this line of thinking further this study proffers a modest proposal for the social-wisdom context of Eliphaz in Job. To lay the groundwork for such a proposal, however, it is necessary to begin with inquiry into the social nexus of the events of the book itself,[124] most notably the social-wisdom context of Job and his interlocutors.[125] Eliphaz is the programmatic counselor who offers a comprehensive theodicy from which the other friends merely tangentially corroborate his theses.[126] As the leading sage and Edomite wisdom counselor his perspective is integral to the author's purpose.[127] Collocating the wisdom perspective of Eliphaz within his

---

122. With respect both to Job and to the Babylonian *Theodicy*, Albertz arrives at his socio-historical reconstruction inversely. That is, he takes the dating commonly assumed by scholars for composition of the work and finds a crisis from that era to serve as the backdrop, creatively finding data to support his hypothesis. Thus, he infers from the scholarly consensus back to the text rather than working from the text outwards. Roberts notes that given the subjective nature of attempts to interpret Job by reference to a particular historical background or linguistic means "one cannot use the date of the book, therefore, to provide a ready-made background for its interpretation" ("Job and the Israelite Religious Tradition," 112–13). Johannes C. de Moor contends that an exilic or post-exilic date is highly unlikely, especially since the book contains no clear allusion to a national calamity which, given the theme, might have been introduced ("Ugarit and the Origin of Job," 227). Furthermore, as Whybray observes "speculative theology was already being written in other parts of the ancient Near East before the first millennium BC" ("Social World," 239), rendering the often held post-exilic date superfluous.

123. Whybray, "Social World," 239. Portions of Job may be compared to a few of the wisdom psalms, but no other book has sustained dialectical dialogue as Job.

124. Such an approach presupposes a gap between the events taking place in the book of Job and the composition of the book. Though this is nearly a consensus among scholars, it is debated (see, e.g., Andersen, *Job*, 23–32). For discussion of the date of the book and lack of consensus, see Moor, "Ugarit and the Origin of Job," 225–27.

125. As Whybray suggests, one of the principal aspects of Job most probable to identify the social background of the author is the figures of Job's three disputant-friends ("Social World," 240).

126. Nicholson, "The Limits of Theodicy," 74; Gordis, *The Book of Job*, 519. This view seems confirmed in that Eliphaz is singled out by Yahweh for rebuke in Job 42:7.

127. Gordis, *The Book of God and Man*, 77; Volz, *Hiob und Weisheit*, 50; Hartley, *The Book of Job*, 103.

social-wisdom context promises to provide potentially a clearer picture of the social milieu standing behind the book of Job.

In terms of its own social-wisdom context, the book of Job uniquely combines elements of the folk and royal wisdom traditions of the ANE. Eliphaz, moreover, is intended to personify and idealize elements of ANE wisdom traditions as the prototype of a wisdom theology most notably consistent with that of the Mesopotamian sage.

Wisdom in the ANE and in Israel

An outline of the contours of wisdom theology within the ancient context is a useful way to begin an analysis of Eliphaz and Job.[128]

The Significance and Development of Wisdom in the ANE

As discussed previously, the book of Job places its characters within the cultural context of the ANE. Hailing from Teman on the northern portion of the Edomite plateau,[129] Eliphaz emerges from the societal matrix of Edom, a region renowned for its wisdom (Jer 49:7; Obad 8).[130] Situated along the King's Highway (Num 20:17), Edom was central in the flow of traffic and commerce in the ancient world, undoubtedly providing much exposure to the cultures and societies of its day.[131] The biblical record states that Edom also had established a monarchy prior to the advent of the Saulite kingdom of Israel (1 Chron 1:43), suggesting that perhaps early on Edom had the societal cohesiveness and structure to support the social context for wisdom that was so emblematic of other corners of the ANE.[132] A major civilization

---

128. In what follows when speaking of wisdom literature, I am referring in particular to the biblical books of Job, Proverbs, and Ecclesiastes, which along with a few wisdom psalms (e.g., Pss 37, 49, 73) constitute canonical wisdom literature. For a helpful overview, see Waltke and Diewert, "Wisdom Literature," 295–328. Mesopotamian wisdom literature is more difficult to elucidate in that it is diffused over a broad swath of genres and settings. Typically the terminology is used for any literary works which encompass themes and ideology of wisdom.

129. Edelman, "Edom," 10.

130. On the Edomite provenance of Eliphaz, see also Clines, *Job 1–20*, 57.

131. See above. This is evident, for example, from theophoric names of Edomite chiefs or clans which were included in topographical lists compiled by Rameses II at Karnak (Oded, "Egyptian References," 47–50).

132. This possibility has been questioned recently, however (Crowell, "A Reevaluation," 404–416). The difficulty with this view, of course, is the lack of inscriptional evidence to support the theory.

The Meaning, Origin, and Theological Provenance of Eliphaz

with which the Edomites would have interacted, particularly in matters of wisdom, was Mesopotamia, a heavyweight of ancient wisdom.[133] A brief survey of the wisdom of Mesopotamia provides insight into the context of the earliest wisdom movements, and the type of wisdom that Eliphaz would have had at his disposal to proffer to Job.

The Meaning of Wisdom in Mesopotamia

The basic meaning of wisdom within the culture of Mesopotamia was "intelligence and skill that enable one to perform practical deeds, particularly deeds for the benefit of the gods."[134] Wisdom was closely linked to special know-how, whether in the sphere of material concerns or in the realm of the gods.[135] Akkadian terms such as *emqu*, "well thought out, deliberate, skilled, experienced, educated," and *hassu*, "intelligent," emphasized "capability, knowledge required of a craft or *techné*, skill, expertise."[136] The terms underscore "*action* and active knowledge" often describing activity in cultic contexts,[137] in which the wise man is the initiate qualified to perform magic, divination, incantation, and exorcism.[138] Special knowledge of the occultic arts, known as mantic wisdom, touched upon the sage's esoteric knowledge of forces beyond the human realm, considered to be singular revelation from the deity.[139] A notable feature of the training of the sage involved acquisition of the skill of careful listening, and the ear was considered the seat

---

133. Anthony Ceresko rightly observes: "Critical scholarship, centered in Europe and the West, has tended to ignore the Bible's own tradition that wisdom comes from the East. Job was 'the greatest of all the people from the East' (Job 1:3), and 'wise men from the East came to Jerusalem' seeking the newborn 'king of the Jews,' according to Matthew's Gospel (2:1-2)" (*Introduction to Old Testament Wisdom*, 13). To these references one may add 1 Kgs 4:30, which affirms that "Solomon's wisdom surpassed the wisdom of all the people of the east."

134. Sweet, "The Sage in Akkadian Literature," 51.

135. Ibid., 65.

136. *CAD*, 6:127-28.

137. Denning-Bolle, *Wisdom in Akkadian Literature*, 38-39, emphasis hers; cf. also Soden, *Akkadisches Handwörterbuch*, 1417. The active element of wisdom was evident also in the skillful, crafty expertise of the gods Marduk and Ea, the latter being especially wily in escaping self-imposed predicaments (ibid., 39-42).

138. Lambert, *Babylonian Wisdom Literature*, 1; Toorn, "Theodicy in Akkadian Literature," 86-89; Denning-Bolle, *Wisdom in Akkadian Literature*, 65.

139. Grabbe, *Priests, Prophets, Diviners, Sages*, 177.

of intelligence.[140] Hearing was central in the pursuit of wisdom as the pupil was to attend assiduously to the ancient secrets of the sages.[141]

Typically the king was the archetype of wisdom, endowed with wisdom from the gods in order to execute various deeds pleasing to the deities, such as the building of temples.[142] Other craftsmen were viewed as partaking of wisdom, particularly as it applied to the employment of their trade.[143] Beyond this, a class of the professional sage, known as the *ummia*, applied sapience in the daily discharge of special skills: (1) collecting proverbs and aphorisms about everyday life; (2) the writing of wisdom tracts, such as disputations between various items, such as between the hoe and the plow or between the cattle and the grain; (3) collecting, compiling, and arranging an extensive collection of archival, historical, and legal documents, wisdom and otherwise, such as royal inscriptions, legal contracts, royal correspondences, king and dynasty lists, and law codes; and, (4) the composition and revision of literary documents: myths and epic tales, hymns, prayers and chants, and laments.[144]

A wide collection of wisdom-oriented literature from Mesopotamia provides insight into the setting and trajectory of its wisdom.[145] The several genres contained in this literature are helpful for appreciating the scope of Mesopotamian wisdom, including incantation texts, divination texts, proverbs, and dialogue-texts.[146] Some notable examples include *Ludlul*

---

140. Thus Marduk is portrayed with four ears (Denning-Bolle, *Wisdom in Akkadian Literature*, 41).

141. As Denning-Bolle suggests: "Ancient Mesopotamian culture placed great importance on the act of hearing: witness the common phrase 'my son' in the instructional texts in which we can visualize the leader or master 'lecturing' to his pupil" (ibid., 36).

142. Sweet, "The Sage in Akkadian Literature," 57. Cf. Solomon's wisdom as applied to the building of the temple in 1 Kgs 5–6.

143. Specific professions identified as enjoying wisdom were (1) craftsmen, (2) architects and builders, (3) soldiers, (4) cult officials, (5) diviners, (6) exorcists, (7) musicians, (8) physicians, (9) scribes, (10) counselors, and (11) teachers (Sweet, "The Sage in Akkadian Literature," 57–64).

144. Kramer, "The Sage in Sumerian Literature," 32–37.

145. *Contra* Lambert, who states that "'Wisdom' is strictly a misnomer as applied to Babylonian literature" (*Babylonian Wisdom Literature*, 1) (although the title of his work contravenes his suggestion). In making this statement, Lambert uses too narrow a definition of wisdom in the Mesopotamian context, owing more it seems to the semantics of Hebrew usage (ibid.). If we use the terminology of "wisdom literature" to denote a specific type of literature that alone defines and is characteristic of wisdom, Lambert is correct. Several works and genres of Mesopotamian literature, however, may be classified as consisting of "Wisdom" according to the definitions we have outlined above (see Buccellati, "Wisdom and Not," 39–40, 44).

146. Denning-Bolle provides a helpful survey of the various types of Mesopotamian

bēl nēmeqi, the Babylonian *Theodicy*, "A Dialogue between a Man and His God," the *Šurpu* incantation series, the DINGIR.ŠA.DIB.BA incantation series, the *Lipšur* litanies, and the *Eršahunga* prayer. These works will be discussed in greater detail below.

The Origins of Mesopotamian Wisdom

The origins of Mesopotamian wisdom were based on Sumero-Akkadian traditions which reach back to sages "before the [Sumerian] Flood" who were known by the term *abgal*, such as Adapa, those responsible for bringing culture and civilization to Sumer and mankind in general.[147] Also designated by the term *apkallu*, these ancient sages occupied an intermediary position between the divine and human spheres as the harbingers of universal laws or truths who were to "insure the correct functioning of the plans of heaven and earth."[148]

From about 2500 BC educational institutions known as the *edubba* or "tablet-house," were established in numerous Sumerian cities for instruction in the scribal arts.[149] Over time the *edubba* matured and evolved into centers of culture and learning, particularly in cities such as Nippur and Ur, where scholars flourished in the arts of academic and humanist studies. Numerous literary works were developed and refined. The headmaster of the *edubba* was the *ummia*, the scholar par excellence who developed the curriculum and closely supervised all elements of training. Graduates of the *edubba* who succeeded were selected for key posts and were influential in shaping Sumerian intellectual and spiritual life.[150]

---

wisdom works (*Wisdom in Akkadian Literature*, 56–67, 85–175).

147. Kramer, "The Sage in Sumerian Literature," 31.

148. Reiner, "The Etiological Myth of the Seven Sages," 2, 4. Cf. *CAD*, 1.2:171–73; Denning-Bolle, *Wisdom in Akkadian Literature*, 48–56.

149. The *edubba* are known from lexical and literary documents excavated at Fara (ancient Šuruppak) and Tell Abu-Salabikh (Kramer, "The Sage in Sumerian Literature," 31). The reader also may find interest in an artist's depiction of the *edubba* in Kramer, "The World of Abraham," 45 [painting by Tom Lovell]. In the artist's rendition the *ummia* is checking the exercise of a pupil in a 2000 BC classroom. The room depicted represents the *edubba* or tablet house, which allowed only boys as students.

150. Ibid., 32. Kramer offers insight into the psyche of students of the *edubba*: "The personalities of these *edubba* graduates had been deeply affected by, and imbued with, the competitive, aggressive drive for preeminence and prestige, for victory and success, that characterized much of Sumerian behavior, and was fostered and nutured by the teachers of the *edubba* who wrote often in ridicule and scorn of the poor, failing student and in lavish praise of the promising student, who would become 'the leader among his brothers, the chief among his friends, the highest among his fellows'" (37).

The Meaning and Development of Wisdom in Israel

While the understanding of wisdom in ancient Israel shared some features with Mesopotamia, unique qualities are evident in a survey of its terminology.

The Meaning of Wisdom in Israel

The Israelite concept of wisdom derives primarily from the meaning of the Hebrew term חָכְמָה, denoting "technical dexterity, skill, experience, cleverness, worldly and pious wisdom."[151] Related biblical terms for wisdom include בִּינָה, "discernment," and תְּבוּנָה, "discernment, cleverness, skill,"[152] along with דַּעַת, "knowledge (technical or otherwise), cognition," and מוּסָר, "chastisement, discipline, warning, admonition."[153] On the negative side terms such as כְּסִיל, "(in practice) foolish, (religiously) impudent," and סָכָל, "foolish, fool," and עָרוּם, "crafty, clever"[154] illustrate the opposite pole to the wise.

The most comprehensive analysis of wisdom terminology remains that of Whybray.[155] He provides an inductive survey of the root and immediate cognates of חכם within OT wisdom literature and elsewhere in the Old Testament, and catalogues the various categories of usage.[156] He argues that,

---

151. *HALAT*, 301–2. Related are the cognates חכם, "to be wise," and חָכָם, "skillful, clever, wise" (ibid.)

152. *HALAT*, 119 and 1548–49. See also von Rad, *Wisdom in Israel*, 53.

153. *HALAT*, 219 and 528.

154. *HALAT*, 465, 713, and 835.

155. Whybray, *The Intellectual Tradition*, 74. Some have questioned his use of the terminology *intellectual tradition* in the title, which suggests a class of the "wise" (a view which Whybray argues against) and presumes an approach to the composition of the OT which compartmentalizes texts into competing traditions without warrant (Zinkand, review of *The Intellectual Tradition*, by R. Norman Whybray, 387–88).

156. His categories of usage for חכם outside of traditional wisdom literature include (1) passages in which חָכְמָה refers to manual skill or other non-intellectual activities including magic (Exod 7:11, 41; 1 Kgs 7:14; Pss 58:6; 107:27; Isa 3:3 40:20 Jer 9:16; 10:9; Ezek 27:8, 9); (2) passages where the root חכם refers to human intelligence in a very general sense, not as applied to deeper existential issues (Exod 1:10; Judg 5:29; Jer 18:18; Hos 13:13); (3) passages which refer to the חֲכָמִים of foreign countries without further effort to define the nature of the wisdom (Jer 49:7; Obad 8; Zech 9:2; Isa 47:10; Isa 44:25; Jer 50:35; 51:57); (4) passages where literary dependence on another source is clearly identified (e.g., Chronicles); and (5) passages in which the term does not bear any special significance (Ezra 7:25; Esth 1:13; Ps 105:22; Deut 16:19; 34:9; Hos 14:10) (83–85). Some of Whybray's categorizations may be called into question, such as his classification of Jer 18:18 as meaning "intelligence" generally, a passage in which חָכָם

The Meaning, Origin, and Theological Provenance of Eliphaz

along with חכם, only terms apparently exclusive to the intellectual tradition[157] are a reliable guide to apprehension of the nature and scope of the wisdom tradition.[158] These terms are בִּינָה, "understanding," בַּעַר, "stupid, brutish," כְּסִיל, "stupid," לֵץ, "scoffer, arrogant man," לֶקַח, "understanding, teaching, persuasiveness," נָבוֹן, "intelligent," סָכָל, "senseless, foolish," עָרוּם, "prudent, shrewd, cunning," and תּוּשִׁיָּה, "wisdom, success."[159]

From the above brief survey we may draw a few observations. First, Israelite wisdom includes a moral element that is largely absent from Mesopotamian wisdom.[160] Wisdom begins with the fear of Yahweh; the fool is he who disregards Yahweh (Prov 1:7). Obedience to the precepts of the Torah is fundamental to wise living. As Kaiser suggests, the fear of Yahweh is a unitive feature of OT theology, "one of the formal connectors between the wisdom writers and the theology of the *tora* and prophets."[161] Second, lesser emphasis is placed in Israelite wisdom literature upon mantic wisdom. While Mesopotamian wisdom encompassed skill in cult and magic lore, Israelite wisdom focused rather upon knowledge acquired through heeding the instruction of the wise (Prov 1:8). More than industrial expertise or initiation into occultic secrets was at stake. Third, Israelite wisdom places greater emphasis on a theology of creation as undergirding its epistemological and theological framework.[162] Thus the Hebrew sage recognizes, for example, that God created the earth by wisdom ("The Lord by wisdom founded the earth; by understanding he established the heavens," Prov 3:19), that man is indebted to express appreciation for the beauty and appropriateness of God's created order ("He has made everything beautiful in its time,"

("the wise") is parallel to the priest and the prophet: "for instruction will not perish from the priest, nor counsel from the wise, nor a word from the prophet" (author's translation). With the terms *priest* and *prophet* constituting distinct figures in Israelite society, it is somewhat doubtful that חָכָם here merely means "intelligent (people)."

157. *The Intellectual Tradition*, 124–49. Whybray has a total of four categories of lexical terms for wisdom. His fourth category is the most salient for our study and consists of "words whose occurrences are restricted to books and passages whose attachment to the intellectual tradition is certain or where such an attachment cannot be ruled out *a priori*" (142). He includes three other categories: (1) terms occurring only in Proverbs, Job, and/or Ecclesiastes; (2) terms occurring frequently in Proverbs, Job, and/or Ecclesiastes as well as in other OT traditions; and (3) terms characteristic of Proverbs, Job, and/or Ecclesiastes but occurring occasionally in other OT traditions.

158. Ibid., 142.

159. Ibid., 142–49.

160. As Lambert argues, while Babylonian wisdom refers in most part to expertise in cult and magic lore, Hebrew wisdom is intellectual ability with emphasis on piety (*Babylonian Wisdom Literature*, 1).

161. Kaiser, "Integrating Wisdom Theology," 199.

162. Zimmerli, "The Place and Limit of Wisdom," 148.

Eccl 3:11]) while enjoying its good gifts ("From the fruit of his lips a man enjoys good things," Prov 13:2 [NIV]), and that man must acknowledge his own inadequacies and limitations in light of God's created order ("[Man] cannot find out what God has done from the beginning to the end," Eccl 3:11. "[God] does great things beyond searching out, and marvelous things beyond number," Job 9:10).[163]

The Sources and Development of the Wisdom Movement in Israel

The Bible extols the wisdom of Solomon and places him squarely in the midst of the origins of wisdom in ancient Israel.[164] In spite of the straightforwardness of the biblical account, a lively debate ensued in the twentieth century concerning the genesis and coalescence of wisdom in Israel.

CRITICAL STUDIES AND THE ORIGINS OF WISDOM

In his study of Israelite wisdom, Whybray lamented that the meaning of the term *wisdom* had become so diffuse that "scholarly confusion may well make the word 'wisdom' useless for the purposes of Old Testament study."[165] This disorientation had set in, according to Whybray, primarily from an unraveling consensus about the fundamental nature of "wisdom" and the sphere in which it had originated and disseminated within Israel. A number of scholars have held that the wisdom movement began in the royal courts of Israel, where it was stimulated by the need to train state administrators and conducted along the lines of the educative wisdom traditions for the scribes of Egypt and Mesopotamia.[166] Challenging this view, however, was a more recent understanding which argued that wisdom evolved over time in the context of Israel's legal tradition, where it was the product of the tribal period and served to regulate life within the context of the family or clan.[167] In Whybray's opinion this more recent understanding threatened to

---

163. See Zuck, "Theology of the Wisdom Books," 217–19.

164. Solomon is reputed for his wisdom, as 1 Kgs 3 onward makes clear, culminating with the account that "God gave Solomon wisdom and understanding beyond measure, and breadth of mind like the sand on the seashore" (1 Kgs 4:29).

165. Whybray, *The Intellectual Tradition*, 2.

166. See, e.g., von Rad, *Wisdom in Israel*, 15ff; Volz, *Hiob und Weisheit*, 101.

167. See, e.g., Westermann, *Roots of Wisdom*, 2–5. According to Westermann, this folk wisdom view was presupposed at the beginning of the twentieth century, while the royal educative wisdom view was of more recent vintage, the product of Gerhard von Rad (*Weisheit in Israel*) and his student H. J. Hermission (*Studien zur israelitischen*

undermine the entire enterprise of wisdom studies by positing an altered trajectory of development and influence upon the OT canon.[168]

An impetus behind distinguishing these sources of wisdom was recognition of two differing strands of wisdom with the canonical wisdom books, namely a corpus of practical wisdom instruction as over against a corpus of speculative wisdom. These allegedly disparate poles—a practical, down-to-earth wisdom dealing with matters of everyday life (folk tradition) vis-à-vis a speculative, abstract wisdom confronting the enigmas of life (royal or scribal tradition)—were the basis for such bifurcation on the origins of wisdom. Nevertheless, though distinct to the modern interpreter, these putative differences were by no means so discrete to the ancient interpreter.[169] A brief survey of both types of wisdom suggests an alternative proposal for the development of wisdom and for Job's and Eliphaz's place within wisdom circles.

Folk Wisdom

In his study of the origins of apodictic law, Erhard Gerstenberger posits an incipient and ancient connection of the law with the motifs of wisdom and wisdom literature, particularly in the warnings to flee sin.[170] Gerstenberger views two types of wisdom as giving impetus and shape to the book of Proverbs: the impersonal, objective style of aphorisms (Prov 10:1–22:16) and the parenetic style of direct address (Prov 1–9; 22:17–24:22).[171] The former style is likely the oldest form of proverbial wisdom, according to Gerstenberger, while the form of direct address is associated with the "education" provided by the father or head of the tribe.[172] Wisdom thus develops from ancient times within the family setting as a means to train up future generations.

Spruchweisheit).

168. Whybray, *The Intellectual Tradition*, 3–5.

169. See, e.g., Denning-Bolle, *Wisdom in Akkadian Literature*, 31–32; cf. Buccellati, "Wisdom and Not," 36. According to Denning-Bolle in the broader ANE context the abstract and concrete pursuits of wisdom were often merged, given the absence of the compartmentalization of the sacred vis-à-vis secular common to the modern era.

170. Gerstenberger, *Wesen und Herkunft*, 49.

171. Ibid., 119–20.

172. Ibid., 121. Gerstenberger proposes that the "Sentenzen" ("aphorisms") of the proverbs in Prov 10:1–22:16 constitute the most basic form of proverbial wisdom and are therefore the authentic and most ancient proverbs (ibid., 120). In time, "the more or less rhetorical 'You' squeezed in between the actual proverbs" leading to a combination of aphoristic and parenetical forms, notable for example in Jesus Sirach, which brings together the ancient and more recent forms in a purposive way (121n1).

Carol Fontaine notes: "While there is no conclusive textual evidence of a formalized position of sage in operation within the family and tribe, there is ample evidence that many roles associated with the sage are carried out by heads of households, mothers, elders, and other tribal leaders."[173]

Royal Wisdom

In his analysis of the historical sources and development of wisdom, William McKane, assumes royal, educative origins of wisdom. He concludes that originally wisdom was primarily "humanistic," a kind of secular empiricism, rising out of commitment to effective administration and policy-making, with little regard to personal piety.[174] The secular character of wisdom, according to McKane's hypothesis, led to an ongoing dialectical confrontation with the Yahwistic prophetic tradition, until at last wisdom succumbed to a sacred overhaul, being incorporated into the prophetic tradition by the introduction of religious perspectives into its otherwise sheerly pragmatic counsel.[175] This view of the development of wisdom was clearly in line with the trajectory of wisdom studies in the twentieth century, which proposed wisdom as springing from the royal court-schools of Egypt and Mesopotmia.

Stuart Weeks, however, questions the "assured results" of McKane and others that wisdom was solely the product of a royal educative context. He argues that the actual material of the canonical book of Proverbs demonstrates little concern for the administrative preoccupation that McKane and others would make front and center, and Weeks concludes that there is no reason to suggest that wisdom was of the exclusive provenance of administrative schools in Israel. Rather, he suggests that the more probable scenario is a royal collocation of proverbs in which sayings were sought far and near for their pointedness or pithiness and then adapted and arranged for pleasing effect, combining pleasing insights with a moral prod.[176]

---

173. Fontaine, "The Sage in Family and Tribe," 164.

174. McKane, *Prophets and Wise Men*, 46, 53–54. Cf. also Westermann, *Roots of Wisdom*, 1. Bruce K. Waltke rightly contends that no such hard and fast distinction is ever made between the secular/profane and religious/pious in ANE literature ("The Book of Proverbs," 302–317). Stuart Weeks finds the theory that Israelite wisdom originally was secular is "wanting in almost every respect" (*Early Israelite Wisdom*, 73).

175. McKane, *Prophets and Wise Men*, 55–57.

176. Weeks, *Early Israelite Wisdom*, 160.

The Meaning, Origin, and Theological Provenance of Eliphaz 153

A Synthetic Approach to the Origins of Wisdom

Others have proposed the origins of wisdom as something of a synthesis between the disparate poles observed above. Ronald Clements, for example, posits that wisdom developed in three stages in ancient Israel.[177] (1) Folk wisdom emerged in clans and families, providing practical advice and intellectual stimulus. This wisdom took the forms of allegory, fable, and aphorism. (2) Monarchical wisdom was nurtured in the royal court and came to be associated with etiquette and court life. Here wisdom took on the character of royal art, with greater sophistication of forms. The king was idealized as the illustrious exponent of wisdom. (3) Post-exilic wisdom became the most consistently literary stage of wisdom, making its most lasting contribution to Israelite intellectual life. The "literary jewel" of Job was produced at this latter stage, according to Clements, along with several significant wisdom pieces. Others have assumed a similar progression in the development of wisdom from its early tribal setting to a more sophisticated royal context. The difficulty on the whole with Clements's view, however, is the presupposition that the lion's share of Israel's literary wisdom output was reserved to the allegedly volatile post-exilic period. In view of the antiquity of several Mesopotamian literary wisdom pieces dating from 1500–1000 BC[178] as well as the literary tradition of Ugarit dating from about the same period,[179] one is shortsighted to assume that Israel was not capable of producing literary wisdom until the fifth century BC.

Anthony Ceresko outlines the development of wisdom along different lines.[180] Early, popular wisdom developed in the family or clan, disseminated primarily by father or mother. The book of Proverbs contains echoes of this early wisdom, as in 1:8, "Hear my son, your father's instruction, and forsake not your mother's teaching." This setting was primary in the education and socialization of younger generations.

---

177. Clements, *Wisdom in Theology*, 23–25.

178. Lambert proposes an early date for two important Mesopotamian wisdom pieces: *Ludlul bēl nēmeqi* somewhere between 1500–1300 BC during the Cassite period (*Babylonian Wisdom Literature*, 26) and the Babylonian *Theodicy* around 1000 BC (ibid., 63).

179. Johannes C. de Moor notes that most of the Ugaritic literature was composed in the fourteenth to thirteenth centuries BC before Ugarit was eradicated by the militant Sea Peoples sometime between 1190 and 1185 BC ("Theodicy in the Texts of Ugarit," 110).

180. Ceresko, *Old Testament Wisdom*, 17–20. I have followed much of Ceresko's observations in the following, although the outline of the wisdom which was part of the village eldership derives from the biblical text.

Another early context was the town council or village elders who sat at the gate.[181] This revered assembly was expected to execute wisdom in the just mediation of disputes, in the observation of the legality of business transactions, and in oversight rendered to the practical, everyday affairs of the village. The origins for elders functioning in this capacity originates in ancient times, as Moses gathers seventy elders from Israel for the Spirit to empower them as judges and mediators in Num 11:16–25. Later, Moses recounts the selection of elders, emphasizing that wisdom was a primary criterion in their choice ("wise, understanding, and experienced men," Deut 1:13). Deuteronomy 25:7–8 provides an example with casuistic law regarding disputes over levirate marriage: "If the man does not wish to take his brother's wife, then his brother's wife shall go up to the gate to the elders and say, 'My husband's brother refuses to perpetuate his brother's name in Israel; he will not perform the duty of a husband's brother to me.' Then the elders of his city shall call him and speak to him."[182]

The village eldership was in many ways the cultural bridge from the folk or clan wisdom to later monarchical wisdom. The assembly of elders utilized the popular wisdom insights that were common stock to the culture and applied them in the practical matters of everyday disputes. For example, in the levirate transaction of Ruth 4:10–12 Boaz redeems Ruth in keeping with Mosaic legal stipulations and then calls upon the village eldership to acknowledge the transaction. The elders in turn eloquently bless the union of Boaz and Ruth using analogical imagery familiar to the ancient wisdom context:[183]

> Then all the people who were at the gate and the elders said, 'We are witnesses. May the LORD make the woman, who is coming into your house, like Rachel and Leah, who together built up the house of Israel. May you act worthily in Ephrathah and be

---

181. On this, see also Fontaine, "The Sage in Family and Tribe," 163–64.

182. On other instances in casuistic law in which elders settle disputes, see Deut 19:12; 21:19; 22:13–21. Evidence elsewhere of the prominence of the village council persists throughout the OT, such as Lot's sitting in the gate of Sodom (Gen 19:1), Job's recollection of his former prestige in the city gate (Job 29:7), and Mordecai's distinguished place at the royal gate (Esth 5:13).

183. The use of image and metaphor, both as word picture and as means for comparing like/unlike things in the pursuit of knowledge, was integral to wisdom. An example is the adept counsel of Hushai to Absalom in which he uses several analogies: "like a bear robbed of her cubs," "like the heart of a lion," "like the sand by the sea shore" (2 Sam 17:7–12) (Ceresko, *Old Testament Wisdom*, 20). The use of such analogy for comparison "suggests a deeper order hidden from the eyes of the naïve and untrained" (ibid., 39). Examples of this use are found also in the proverbs: "Like a dog that returns to his vomit is a fool who repeats his folly" (Prov 26:11).

renowned in Bethlehem, and may your house be like the house of Perez, whom Tamar bore to Judah, because of the offspring that the LORD will give you by this young woman (Ruth 4:11–12, ESV).

An implication of this is evident as well in the shrewd dealings of Absalom while out of favor with the Davidic court, illustrating the cunning described earlier as the negative side of wisdom. In 2 Samuel 15 Absalom stands by the gate to intercept litigants entering Jerusalem to seek judgment from the king. Absalom advises them that the king has no one appointed to resolve their disputes—adding innocuously that if he were king such would not be the case. Thus, through his chicanery Absalom "stole the hearts of the men of Israel" (v. 6). The longest description of the esteem bestowed upon the village elders for their wisdom is found in Job 29, where Job describes his former splendor as an elder in the gate (likely underscoring the account for effect): "When I went out to the gate of the city, when I prepared my seat in the square, the young men saw me and withdrew, and the aged rose and stood; the princes refrained from talking and laid their hand on their mouth; the voice of the nobles was hushed, and their tongue stuck to the roof of their mouth" (vv. 7–10).

In addition to the elders, occasionally notable individuals obtained a reputation for wisdom and were sought after for counsel. Two such figures renowned for wisdom were Ahithophel and Hushai the Archite, who pit their wise counsel to Absalom against one another in 2 Sam 16–17 (Hushai's counsel as subterfuge to deliver David). It is unclear whether these men were professional advisers to the king or merely elders with a reputation for sapience whom the king consulted (cf. 1 Chron 27:33). Also in 2 Samuel two wise women were identified, including a wise woman of Abel (2 Sam 20:14–22) and a wise woman of Tekoa, the latter summoned by Joab as part of his plot to seat Absalom on the throne through political intrigue (2 Sam 14).

The most significant development of wisdom came with the advent of the "scribal school," an integral part of the royal court in ancient times. As Ceresko observes, "When Israel made the fateful step across the line from the decentralized organization of the tribal confederacy to the increasingly centralized and authoritarian state under David, the need arose for a more complex administrative apparatus."[184] Within this context scribes and overseers were accorded a prominent position in the administration of the kingdom (2 Sam 20:23–25). Solomon further consolidated and bolstered the monarchical bureaucracy with his extensive building projects, wide ranging

---

184. Ceresko, *Old Testament Wisdom*, 18.

trade network, and division of the nation into tax districts (1 Kgs 3–11). The tasks of these scribes encompassed at least three activities: (1) Daily administration of the state, including royal correspondences, record keeping, and organization of the royal archives; (2) education of future scribes as well as leaders and administrators for roles as governors, ambassadors, or advisors to the king; (3) literary output, which included instructional material for the aforementioned training, as illustrated in the identification of provenance in Prov 1:1, 10:1, and 25:1. Undoubtedly literary wisdom compositions were a significant feature of the scribal period.[185]

Thus, we have observed two distinct approaches to the wisdom of ancient Israel. Critical scholars have typically posited on one hand a clan model in which wisdom evolved along with the law of Israel from its inceptive days to be used pragmatically in training clan chiefs of the loosely confederated tribal amphictyony. Or, wisdom is viewed as having originated as a purely secular enterprise valuable for the training of officials and diplomats and only at a very later stage inseminated with a religious disposition. Distinct from these approaches, however, is the foregoing sketch, which views the development of wisdom as one of organic continuity, beginning with the family framework and culminating in the royal wisdom of the Solomonic and later eras. In addition, this outline of the progression of wisdom has the advantage of according with the biblical record, and thus is to be preferred to the critical reconstructions.

The Place of Job and His Friends in the Wisdom Movement

The remaining task before us is to collocate Job and his friends in the stream of wisdom progression outlined in the preceding section. If the book of Job is a product of scribal tradition, one might posit that Job and his friends ought to be considered professional sages, part of a class of the vocational wise. As Whybray notes, however, the evidence of the book runs contrary to this: "The dialogue in Job is represented as taking place not between 'learned men' belonging to a professional class, but between a (once) wealthy landowner and his friends: that is, between educated farmers."[186] He concludes:

---

185. Ceresko is more tentative on this point than he should be, positing only the Yahwist epic of the Pentateuch, assorted collections of the sayings of Prov 25–29, and the Throne Succession Narrative (2 Sam 9–20; 1 Kgs 1–2) as emerging from this period (ibid., 19). There is no reason to reject that other significant works such as Job and Ecclesiastes were composed during this period.

186. Whybray, *The Intellectual Tradition*, 65.

"If a precise context is presupposed, this might well be the *sōd*, or friendly discussion among equals by the elders of the city 'in the gate.'"[187]

It is evident from a survey of the book of Job that the prominence of elders at the city gate was a significant concept, a key component to recognizing the social setting of Job and Eliphaz. In Job 5:4 Eliphaz portrays the inescapable plight of the wicked, affirming that "his children are far from safety; they are crushed in the gate, and there is no one to deliver them." Though depicting the fate of the godless, it is clear that Eliphaz and the others consider themselves to be of equal, if not superior, social standing than the rogue evildoer. In his second speech, Eliphaz appeals to ancient traditions which have been handed down from generations, a likely reference to the distilled wisdom which he inherited from the village elders: "I will show you; hear me, and what I have seen I will declare (what wise men have told, without hiding it from their fathers)," Job 15:17-18.[188]

As we have already observed, Job recalls his former prestige at the gate in Job 29, claiming that "men listened to me and waited and kept silence for my counsel. After I spoke they did not speak again, and my word dropped upon them" (vv. 21-22). He concludes that he "chose their way and sat as chief, and . . . lived like a king among his troops, like one who comforts mourners" (v. 25). As Job recounts his own actions, the just and sapient mediation of disputes is within purview of the elders: "I put on righteousness, and it clothed me; my justice was like a robe and a turban. I was eyes to the blind and feet to the lame. I was a father to the needy, and I searched out the cause of him whom I did not know" (29:14-16). Further, in 31:21 Job adjures that he never mistreated orphans even though he might have counted on the nefarious support of his alliances at the city gate.[189] This allusion underscores the power of the town council for good or ill. The preceding passages suggest a *Sitz im Leben* for Job and his friends within the context of the village eldership, those who resorted to wisdom and insight in dealing with day-to-day matters of governance and legal disputes.

Thus, it is most likely that Job and his friends reflect the pastoral wisdom of the village eldership. Thus Eliphaz was for his part, if one may infer from the biblical account, most likely a chieftain and elder from Teman (Job

---

187. Ibid.

188. One might argue nonetheless that Eliphaz has a rather narcissistic predilection for his own version of the ancients' wisdom, as observable in his multiple use of personal pronouns for emphasis (for a similar interpretation, see Caesar, "Job," 435-47). On the notion of Eliphaz's reference being to the wisdom of the town eldership, see Whybray, *The Intellectual Tradition*, 65.

189. For the difficulties and various interpretations of this verse, see Clines, *Job 21-37*, 1023.

2:11). He would have been highly esteemed for his wise and righteous counsel, as well as his ability to resolve disputes and legal grievances in a pleasing way. He was a man of prestigious social standing. This understanding clears the way for an analysis of Eliphaz's wisdom perspective as a renowned elder who is called upon to settle the dispute underlying the book of Job; it is a dispute ultimately between Job and God.

Eliphaz in the Context of Ancient Wisdom

As we have observed, Eliphaz was likely a town elder who was eager to dispense of his counsel. But further clues to Eliphaz's wisdom perspective will be adduced in the following discussion.

The Gentile Provenance of Eliphaz

Eliphaz is identified in rabbinical literature as one of only a handful of Gentiles in human history who will testify at the end of the age on behalf of Israel that she observed the Torah in its entirety.[190] The amusing claim notwithstanding, the interpretation is of interest in that it presupposes an early understanding of Eliphaz as a leading representative of the Gentiles. This understanding undoubtedly arose in part due to Eliphaz's provenance in the book of Job as a Temanite of Edomite nationality. To the Jewish people Edom came to represent metonymically the nations at large and specifically Israel's antagonist.[191]

Mayer Gruber develops this Gentile-Israelite dialectical perspective in Job, arguing contrary to previous scholars,[192] who see in Job the outlook of the unconventional Israelite challenging the orthodox view of his day. In reality, however, Gruber argues that "Job's point of view, which, in the end,

---

190. *'Abodah Zarah*, 3a. Eliphaz elsewhere is identified as one of seven Gentile prophets who uniquely prophesied to the heathen, vis-à-vis Israelite prophets who prophesy primarily to Israel (*Baba Bathra*, 15b).

191. Evidence, for example, is found in Isa 34, in which the opening of the oracle is addressed to the "nations" and "peoples" and the Lord is said to be "enraged against all the nations" (vv. 1, 2), while the remaining oracle specifies only Edom and Bozrah as targets of judgment (vv. 5, 6, 9). A similar metaphorical use is employed by Ezekiel in Ezek 35–36, where a prophecy of judgment against Mt. Seir (chap. 35) is followed by a prophecy of comfort to Israel that she will see similar desolation taking place in all the surrounding "nations" (36:5–7). See Dicou, *Edom, Israel's Brother and Antagonist*, 17, 49.

192. E.g., Gordis, *The Book of God and Man*, 48–52; Tsevat, "The Meaning of the Book of Job," 101–3; Whybray, *Two Jewish Theologies*, 4.

is supported by God in Job 42, is the traditional and authentic Torah of God and Israel, while the rantings of Job's three friends represent human wisdom or Gentile wisdom, which, from a biblical point of view, is inferior to divine wisdom."[193] Gruber's view, which appears to be on the right track, has two significant components which will be explored in what follows. First, the tenor of the book of Job is Semitic in orientation. That is, the perspective of Job, God, and the human author is ultimately in line with the later normative trajectory of Israel's theological perspectives, although set in a context of extreme suffering and theodicy.[194] Second, Eliphaz and the other friends represent human or Gentile wisdom, which the book portrays as ultimately inferior to the divine wisdom culminating in the Yahweh speeches of Job 38–41. I will take this a step further to argue that Eliphaz is in fact a specimen of the finest sapience that Gentile wisdom had to offer.[195] He holds numerous elements of the theological perspective of the wisdom specialist from the ANE, incorporating sapiential viewpoints from Mesopotamian wisdom. From this, a conclusion will be drawn that an overlooked purpose of Job is its polemical defense of Yahweh's divine wisdom as over against the human wisdom and counsel of the nations.

The Jewish Orientation of the Book of Job

John Walton has written a useful essay on the book of Job in which he outlines the Jewish features of the writing.[196] While recognizing numerous points of contact between Job and Ugaritic language and literature on the one hand, Walton emphasizes a set of uniquely Semitic perspectives which hint at Jewish authorship.[197] (1) Through Job's three friends the book seeks to defend the justice of God, which is at odds with the perspective of other

193. Gruber, "Human and Divine Wisdom," 92.

194. On this, see the section below "The Jewish Orientation of the Book of Job."

195. As Joseph Blenkinsopp contends, Eliphaz and his fellow counselors "are not straw men, set up just to be knocked down by Job's arguments. On the contrary, they represent the best thinking available at that time within the intellectual tradition of the sages" (*Sage, Priest, Prophet*, 52). See also Newsom, "Job and His Friends," 239–40.

196. Walton, "Job 1: Book of," 344. Not all of Walton's arguments are equally compelling, nor does the present writer agree *en toto* with Walton's conclusions. His arguments are presented here merely to present the logic of his position and to draw inferences from the tenable portions of his argumentation.

197. Although Walton argues for a provenance likely during the monarchical period, when he suggests a religious context existed which could give expression to the outlook of the book, I contend for a much earlier date (sixteenth–fifteenth century BC) when several similar Babylonian works of theodicy were written. This approach also accounts for the unusual linguistic and semantic features of the book.

ANE cultures and suggests a distinctly Jewish perspective. Usually in the ANE the gods were considered to be interested in social justice, people prayed to them for the bestowal of justice, and the king was distinctively seated by them to establish justice for the commonweal of the people. Yet the gods themselves were often capricious, not necessarily considered just nor in need of any efforts to defend their inherent justice. Furthermore suffering was not tied as integrally to divine justice, so the impetus behind the book that God's justice must be exonerated is distinctly Jewish.[198] (2) Job denies paying homage to the sun or moon, indicating that to do so would be an act of infidelity to God (Job 31:26–28).[199] Such scruples were not common to the ANE, as faithfulness to one deity above another was not an issue. Walton concludes that only in Jewish theology would worship of celestial deities be considered an offense. (3) The book's view of God demonstrates a uniquely Jewish perspective. Although the friends argue in favor of appeasement, they do not prescribe a ritual remedy, which would have been the norm in the ANE. Furthermore, throughout the book God is acknowledged not to be dependent in any way upon human activities, a concept which is difficult to identify outside the Jewish people. (4) The fact that the appeasement solution offered by the friends is rejected indicates that a Jewish perspective is underscored. Orthodox Jewish theology deemed appeasement to God to be reflective of a flawed perspective. Within this framework it is apparent that the book and author provide persuasive clues to a Jewish provenance. If the main thrust of Walton's proposal is accepted, the role of Eliphaz and the purpose for the book come more clearly into focus.

Eliphaz's Mesopotamian Wisdom Perspective

Earlier the study sought to establish that Eliphaz exhibits an affinity to traits of the so-called Edomite wisdom perspective and that this wisdom perspective was likely tied closely to Mesopotamian views due to contact between the peoples and cultures along prominent trade routes. A close analysis of Eliphaz's wisdom perspective corroborates several points of contact with the wisdom tradition of Mesopotamia.

---

198. E.g., as Karel van der Toorn argues, the concern of Mesopotamian wisdom was not so much the righteousness of the gods themselves as the soundness of its cherished tenet of retribution, viz., that no evil deed (i.e., offence to the god) would be unrequited with commensurate punishment ("Theodicy in Akkadian Literature," 59).

199. This is the weakest of Walton's arguments—all of the friends brook no allowance of polytheism although they are not purported to be Jewish. One might argue that this perspective is Edomite also.

The Use of the Retribution Model

Frequently in the literature on the book of Job Eliphaz and the other interlocutors are identified as purveyors of the so-called Deuteronomic canon of retribution which prescribes that in this life the wicked and righteous are punished or rewarded by Yahweh in accordance with their deeds.[200] In what follows I will argue that while Eliphaz holds to a doctrine of retribution, it is not the retribution of the Deuteronomists but rather the retribution perspective common to several ANE cultures, most notably Mesopotamia.

Retribution in Mesopotamia

As previously observed, the tenet of retribution was integral to the philosophical outlook of ancient Mesopotamia. No doubt existed in the mind of the ancients about the existence of the gods or their rule over the realm of mankind. Rather, the ideological struggle which gave birth to a compendium of ancient Near Eastern wisdom writings was the integration of that understanding with other observations regarding the occasional inconsistency of the outworking of retribution.[201] Toorn observes that the retribution model derives from a basic presupposition of similarity between the human and divine realms: "According to the common ANE principle of similarity, gods exceeded humans in strength, longevity, beauty, size, and appetite, but their emotions and values mirror those of their human servants."[202] The correspondence between gods and humans extends beyond a likened perception of right and wrong to the more basic level of impulse: the gods experience pleasure, revulsion, or anger in ways equivalent to those of humans. The god

---

200. Perdue, *Wisdom in Revolt*, 118; Scott, *The Way of Wisdom*, 136; Rankin, *Israel's Wisdom Literature*, 91; Parsons, "Guidelines for Understanding," 403.

201. Toorn contends: "What is at stake, in the Mesopotamian theodicy texts, is the validity of the retribution model and the notion of divinity it implies. According to the prevalent conception in modern times the co-existence of moral integrity and suffering precludes divine providence or the existence of God altogether; in the view of the ancients unmerited suffering called into question the validity of the premises underlying the doctrine of retribution" ("Theodicy in Akkadian Literature," 59). The Mesopotamian perspective at its core is tied to its particular view of Fate. As Buccellati observes, Fate is not a god in the personal sense but rather an "ultimate referent" in conditioning the behavior of the gods: it is "more divine than the gods in its degree of absoluteness" ("Wisdom and Not," 36). Walton refers as well to these "control attributes" (Sumerian *me*) which exist outside the jurisdiction of the gods and to which the gods themselves are obligated ("Retribution," 648).

202. Toorn, "Theodicy in Akkadian Literature," 60.

Erra, for example, a unique god in the Babylonian pantheon,[203] experiences various passions which are analogous to those of humans as he prepares for battle in the later legend which bears his name:

> —Arise, Erra! By laying waste the country
> How relieved your mind will be, how much your heart will rejoice—
> Erra's limbs are wear[y] like those of one who cannot fall asleep.
> 'Shall I get up? Shall I keep on lying,' he wonders.
> To his weapons he says: 'Stay in the racks!'
> To the Sibitti, unrivalled heroes: 'Back to your seats!'
> Until you (=Išum) rouse him, (Erra) will lie in his chamber:
> With Mami, his consort, he will indulge in pleasure.[204]

Erra experiences joy, fatigue, indecisiveness, and sexual pleasure in much the way humans do. In the area of retribution, one builds upon this notion of likeness to posit further that the gods and humans likewise share in the appreciation of social norms which involves the ethics of beneficence toward others, especially those of a lower class or position. An example of the latter is found in the Babylonian *Counsels of Wisdom* in which retribution according to deeds is assumed to derive from the analogous moral assessments of the gods, particularly Šamaš, the god most responsible for the administration of justice:

> Do not insult the downtrodden and [...]
> Do not sneer at them autocratically.
> With this a man's god is angry,
> It is not pleasing to Šamaš, who will repay him with evil.
> Give food to eat, beer to drink,
> Grant what is asked, provide for and honour.
> In this a man's god takes pleasure.
> It is pleasing to Šamaš, who will repay him with favour.[205]

Thus the gods value charitable deeds toward the distressed but disapprove of scorn toward the needy. Pleasure or repulsion are the poles which move the god to action, and so it is incumbent upon the human servant to align his behavior with what is pleasing to the god. From this understanding, the code of retribution naturally flows. If one is suffering, the god is

---

203. See Cagni, *The Poem of Erra*, 14–16. Cf. also Burns, "The Chastening of the Just," 20.
204. "The Poem of Erra," lines 13–20 (*The Poem of Erra*, 26).
205. Lambert, *Babylonian Wisdom Literature*, 100–3 (lines 57–64).

revulsed; if one is rewarded, the god is pleased. Personal observation becomes the means by which one is assessed to be pleasing or displeasing to the god. Toorn draws out the implications:

> According to the traditional theology of the Mesopotamian scholars the doctrine of retribution is a law of nature, so to speak, that does not require an act of disclosure on the part of the gods. It can be known from observation, extrapolation, and speculation on the principle of similarity. Divine retribution is *Erfahrungswissen*, knowledge from experience.... It is the common view of ancient Near Eastern wisdom traditions that retribution belongs to the realm of visible facts; it is no secret that needs to be revealed. The cause-and-effect model of retribution creates the collective conviction that a happy life is the consequence of correct behaviour, and that suffering is on principle merited.[206]

Consequently, the value judgment placed by the god upon one's behavior is duly observable in the outward circumstances of one's life. Those who are happy and successful have been rewarded in kind; those who are despondent and suffering have been punished in kind.

Retribution in Eliphaz

The norm of retribution likewise undergirds much of Eliphaz's wisdom outlook. He sets this tone early in the first round of dialogue: "Is not your fear of God your confidence, and the integrity of your ways your hope? Remember: who that was innocent ever perished? Or where were the upright cut off? As I have seen, those who plow iniquity and sow trouble reap the same" (Job 4:6–8). This passage leads directly into the core of Eliphaz's retributive doctrine in 4:7–9, as discussed above. So then, one may discern in Eliphaz, as noted above, both personal observation as determinative for value judgment ("As I have seen") and the integral connectivity placed between deed and consequence ("who that was innocent ever perished?" and "those who plow iniquity ... reap the same"). The significance of personal observation in Eliphaz's interpretation of Job's plight becomes especially evident at the culminating close to his first speech "Behold, this we have searched out; it is true. Hear, and know it for your good" (5:27). In the second speech Eliphaz provides an extended and eloquent peroration concerning the retribution requited upon the evildoer, using analogies from war and famine to depict

---

206. Toorn, "Theodicy in Akkadian Literature," 61.

his utter desolation. He sums up the plight of the wicked: "For the company of the godless is barren, and fire consumes the tents of bribery. They conceive trouble and give birth to evil, and their womb prepares deceit" (15:34–35). The impending destruction for the evildoer is inexorable. In his final speech Eliphaz applies the retribution principles unilaterally. Job is in agony precisely because of his sin: "Is not your evil abundant? There is no end to your iniquities." Yet he offers hope to Job in that if he turns back to God, good will come to him since the righteous are duly rewarded. "Agree with God, and be at peace; thereby good will come to you. Receive instruction from his mouth, and lay up his words in your heart. If you return to the Almighty you will be built up" (22:21–23a). Thus, we have seen that in his understanding of retribution, Eliphaz is much in line with the perspective of Mesopotamian wisdom and its code of divine reprisal for one's deeds.

The Use of Prayer or Incantations

Another area of concord between the perspective of Eliphaz and that of Mesopotamian wisdom is the use of prayer to rid oneself of evil and regain the favor of the deity. In Mesopotamia these prayer formulae took the form of incantations which were spoken aloud by the religious specialist to extirpate the evil which had befallen the victim and to ritually purify him.[207] Prayers or incantations were the means to regain the favor of the gods. As the counselor in the Babylonian *Theodicy* admonishes, "Seek the kindly wind of the god, what you have lost in a year you will make up in a moment."[208]

Mesopotamian Incantations

One notable incantation series is *Šurpu*, an incantation prescribed when the sufferer does not know by which deed he has offended the god and/or the existing world-order.[209] In response to his plight, the sufferer delineates a long list of all possible sins, ranging from violation of religious taboos to violations of societal moral norms. The victim additionally adds request for release from inadvertent oaths which may have conjured up evil, occultic powers against him. As Denning-Bolle observes:

---

207. Denning-Bolle, *Wisdom in Akkadian Literature*, 57.
208. "Babylonian *Theodicy*," lines 241–42 (*BWL*, 85).
209. Reiner, *Šurpu*, 3.

> What is interesting is that, when the rites are described, all possible offences are listed as being absolved by those rites. It is obvious that the victim who requires these services has not committed so many offences. The prevalent theme in this series is that of not knowing what transgression a man has done, what evil he is guilty of. The only way to solve this dilemma is to enumerate all possibilities."[210]

In the incantation the sufferer acknowledges both his culpability before the gods and his ignorance of the nature of the misdeed:

> He does not know what is a crime against god,
> He does not know what is a sin against the goddess.
> He scorned the god, despised the goddess,
> His sins are against his god, his crimes are against his goddess.[211]

After pointing out his inadvertent scorn of the god, the sufferer goes on to confess to a litany of sins perpetrated against others. Although it is certain that in reality he did not commit all these deeds, he enumerates them as personal sins. He confesses to family strife and hatred, lying, deceptive business dealings, removing boundary markers, extortion, immorality, murder, oppression of the needy, gossip, sorcery, violation of religious taboos, neglect of the gods, political insubordination, broken vows, impermissible affiliation with the accursed, and misuse of omens:[212]

> He took money that was not due to him
> (but) [did not ta]ke mo[ney due to him],
> he disinherited the legitimated son (and)
> [did not est]ablish (in his rights) the le[gitimated] son.
> He put on (var.: took away) his neighbor's clothes,
> (and) did not clothe a young man when he was naked.
> He ousted a well-to-do young man from his family,
> Scattered a gathered clan.[213]

The incantation ends with an appeal to over fifty gods in the pantheon to release the evil, followed by a final plea for the god and goddess to stand by him and to extirpate the crimes.[214]

---

210. Denning-Bolle, *Wisdom in Akkadian Literature*, 57.
211. Šurpu, tablet II, lines 32–34 (Reiner, Šurpu, 13–14).
212. Šurpu, tablet II, lines 35–128 (ibid., 14–15).
213. Šurpu, tablet II, lines 43–44, 50–53 (ibid., 14).
214. Surpu, tablet II, lines 129–192 (ibid., 16–18).

The DINGIR.ša.dib.ba incantations are a series of incantations whose title means "incantation for appeasing an angry god."[215] Lambert states the purpose of the rite:

> The point of these prayers in every case is derived from the misfortune or suffering of the speaker. It is presumed that this had occurred and that the personal god (sometimes coupled with the personal goddess) was angry. This anger, then had to be appeased. The basis for this anger is variously explained. Occasionally the sins of parents or other relatives are suggested as the cause (I 115–18). More commonly the sufferer assumes that he himself must be at the root of the trouble. Sometimes he simply confesses his many sins in the hope that confession alone will appease the angry god.[216]

The sufferer again seems unaware of the exact crimes committed but all possibilities are explored for resolution:

> My iniquities are many: I know not what I did.
> My god, expunge, release, suppress the anger of your heart,
> Disregard my transgressions, receive my prayers,
> Turn my sins into virtues.[217]

The victim pleads with the deity for clemency in view of the universality of human sinfulness:

> In respect of offence, iniquity, transgression, and sin
> I have offended against my god, sinned against my goddess, have committed
> [All] my iniquities, all my sins, all my transgressions.
> I promised and then reneged; I gave my word but then did not pay.
> I did wrong, I spoke improper things,
> I repeated [what should not be uttered], improper things were on my lips.
> In innocence I went too far.
> . . .] . . . my god, forgive.
> May [my transgressions] be released, [turn] my sins into virtues.
> . . .] . . . you determine.
> . . .] . . . who sinned, save completely.

---

215. Lambert, "Dingir.ša.dib.ba Incantations," 267.
216. Ibid., 270.
217. Tablet I, lines 29–32 (ibid., 275).

> Who is there who has not sinned against his god?[218]

He enumerates specific sins committed in an effort to gain the god's favor:

> I committed offence against the god who created me,
> I did an abomination, ever doing evil.
> I coveted your abundant property,
> I desired your precious silver.
> I raised my hand and desecrated what should not be so treated.
> In a state of impurity I entered the temple.
> Constantly I committed a terrible abomination against you,
> I transgressed your rules in what was displeasing to you.
> In the fury of my heart I cursed your divinity,
> I have continually committed iniquities, known and unknown.[219]

Another series of incantations, the *Lipšur* litanies, includes a long succession of incantations which were to be spoken over the sufferer to exorcise the sin and curse.[220] The opening rite of purification for the victim is described as follows:

> If NN, son of NN, has sinned, may he be absolved, may he be wiped clean;
> If he was negligent, if he committed errors, same (=may he be absolved, may he be wiped clean);
> If he committed assault, if he committed murder, same;
> If he ate unwittingly what is taboo to his god,
> If he had intercourse with the priestess of his god, same;
> If he had intercourse with the wife of his friend,
> If his actions were displeasing to his god, same;
> If he talked to an accursed man.[221]

The incantation again goes on to list any and all possible sins from which the worshipper seeks divine resolution.

Lastly, the *Eršahunga* prayer offers insight into the type of hymnic prayer the sufferer was to offer to appease the god:

> You look with favour, look with steadfast favour on me.

---

218. Tablet I, lines 121–32 (ibid., 281).
219. Tablet I, lines 139–48 (ibid., 283).
220. Erica Reiner, "*Lipšur* Litanies," 129–49.
221. *Lipšur*, lines 81–85 (ibid., 137).

> Lord god, you look with favour, look with steadfast favour on me.
> When you look with favour, that man lives. Look with steadfast favour on me.
> The man on whom you look with favour lives. Look with steadfast favour on me.[222]

By gaining the favor of the god the victim would be restored to a righteous and happy path as evidenced in his outward circumstances.

Prayer Resolution in Eliphaz

The preceding analysis offers insight at a few points into Eliphaz's admonitions to Job. First, as in the method of the incantations, Eliphaz repeatedly reminds Job to turn to God in prayer. In his first speech Eliphaz exhorts Job: "As for me, I would seek God, and to God would I commit my cause" (5:8). He follows up this insistence with a reminder that submission to God brings blessing: "Behold, blessed is the one whom God reproves; therefore despise not the discipline of the Almighty" (5:17). Although not using the explicit terminology of prayer, the suggestion is that if Job would submit to the ways of God—by inference in humble prayer—all would be well. Nevertheless, Job is belligerent. So Eliphaz must return with a warning in his second speech regarding Job's perilous refusal to submit in prayer: "Why does your heart carry you away, and why do your eyes flash, that you turn your spirit against God and bring such words out of your mouth?" (15:12–13). The implication is that rather than obtaining reconciliation through acquiescent prayer, Job is further offending God by his continued impious outbursts.

In his third speech Eliphaz returns to his more urbane urging of Job to call upon God, with an extended call to pray as the climax of his oration: "Agree with God, and be at peace; thereby good will come to you. Receive instruction from his mouth, and lay up his words in your heart. If you return to the Almighty you will be built up" (22:21–23). Eliphaz follows up with one final plea for the happy outcome that awaits penitent prayer: "You will delight yourself in the Almighty and lift up your face to God. You will make your prayer to him, and he will hear you, and you will pay your vows" (22:26–27). It is clear that Eliphaz understands that resolution to Job's plight rests in restorative prayer, likely modeled in some respect after the incantational prayers. An invocation by Job in line with the *Eršahunga* prayer will provide a ready-made blessing.

---

222. "*Eršahunga* prayer," lines 29–32 (Lambert, "Dingir.ša.dib.ba Incantations," 291).

Second, the Mesopotamian incantation series provides insight into Eliphaz's most pointed remonstrance with Job. In his third speech Eliphaz delineates to Job a lengthy list of evils which Job has committed. "For you have exacted pledges of your brothers for nothing and stripped the naked of their clothing. You have given no water to the weary to drink, and you have withheld bread from the hungry. The man with power possessed the land, and the favored man lived in it. You have sent widows away empty, and the arms of the fatherless were crushed" (22:6–9). In light of the incantation series, it is likely that since Job has refused to confess any sins to God, Eliphaz is more than willing to provide some prodding. Rather than merely an outline of sins which he imagines Job to have committed,[223] Eliphaz is preparing the way for Job's reversal by offering a generic listing of evil acts to which Job can concede. In doing so Job is assured restoration to divine approval as well as extirpation of the harrying evil.

The Use of Revelation / Divination

Another link between the wisdom of Mesopotamia and that of Eliphaz is found in mantic wisdom, that wisdom which is associated with special revelation from the divine.

Divination in Mesopotamia

Toorn notes the importance divination occupied in the wisdom perspective of Mesopotamia:

> The traditional science of divination (*bārûtu*) was claimed to have a celestial origin. It was traced back to Enmeduranki, once king of Sippar, who owed his knowledge to a heavenly revelation. The Enmeduranki myth applies the concept of revelation only to part of the body of religious lore—albeit an essential one. Divination played a crucial role in the religious practice of Mesopotamia since it allowed human beings to discover the purposes and plans of the gods. It was thus an essential channel of communication.[224]

Divination formed a connectivity between the wisdom of practical affairs and the mysteries of the cult, and the wise was the initiate who was able

---

223. So Clines, *Job 21–37*, 555.
224. Toorn, "Theodicy in Akkadian Literature," 87.

to span the divide successfully.²²⁵ Furthermore, divination provided insight into the nature of reality, thus creating a revelatory means to acquire knowledge of the mundane yet unalterable aspects of reality.²²⁶ As Lester Grabbe observes:

> 'Wisdom/sage' overlaps both the supernatural and mundane spheres. In the same way it overlaps the functions of priests, prophets, diviners, and the like. Wisdom might be acquired through lore passed down by priests or by prophets to their disciples or by diviners from their teachers or by diviners on the basis of spirit revelation. The term 'wise' could apply to counsellors and scribes but also to any person with special knowledge or skills above the ordinary. Those able to contact and in some way harness the supernatural, such as priests, prophets, and diviners, were in a special position to acquire wisdom and be called 'wise.'²²⁷

The sufferer in *Ludlul bēl nēmeqi* recognizes the significance of divination as a means of restoration and therefore appeals to this means as an avenue for appeasement of the offended deity (although to no avail).

> The omen organs are confused and inflamed for me every day.
> The omen of the diviner and dream priest does not explain my condition.²²⁸

> The diviner with his inspection has not got to the root of the matter,
> Nor has the dream priest with his libation elucidated my case.
> I sought the favor of the *zaqīqu*-spirit, but he did not enlighten me;
> And the incantation priest with his ritual did not appease the divine wrath against me.²²⁹

The special knowledge of divination could occur through various means, one of which was dreams through which the god revealed. For example, the aforementioned sufferer in *Ludlul bēl nēmeqi* has revealed to him through a series of dreams that Marduk intends to restore him. He describes the spectral aura of the dream experience:

---

225. Denning-Bolle, *Wisdom in Akkadian Literature*, 65–66.
226. As Buccellati notes: "Rather than an attempt to bend reality, divination may be viewed as the ability to perceive laws which *de facto* link the various aspects of reality" ("Wisdom and Not," 36).
227. Grabbe, "Prophets, Priests, Diviners, and Sages," 58.
228. *Ludlul bēl nēmeqi*, tablet I, lines 51–52 (*BWL*, 33).
229. *Ludlul bēl nēmeqi*, tablet II, lines 6–9 (ibid., 39).

The Meaning, Origin, and Theological Provenance of Eliphaz

> His hand was heavy upon me, I could not bear it.
> My dread of him was alarming, it [. . . . . me].
> His fierce [.] .. was a tornado [. . . . .]
> [. . .] . . . he stood over me,
> [I . . .] and [my] body was numbed.[230]

Interestingly, as part of this dream-experience, an incantation priest is used to deliver to the sufferer the good news that Marduk has seen fit to restore him:

> An incantation priest, carrying a tablet,
> 'Marduk has sent me.
> To Šubši-mešrê-Šakkan I have brought prosperity,
> From Marduk's pure hands I have brought prosperity.'[231]

Thus, dream experience was an important part of revelation from the divine and an integral component to Mesopotamian wisdom.

Related to the concept of revelation/divination was the notion of intercession and protection by a personal, watchful angel, who was charged with closely guarding the devotee of the god. The sufferer in *Ludlul bēl nēmeqi* mourns that even his "protecting spirit" (*lamassi*)[232] had abandoned him to his fate:

> The benevolent angel who (walked) beside [me] has departed,
> My protecting spirit has taken to flight, and is seeking someone else.[233]

For the sufferer this fate is a foretoken of the severity of his agony and sure abandonment by the displeased deity. The sage counselor in the Babylonian *Theodicy* likewise recognizes the significance of the protective spirit: "He who waits on his god has a protecting angel."[234] For the sufferer in *Ludlul* the only certain solution to his predicament was intercessory prayer to the god, counsel which sounds strikingly similar to the advice proffered by Eliphaz:

> For myself, I gave attention to supplication and prayer:

---

230. *Ludlul bēl nēmeqi*, tablet III, lines 1–3, 13–14 (ibid., 48–49).

231. *Ludlul bēl nēmeqi*, tablet III, lines 41–44 (ibid., 51).

232. Rykle Borger translates similarly "Schutzgeist" (*Mesopotamisches Zeichenlexikon*, 567).

233. *Ludlul bēl nēmeqi*, tablet I, lines 45–46 (*Babylonian Wisdom Literature*, 33).

234. The Babylonian *Theodicy*, line 21 (ibid., 71).

> To me prayer was discretion, sacrifice my rule.[235]

These means of restitution were the only hope for the hapless sufferer.

Special Revelation in Eliphaz

Eliphaz recounts in his opening speech a unique experience of revelation which he received apparently from an apparition that appeared to him during the night. "Now a word was brought to me stealthily; my ear received the whisper of it. Amid thoughts from visions of the night, when deep sleep falls on men, dread came upon me, and trembling, which made all my bones shake" (4:12–14). He describes this visitor as a "spirit" and a "form" (vv. 15, 16). Given the similarities in Eliphaz's description of his nocturnal visit to the descriptions in *Ludlul bēl nēmeqi*, it is quite likely that Eliphaz has experienced a dream. The dream provides an extraordinary revelatory context to communicate to Eliphaz the rather banal truth of the universality of human sinfulness. Thus, Eliphaz leverages this experience to heighten his credibility and add weight to his counsel to Job. Eliphaz's use of special revelation is unusual in the corpus of Hebrew wisdom literature but makes sense against the backdrop of Mesopotamian wisdom. The similarities provide further suggestion that Eliphaz is smugly within the tradition of Mesopotamian wisdom.

In addition, Eliphaz makes allusion to the departure of the benevolent angel from Job, a certain sign that the deity is displeased. In the midpoint of his first speech Eliphaz alludes to the sufferer's loss of angelic protection and intercession: "Call now; is there anyone who will answer you? To which of the holy ones will you turn?" (Job 5:1). There are other hints of this idea along the course of his speeches. For example, in expounding upon his doctrine of remedial suffering, Eliphaz appears to suggest protection from demons who are feared as wreaking destruction upon mankind (see exegesis below for a fuller treatment): "You shall be hidden from the lash of the tongue, and shall not fear destruction when it comes. At destruction and famine you shall laugh" (5:21–22a). This protection likely comes from the presence of a protective spirit/angel who watches over the upright if he sustains the favor of God. Perhaps an allusion to this is also to be found in Eliphaz's promise of restoration for Job should he heed the former's counsel: "You will pray to him, and he will hear you" (22:26). Given the utter transcendence of Eliphaz's deity, one may posit that this is accomplished through the agency of his protective spirit being.

---

235 *Ludlul bēl nēmeqi*, tablet II, lines 23–24 (ibid., 39).

Lastly, Eliphaz appeals to intercessory prayer as the only certain means of restitution. "As for me, I would seek God, and to God would I commit my cause" (5:8). In the final entreaty of his third speech, Eliphaz offers one final solicitation. "Agree with God, and be at peace; thereby good will come to you" (22:21). As a result "you will make your prayer to him, and he will hear you, and you will pay your vows" (22:27). Eliphaz's counsel is conspicuously similar to the approach of the sufferer in *Ludlul bēl nēmeqi*.

Conclusion

This section has traced the contours of wisdom in Israel and the ancient Near East to suggest that in the book of Job Eliphaz is intended to be representative of Gentile wisdom. As part of this purpose, Eliphaz exhibits numerous wisdom traits which link him closely to the wisdom tradition of Mesopotamia. If the reader accepts that Job was written within an Israelite context but that Eliphaz, the chief antagonist to Job, was representative of ANE wisdom, a proposed social milieu for Job becomes possible.

First, the canonical book of Job was composed likely during a period in which didactic theodicy was flourishing in the ANE, given the polemic for Yahweh's wisdom vis-à-vis that of the nations, as I have suggested. Most of the so-called ANE wisdom literature of this sort originated from as early as the Third Dynasty of Ur onward into the Cassite era, 2000–1500 BC, a period in which the development and spread of Babylonian literature was most prevalent.[236] Although issues of authorship are largely beyond the pale of the present study, such a provenance aligns most readily with a sixteenth- to fifteenth-century authorship of Job by Elihu.[237]

Second, this interpretation suggests a clearer purpose for the book of Job, in addition to the usual themes offered, as a polemic for the divine wisdom of Yahweh vis-à-vis the alleged wisdom of other peoples and their distinctive gods. A similar polemic lies behind the claim centuries later that Solomon's wisdom surpassed the wisdom of all the peoples of the East (1 Kgs 4:30). In the book of Job the Yahweh speeches constitute the apex of the book, while in the end Eliphaz is soundly reproved (42:7). This perspective emphasizes further that true wisdom recognizes the sovereign knowledge and freedom of the Lord, while inferior human insight lays but empty claim to true wisdom and knowledge. Having proposed a background and social

---

236. *Babylonian Wisdom Literature*, 10–11. Foster, "Dialogue Between a Man and His God," 485; Nougayrol, "Une Version Ancienne du 'Juste Souffrant,'" 240.

237. On this, see the Appendix. For several cogent arguments *against* Elihuan authorship, see McCabe, "Elihu's Contribution to the Thought of Job," 47–80.

setting for Eliphaz and his wisdom, the stage is set for a closer look at the content of his speeches. Exegesis of his discourses will provide additional insights into the nature of this enigmatic sage.

5

Exegesis and Correlation of the Eliphaz Speeches

WITH A FRESH UNDERSTANDING of the background and orientation of Eliphaz gained in the preceding analysis, we now turn to a more detailed investigation of salient portions of the Eliphaz speeches in Job. The following includes my own translation of the text of Eliphaz's speeches combined with exegetical notes based upon the understanding gained in the preceding of Eliphaz's role as the ANE wisdom counselor. The textual basis for this analysis is the MT. My particular focus is upon those passages identified in the opening chapters as pivotal for one's overarching interpretation of Eliphaz: (1) Eliphaz's archetypal retributive doctrine in 4:5–11; (2) Eliphaz's special revelatory experience in 4:12–21; (3) Eliphaz's doctrine of remedial suffering in 5:17–27; (4) Eliphaz's status as doyen and proponent of ancient wisdom traditions in 15:7–19; (5) Eliphaz's use of the sin listing in 22:2–12; and (6) Eliphaz's rebuke from Yahweh in 42:7.

Eliphaz's First Speech (Job 4–5)

Consensus generally is held that Eliphaz's first speech (Job 4–5) contains two distinct sections (4:2–21 and 5:1–27), neatly separated according to the chapter division.[1] These sections often are classified under the larger genre of "disputation speech," a *Gattung* that involves an argument between two (or more) parties who hold to differing points of view, and is typical of the

---

1. Course, *Speech and Response*, 17–20; Fokkelman, *Major Poems of the Hebrew Bible*, 326, 330; Lugt, *Rhetorical Criticism*, 61.

dialogue among wise men, litigates in court, or prophets and the people.² Following the introductory formula which occurs at the commencement of each of Eliphaz's speeches ("Then Eliphaz the Temanite answered and said"), chapter 4 consists of two larger stanzas (4:2-11; 4:12-21) with four substanzas (vv. 2-4; 5-11; 12-16; 17-21).³ Thus the first section may be classified in the following manner: (1) admonition to Job on the basis of his past righteous deeds that hope lies ahead if he should repent and submit (4:2-4); (2) the archetypal paradigm of Eliphaz's retributive argument that the innocent cannot perish as the wicked do (4:5-11); (3) a depiction of Eliphaz's nocturnal "auditory dream vision" as substantiation of his claim (4:12-16); and (4) the special revelatory content of the dream experience of which Eliphaz has been the select recipient (4:17-21).⁴

Chapter 5 consists of three larger stanzas: (1) the certain and grim outcome of continued punishment for evildoing if divine appeasement is not attained (5:1-7); (2) a hymnic appeal to seek God in light of the obvious divine disapprobation (5:8-16); and (3) a psalm cautioning repentance and acceptance of divine reproof as a means of obtaining divine favor in view of God's remedial yet rather capricious chastening (5:17-27).⁵ My analysis of chapter 5 will confine itself to the final stanza.

Eliphaz's Archetypal Retributive Doctrine (4:5-11)

In this portion Eliphaz outlines the principal theological tenets of his retributive doctrine. The new section is marked in verse 5 by the contrastive conjunction כִּי along with the topical transition from Job's past deeds to his present situation. This shift provides Eliphaz an opportunity to expound more fully upon his cherished doctrine of retribution. The section ends in verse 11 as Eliphaz perorates using the analogy of wild lions to buttress his observations regarding divine retribution in human affairs.

As argued in the opening chapters, the manner in which an interpreter reads this section determines largely his or her understanding of the

---

2. Murphy, *Wisdom Literature*, 175-76; Course, *Speech and Response*, 21. Georg Fohrer identifies Eliphaz's initial speech as comprising in its first section "Streitgespräche der Weisen" ("disputation speeches of the wise") and in its second "Redeund Stilformen der Psalmen" ("speech and style forms of the Psalms") (*Das Buch Hiob*, 50-51).

3. Fokkelman divides each substanza further into two strophes (*Major Poems*, 326).

4. Murphy, *Wisdom Literature*, 23-24; Hartley, *Job*, 111; Lugt, *The Poetry of the Book of Job*, 62.

5. Hartley, *Job*, 115-23. *Contra* Murphy, *Wisdom Literature*, 24.

purpose and significance of Eliphaz. The lead counselor outlines his thesis and corroborates it with pointed illustrations gleaned empirically from nature (specifically the fate of the ravenous lion). There is hope for Job should he repent due to the demonstrable reality that only the wicked perish. Job is limping down the path to perdition but has a slender opportunity to reverse his fortunes should he acquiesce to the offended deity. This course of action alone will assuage God's wrath and restore Job to a life of blessing.

Translation

4:5 But now it comes to you, and you cannot make due;
It touches you, and you become dismayed.
4:6 Surely your fear is your source of confidence,
And the integrity of your ways is your hope!
4:7 Remember, who that was innocent has ever perished?
Or where have the upright been effaced?
4:8 Just as I have seen, those who plow wickedness
And sow trouble, reap the same.
4:9 By the breath of God they perish,
And by the gust of his anger they come to nothing.
4:10 The roaring of the lion, the sound of the savage lion,
And the teeth of the young lions are broken.
4:11 The lion perishes for lack of prey,
And the cubs of the lioness are scattered.

Exegetical Notes

In this section Eliphaz sets the tone of the eloquent ANE counselor who is to lead the sufferer back to a correct view of his sin and back ultimately to necessary capitulation to the caprice of the offended deity. To add persuasive sophistication to his argument, Eliphaz employs imagery to be observed from the natural and predictable patterns of agriculture and animal life (the latter constituting an adumbration of the Yahweh speeches). These *Sprachbilden* are included by the sage both to bolster his teaching on the fate of the wicked and to augment the need for Job to mollify the angered deity. They are anchored in themes common to the ANE context in which Eliphaz is rooted and from which he emerges.

Verse 5

כִּי עַתָּה ׀ תָּבוֹא אֵלֶיךָ וַתֵּלֶא תִּגַּע עָדֶיךָ וַתִּבָּהֵל

Eliphaz refers to the trouble which "comes" to Job, a Qal impf 3fs from בוא, here to be rendered in the sense of a present verb.[6] The second verb in the sentence, תֵּלֶא, derives from the root לאה, which, as Gordis argues persuasively, cannot be rendered "be weary" as it is traditionally translated (KJV, ASV "faintest"; NKJV "be weary"; cf. ESV, NASB "are impatient" and NIV "be discouraged") since such a meaning "is actually nonexistent in biblical Hebrew."[7] The term denotes rather, "to be unable" as evident when used complementarily in the phrase "they were unable to find the entrance" (וַיִּלְאוּ לִמְצֹא הַפָּתַח) in Gen 19:11. Driver and Gray take notice that the verb תִּבָּהֵל, the Niphal stem of the root בהל is a more forceful word than most English versions convey, signifying "be dismayed, thrown into alarm,"[8] underscoring that Eliphaz perceives that a profound instability has overtaken Job.

Verse 6

הֲלֹא יִרְאָתְךָ כִּסְלָתֶךָ תִּקְוָתְךָ וְתֹם דְּרָכֶיךָ

The opening interrogative particle is really to be rendered an emphatic "indeed."[9] The concept of "your fear" (יִרְאָתְךָ) simply describes Job's piety[10] which is to be a source of confidence in the midst of his ordeal. These dual themes of "the fear of God" and its corollary, "hope," are pervasive throughout the Eliphaz speeches.[11] These virtues are integral to Eliphaz's counsel

---

6. Fohrer, *Hiob*, 130.
7. Gordis, *Job*, 46.
8. Driver and Gray, *Job*, 2:24.
9. Gordis, *Book of Job*, 47.
10. Terrien, *Job*, 90.
11. As Jürgen Ebach contends: "Gottesfurcht und Hoffnung sind die Leitprinzipien der ganzen Elifasrede. Tatsächlich war die Überzeugung, daß der Guttäter und der Übeltäter mit ihrem Tun ihr Geschick (und das ihrer Nachkommen) selbst bewirken, die gemeinsame Grundüberzeugung Hiobs und seiner Freunde" ("The fear of God and hope are the leading principles of the entire speeches of Eliphaz. In reality, the conviction that the welldoer and the evildoer by their deeds bring about their fate (and that of their descendants) was the common basic conviction of Job and his friends") (*Streiten mit Gott*, 60). Yet in this Eliphaz is not simply a rigid dogmatist: "Die Auffassung vom Zusammenhang von Tun und Ergehen, Saat und Ernte ist nicht naiv; sie schließt Erfahrung und Hoffnung zusammen" ("The view of the connectivity of deed and outcome, seed and harvest, is not naïve; it joins experience and hope together"). Indeed, the "sprachbild von Saat und Ernte" ("the figure of speech of seed and harvest")

as well as to his role as the restitutionary sage in bringing Job to restoration through cultic means. The term כִּסְלָתֶךָ from the root כִּסְלָה has generated much discussion, as the lexeme may connote "foolishness" on the one hand or "hope, confidence" on the other.[12] Dhorme is persuasive that the latter meaning of "confidence" is suitable to the immediate and larger context and is therefore intended.[13] Eliphaz is appealing to what is Job's basis of hope for a good outcome: his proven integrity must now be his guide back to the favorable sphere of restitution with the deity who has for an unknown reason become displeased with Job.

Verse 7

זְכָר־נָא מִי הוּא נָקִי אָבָד וְאֵיפֹה יְשָׁרִים נִכְחָדוּ

Dhorme identifies correctly the pivotal nature of the retributive doctrine which Eliphaz brings out in this statement.[14] He points further to the foundation of this insight in the cultural context of the ANE: "This is exactly the ethic of the Babylonians and Assyrians as it is disclosed in magical or religious texts."[15] Eliphaz delivers his retributive doctrine through the eloquent presentation of two rhetorical questions, both of which anticipate a negative reply: Job can be certain that the innocent (נָקִי) have never perished and

---

is found throughout the Hebrew Scriptures often in wisdom settings, including Hos 8:7; 10:12; Ps 126:5; Prov 22:8 (ibid., 61).

12. Cotter, *A Study of Job 4–5*, 162–63; Dhorme, *Job*, 45.

13. "The masculine כֶּסֶל is found in the Book of Job with the meaning of 'confidence' (8:14; 31:24), and as a parallel it has the word מִבְטָח 'security.' It is clear that כִּסְלָתֶךָ, which, in virtue of antithetic parallelism, has as a parallel תִּקְוָתֶךָ 'your hope,' is used here in the sense of confidence" (Dhorme, *Job*, 44).

14. In drawing out the retributive orientation Dhorme appeals to Thomas Aquinas, who describes the view of Eliphaz and his friends as "opinionem . . . quod adversitates hujus mundi non adveniant alicui nisi in poenam peccati et e contrario prosperitates pro merito justitiae" ("opinions . . . that the adversities of this world overtake no one except in punishment of sins and on the contrary prosperity [only] for rewarded righteousness") (*Job*, 45).

15. Dhorme, *Job*, 45 (cf. that Habel calls this doctrine "widespread in the ancient Near East" and points to the Babylonian *Theodicy* as an exemplar [*Job*, 125]). Dhorme does not on this basis reject the validity of Eliphaz's theological perspective, however. "Ps 37 develops fully the thesis of the relation between moral good and good fortune and between moral evil and misfortune. Even if appearances suggest that good fortune comes at times to the wicked and misfortune to the righteous, this is only a false and transient illusion. The last word remains with God, who on this earth rewards the just and punishes the wicked. The author of the Psalm also appeals to his personal experience: 'I have been young and now am old, yet I have never seen the righteous forsaken' (Ps 37:25; cf. Sir 2:10f.). Thus the ideas of Eliphaz are current coin" (*Job*, 45).

that the upright (יְשָׁרִים, cf. Job 1:1 where Job is described as יָשָׁר) have never been effaced (נִכְחָדוּ, Niph impf 3mp from כחד, "be destroyed, wiped out").[16] Here the chief counselor attempts an air of sophistication as he reminds Job of familiar truths as a means by which to restore Job's confidence and lead him back to repentance/reconciliation,[17] noted by his conspicuous use of זְכָר־נָא ("recall now") to point to common tradition held by the friends.[18] He has provided the sufferer with surer ground and space to realize that while his situation is dire it is not hopeless. The offended God may yet be appeased if Job is careful, holds his temper, and heeds Eliphaz's counsel.

Verse 8

כַּאֲשֶׁר רָאִיתִי חֹרְשֵׁי אָוֶן וְזֹרְעֵי עָמָל יִקְצְרֻהוּ

Although Duhm opines that the twin quatrains of verses 8–9 and 10–11 are "clumsily constructed" so that "one might be pleased to do without them,"[19] we find in these lines the fundamental core of Eliphaz's retributive dogma. Whether in these verses Eliphaz is kindly or harsh determines largely one's understanding of his tone. Whether he is incisive and truthful or ill-advised and erroneous determines one's view of the legitimacy of his wisdom perspective.

Eliphaz begins with a subordinating conjunction כַּאֲשֶׁר as a means of interjecting his personal observation and opinion ("just as I have seen"), an approach which is characteristic of his method as observed previously.[20] Duhm would prefer here to render the first person רָאִיתִי as second person "du selbst hast es gesehen" ("you yourself have seen it") on the basis

---

16. This is a recurring term and motif of Eliphaz, as he uses כחד with the same significance in 15:28 and 22:20 (Horst, *Hiob 1–19*, 68).

17 Newsom, *Job*, 101; Hartley, *Job*, 107.

18 Habel, *Job*, 125; Duhm, *Hiob*, 26; Clines, *Job 1–20*, 124. Horst notes that they hold to "die bisher gemeinsame, verbreite und durchaus eingängige religiöse Lehrmeinung vor, daß Gott die Frommen erhält, hingegen den Sündern Glück und Leben mindert und gar entzieht" ("the before now common, current, and by all means plausible religious doctrine that God preserves the godly and on the contrary diminishes and altogether deprives the sinner of happiness and life") (*Hiob 1–19*, 69).

19 Duhm contends that "die beiden folgenden Vierzeiler v. 8 9 und v. 10 11 sind so holprig gebaut und der Inhalt entspricht so wenig dem Aufwand an pathetischen Worten, dass man sie gern missen möchte" ("both of the following quatrains v. 8–9 and v. 10–11 are so clumsily constructed and their content corresponds so little to the effort at emotive words that one might be pleased to do without them" (*Hiob*, 26).

20. Lael Caesar, "Job: Another New Thesis," 437.

of verse 7, but this is unjustified.²¹ And although Delitzsch connects the conjunction כַּאֲשֶׁר, which he deems to be a temporal marker, to the verb רָאִיתִי as syntactically governing that which immediately follows, thus rendering along the lines of "every time I have seen such (evildoers) plowing,"²² Dhorme contends that such a construction makes the statement "curiously heavy." He suggests instead that the phrase is subordinate to the rest of the sentence and that the implied subject of חֹרְשֵׁי and זֹרְעֵי is the subject also of יִקְצְרֻהוּ so that "the verbs חרש 'plough,' 'cultivate,' זרע 'sow,' קצר 'reap,' mark very clearly the successive actions of the sinner."²³ Eliphaz is outlining the consecutive deeds which characterize the sinner as a means of persuading Job that he must re-assert his pious devotion, a source of confidence in the face of the offended God, in order to prevent this downward spiral toward unmitigated ruin. Fortunately Eliphaz is able wisely to prescribe this remedy insofar as he has personally observed the end of evildoers and is for this reason confident that if Job heeds his advice good may yet come of this disaster. Job is not too far down that path to pull back, but a repeat of his ill-advised outburst (Job 3), would be, in Eliphaz's "humble opinion," calamitous.

Verse 9

מִנִּשְׁמַת אֱלוֹהַ יֹאבֵדוּ וּמֵרוּחַ אַפּוֹ יִכְלוּ

Dhorme sees in this and the following verses an elucidation upon the way in which "misfortune is the consequence of sin. The mediating agent is the divine anger manifested by the same symptoms as among human beings. Sin provokes God and He avenges Himself. We find the same thought among the Assyrians and Babylonians."²⁴ The choice of the terms נְשָׁמָה signifying "breath" and רוּחַ signifying "spirit, wind, breeze" is unfortunate in light of the disaster that has claimed the lives of Job's children, but Eliphaz likely

---

21. Duhm, *Hiob*, 26. Duhm fails to convince Dhorme (*Job*, 46).

22. Delitzsch argues: "In v. 8 ist כַּאֲשֶׁר nicht vergleichend, sondern zeitlich gemeint, so aber dass es, wie gewöhnlich, unmittelbar auf einander Folgendes und in Folgenzus. Stehendes verknüpft: als, so wie, so oft ich gesehen hatte solche die Böses entwarfen und ausführten (vgl. Spr 22,8), bekam ich auch zu sehen, dass sie es ernteten" ("In verse 8 כַּאֲשֶׁר is not meant as comparative, but temporal, yet so that it concatenates as customarily, what stands in close connection with and follows directly upon the preceding: 'When just as so often I have seen those who planned and worked out evil (cf. Prov 22:8), I saw also that they reaped it.'") (*Hiob*, 60).

23. Dhorme, *Job*, 46.

24. Ibid., 46.

does not intend to refer to this tragedy.²⁵ Eliphaz bases his argument upon the "organic fabric of order" that guarantees by the outcome of one's life that God's will is revealed.²⁶

Verse 10

שַׁאֲגַת אַרְיֵה וְקוֹל שָׁחַל וְשִׁנֵּי כְפִירִים נִתָּעוּ

Eliphaz selects the lion as an example of the universal truths he is seeking to inculcate. In the ANE *Panthera leo persica* (the Asiatic lion) was a revered beast, inspiring fear and awe among the inhabitants of Mesopotamia up until the twentieth century. Frequently in ANE mythology the animal symbolized chaos as well as the harsh and expansive wilderness.²⁷ In the later Erra *epos* the god Erra would be symbolized by the lion in his efforts to exert hegemony over the earth: "In the heavens I am a wild bull; in the land (*erṣetu*) I am a lion; in the homeland (*mātu*) I am king . . . ." (*ina šamê rīmāku ina erṣetim labbāku ina mātim šarruku*).²⁸ From earliest recorded human history, the monarch, in his quest to extend his dominion beyond his own city, would symbolize his power and authority with the lion.²⁹ As Dick observes, the lion was identified specifically with royal potency and alacrity:

> From our earliest artistic and textual evidence the Asiatic lion has been linked with kingship. The famed mace head of Mesilim, the twenty-sixth-century B.C.E. king of Kiš (AO 2340; see fig. 1), found at a possible Ningirsu shrine in Girsu, bears six intertwined lions on its sides and the lion-eagle Anzû (Imdugud) on its top. Its inscription clearly links it with kingship: 'Mesilim king of Kiš, builder of the temple of the God Ningirsu.'³⁰

Stefan Maul also points up the significance in later ninth-century through seventh-century BC neo-Assyrian royal seals: "The Neo-Assyrian royal seal

---

25. Hartley, *Job*, 108.

26. Horst, *Hiob 1–19*, 70.

27. Dick, "Neo-Assyrian Royal Lion Hunt," 245, 269. Cf. Prov 30:30 "The lion . . . is mightiest among beasts and does not turn back before any."

28. "The Poem of Erra," lines 109–10. Cf. *CAD*, 14:361; *CAD*, 9:24.

29. As Elena Cassin writes, "En définitive, par le truchement de le comparaison du roi avec le lion, on cherche toujours à exprimer le même aspiration à une souveraineté universelle" ("Above all, by means of the first comparison of the king with the lion, one seeks always to express primarily the same pursuit of universal sovereignty") ("Le roi et le lion," 400).

30. "Neo-Assyrian Royal Lion Hunt," 245.

with [this] royal hero symbolized clearly royal authority *in itself*."[31] Eliphaz has chosen a revered and distinguished beast, associated formally with imperial power and prestige, to impress upon Job the ineluctable ends about which he is arguing. No living thing, even the most powerful of beasts, can escape the fury of an offended God. Job has no hope, therefore, but to surrender himself to the divine will if is he is to have any hope of restitution to his prior dignity. This important connection is proved out by the counsel provided from the friend of the sufferer in the related Babylonian *Theodicy*, counsel which runs along similar lines:

> Come, consider the lion that you mentioned, the enemy of cattle,
> (*gi-ir bu-li la-ba š á taḫ-su-su ga-na bit-ru*)
> For the crime which the lion committed the pit awaits him.
> (*gi-il-lat nēš u i-pu-š u pi-ta-as-su ḫaš-tum*).[32]

In this admonition the friend of the sufferer chides the victim in much the same way Eliphaz reproves Job. The lion is a picture of the evildoer; for his act of thievery and pillaging, the lion will be duly recompensed. As a concrete case in point of "deed-outcome connectivity" (*Tun-Ergehen-Zusammenhang*), Job can expect no less.[33] Furthermore, a comparison of 4:10b with Psalm 58:6 suggests that Eliphaz's allusion to the breaking of the lion's teeth denotes an act of divine vengeance: "O God, break the teeth in their mouths; tear out the fangs of the young lions, O Lord!"[34]

Eliphaz's eloquence in these verses is frequently observed.[35] A total of five synonyms for "lion" are used in verses 10 and 11 (לַיִשׁ, כְּפִיר, שַׁחַל, אַרְיֵה, and לָבִיא).[36] The term אַרְיֵה is the most common in the OT, employed nearly forty times, with the general meaning of "lion."[37] The more semantically

---

31. "Das neuassyrische Königssiegel mit dem königlichen Helden symbolisierte ganz offensichtlich die königliche Autorität *an sich*" ("Das 'dreifache Königtum,'" 396, emphasis his).

32. Lambert, *BWL*, 75.

33. Gradl, *Das Buch Ijob*, 83.

34. Hartley, *Job*, 108.

35. Budde claims it is "unnachahmlich die Menge der Bezeichnungen für die Löwen" in vv. 10–11 ("inimitable the amount of expressions for the lion") (*Hiob*, 18). Cf. Gordis, *Job*, 47.

36. Hartley proposes that the different terms may relate to developmental stages of the lion (*Job*, 108, n. 4), but this seems difficult to justify as Eliphaz refers to the "lioness" as well as the "lion" and seems only to be extending the vividness of his analogies through the rich vocabulary available to him rather than explaining anything in more detail about the beast.

37. *HALOT*, 87–88.

precise synonym שַׁחַל is often compared to the Arabic *saḥala* "to bray" suggesting that in its etymology the root may denote the roaring of the beast.³⁸ We find an instance in this verse of zeugma, in which the subjects "roaring" and "cry" of the first clause, along with "teeth" in the second clause depend upon the same verb.³⁹

Verse 11

לַיִשׁ אֹבֵד מִבְּלִי־טָרֶף וּבְנֵי לָבִיא יִתְפָּרָדוּ

The term לַיִשׁ is used only three times in the OT (Isa 30:6; Job 4:11; Prov 30:30) to denote a "lion,"⁴⁰ and לָבִיא is used about a dozen times in poetic texts to describe a "lioness."⁴¹ Psalm 92:10 (EVV, 92:9) underscores the conceptual affinity of the two verbs "perish" (אבד) and "be scattered" (פרד) as the same verbs are used in parallelism:

> Your enemies shall perish;
> All evildoers shall be scattered.

Eliphaz's Nocturnal Dream Vision (4:12–16)

Verse 12 is the introduction of a substanza, as is clear by the marked shift of topic⁴² as well as the fact that verses 12–16 form a semantic inclusio.⁴³ Eliphaz begins the incorporation of his dream-visionary experience with a brief description of the encounter he has had with a revelation-bearing spirit-being.

Translation

> 4:12 A word came to me stealthily;
> My ears caught only a whisper of it,
> 4:13 Amid alarming thoughts arising from visions of the night,
> When deep sleep falls upon men.

---

38. Driver and Gray, *Job*, 2:24.
39. Buttenwieser, *Job*, 162.
40 *HALOT*, 529.
41 *HALOT*, 517. Cf. Ugaritic term *lbit*, "lioness" (Cyrus H. Gordon, *Ugaritic Textbook*, §19:1347).
42. Reyburn, *Handbook on the Book of Job*, 97.
43 Lugt, *The Poetry of the Book of Job*, 64.

4:14 Dread came over me, and trembling—
My entire frame shook.
4:15 A spirit glided past my face;
It made the hair of my flesh stand on end.
4:16 It stood still, but I could not recognize its features—
A form was before my very eyes! A hush, then I heard a voice:

Exegetical Notes

The vivid dream encounter comprises this section of Eliphaz's first speech. His depiction of the brush with the divine is one of the most extraordinary in all of Scripture.

Verse 12

וְאֵלַי דָּבָר יְגֻנָּב וַתִּקַּח אָזְנִי שֵׁמֶץ מֶנְהוּ

In verse 12, Eliphaz describes the reception of the visionary experience as a word coming to him furtively. The verb גנב ("to bring secretly," "be brought by stealth")[44] is rather uncommon, found here in the Pual imperfect, the only other occurrences of the word in this stem being found in Gen 40:15 and Exod 22:7 (Heb. 6).[45] Some posit that the word came to be used as a technical term for revelation.[46] However, the abnormal description of the transmission of the revelation inherently discredits to an extent the viability of its authority.[47] The word שֵׁמֶץ has also received quite a bit of attention. Rowley contends that the meaning here is "whisper" based upon a related cognate (so most EVV, including NIV, NASB, ESV, and NRSV).[48] Oth-

---

44. *HALAT*, 190; BDB, 170.

45. Alden, *Job*, 86.

46. Michel, *Job in the Light of Northwest Semitic*, 87; Werblowsky, "Stealing a Word," 105–6.

47. Gordis comments: "It is noteworthy that the most graphic and circumstantial description of the process of revelation occurs not in the Prophets, but here in Wisdom literature!" (*Job*, 519). He adds that usually prophets were more concerned with the *content* rather than the *mode* of divine revelation (ibid.). H. D. Preuss also points out the abnormality of this visionary experience vis-à-vis that of the true prophets: "The messenger formula ('thus says the words of YHWH') and the messenger oracle make it even clearer that the prophets were understood more as the intermediary of the word than as the speaker encountered by YHWH" (*Old Testament Theology*, 2:74).

48. Rowley, *The Book of Job*, 47.

ers have demonstrated, however, that the meaning of the word is simply "a little."⁴⁹ Michel observes that the word occurs elsewhere in Job only in 26:14, where it is placed parallel to קָצוֹת ("extremities, fringes" [most EVV "outskirts"]).⁵⁰ Furthermore, in Sirach 10:10 and 18:32, as well as in the Talmud, the word connotes "a little, a particle." As Dhorme suggests: "In consequence of the mysterious character of the communication made to him, Eliphaz has only been able to grasp a fragment."⁵¹

Verse 13

בִּשְׂעִפִּים מֵחֶזְיֹנוֹת לָיְלָה בִּנְפֹל תַּרְדֵּמָה עַל־אֲנָשִׁים

The phrase בִּשְׂעִפִּים מֵחֶזְיֹנוֹת ("amid disquieting thoughts⁵² from visions," v. 13) is taken by Dhorme to mean "amid nightmares caused by visions" with the preposition מִן conveying causative force, as in verse 9.⁵³ Michel contends that "when deep sleep falls upon men" is epexegetical of "night," only providing a general statement of when the vision occurred rather than suggesting a dream which takes place *during* deep sleep.⁵⁴ Other scholars attach greater significance, however, to the connotation of תַּרְדֵּמָה ("deep sleep"). The term תַּרְדֵּמָה is connotative elsewhere of encounter with the divine,⁵⁵ the most vivid connection being the distinct account of the initiation of the Abrahamic covenant in Genesis 15. The use of the term in Genesis 15:12 is particularly poignant, bearing remarkable affinities to Eliphaz's portrayal:

> Now when the sun was going down, a deep sleep fell upon Abram;
> וַיְהִי הַשֶּׁמֶשׁ לָבוֹא וְתַרְדֵּמָה נָפְלָה עַל־אַבְרָם
> And, behold, terror and great darkness fell upon him (NASB)
> וְהִנֵּה אֵימָה חֲשֵׁכָה גְדֹלָה נֹפֶלֶת עָלָיו

Both the Genesis and the Job account use the term תַּרְדֵּמָה to describe the divine revelatory ambience, and both records depict the emotive element of terror (Eliphaz uses the term פַּחַד [v. 14] while the Genesis account uses אֵימָה). Jürgen Ebach most thoroughly traces the interrelation between the

49. See Gordis, *Job*, 48; Dhorme, *Job*, 49; Driver and Gray, *Job*, 2:24.
50. Michel, *Job in the Light of Northwest Semitic*, 87.
51. Dhorme, *Job*, 49.
52. BDB, 972; *HALOT*, 1343.
53. Dhorme, *Job*, 50. Cf. also Clines, *Job 1-20*, 111.
54. *Job*, 89.
55. Gordis, *Job*, 48.

descriptions.⁵⁶ He sees not only an affiliation in the dream encounters experienced by both men, but also a conceptual affinity which permeates both passages:

> Near with our text, however, is above all the depiction given in Gen 15 of a nocturnal revelation to Abraham. As Job 4 so also is Gen 15, the promise to Abraham, presumably a young literary narrative in ancient garb. By the documented usage of the word *tardema* (perhaps: deep sleep) in both texts and the observable emphasis in both locations on terror, which the nocturnal revelation triggers, the substance of the promise of a fortunate outcome reaches out in spite of intervening anguish. One may compare the respective announcements of dying in peace at an advanced age (Gen 15:15; Job 5:22ff.) and the promise of numerous descendants, central in Gen 15 and consistent with Job 5:25.⁵⁷

Ebach's insights are in the main helpful, although he misses the mark when he infers that the connection pertains only superficially to the level of literary convention rather than to comparable time periods. Rather than seeing in this a "misplacement" (*Verlegung*) by the Joban writer of Eliphaz's account into the historical milieu of the patriarchal period, the simpler solution is to observe a more profound correspondence. The manner in which the revelation is received, the terminology used to depict the brush with deity, and the dread/terror associated with the divine encounter all point to a chronological affinity which is favorable to an early date (15th century or earlier) for the material of the Eliphaz speech.

---

56. Although clearly seeing the connectivity between the passages, unfortunately Ebach is tied to a late date for the composition of Job and thus sees the resemblance merely as that of literary connection whereby for effect the events are depicted anachronistically with the conventions of ancient parlance. I would prefer to see the connection instead as pointing up a more plausible chronological affinity, thus supporting my contention for an early date for the composition of the book.

57. "Nahe bei unserem Text aber vor allem die in Gen 15 gegebene Schilderung einer nächtlichen Offenbarung an Abraham. Wie Hi 4 ist auch Gen 15, die Verheißung an Abraham, vermutlich eine literarisch junge Erzählung in altem Gewand. Über die in beiden Texten belegte Verwendung des Wortes *tardemā* (etwa: Tiefschlaf) und die an beiden Stellen zur beobachtende Betonung des Schreckens, den die nächtliche Offenbarung auslöst, hinaus weist der Inhalt der Verheißung eines glücklichen Ausgangs trotz dazwischenliegender Qual. Man vergleiche die jeweilige Ankündigung des Sterbens in Frieden, in hohem Alter (Gen 15,15; Hi 5,22ff.) und die in Gen 15 zentrale, in Hi 5,25 anklingende Verheißung zahlreicher Nachkommen" (*Streiten mit Gott*, 62).

Verses 14–15

וְרוּחַ עַל־פָּנַי יַחֲלֹף תְּסַמֵּר שַׂעֲרַת בְּשָׂרִי פַּחַד קְרָאַנִי וּרְעָדָה וְרֹב עַצְמוֹתַי הִפְחִיד

In verse 14 Eliphaz states literally that "dread encountered me" (פַּחַד קְרָאַנִי). Gordis notes interestingly that the same word is used of God's "encounter" with the Gentile prophet Balaam in Num 23:3.[58] "My bones" (עַצְמוֹתַי) refers by synecdoche to the whole body.[59] The point is that dread and trembling came over him, causing his whole body to quake. Much consideration has been given to the meaning of רוּחַ ("breath, wind, spirit") in verse 15. Solomon Freehof understands the specter to be an angel.[60] Andersen posits that, in light of the masculine verbal form used, the meaning is the particular personal Spirit, viz., the Spirit of God.[61] These views are difficult to accept, however. The more common nuance of רוּחַ is "breath" or "wind,"[62] both of which can accompany supernatural activity. Additionally, the masculine usage of the term nearly always means "wind" or "breath" (cf. Job 41:8; Exod 10:13; Eccl 1:6; 3:19).[63] Others note that more commonly the word carried the connotation of an impersonal force or power rather than a personal being, especially in early Hebrew.[64] Given the nature of the revelatory process, however, I am inclined to favor the meaning of personal spirit-being who conveys special revelation to Eliphaz. Dahood argued that שַׂעֲרַת in verse 15 should be read to mean "storm," stemming from a variant vocalization and a preserved feminine ending ת-, as in Phoenician and Ugaritic.[65] However, the normal meaning "hair" makes good sense in the text, and can be used collectively to denote the hairs of the body.[66] The verb תְּסַמֵּר ("stand on end," "bristle")[67] is Piel transitive, signifying that the "breath of air" is still the subject (or that the subject is indefinite), causing the hairs of the flesh to stand erect.

---

58. *Job*, 49. *Contra* Andersen, *Job*, 113.

59. Rowley, *Job*, 48.

60. *Book of Job* (New York: Union of American Hebrew Congregations, 1958), 66.

61. *Job*, 114n1.

62. Gordis, *Job*, 49.

63. Clines, *Job 1–20*, 111; Dhorme, *Job*, 50.

64. Albertz and Westermann, "rûah," 3:1211.

65. "S'RT 'Storm' in Job 4,15," 544–45. This has been followed by Gordis, *Job*, 49; Michel, *Job*, 92; Blommerde, *Northwest Semitic Grammar and Job*, 40. The Targum makes a similar suggestion, although changes to the more common ה- ending.

66. So Clines, *Job 1–20*, 111; Dhorme, *Job*, 50; *HALOT*, 1345.

67. *HALOT*, 760; BDB, 702.

Verse 16

יַעֲמֹד ׀ וְלֹא־אַכִּיר מַרְאֵהוּ תְּמוּנָה לְנֶגֶד עֵינָי דְּמָמָה וָקוֹל אֶשְׁמָע

In verse 16, the LXX, Aquila, and Symmachus read "I stood up" (ἀνέστην) rather than "it stood still." The MT is to be preferred here, however, given the inconsistency of the LXX as a literal translation and the shift in the text that marks transition from the movement of the apparition to Eliphaz's reaction to it.[68] Several have proposed that the phrase דְּמָמָה וָקוֹל ("silence and a voice") should be connected as a hendiadys, meaning that Eliphaz heard "a whispering voice."[69] Johann Lust, on the other hand, proposed that דְּמָמָה derives from a different nuance of the stem דמם, meaning "to roar" in keeping with an Akkadian cognate.[70] Several factors persuade, however, to disjoin the "silence" from the "voice." Gordis notes that the MT's vocalization joins "voice" to the verb אֶשְׁמָע ("I heard"), rather than to "silence."[71] Pope argues, in addition, that דְּמָמָה functions as a *casus pendens*, signifying "in a hush."[72] The eerie recounting of the visionary experience is further intensified if Eliphaz is depicting a ghastly hush, followed by a voice.

The Content of Eliphaz's Special Revelation (4:17–21)

Eliphaz now relays to his audience the substance of what was revealed to him by his nocturnal visitor.

Translation

> 4:17 How can a mortal human be just before God?
>
> How can a man be clean before his Maker?
>
> 4:18 If God does not trust His servants,
>
> And attributes folly to His angels,
>
> 4:19 How much more those who dwell in houses of clay, which have a foundation of dust?
>
> They are liable to be crushed like a moth!

---

68. Hartley, *Job*, 109n6.
69. So NIV; *NET*; Dhorme, *Job*, 52; Williams, *Hebrew Syntax*, §72.
70. "A Gentle Breeze or a Roaring Thunderous Sound?" 111. Cf. Clines, *Job 1–20*, 112.
71. Gordis, *Job*, 50.
72. Pope, *Job*, 37.

4:20 In the space of a dawn to dusk they may be pulverized.
They would perish forever without anyone noticing.
4:21 Would they not die if their tent-cord were plucked up from them?
Yet not because of wisdom!

Exegetical Notes

The content of the special revelation delivered to Eliphaz is frequently characterized as trite. It expounds again on the recurrent motif of divine retribution crucial to Eliphaz in his first speech.

VERSE 17

הַאֱנוֹשׁ מֵאֱלוֹהַ יִצְדָּק אִם מֵעֹשֵׂהוּ יִטְהַר־גָּבֶר

Job 4:17 has received the most attention of any verse in its immediate pericope. It is the pivotal verse for this substanza, giving the heart of the phantom's revelation; verses 18–21 simply reinforce its message.[73] Yet it also contains the most difficult interpretive crux. The difficulty lies in whether the preposition מִן affixed to אֱלוֹהַ ("God") carries the normal comparative sense of "more than" (i.e., can a mortal man be more just than God?) or a relational sense of "before, in the sight of" (i.e., can a mortal man be just in the eyes of God?). Wolfers contends that the normal comparative sense should carry here, because this is the sense when Elihu asks the question in 35:2 and the same expression means "more than" in Num 32:22 and Jeremiah 24:25–27.[74] The text tells against such an understanding in this verse, however. Grammatically an understanding of "before" is possible. Williams categorizes this usage of מִן as that of "relationship," which can have three nuances: (1) in space (Josh 8:13; Num 32:19), (2) in time (Gen 19:34; 2 Sam 15:34), and (3) in point of view, meaning "before, in the sight of, from the standpoint of" (Num 32:22; Sir 10:7).[75] Job 4:17 falls into the last category. Two passages in Job parallel to the concept of this verse are 9:2 ("how can a mortal be righteous before God?") and 25:4 ("how then can a man be righteous before God?"). In both instances the preposition מִן ("with, before") is used, but the semantic force seems to be the same as in this passage. Contextually, the sense of "before" correlates better since Job

---

73. Whybray, *Job*, 43.
74. *Deep Things out of Darkness*, 381. Cf. KJV; Reyburn, *Job*, 101.
75. *Hebrew Syntax*, §323.

has never said, nor probably imagined, that he is *more* just than God.⁷⁶ As Dhorme states: "Verses 18ff. aim at showing that before God nothing and no one can claim either justice or purity. It has never occurred to Job to compare his perfection with that of God."⁷⁷ Two other items in the verse merit mention. Williams argues that the imperfect verbs here emphasize *potentiality*, expressing ability, hence the translation value of "how can a [mortal human] be righteous."⁷⁸ Also, Eliphaz uses a less common word for "man" at the beginning of the verse, אֱנוֹשׁ ("human being, man"),⁷⁹ to underscore the finitude and mortality of mankind (vis-à-vis the deity).

Verses 18

הֵן בַּעֲבָדָיו לֹא יַאֲמִין וּבְמַלְאָכָיו יָשִׂים תָּהֳלָה

In verses 18 and 19 the visitor argues *a fortiori* that if God does not trust angels, superior creatures to man, how much less should mankind expect itself to be highly regarded in the divine economy. Michel and Blommerde point out the probability that the particle הֵן in verse 18 ought to be conditional as in 15:15 and 25:6.⁸⁰ Grammatically this is preferable, in that when הֵן is followed by the preposition + article בְּ as here, the first clause must be a premise.⁸¹ Thus, the *a fortiori* argument is strengthened, with the apodosis in verse 18 ("if he does not trust") leading to the protasis in verse 19 ("how much less"). A minor question has persisted as to the identity of the servants in the first stich of verse 18. The Targum identifies these servants as the prophets, but most scholars, in view of the parallelism, understand the servants to be angels (cf. Ps 104:4).⁸²

More attention has focused in verse 18 on the meaning of the *hapax legomenon* in the final word תָּהֳלָה ("folly, error").⁸³ The difficulty lies in ascertaining to which stem and cognate the word belongs. Michel suggests a repointing of the word to תְּהִלָּה ("praise") and a carrying over of the negative from the first line to mean "he does not ascribe praise to his angels."⁸⁴ Few

---

76. Rowley, *Job*, 49; Habel, *Job*, 116; Gordis, *Job*, 50.
77. *Job*, 52.
78. *Hebrew Syntax*, §169.
79. *HALOT*, 70.
80. Michel, *Job*, 95; Blommerde, *Job*, 41.
81. Clines, *Job*, 112.
82. Hartley, *Job*, 114; Reyburn, *Job*, 102; Dhorme, *Job*, 52.
83. *HALOT*, 1691.
84. *Job*, 96.

have followed his lead, however.⁸⁵ BDB suggest an emendation of the word to תִּפְלָה ("error").⁸⁶ Others arrive at the same basic meaning of "error" but apart from the emendation by relating the word to an Ethiopian cognate meaning "to wander" (so RSV, NIV).⁸⁷ Clines disfavors this nuance, however, since such a cognate is never used in Semitic languages.⁸⁸ Probably the best understanding is that advanced by Gordis and Dhorme, that the stem of the word is הלל ("to be mad"), hence "folly, madness."⁸⁹ In either case, whether "error" or "folly," the thought is parallel to that of the first line, viz., that God, who is "wholly other," does not completely endorse any of his created beings.

Verse 19

אַף ׀ שֹׁכְנֵי בָתֵּי־חֹמֶר אֲשֶׁר־בֶּעָפָר יְסוֹדָם יְדַכְּאוּם לִפְנֵי־עָשׁ

In verse 19 man is depicted as those who dwell in houses of clay.⁹⁰ Most scholars understand this allusion to be a reference to the human body.⁹¹ The speech emphasizes the frailty and mortality of man by speaking of the human body as that which possesses a foundation of dust.⁹² Dhorme poignantly summarizes the meaning: "Since God finds defects in the angels, who are superior beings, sons of God (1:6), how much more will He find defects in frail creatures who dwell in a body of clay and whose foundation and support is but the dust."⁹³ Eliphaz's thinking in these verses is similar to the counselor in the Babylonian *Theodicy*, who links the perversity of man inseparably to his mortality:

> Narru, king of the gods, who created mankind,

---

85. Habel follows Michel, namely because for him "the significance of mad angels in this context . . . remains obscure" (*Job*, 116).

86. BDB, 1062.

87. Hill, "4:278 ",תהלה.

88. *Job 1–20*, 112.

89. Gordis, *Job*, 50; Dhorme, *Job*, 52.

90. Crenshaw suggests the unusual possibility that Eliphaz makes reference here to the death of Job's children, as those who live in houses that fall down (*Old Testament Wisdom*, 96). This understanding seems to miss the point that "houses of clay" is most likely a reference to the human body, not to the domiciles of ancient man.

91. E.g., Pope, *Job*, 37; Whybray, *Job*, 43; Gordis, *Job*, 50; contra Andersen, *Job*, 115n1.

92. Clines rightly points out that "foundation" is a reference to "houses," not to "dwellers" (*Job 1–20*, 113).

93. *Job*, 54.

And majestic Zulummar, who dug out their clay,
And mistress Mami, the queen who fashioned them,
Gave perverse speech to the human race,
With lies, and not truth, they endowed them forever.[94]

Eliphaz is also equating man's mortality (made of clay) with his ineluctable iniquity and concomitant suffering.

The quotation from the spirit emphatically punches its assertion by exclaiming, "They are crushed like a moth!" Much ink has been spilled over attempting to arrive at the meaning of this phrase, יְדַכְּאוּם לִפְנֵי־עָשׁ ("they crush them before a moth"). GKC assert that the subject is indefinite for which the verb carries the sense of passive ("they are crushed").[95] The greater difficulty lies in interpreting the final phrase לִפְנֵי־עָשׁ ("before a moth"). Typically לִפְנֵי carries a temporal or spatial connotation ("before"). The difficulty lies in understanding how one is crushed in the presence of a moth. Rimbach suggests a refiguring of the text to make it read "before their Maker."[96] He bases his argument primarily on the symmetry of the lines, but, as Habel points out, the flaw of his argument is to assume that symmetrical poetry is more likely to be original than asymmetrical poetry.[97] In any event, his case is not compelling. Gordis uses an Arabic cognate to argue for a meaning of "bird's nest" instead of "moth" ("they are crushed like a bird's nest").[98] This suggestion is possible, but unnecessary: the text as it stands clearly refers to the moth.

Reyburn preserves the temporal connotations of לִפְנֵי with the meaning "people are crushed more quickly than a moth is crushed."[99] The preferable understanding, however, is to see comparison in the analogy: man may be crushed as easily as a moth is crushed. The comparative sense of לִפְנֵי is already established in the book in 3:24 (sighing comes as/instead of food). Williams demonstrates that the word has this connotation elsewhere as in 1 Samuel 1:16, "do not treat your servant as a base woman."[100] So then, the spirit asserts that man is liable to be crushed like a moth.

---

94. "Babylonian *Theodicy*," lines 276–80 (*BWL*, 89).

95. GKC, §144g.

96. J. Rimbach, "Crushed Before the Moth (Job 4:19)," *JBL* 100 (June 1981): 244–46.

97. Habel, *Job*, 116.

98. Gordis, *Job*, 50.

99. Reyburn, *Handbook on Job*, 103.

100. Williams, *Hebrew Syntax*, §373.

Verse 20

מִבֹּקֶר לָעֶרֶב יֻכַּתּוּ מִבְּלִי מֵשִׂים לָנֶצַח יֹאבֵדוּ

The greatest difficulty in verse 20 is the phrase מִבְּלִי מֵשִׂים ("without setting"). While some have suggested here an ellipsis for "without setting [one's heart]" = "without paying attention," Dhorme objects that such an elliptical construction is "rather too violent."[101] He reluctantly suggests rather that the LXX is to be followed, rendering the phrase "without a Savior" (i.e., "they perish forever from lack of a Savior").[102] As previously noted, however, it is notoriously tenuous to side with the LXX against all other versions. Dahood and Pope have suggested that the preformative מ on מֵשִׂים should be viewed as an enclitic מ and the phrase then taken to mean "without a name."[103] This is possible, but as Gordis argues the emendation is unnecessary and breaks up the parallelism.[104] The best solution is to view this phrase as an elliptical construction, signifying that death may come without any particular notice. Michel points to Isaiah 53:8 as a parallel to this passage, with similar ellipsis.[105] So, as Whybray notes, the import of the phrase is that "death is too commonplace to be especially remarked upon by others."[106]

Verse 21

הֲלֹא־נִסַּע יִתְרָם בָּם יָמוּתוּ וְלֹא בְחָכְמָה

The crux of verse 21 is the meaning of יִתְרָם ("their tent cord").[107] The *NET* has followed Dhorme and the Targum in rendering this phrase "Is not their excess wealth taken away from them?" This interpretation arises from the more common meaning of יֶתֶר ("remainder").[108] But while "remainder" may be the more common semantic connotation in sheer number of occurrences in the Hebrew Scriptures, this does not necessitate such an understanding here. The only other occurrence of the word יֶתֶר in Job is in 30:11, where it denotes "bow-string." The semantic similarity would suggest a meaning of

---

101. Dhorme, *Job*, 55.
102. Ibid.; cf. Rowley, *Job*, 50.
103. See Pope, *Job*, 38; Dahood, "Northwest Semitic Philology and Job," 55–56.
104. Gordis, *Job*, 51.
105. Michel, *Job*, 99.
106. Whybray, *Job*, 44.
107. So *HALOT*, 452; BDB, 452.
108. See ibid.

"cord, tent cord" here. Furthermore, reference to superfluous wealth would contravene the thought-flow of the pericope. Eliphaz has just compared the human body to a house of clay, and his emphasis is on the perishability of man, not his overabundance of wealth. In like manner Isa 38:12 equates the brevity of life to a tent. Most viable, therefore, is a rendering of "tent cord."[109]

Clines has argued persuasively that the verbs here are modal, expressing particular possibility rather than general actuality, viz., that it is possible that some men (viz., the wicked) will die in this way but not that all men actually will.[110] He argues for this insofar that Eliphaz otherwise would be using in support of his invective a quotation which contradicts his main premise. That is, Eliphaz harbors a strict view of divine retribution: the righteous prosper, the wicked suffer (5:2–3, 17–18). If he posits here that all men suffer simply because they are human (good or evil notwithstanding), he has challenged his main premise. I have extended the modal sense to verse 19 for conformity sake.

GKC argue that the negative interrogative marker at the beginning of verse 21 ("does not") is to be joined to the verb "die," with the intervening clause subordinate in a conditional manner. Thus, I have combined these twin ideas in my translation, "Would they not die if their tent cord were plucked from them?" Dhorme suggests also that the prefixed preposition בְּ on the word בְחָכְמָה ("with wisdom") connotes, as is commonly the case after the verb מות ("die"), the cause of death.[111] So then the meaning is "they die and not because of wisdom," (i.e., wisdom is not the perpetrator of the untimely death) rather than "they die without wisdom."

Eliphaz's Psalm Admonishing the Acceptance of Divine Reproof (5:17–27)

Eliphaz ends his first speech with an eloquent and poignant concluding appeal to Job to accept divine reproof, to confess his sins, and thereby through cultic means to regain the divine favor which has abandoned him.

Translation

5:17 Behold, how blessed is the man whom God reproves,
So do not reject the chastening of the Almighty.

---

109. Pope, *Job*, 38; Habel, *Job*, 117; Gordis, *Job*, 51; Hartley, *Job*, 110n12.
110. "Verb Modality," 354–57.
111. *Job*, 57. Cf. Judg 15:18; Isa 50:12.

5:18 For he causes pain but he binds up;
He strikes but his hands heal.
5:19 From six troubles he will deliver you,
And in seven no evil will touch you.
5:20 In famine he has redeemed you from death
And in battle from the blow of the sword.
5:21 From the lash of the tongue you will be hidden,
And you will not fear when devastation comes.
5:22 At devastation and famine hunger you will laugh,
And you shall not fear the beasts of the earth.
5:23 For your covenant will be with the stones of the field,
And the beasts of the field will live at peace with you.
5:24 You will know that your tent is at peace;
You will attend to your property and not be missing a single thing.
5:25 You will know that your seed will be many,
And your offspring as the grass of the earth.
5:26 You shall come with vigor to the grave,
Like a sheaf gathered up in its time.
5:27 Behold this! We have searched it out, and it is true.
You had better listen and apply it for your own good!

Exegetical Notes

Eliphaz is drawing here again from the conceptual currency of ANE thought. His motif concerns the salutary effect that accompanies confession of sin before God specifically in light of umbrage the deity has taken with Job. And although Eliphaz expounds upon the chastening of God as having an ameliorative effect on its recipient, I also see lying here under the surface an element of caprice attributed to the deity, an arbitrariness most evident in verses 17–18. This distinction will be developed more fully in the immediately following discussion.

Verse 17

הִנֵּה אַשְׁרֵי אֱנוֹשׁ יוֹכִחֶנּוּ אֱלוֹהַּ וּמוּסַר שַׁדַּי אַל־תִּמְאָס

Eliphaz begins the section with an emphatic marker הִנֵּה followed by the beatific term of promised blessing, אַשְׁרֵי, marking the construction as a beatitude: "how happy," "how blessed."[112] The terms יכח ("to reprove") and מוּסָר "chastisement, instruction" introduce the motif of "inflicting pain" which Eliphaz takes up at present.[113] As part of his overarching doctrine of retribution, Eliphaz presents this remedial chastening as the felicitous "erziehliche Maßnahme" ("educative step/strategy") in attaining reconciliation with the deity.[114] His hymnic eloquence betrays a pious (though off-putting) certainty in his counsel—he is convinced his advice to Job is foolproof.[115] Although some commentators, such as Hartley, argue that Eliphaz is portraying God's "loving care for humanity" in that the deity strives to "make that person aware of the consequences of his sinful acts,"[116] I contend instead that under the surface lurks more ominous counsel.

Eliphaz lays out his own theological viewpoint that the reproof of God is useful to mankind in general and to Job in particular, but he fails to ground this assertion in the character of God, exhibited, for example, in his providential care of creation or in privileged covenant love. No explicit mention is made of the greater divine purposes or of God's special notice of the created order nor in particular of humanity. In other words, God "disciplines," "reproves," "causes pain," and "strikes," but we are left to wonder why he does so. There appears to be no virtue nor moral excellence in the divine action—insofar as Eliphaz portrays it—because it is rooted ultimately in a capricious deity whom no man can fathom. This reality is observed most readily when comparison is drawn to other OT passages which expound upon the value of God's remedial chastening, most notably Proverbs 3:11–12, which has striking textual affinities to the present passage. In that passage the sage counsels:

> My son, do not reject the chastening of Yahweh, and do not loathe his reproof
>
> מוּסַר יְהוָה בְּנִי אַל־תִּמְאָס וְאַל־תָּקֹץ בְּתוֹכַחְתּוֹ

---

112. Hartley demonstrates that the beatitude form is quite at home in the Wisdom tradition (cf. Prov 3:13; 8:32, 34; 28:14; 29:18; Pss 1:1; 32:1–2; 94:12) (*Job*, 124n13). Habel labels this form as a macarism (*Job*, 134).

113. Gordis, *Job*, 58.

114. Horst, *Hiob 1–19*, 86. Hartley calls this the "intermediate step" (*Job*, 125).

115. As Ebach notes: "So certain is Eliphaz of the 'sturdiness' of his counsel that he can strike up a hymn, in which he can speak of God's great acts and—almost in comparably hymnic tone—of Job's future welfare" ("So gewiß ist Elifas der Tragfähigkeit seines Rates, daß er einen Hymnus anstimmen kann, in dem er von Gottes großen Taten und—fast im gleichen hymnischen Ton—von Hiobs dereinstigem Wohlergehen reden kann") (*Streiten mit Gott*, 66).

116. Hartley, *Job*, 125.

> For Yahweh reproves the one he loves, just as a father the son he delights in.
>
> כִּי אֶת אֲשֶׁר יֶאֱהַב יְהוָה יוֹכִיחַ וּכְאָב אֶת־בֵּן יִרְצֶה

The semantic correspondence is obvious. Both Job 5:17 and Prov 3:11–12 share the Hebrew term מוּסָר ("chastening"), the Hiphil-stemmed verb יכח (with its cognate noun תּוֹכַחַת also in Prov 3:11, "reprove," "reproof"), and the negative admonition אַל־תִּמְאָס ("do not reject/despise"). Yet, the distinctions also are readily apparent. Solomon grounds his admonition in the fatherly love of Yahweh: "Yahweh reproves the one he loves." For Eliphaz, there is no fatherly love nor filial delight. The chastening comes instead from the transcendent and impersonal שַׁדַּי ("the Almighty One").[117] The chastening may have a salutary effect, but it is purely pragmatic—good may come of it in outward prosperity and welfare, not in consecrated observance of covenant.[118] Psalm 94:12, a similar beatitude extolling the chastening provision of God, reinforces this distinction: "Blessed (אַשְׁרֵי) is the man whom You chasten (יסר), O LORD, and whom You teach out of Your law" (NASB). Here the semantic terms אַשְׁרֵי and יסר (cf. with cognate מוּסָר) correspond to key terms in Job 5:17. Yet the psalmist roots divine chastening theologically in the teaching and application of the Torah and, a few lines later, in Yahweh's covenant love: "For Yahweh will not abandon his people." Eliphaz, on the other hand, has rooted his counsel simply in the transcendentally sovereign and impersonal acts of אֱלוֹהַּ ("God") and שַׁדַּי ("the Almighty One"), divine operations which may yet issue in Job's well-being, yet on what basis?

So although Eliphaz is attempting to persuade Job that what has happened is "for his own good" (cf. 5:27) in that the divine correction is likely

---

117. The use of the term שַׁדַּי (used 31 times in Job out of 48 times total in the OT), if taken seriously, favors placing Eliphaz linguistically in the general period of the patriarchs (Hartley, *Job*, 123, n. 1), as the term appears frequently in accounts of that era (cf. Gen 17:1; 28:3; 35:11; 43:14; 48:3; 49:25; Exod 6:3; Num 24:4, 16; normally preceded by אֵל). Although Koehler and Baumgartner contend that the term is pre-Israelite (later appropriated by Israel from her Canaanite neighbors) referring originally most likely to the Syrian weather god Baal-Hadad, whose dwelling was on the slopes of Ṣāpōn (*HALOT*, 1422), the lexeme appears to derive etymologically from the Akkadian *šadû* "mountain" (Friedrich Delitzsch was the first to propose this in 1886. See Albright, "The Names Shaddai and Abram," 180–193; Cross, *Canaanite Myth and Hebrew Epic*, 52–58) (cf. Ugaritic *td* "breast"). It is quite likely that the term, like אֵל, was a common epithet for God among several cognate languages, not necessarily tied to any singular deity (see Albright, "The Names Shaddai and Abram," 191).

118. As Habel notes, "The image of God as a loving father in Prov 3:12 has been replaced by Shaddai, the grand controller of all cosmic events that affect human lives" (*Job*, 134–35). My only quibble with Habel's insight is his use of the word *replaced* to suggest later chronology and appropriation on the part of Eliphaz. I am suggesting that any intertextuality or allusion works the other way.

to have a salubrious outcome, in reality no solace or hope is offered. Job is left feeling much the same in spite of Eliphaz's fair show of eloquence. Much to his dismay Job is still at the wiles of an arbitrary God who appears to have no greater purposes or concerns behind his dark providences other than evidential traces of his sheer sovereignty.

Verse 18

כִּי הוּא יַכְאִיב וְיֶחְבָּשׁ יִמְחַץ וְיָדָיו תִּרְפֶּינָה

Although Hartley again observes in this text a "hymnic line lauding God's way of acting," exemplifying his role as "the great disciplinarian and the great healer,"[119] we prefer to see more inauspicious counsel. The deity does as he wishes not because he has obligated himself to a covenant—as he has done with Israel and which is the grounding of his redemptive acts throughout the OT—but simply because he is almighty, transcendent, sovereign. God is infinite but impersonal, a trait common to many pseudo-religions particulary religious traditions originating in the East.[120] The Hiphil stem of כאב ("wounds") conveys the notion of physical pain caused by a wound.[121] Eliphaz, although offering a sure remedy to Job's predicament, is thinking in pragmatic terms of restitution, repentance, and abeyance, so that Job's strife with God may be renounced and the divine hand which has battered Job may now restore him.[122]

Verse 19

בְּשֵׁשׁ צָרוֹת יַצִּילֶךָּ וּבְשֶׁבַע׀ לֹא־יִגַּע בְּךָ רָע

To elucidate upon his motif regarding the nature of pragmatic blessing which accompanies divine favor, Eliphaz uses the common Semitic poetic device, traditionally associated with wisdom, of ascending enumeration x +

---

119. Hartley, *Job*, 125.

120. Only the true depiction of the biblical God as presented in the OT and NT balances properly an infinite God who is at the same time personal. All other religions hold, like Eliphaz, to a god who is infinite but impersonal (e.g., Islam, Buddhism, deism) or who is personal but finite (e.g., open theism, Socianism, and, to some extent, process theology). The paradox of an infinite God who is simultaneously personal is exhibited most vividly and beautifully in the incarnation and atonement of Jesus Christ.

121. Dhorme, *Job*, 68.

122. Horst, *Hiob 1–19*, 86.

(x + 1):[123] "From six troubles he will deliver you, and in seven no evil will touch you." Gordis notes that two types of poetic enumeration are used in the Hebrew Scriptures: (1) ascending numbers used rhetorically to connote "several" with no effort to correlate the numerals to the exact number of items delineated (e.g., Amos 1:3–2:6; Mic 5:4; cf. Eccl 11:2; Sir 25:7) and (2) ascending numbers used concretely to list out items corresponding exactly to the higher figure given (x + 1; e.g., Prov 6:16; 30:5, 18, 21, 24).[124] Much discussion has centered upon whether Eliphaz is using the former convention or the latter, and, if the latter, which precisely are the seven items he intends to spell out. Habel, following Dhorme, sees no need to conform the number of redemptive acts to the precise numerals given, as he judges the poetic device to be merely rhetorical, an emphasis upon the scope of disasters (and divine deliverances) encountered by mankind.[125] Steinmann has argued persuasively, however, that each of the four occurrences of the graded numerical saying in Job is an enumeration of the second variety, as the book never uses a graded numerical saying as merely rhetorical convention for "several" but always matches the list precisely to the higher numeral given.[126] Steinmann posits additionally that the author or final editor of the book has prudently utilized the graded numerical saying as a structural marker to point the reader to significant junctures in the movement of the book. Individually the sayings function as a forceful feature in their immediate context. Collectively they mark out "signposts" that point the reader to the larger concerns (and trenchant portions) of the book.[127]

Those who see Eliphaz as delineating seven items have disagreed widely on the intended seven, especially as an initial reading of the passage appears to bring to light nine items.[128] N. H. Tur-Sinai argues that the list encompasses (1) famine, (2) war, (3) evil tongue, (4) destruction by God, (5) stones, (6) wild beasts, and (7) bereavement (parental and conjugal).[129] The difficulty with his proposal, however, is that vv. 24–26 must be conflated to expound a single item, while several previous acts comprise a single stich. Second, protection from wild beasts, delineated twice in slightly different ways, is reduced to a single aspect. Hartley falls into much the same pattern

---

123. See Roth, "The Numerical Sequence X/X+1 in the Old Testament," 300–11.
124. Gordis, *Job*, 58.
125. Habel, *Job*, 135; cf. also Dhorme, *Job*, 69.
126. The graded numerical saying is used in Job 5:19–26 (numbers 6/7); 33:14–15 (1/2); 33:29–30 (2/3); and 40:5 (1/2) (see Steinmann, "Graded Numerical Sayings," 288).
127. Ibid., 297.
128. Clines, *Job 1–20*, 151.
129. Tur-Sinai, *The Book of Job*.

in observing the following seven disasters: (1) famine, (2) war, (3) scourging of the tongue, (4) destruction, (5) drought, (6) beasts of the land, and (7) stones.[130] Hartley's suggestion is unlikely as well; he does not observe any calamities meriting divine intervention in verses 24–26. Second, his identification of drought in verse 22 is interpretively improbable.[131] Clines gets creative, offering two possible lists. First, he suggests that the calamities are (1) famine; (2) war; (3) tongue; (4) wild animals; (5) loss of property; (6) loss of offspring; (7) premature death. Second, he modifies the list given the significance of Eliphaz's repetition of the theme of hunger for another suggested enumeration: (1) war; (2) tongue; (3) destruction (? or flood); (4) wild animals; (5) loss of descendants; (6) premature death; and, (7) hunger.[132] Clines's own indecisiveness is telling. And although he incorporates all the verses of the pericope in his proposal, he needs to rearrange the material somewhat to accommodate his proposed enumeration.

After examining several of the previous—and inadequate—attempts to correlate Eliphaz's numerals with his listing, Steinmann concludes that prior efforts have fallen short out of failure to recognize the structure of the passage. Although the eight verses following 5:19 are typically thought to spell out the number of divine acts in the passage, many fail to see verse 27 as a summary statement, with the preceding seven verses, consisting of two lines each, each identifying a specific act of divine deliverance.[133] In favor of Steinmann's proposal is that he is sensitive to the structure of the passage and the thought-flow of Eliphaz's enumeration rather than randomly selecting seven nouns commensurable to the higher numeral. Steinmann takes each couplet on its own as portraying an intended calamity and divine deliverance. Syntactically, support for this approach may be adduced in the observable structure of the pericope: the first three verses (vv. 20–22) begin with a preposition, the fourth and central verse (v. 23) begins with the transitional syntactical marker כִּי עִם, and the final three verses (vv. 24–26) begin with a verb. He thus identifies the seven acts of divine deliverance proposed as the following: (1) safety from scourges that affect entire populations: famine and war (v. 20); (2) safety from verbal attack turning into physical harm (v. 21); (3) safety from scourges that affect individuals (v. 22); (4) safety away from home (v. 23); (5) safety in one's home (v. 24); (6) many children (v. 25); and, (7) long life (v. 26).[134] Steinmann summarizes the seven redemptive

---

130. *Job*, 126–27.
131. Clines, *Job 1–20*, 151.
132. Ibid.
133. "Graded Numerical Sayings," 291.
134. Ibid., 291–92.

acts as "an enumeration of the seven ways God protects his people. Thus, the graded saying and its accompanying enumeration serve to drive home the point of Eliphaz's discourse: God uses suffering to correct those who err, but he also protects his people from all real harm."[135] I follow the general contours of Steinmann's proposal in the following exegesis, although his third and fourth points need minor modification. It is difficult to concur in verse 23 that a covenant with stones of the field and living at peace with wild beasts constitute safety away from home. It is preferable to see this as promised peace and productivity in one's agricultural endeavors.

Verse 20

בְּרָעָב פָּדְךָ מִמָּוֶת וּבְמִלְחָמָה מִידֵי חָרֶב

In the first couplet Eliphaz pictures redemptive deliverance (פָּדְךָ, "he has redeemed you") from "famine" (a divine act) and "the power [lit. 'hands of'] the sword" in war (a human act).[136] Clines points out the use of the verb פדה as the "perfect of certitude," pointing up the surety of the deliverance Job will experience if he heeds Eliphaz's counsel.[137]

Verse 21

בְּשׁוֹט לָשׁוֹן תֵּחָבֵא וְלֹא־תִירָא מִשֹּׁד כִּי יָבוֹא

Driver and Gray emend בְּשׁוֹט to מִשּׁוֹט to achieve the meaning of "from,"[138] but this is unnecessary as the contextual meaning of מִן may be postulated from the following verb.[139] Habel alleges greater parallelism by reading שׁוֹט

---

135. Ibid., 292.

136. See Hartley, *Job*, 125. Cf. Jer 18:21 "Therefore deliver up their children to famine; give them over to the power of the sword."

137. Clines, *Job 1–20*, 151. Clines contends that the term "belongs to the realm of the law and of psalmody, not to the wisdom material." Dhorme allows that the perfect form emphasizes the certainty of an affirmation which in effect is a prophecy (*Job*, 69; cf. Gordis, *Job*, 59).

138. Driver and Gray, *Job*, 2:32. A comparison of the authors' comments on vv. 19 and 21 is telling. In v. 19 they argue that emendation of the Hebrew from בְּ to מִ "is not necessary: בְּ followed by בְּ is an effective repetition; and LXX may have rendered freely." In v. 21 they claim, however, that changing from בְּ to מִ is "a necessary connection. Confusion of בּ and מ is common: LXX often expresses one (not always rightly) where MT has the other" (*Job*, 2:32). Their comments reveal an inconsistency, especially in light of the fact that the בְּ in v. 21 is a repetition of the dual uses of בְּ from v. 20.

139. Dhorme, *Job*, 70.

as deriving from the verb שׁוט "to rove" rather than from the nominal homonym meaning "scourge" or "lash" and by repointing שֹׁד ("devastation, violence") as שֵׁד ("demon"), thus proposing that Eliphaz is offering deliverance from the roaming ravishment caused by demons. Even without the repointing, however, it is quite possible that demons are in view as wielding violence and devastation against mankind, a common conceptual connection in the ANE.[140] On this basis Duhm wishes to emend לְשׁוֹן to a word for "pestilence" such as רֶשֶׁף,[141] but this is an arbitrary and gratuitous change.[142]

---

140. One may compare the Kirta Epic (1:17–19), in which various demons are perpetrators of destruction against Kirta and his extended family:
    One-fourth the Zebulonim (slew),
    One-fifth Resheph gathered to himself,
    One-sixth the servants of Yam (swept away).

On the numerals as fractions, see Segert, *Basic Grammar*, 54; Finkel, "A Mathematical Conundrum," 109–149. Pardee interprets the numerals as referring to successive brides of Keret who perish in various ways ("The Kirta Epic," 1:333; cf. also Halayqa, *Lexicon*, 63). The context is rather unclear whether in fact the epic refers here to Kirta's wives, offspring, or kindred generally (e.g., the brothers mentioned in lines 8–9). I prefer the latter because (1) most likely the numerals are fractions, suggesting that wives are not in view (that one-fifth of a harem were taken by pestilence is impossible from the context) and (2) it does not appear that Kirta has sired any progeny to this point (later in the myth numerous children are born to him and his wife Ḥurayya (column iii, lines 20–25). Thus, the lines seem most likely to be a reference to Kirta's kinsfolk in general, leaving him without family. I follow M. Tsevat's suggestion that all of the perpetrators of death in the list are various deities of the Canaanite pantheon ("Additional Remarks," 322; cf. also Gordon, *Ugaritic Textbook*, 393), a view which accords well with the parallelism in the context. Thus "*Zebulonim*," which is related to the term *zbl*, meaning "prince," is quite possibly "personified as the deity 'Disease'" (Gordon, UT, 393). The plural form is likely analogous to the use of Rephaim, a plurality of "all the [warrior] gods who assemble at El's invitation" (L'Heureux, "Ugaritic and Biblical Rephaim," 272). Resheph, the god of pestilence and the Netherworld, was a significant divinity of antiquity. See Albright, *Yahweh and the Gods of Canaan*, 139; Fulco, *The Canaanite God Rešep* 1–22, 33–55; Day, *Yahweh and the Gods*, 197–208. Resheph is attested as early as the third millennium BC at Ebla where he appears to have been a popular deity (Xella, "Resheph," 701). Giovanni Pettinato notes that Resheph occupies the second position in the Eblaite pantheon, which numbered about 500 gods ("Royal Archives of Tell Markikh-Ebla," 48). As Pomponio and Xella summarize: "Rasap est parmi les divinités les plus importantes et populaires de la tradition religieuse de la Syro-Palestine et ce n'est pas une surprise de la trouver dans le panthéon d'Ebla avec un rôle de premier plan" ("Resheph is among the most important and popular divinities of the religious tradition of Syro-Palestine, and it is not a surprise to find him with a leading role in the pantheon of Ebla") (*Les dieux d'Ebla*, 313–14). Yam is the well-known god of the sea who battles with Baal over hegemony of the created order in the Baal myth.

141. Duhm, *Hiob*, 34.

142. Clines, *Job 1–20*, 117.

Verse 22

לְשֹׁד וּלְכָפָן תִּשְׂחָק וּמֵחַיַּת הָאָרֶץ אַל־תִּירָא

The term שֹׁד ("devastation, destruction") is repeated here (unless one accepts Habel's repointing in the previous verse) and linked to another sort of dearth. The term כָּפָן is similar to רָעָב and debated in the literature, referring likely to hunger caused by crop failure.[143] Dhorme notes that syntactically this verse bridges verses 21 and 23.[144] From verse 21 the term שֹׁד is repeated, the Aramaic synonym כָּפָן is substituted for רָעָב, and לֹא־תִירָא ("you will not fear") becomes אַל־תִּירָא ("you shall not fear"). Anticipating verse 23 is mention of the חַיַּת הָאָרֶץ ("wild beasts of the earth") for חַיַּת הַשָּׂדֶה ("wild beasts of the field"). Dhorme argues, however, that the repetition is not unjustified but rather is intended to heighten the effect and connectivity of the verses: "It is easy to see that v. 23a gives the reason for v. 22a, whilst v. 23b explains v. 22b."[145]

Verse 23

כִּי עִם־אַבְנֵי הַשָּׂדֶה בְרִיתֶךָ וְחַיַּת הַשָּׂדֶה הָשְׁלְמָה־לָךְ

Building upon the immediately preceding comments, we observe here a close connection to the preceding verse 22 as a basis and explanation of the antecedent couplet. Thus, the reason that dearth will not decimate the penitent sinner is that he enjoys a covenant with the stones of the field, and the basis for which he need not fear the wild beasts of the earth is that they shall be living at peace with him. Modifying Steinmann's approach above, we see in this couplet promised peace and productivity in agricultural endeavors.

The first hemistich is lacking completely in the LXX, perhaps owing to haplography from the repetition of הַשָּׂדֶה in the second hemistich.[146] Interpretations of the first phrase ("Your covenant [will be] with the stones of the field") have abounded. In light of the difficulties, various emendations have been proposed, including a reading from the Targums of אֲדֹנֵי

---

143. Gordis exhibits this by various explanations of the terms in the Targums (*Job*, 59). Duhm identifies כָּפָן as an Aramaism synonymous to רָעָב (*Hiob*, 34; cf. Dhorme, *Job*, 70; Budde, *Hiob*, 24).

144. Budde sees in the "unmittelbare Wiederholung" ("immediate repetition") of terms from the directly preceding and following verses sure signs of "Einschub" ("[redactive] insertion") (*Hiob*, 24).

145. Dhorme, *Job*, 70.

146. Dhorme, *Job*, 71.

הַשָּׂדֶה ("mountain-men"; "satyrs")¹⁴⁷ and a suggested בְּנֵי הַשָּׂדֶה ("sons of the field" or "spirits of the field").¹⁴⁸ Gordis dismisses both proposals.¹⁴⁹ Dhorme contends that the covenant with the stones of the field signifies protection from scourge, as one makes a covenant with death to obtain protection from its bane (Isa 28:15). Stones of the field produce infertility (Matt 13:5) and are sown to devastate a hostile country defeated in battle (2 Kgs 3:19). Thus to have a covenant with the stones of the field entails protection from infertility and devastation.¹⁵⁰ In another way, wild beasts threaten decimation to one's livestock and impede one's ability to produce flourishing crops. Eliphaz seems to be drawing from ANE concepts of primal harmony with nature,¹⁵¹ a promised blessing for Job as "all of nature will stand in a peaceful relationship to you: the stones of the field in that they do not hinder the fertility of your fields, the wild beasts of the field in that they do not injure you or your herds."¹⁵² Eliphaz promises complete peace and productivity in farming and animal husbandry, i.e., protection from stones that produce infertility and from wild beasts that threaten livestock, for those who are favored by God.

VERSE 24

וְיָדַעְתָּ כִּי־שָׁלוֹם אָהֳלֶךָ וּפָקַדְתָּ נָוְךָ וְלֹא תֶחֱטָא

Eliphaz promises certainty ("you will know") of divine blessing should Job heed his counsel. The concept of "tent" (אָהֳלֶךָ) often means simply "home" and together with "habitation" (נָוְךָ) signifies household and property, meaning that, if reconciled, Job may expect the pleasure of inspecting his property and finding all in order, exactly what he anticipated and hoped for, and moreover a robust and healthy herd.¹⁵³ Thus the term שָׁלוֹם connoting complete well-being in every aspect of the household.¹⁵⁴ The verb

---

147. So Rashi (see Habel, *Job*, 136).
148. So Pope, *Job*.
149. Gordis, *Job*, 60.
150. Dhorme, *Job*, 71.
151. Habel, *Job*, 136; Hartley, *Job*, 127.
152. "Die ganze Nature wird in Friedensverhältniss zu dir stehen: die Steine des Feldes, dass sie die Fruchtbarkeit deiner Felder nicht beeinträchtigen, das Wild des Feldes dass es dich und deine Heerden nicht beschädigt" (Delitzsch, *Hiob*, 67; cf. also Fohrer, *Hiob*, 155).
153. Fohrer, *Hiob*, 155–56.
154. Hartley, *Job*, 127.

תֶחֱטָא carries its primarily physical meaning of "to miss" as illustrated in the sharpshooting Benjamites in Judg 20:16 "everyone could sling a stone at a hair and not miss" (ESV). Nothing will come up missing in the most meticulous inspection when God's blessing returns to Job.

VERSE 25

וְיָדַעְתָּ כִּי־רַב זַרְעֶךָ וְצֶאֱצָאֶיךָ כְּעֵשֶׂב הָאָרֶץ

Eliphaz repeats his confident certainty יָדַעְתָּ ("you will know") to evidence that, furthermore, at home Job's offspring (זֶרַע lit. "seed") will be abundant, as plentiful as the "grass of the earth."[155] The analogy is strengthened by the use of the term צֶאֱצָא which may refer to human descendants or to the produce of the field.[156] The twin terms for descendants, זֶרַע and צֶאֱצָאִים, are frequently used together in Job and Isaiah, as in Job 21:8; Isaiah 44:3; 48:19; 61:9; 65:23.[157]

VERSE 26

תָּבוֹא בְכֶלַח אֱלֵי־קָבֶר כַּעֲלוֹת גָּדִישׁ בְּעִתּוֹ

The LXX is modified somewhat here, which has led to a measure of speculation. The Hebrew phrase "you shall come with vigor [? or "full age"] to the grave like a sheaf gathered up in its time") is concretized in the Greek version: ἐλεύσῃ δὲ ἐν τάφῳ ὥσπερ σῖτος ὥριμος κατὰ καιρὸν θεριζόμενος ἢ ὥσπερ θιμωνιὰ ἅλωνος καθ' ὥραν συγκομισθεῖσα ("and you shall come into the grave just as ripe wheat harvested in season").[158] On the basis of the LXX, Herz suggested emendation of the Hebrew בְּכֶלַח ("with vigor") to כאביב לח ("as a fresh ear of corn"), but Dhorme calls this change impossible due to the unreliability of the LXX.[159] Although questions linger regarding the etymology of the term כֶּלַח, it is typically construed in one of two ways.[160] Comparison to Job 30:2 favors a meaning of "vigor," often likened to the Arabic cognate *kalaḥa* denoting "firm, hard" especially in the context of showing

---

155. Hartley, 128.
156. *HALOT*, 993–94.
157. Horst, *Hiob 1–19*, 88.
158. The LXX is followed by Aquila, Sahidic Coptic, Jerome, and Syro-hexapla (see Dhorme, *Job*, 72).
159. Dhorme, *Job*, 73.
160. See Horst, *Hiob 1–19*, 89.

oneself to be strong and firm against another, hence the idea here of coming to the grave with full bodily vigor and firm strength.[161] Jewish Targums, on the other hand, assigned to the term a meaning of "fullness of years," with additional recourse to a different potential Arabic cognate, which led Dhorme to translate "in old age."[162] The closer context of Job 30:2 prefers a meaning of "vigor" (so NASB, NIV), although most English translations opt for "full age" or "ripe age" (so ESV, NET, NJB, JPS, NLT, NRSV, NKJV, KJV, ASV). As for the German versions, Luther translated "Alter" (1545 edition and *Revidierte Lutherbibel* [1984]; followed also by the Schlachter version [1951]), while more contemporary versions render "Rüstigkeit" (*Revidierte Elberfelder* [1993]; cf. "Kraft" in *Einheitsübersetzung* [1980]).

Verse 27

הִנֵּה־זֹאת חֲקַרְנוּהָ כֶּן־הִיא שְׁמָעֶנָּה וְאַתָּה דַּע־לָךְ

Eliphaz ends his speech emphatically with an exhortation to accept his counsel, thus providing a bookend to his opening urge to extend counsel (4:2).[163] By using the first person plural ("we have searched it out") as the basis for his counsel, Eliphaz connects himself to the stream of common ancient wisdom for the grounding of the truth of his assertions.[164] Additionally, he is linked to the later wisdom tradition through his use of the terms שְׁמַע ("hear") and דַּע ("know") (cf. Prov 1:8; 4:1; 24:14).[165] Eliphaz exhibits characteristics that make him "as a representative of their standing, the standing of the wise."[166] Based on the preceding, we would argue that Eliphaz is in fact an archetype of the wise. As Habel notes of Eliphaz's conclusion:

> The phrase הִנֵּה־זֹאת, "behold this," "this indeed," or "yes, this," is a typical summative introduction to the closing message of Eliphaz (cf. 20:29; 33:12, 29). Just as at previous points where he validated his teaching with an appeal to personal experience (4:8; 5:3), Eliphaz now concludes by asserting that all the prior

---

161. Driver and Gray, *Job*, 2:33.
162. Dhorme, *Job*, 73; cf. Gordis, *Job*, 60.
163. Habel, *Job*, 137.
164. Hartley, *Job*, 128; Clines, *Job 1–20*, 154.
165. Habel, *Job*, 137.
166. "Als Vertreter ihres Standes, des Standes der Weisen" (Horst, *Hiob 1–19*, 89).

teaching which underlies his counsel has been tested by careful investigation.[167]

Therefore, Eliphaz concludes his initial peroration exhorting Job toward repentance and appeasement of God if he is to have his fortunes restored.

Eliphaz's Second Speech (Job 15)

The genre of Eliphaz's second discourse is again that of disputation speech, which Horst defines more precisely as *Verweisrede* ("reprimand speech").[168] Following the customary introductory formula (v. 1), Eliphaz's second speech consists of two large stanzas along with several subunits.[169] In 15:2–19 Eliphaz reprimands Job for his apparent refusal to submit to the friends' counsel and, moreover, to accede to the obvious divine displeasure by means of appeasement. The section may be categorized further as a semi-chiastic structure in which Eliphaz alternates between ridiculing Job by asking a series of pointed rhetorical questions and accusing Job by blaming him of outright sin:

Ridicule through rhetorical questions (15:2–3)
Accusation of sin (15:4–6)
Ridicule through rhetorical questions (15:7–11)
Accusation of sin (15:12–16)
Summary of Qualifications as Wisdom Teacher (15:17–19)

Finally, in the concluding section, vv. 20–35, Eliphaz turns once again to his retributive doctrine by warning Job from the hallowed counsels of the Edomite wisdom tradition, a tradition of which Eliphaz is a most dignified proponent.

Translation

15:7 Were you the first man ever born?
Were you brought forth before the hills?
15:8 Have you listened in on the council of God?
Have you so hoarded wisdom to yourself?
15:9 What do you know that we do not?

---

167 Habel, *Job*, 137.
168 *Hiob 1–19*, 220.
169 Murphy, *Wisdom Literature*, 31; Horst, *Hiob 1–19*, 220.

What do you discern that is not apparent to us also?
15:10 Both the gray-haired and the aged are among us,
Greater in days than your father!
15:11 Are the consolations of God too few for you?
Even the word intended for a gentle end?
15:12 Why does your heart carry you away?
Why do you flash your eyes?
15:13 For you turn your spirit against God—
Spewing such words from your mouth!
15:14 What is man that he should be pure?
Or one born of woman that he should be righteous?
15:15 Behold, God does not trust his holy ones;
The heavens are not pure in his eyes.
15:16 How much worse that which is abhorred and corrupt—
Man, who gulps down iniquity like water!
15:17 Let me declare this to you—listen to me!
I have seen this and have recounted it.
15:18 What wise men have declared—
And have not hidden—from their fathers.
15:19 To them alone the land was given,
And no stranger passed through their midst.

Exegetical Notes

Here Eliphaz is more pointed in his assertions and indignant in his counsel to the recalcitrant Job.

Verse 7

הֲרִאישׁוֹן אָדָם תִּוָּלֵד וְלִפְנֵי גְבָעוֹת חוֹלָלְתָּ

Eliphaz begins the section with a series of rhetorical and ironical questions, anticipating a negative reply, a device used commonly in his second speech in an effort to keep Job off-balance. He is hard pressing Job as a grand inquisitor, as he perceives the sufferer to be contravening the cherished premises of Wisdom,[170] meanwhile unbearably pretentious in his (in-

---

170. Ebach, *Hiob*, 131.

valid) claims to wisdom.¹⁷¹ The term הָרִאישׁוֹן has an unusual morphology, as Duhm observes.¹⁷² Together the construction הָרִאישׁוֹן אָדָם is a construct phrase meaning "the first of mankind" or, in essence, "the first man, Adam."¹⁷³ Clines sees here reference to the primordial First Man myth, presaging a personage known as *Urmensch*,¹⁷⁴ "a mythical figure endowed with supernatural wisdom."¹⁷⁵ Others elaborate upon this to propound the myth of a "heavenly Adam" who sits in the heavenly council and has direct access to God, thus the apogee of human wisdom. This heavenly Adam was essentially primordial man, a model for the later earthly Adam.¹⁷⁶ Habel, in fact, sees four characteristics of this (primordial) *Urmensch*: (1) he is the first of all who are born); (2) his origin precedes the construction of the hills; (3) he has direct access to the council of heaven; and (4) he has the possibility of usurping primordial "Wisdom."¹⁷⁷ Habel elaborates upon this mythological cosmogony:

> This Primal Human is apparently a figure born of the gods or Mother Earth (cf. 1:21) rather than one 'born of woman' like normal mortals (v. 14). He is described in terms of pre-existence comparable to those of Wisdom. Like her, he exists 'before the hills' (Prov. 8:25; cf. Ps. 90:2). Like her he is with God at the time of creation and therefore a potential counselor (Prov. 8:30). The same myth of a Primal Human present with God at creation is suggested by the challenge of Yahweh from the whirlwind.¹⁷⁸

Habel's proposal goes beyond what the data allows, however. A better solution is to perceive an allusion to Hebrew-Semitic traditions already in currency, which understand Adam, viewed in his original state, as the apex of human wisdom and perfection prior to the Fall. In light of later wisdom traditions regarding the genesis of wisdom prior to and then integrally involved in the creation of the world (cf. Prov 8:22–31), Adam, as the first and archetypical man, has prime access to the pristine fountains of divine sapience (immediate contact with the Creator; cf. Gen 2:15–20) and

---

171. Dhorme, *Job*, 210.

172. Duhm remarks that the term exhibits "a double orthography, the phonetic with י, the etymological with א" (*Hiob*, 81).

173. Gordis, *Job*, 161.

174. Ebach, *Hiob*, 132.

175. Clines, *Job 1–20*, 349.

176. Hartley, *Job*, 245.

177. Habel, *Job*, 253.

178. Ibid.

is thus the prototype of the true sage.[179] The second hemistich reinforces his point, reaching back before the birth of creation itself: "Were you brought forth before the hills?"[180] Eliphaz is in essence asking Job whether he fancies himself to be older than creation, as old as and wiser than Wisdom itself.[181]

Verse 8

הַבְסוֹד אֱלוֹהַ תִּשְׁמָע וְתִגְרַע אֵלֶיךָ חָכְמָה

The customary interrogative הֲ is repointed הַ due to the *shewa* which follows,[182] and the preposition בְּ suggests an eavesdropping or listening in.[183] The term סוֹד may denote either "secret" or "secret counsel," a semantic range evident from the variety of translations which have been adduced.[184] The phrase סוֹד אֱלוֹהַ connotes here "the circle of those who are admitted to intimacy with Yahweh and so obtain knowledge that is hid from other men."[185] The incongruity in this statement is obvious. Eliphaz is accusing Job of hubris for insinuating that he has listened in on those secret councils to which Eliphaz presumes Job to have no access. Yet the irony is that Eliphaz, by means of his nocturnal dream encounter, is essentially arrogating this privilege to himself in a shaded sense, while in reality the reader is the only onlooker who has enjoyed this exclusive vantage point from the outset of the book. The two phrases of verse 8 may be read either as (1) vividly depicting the specific primeval divine council which brought to fruition the created order (e.g., the "Let us" in Gen 1:26) or (2) a recurrent eavesdropping of the divine councils.[186] The first sense is preferred as it anticipates Yahweh's eloquent allusion to this background in Job 38:4–5 ("Where were you when I laid the foundation of the earth? Tell me, if you have understanding. Who determined its measurements—surely you know! Or who stretched the line upon it?"). The second hemistich in verse 8 is most likely consecutive, relating

---

179. Gordis, *Job*, 160. Gordis points to Ezek 28:12–19 and Ps 82:6–7 to support this argument, but corroboration from these passages is tenuous. It is significant to note that the theme of creation is recurrent in wisdom traditions.

180. Dhorme, *Job*, 210. Cf. the common English idiom of one's being "older than the hills."

181. Ebach, *Hiob*, 131.

182. Dhorme, *Job*, 211.

183. Gordis, *Job*, 161.

184. Dhorme, *Job*, 211.

185. Driver and Gray, *Job*, 2:96. Cf. Ps 25:14 where the NRSV translates סוֹד יְהוָה "the friendship of the LORD."

186. Driver and Gray, *Job*, 2:96.

to the action which Job would have taken in light of having listened to the divine council, viz., hoarding for himself a piece of divine insight.[187]

Verse 9

מַה־יָּדַעְתָּ וְלֹא נֵדָע תָּבִין וְלֹא־עִמָּנוּ הוּא

Eliphaz disparages the pretention that Job has discovered—much less enjoys any real access to—the secrets of true wisdom, as Eliphaz and his confidants are the only esteemed holders of the keys to this kingdom. Job's knowledge falls short; what little insight he has gained through the maturation process of his experiential suffering is completely outweighed by the logically consistent norms of Eliphaz's wisdom. This is the case, as Ebach observes, "because Eliphaz can discern in Job no 'mythical' advance in knowledge and can allow for him no more than an advanced understanding matured from the experience of suffering he measures—within his logically consistent categorical system—Job's knowledge and the traditional norms"[188] Although Dhorme sees Eliphaz as alluding to himself and his immediate friends,[189] he is likely referring to a larger class of sages as he makes clear in the following verses. Job has threatened Eliphaz's very epistemology by his rash words, and his pseudo-wisdom must be summarily abrogated.[190]

Verse 10

גַּם־שָׂב גַּם־יָשִׁישׁ בָּנוּ כַּבִּיר מֵאָבִיךָ יָמִים

The participle שָׂב from the verb שׂיב ("to have white hair"; cf. the cognate noun שֵׂיבָה "white hair") is rare (only elsewhere in Sir 32:3).[191] The terminology of יָשִׁישׁ ("aged") is used also in Job 12:12. Job ought to have more respect for the words of Eliphaz since he is older than Job's father and therefore certainly wiser than Job.[192] As Gordis observes: "Here Eliphaz delivers

---

187. Ibid.
188. "Da Elifas Hiob keinen «mythischen» Vorsprung an Wissen zuerkennen und ihm ebenso wenig einen aus seiner Leidenserfahrung erwachsenen Verstehensvorsprung zubilligen kann, mißt er—innerhalb seines Kategoriensystems konsequent—Hiobs Wissen und den tradierten Normen" (Ebach, *Hiob*, 132).
189. Dhorme, *Job*, 211.
190. Habel, *Job*, 254.
191. Dhorme, *Job*, 211.
192. Duhm, *Hiob*, 81. *Contra* Hartley, who points to hyperbole here and dismisses

himself of what is the decisive argument in the ancient world—Wisdom is synonymous with age."¹⁹³

Verse 11

הַמְעַט מִמְּךָ תַּנְחֻמוֹת אֵל וְדָבָר לָאַט עִמָּךְ

Eliphaz now grows still sharper in tone.¹⁹⁴ The LXX is markedly different in this verse as noted above.¹⁹⁵ The phrase תַּנְחֻמוֹת אֵל ("consolations of God") refer to the constituent elements of Eliphaz's retributive doctrine regarding the necessary correlation of deed and outcome (*Tun-Ergehen-Zusammenhang*):¹⁹⁶ the righteous must be rewarded and the evildoer must be punished. This is pristine, divine truth for Eliphaz, delivered to him personally through direct revelation (4:16–21) and full-brewed to perfection in the unassailable sapience of the ancients (15:10, 17–18).¹⁹⁷ In this tit-for-tat discourse Eliphaz will not relinquish his trump card. The term לָאַט is a difficult one, generally rendered "act gently" (cf. 2 Sam 18:5; Isa 8:6) and thus likely here "speak gently."¹⁹⁸ This is likely a subtle reference to Eliphaz's visionary dream encounter.¹⁹⁹

Verse 12

מַה־יִּקָּחֲךָ לִבֶּךָ וּמַה־יִּרְזְמוּן עֵינֶיךָ

Eliphaz confronts Job on his settled anger, which is a further affront to the offended deity. The pronoun מָה is used here in the sense of "why?"²⁰⁰ The heart and the eyes were conceived in ancient times as the sources of desire and passion, spoken of in the Targums as "the middle men of transgression"

---

the notion that Eliphaz is older than Job's father (*Job*, 246).

193. Gordis, *Job*, 161. As Dhorme adds: "It is always in going back to the preceding generations that one finds more and more of wisdom" (*Job*, 212).

194. Ebach, *Hiob*, 133. Habel perceives "a measure of hurt and disappointment" (*Job*, 254), but Eliphaz seems to be on the offensive rather than defensive.

195. See Dhorme, *Job*, 212.

196. Gradl, *Ijob*, 83.

197. Gordis, *Job*, 161.

198. Ibid.

199. Dhorme, *Job*, 212.

200. Ibid.

(סרסורי עבריה).²⁰¹ The heart in particular is the seat of one's volitional and rational life, and the eyes reveal the contents of the heart.²⁰² For Eliphaz the carrying away of the heart and the flashing of the eyes mean that Job has clearly transgressed. In his accusation that Job's heart has "carried him away," Eliphaz is similar to the friend in the Babylonian *Theodicy* who likewise exhorts, "You have let your subtle mind go astray, [. . .] you have ousted wisdom."²⁰³ Earlier the counselor had impugned the sufferer for his dementia, another topic at which Eliphaz hints at in this couplet:

> What I say is restrained . . . . [. .]
> But you [. . .] your balanced reason like a madman.
> You make [your . . . .] diffuse and irrational,
> You [turn] your select . . . blind.²⁰⁴

The verbal form יִרְזְמוּן presumably from the lexeme רזם, a *hapax* root, has been widely discussed in the literature. Ebach conjectures here that in the flashing of the eyes Eliphaz is suggesting an allusion to the Sumerian *engalgalutim*, meaning "the very great eye" (sehr großes Auge), as a symbol of wisdom and insight.²⁰⁵ This would be taken ironically as Eliphaz's asking Job if he really imagines himself to be a fountain of sapience. Tur-Sinai connects to an Arabic cognate *razama*, "dwindle away, become weak," which he argues signifies that Eliphaz observes weakening perspicacity in Job, the basis for his foolish and wanton rebellion against God.²⁰⁶ The difficulty with this proposal, however, is that it does not fit the context of vented anger against the offended deity. Dhorme attaches the term instead to רמז in Aramaic, Syriac, and New Hebrew to connote "make signs," "blink," or "wink."²⁰⁷ Others nuance this meaning to propose a rolling or flashing of the eyes which Eliphaz indignantly confronts.²⁰⁸ Kotzé elaborates upon this final suggestion to propose that Eliphaz refers here to an "evil eye" in Job, tied to ANE beliefs regarding witchcraft and black magic.²⁰⁹ He points to the Syriac root רמז, which is used to translate the closely related term קרץ, and

---

201. Gordis, *Job*, 161.
202. Hartley, *Job*, 247.
203. "Babylonian *Theodicy*," lines 212–13, (*BWL*, 83).
204. Ibid., lines 34–37 (*BWL*, 73).
205. Ebach, *Job*, 133. Oppositely, a narrowing of the eyes would suggest a fool's *Dummheit*.
206. Tur-Sinai, *Job*, 250. Cf. Pope, *Job*, 15; Clines, *Job 1–20*, 342.
207. Dhorme, *Job*, 213. So also Driver and Gray, *Job*, 2:96–97.
208. Fohrer, *Hiob*, 270; Horst, *Hiob 1–19*, 225; Kissane, *Job*, 90.
209. Kotzé, "Magic and Metaphor," 152–57.

proposes a meaning of "stinging eye," a euphemism in ANE magic texts for the baleful eye which projects evil and harm by a mere glance.[210] Although Kotzé's suggestion that Eliphaz is openly accusing Job of witchcraft is somewhat suspect, he has, in my opinion, correctly identified the context from which this term arises. Eliphaz is steeped in the customary ANE methods for restoring favor to the offended deity, including as we will see below, the ritualistic purging methods of incantation. He is therefore quite possibly contending that Job is further alienating himself by flashing his eyes in anger toward the displeased deity rather than following submissively Eliphaz's prescribed means of repentance and restoration.

Verse 13

כִּי־תָשִׁיב אֶל־אֵל רוּחֶךָ וְהֹצֵאתָ מִפִּיךָ מִלִּין

Dhorme points out that רוּחַ is occasionally used in the sense of "anger" (Judg 8:3; Prov 16:32), as the terms θυμός and *animus* "animosity," and should here be translated "when you turn against God your animosity and allow such words to proceed out of your mouth."[211] Again, the counsel of the friend in the Babylonian *Theodicy* runs along similar lines:

> My reliable fellow, holder of knowledge, your thoughts are perverse.
> You have forsaken right and blaspheme against your god's designs.
> In your mind you have an urge to disregard the divine ordinances.
> [. . . . .] the sound rules of your goddess.[212]

Eliphaz perceives a dangerous hubris and renegade spirit in the sufferer, and for Job's own good Eliphaz must challenge his pugilism. The counselor in the Babylonian *Theodicy* likewise reprimands that "in your anguish you blaspheme the god."[213]

---

210. Ibid., 155.
211 Dhorme, *Job*, 213.
212. "Babylonian *Theodicy*," lines 78–79 (*BWL*, 77).
213. Ibid., line 255 (*BWL*, 87).

Verse 14

מַה־אֱנוֹשׁ כִּי־יִזְכֶּה וְכִי־יִצְדַּק יְלוּד אִשָּׁה

Eliphaz presents here a reformulation of the syllogism presented to him by his nocturnal visitor, reported previously in 4:17–19.[214] Eliphaz recycles the material for fresh emphasis. While the former accent was on the inescapable inferiority of mortals made of clay vis-à-vis the transcendent purity of the Creator, here the focus moves to the inner impulses which distinguish this loathsome, mortal man "born of woman."[215] Job, of course, is the prime specimen for observation in this regard. Gordis renders the first stich "What is man that he should be pure?"[216] The parallelism signals that וְכִי is to be taken as a question also, a common usage in Mishnaic Hebrew.[217] In the second hemistich woman is a source of impurity (cf. 14:4).[218] The counselor in the Babylonian *Theodicy* serves as a striking foil:

> Narru, king of the gods who created mankind,
> And majestic Zulummar, who dug out their clay,
> And Mistress Mami, the queen who fashioned them,
> Gave perverse speech to the human race.
> With lies, and not truth, they endowed them forever.[219]

Both Eliphaz and the Babylonian counselor view humanity as innately perverse and therefore susceptible to the capricious whims of the divine realm.

Verse 15

הֵן בִּקְדֹשָׁיו לֹא יַאֲמִין וְשָׁמַיִם לֹא־זַכּוּ בְעֵינָיו

The emphatic הֵן is another clue that this is a reformulation of the divine disclosure received in his night-time dream-vision. The first hemistich reproduces 4:18a, but with בִּקְדֹשָׁיו ("in his holy ones") rather than בַּעֲבָדָיו ("in his servants").[220] Eliphaz is re-asserting the universal depravity of the created order. Again this is an avowal of God's capricious transcendence: nothing of

---

214. Hartley, *Job*, 247; Dhorme, *Job*, 213.
215. Habel, *Job*, 255–56.
216. Gordis, *Job*, 161.
217. Ibid., 162.
218. Dhorme, *Job*, 213.
219. "Babylonian *Theodicy*," lines 276–280 (BWL, 88).
220. Ibid., 214.

the created order is "good" as it is *en toto* a perishable entity disconnected from the sovereign "otherness" of the Almighty, who may be pleased or displeased randomly according to the dictates of his whim. Likewise the counselor in the Babylonian *Theodicy* advises the sufferer:

> The divine mind, like the centre of the heavens, is remote;
> Knowledge of it is difficult; the masses do not know it.[221]

Elsewhere this sage muses: "The plan of the gods is remote."[222] In a comparable manner the sufferer in *Ludlul bēl nēmeqi* laments, "Who knows the will of the gods in heaven?" and asks again "Where have mortals learnt the way of a god?"[223] Eliphaz is similarly stressing the utter transcendence of God. Divine transcendence must equate to the impurity of the created order. This is applied to Job in a direct manner. The issue now at hand is not proof of Job's guilt; this is evident to anyone with eyes. The means of reversing the divine displeasure must now be addressed.

Verse 16

אַף כִּי־נִתְעָב וְנֶאֱלָח אִישׁ־שֹׁתֶה כַמַּיִם עַוְלָה

Eliphaz employs *a fortiori* argument "how much more so." Eliphaz has gone from generalities concerning universal human peccability in 4:19 to specific application: Job is a deliberate sinner.[224] The lexeme נִתְעָב conveys that which disgusts or horrifies, "abominable."[225] The term נֶאֱלָח is related to an Arabic cognate "to grow sour (of milk)" and thus "loathsome."[226] The metaphor of drinking iniquity like water is a picturesque way of describing the human bent toward evil.[227] In its practical application Job has gulped down his iniquity, imbibed its perversion, and is now spewing forth corrupt speech. Likewise the counselor in the Babylonian *Theodicy* advises the sufferer that his intrinsic evil has landed him afoul of the gods:

> My reliable fellow, holder of knowledge, your thoughts are perverse.
> You have forsaken the right and blaspheme against your god's designs.

---

221. "Babylonian *Theodicy*," lines 256–57 (*BWL*, 87) (cf. line 82).
222. Ibid., line 58 (*BWL*, 75).
223. *Ludlul bēl nēmeqi*, lines 36, 38 (*BWL*, 41).
224. Gordis, *Job*, 162.
225. Dhorme, *Job*, 214.
226. Gordis, *Job*, 162.
227. Hartley, *Job*, 248.

In your mind you have an urge to disregard the divine ordinances.
[. . . . .] the sound rules of your goddess.[228]

Verse 17

אֲחַוְךָ שְׁמַע־לִי וְזֶה־חָזִיתִי וַאֲסַפֵּרָה

The term אֲחַוְךָ ("Let me explain to you") is found frequently later in the Elihu speeches (32:6, 10, 17; 36:2). The sage is fond of arguing on the basis of his own personal experience ("I have seen this and will recount it now") (cf. 4:7, 8; 5:1, 3, 8, 17, 27), and this portion is no exception. The particle זֶה is the relative "that which,"[229] here a likely reference to the dream encounter which Eliphaz is newly expounding upon. The term חזה ("I have seen [in a vision]") is thus an allusion to Eliphaz's shadowy brush with the revelatory spirit from God and he is propounding additional truth that was afforded him by the divine disclosure.[230]

Verse 17 is transitional, as Eliphaz moves from a reformulation of the content of his visionary experience to expound now in the immediately following verses upon the trustworthiness of his wisdom as distilled from the reservoir of ancient sapience. As Ebach notes, this wisdom is for Eliphaz doubly reliable: "The wisdom of the fathers is therefore so reliable because (1) it descends from men to whom the administration of the entire land was entrusted and (2) it descends from a time in which there was not even a stranger in the land."[231] Eliphaz is absolutely entrenched in his position, as he after all has both God and the fathers on his side!

---

228. "Babylonian *Theodicy*," lines 78–81 (*BWL*, 77).

229. Dhorme, *Job*, 214.

230. Habel, *Job*, 257. Habel sees the additional revelation as contained in vv. 20 and following. It is better to understand the revelation as what has preceded in vv. 14–16, on the basis of at least two factors. First, the content of vv. 14–16 is very similar to 4:17–19, suggesting that this is a direct reference back to the content of that revelation. Second, v. 17 ("Let me declare this to you—listen to me! I have seen this and have recounted it") is best posited as a summary statement—as Eliphaz is wont to make elsewhere (cf. 5:27)—which refers to the content that has preceded immediately. Eliphaz is seeking to reinforce the validity of this nocturnal encounter by exaggerated claims of empirical trustworthiness.

231. "Die Weisheit der Väter ist deshalb so vertrauenswürdig, weil sie 1. von Männern stammt, denen die Leitung des ganzen Landes anvertraut war, und 2. aus einer Zeit stammt, in der es noch nichts Fremdes im Lande gab" (Ebach, *Hiob*, 133–34).

Verse 18

אֲשֶׁר־חֲכָמִים יַגִּידוּ וְלֹא כִחֲדוּ מֵאֲבוֹתָם

This verse is difficult in light of its word order and syntax. A straightforward reading is not easily comprehended on its face, as it conveys that Eliphaz is about to provide momentous insights "which wise men declared and did not hide *from their fathers.*" But this meaning seems out of place. Hallowed traditions are those very things which are *received from* the fathers rather than *hidden from* the fathers, and thus the *prima facie* sense would contravene Eliphaz's overall import.[232] He is marshalling, instead, those very sapient traditions which have been handed down from his esteemed mentors and forebears rather than appealing to esoteric insights obscured from them which would place him out of line with that tradition. Another option is to understand the מִ as denoting time, hidden from the *time* of the fathers. This meaning would belie Eliphaz's purpose of crystallizing the very insights which his forebears had bequeathed to him. He does not suggest to unearth new insights which had fallen out of use since the time of the fathers. The best solution is to take וְלֹא כִחֲדוּ ("and have not hidden") as parenthetical, in which case Eliphaz is appealing to that which the wise men have openly declared—without hiding anything—(that is to say, hallowed counsels) from their fathers.[233]

Verse 19

לָהֶם לְבַדָּם נִתְּנָה הָאָרֶץ וְלֹא־עָבַר זָר בְּתוֹכָם

The meaning of this verse is unclear, and has been interpreted variously as an allusion to a pure community of believers or Eliphaz's home country. Although Dhorme sees this as referring to Israel,[234] nothing in the text points definitively to this, as there are abundant examples of xenophobia and of the mixture and dilution of people groups in ancient times as migrations took place and empires were established.[235] Eliphaz's argument seems to point, rather, to the unequivocally pristine nature of wisdom that is distilled from the ancient epochs.[236] Eliphaz is referring to "remote ancestors who

---

232. Gordis, *Job*, 162.
233. Driver and Gray, *Job*, 2:97.
234. Dhorme, *Job*, 215.
235. Hartley, *Job*, 251n21.
236. Horst, *Hiob 1–19*, 228.

lived long ago, at a time when men were few on the earth, unlike its present crowded condition. The earlier the period of the ancestors, the greater their wisdom."[237] Eliphaz is clearly relying upon his ancestors' "store of doctrines and norms."[238]

Eliphaz's Third Speech (Job 22)

In the third speech the genre remains that of *Streitgespräche* but Eliphaz incorporates—as he does in the first discourse—several elements of hymn, reminiscent of the style and form of the Psalms. The structure of the speech is difficult to classify. It consists of an opening series of rhetorical questions (22:2–5), followed by the main body of the speech, which Murphy partitions into five subunits:[239] (1) specific accusations against Job (22:6–9); (2) threats to Job regarding his persistent refusal to submit as his present trials result from his sinfulness (22:10–12); (3) accusations of Job's claims that God is ignorant (22:13–14); (4) a final warning to Job based on the end of the wicked (22:15–20); and (5) conclusive instruction to Job with a conditional promise of restoration should he seek renewed divine approbation through appeasement (22:21–30). We will survey first the series of opening rhetorical questions, followed by the first two subunits of the main body of Eliphaz's third speech.

Translation

22:2 Can man be useful to God?
Indeed can the insightful be useful to him?
22:3 Is it any delight to the Almighty if you are righteous?
Does he profit when you are upright in your ways?
22:4 Is it because of your piety that he would arraign you,
Entering litigation with you?
22:5 Is not your wickedness great?
Your iniquity limitless?
22:6 For you have gratuitously taken pledges from your brothers.
The garment of the naked you have stripped off.
22:7 You have denied water to drink to the faint;

---

237. Gordis, *Job*, 162.
238. "Vorrat an Lehren und Normen" (Ebach, *Hiob*, 134).
239. Murphy, *Wisdom Literature*, 34.

You have withheld food from the hungry.
22:8 To the man of strength the land belonged;
The prejudiced man lived in it.
22:9 You have sent away widows empty-handed;
The arms of orphans were crushed.
22:10 Therefore snares encircle you;
Suddenly dread dismays you.
22:11 Whether or not there is darkness, you do not see.
A flood of water encompasses you.
22:12 Is not God high in the heavens?
See the chief stars how lofty they are!

Exegetical Notes

Eliphaz turns now to prescribe the ritual means by which Job may regain favor with the offended deity.

Verse 2

הַלְאֵל יִסְכָּן־גָּבֶר כִּי־יִסְכֹּן עָלֵימוֹ מַשְׂכִּיל

In a return to the acrimonious approach of his second speech, Eliphaz poses a series of pointed rhetorical questions to Job as a means of vitiating the epistemological foundations to his spurious claims of wisdom. Here the first four verses are rhetorical questions: verses 2–3 query the advantage of righteous deeds, while verses 4–5 question the basis for Job's deplorable plight.[240] Eliphaz holds tightly to his view of a transcendent God, pressed harder in light of Job's continued protestations of innocence. Eliphaz wants to prove to Job (and the others) that God is "wholly other," sufficiently removed and disinterested in the created order as in no way beholden to it, insofar only as to mete out punishment and reward as he wills. Yet the divine disinterest only further substantiates Job's guilt.[241] In light of the divine test revealed in

---

240. Hartley, *Job*, 324.

241. As Duhm notes, for Eliphaz "God is an entirely objective, uninterested being, who therefore also handles men objectively according to their conduct so that the cause of human fate always is to be sought in the humans themselves and the friends rightly found 'the root of the matter' in Job" ("Gott ist ein ganz objektives, uninteressiertes Wesen, das darum auch die Menschen objektiv nach ihrem Verhalten behandelt, so dass die Ursache des menschlichen Geschickes immer im Menschen zu suchen ist und die Freunde mit Recht 'die Wurzel der Sache' in Hiob fanden") (*Hiob*, 114).

the prologue, however, Eliphaz's question is ironic: God indeed has a vital stake in the integrity of his servant.²⁴²

Dhorme observes that the LXX rendering of verse 2 (πότερον οὐχὶ ὁ κύριός ἐστιν ὁ διδάσκων σύνεσιν καὶ ἐπιστήμην;) ("Is not rather the Lord the teacher of insight and knowledge?") presupposes the translator's reading הלא אל (double א).²⁴³ The verb סכן ("to be useful, profitable"), which is used twice here and once earlier in 15:3, is disputed due to the range of meanings evident in the root.²⁴⁴ The key to its significance in our context lies in Elihu's later riposte (34:9), which uses the term with the clear import of "be of use":

> For he has said, 'It is of no use for man
> (כִּי־אָמַר לֹא יִסְכָּן־גָּבֶר)
> When he is in favor with God'
> (בִּרְצֹתוֹ עִם־אֱלֹהִים)

Elihu utilizes the same term in 35:3 with similar significance: "What advantage have I?" (ESV).²⁴⁵ The conjunction כִּי is used here in the conditional sense of "if, whether." The final term in the stich, מַשְׂכִּיל (lit. "sage, wise man"), is frequently synonymous in the wisdom corpus with the righteous (cf. Ps 14:2; Dan 11:33, 35; 12:3, 10). Gordis renders the latter term adverbially and proposes a different sense for סכן in the second hemistich to pose "Is it God whom man benefits when he wisely puts himself in harmony with him?"²⁴⁶ The particle כִּי which begins the second hemistich, however, anomalously suggests a double question (as rendered above),²⁴⁷ and thus the sense is in line with our translation above. Habel emends עֲלֵימוֹ to read the term עוֹלָם "the Eternal One," thus placing Eliphaz in the patriarchal era by means of a common epithet for God (cf. Gen 21:33). Although we have placed Eliphaz closely in line with the patriarchal era, there is no need to

---

242. Habel argues that God is seeking some gain by his wager with the adversary concerning Job's integrity (*Job*, 338).

243. Dhorme, *Job*, 326. The Hebrew sense of the verse seems entirely to have escaped the LXX translator.

244. Although *HALOT* defines the various meanings of סכן under a single heading, the divergence of sense suggests multiple roots (Gordis, *Job*, 244). *HALOT* provides the following glosses: "be of use, run into danger, have the habit of, be acquainted with, be reconciled with" (755). E. Lipiński suggests that all four occurrences of סכן in Job (15:3; 22:2; 34:9; 35:3) signify "run a danger" ("courir un danger") ("*skn* et *sgn*," 191–92), but this is unconvincing.

245. Gordis, *Job*, 244.

246. Gordis, *Job*, 245. Gordis derives the meaning of the second סכן as a metaplastic form of סכם "to agree." Clines points out that Gordis's proposal is tenuous as such a meaning for סכן is unattested (*Job 21–37*, 540).

247. Clines, *Job 21–37*, 540.

emend the text, as to do so fails to obtain better sense of the passage or to align with alternate readings in any ancient version.

Verse 3

הַחֵפֶץ לְשַׁדַּי כִּי תִצְדָּק וְאִם־בֶּצַע כִּי־תַתֵּם דְּרָכֶיךָ

Verse 3 develops further the thought of verse 2. God derives neither benefit nor pleasure in the integrity (כִּי תִצְדָּק "that you are righteous") of loathsome mankind. Several interpret חֵפֶץ as "special benefit, favor, advantage" in light of the parallelism with בֶּצַע, "profit, gain" in the second hemistich.[248] It is preferable to see the term as meaning "pleasure, delight," however, as this is consistently its import in the book.[249] Eliphaz again uses the divine name שַׁדַּי to underscore the transcendence of God (see above). God derives no delight from the character of mankind, as if Job's specious claims to innocence really mattered. The term תַתֵּם is an Aramaizing Hiphil from תמם,[250] a tendency attested in early Hebrew and not indicative of a later date (cf. Exod 13:18).[251]

Verse 4

הֲמִיִּרְאָתְךָ יֹכִיחֶךָ יָבוֹא עִמְּךָ בַּמִּשְׁפָּט

Eliphaz continues with his "bitterly ironic taunt," confronting Job further about his misinformed claims to innocence.[252] Here again יִרְאָתְךָ ("your fear") denotes "your piety" (cf. 4:6; 15:4). The terminology of יכח and בוא בַּמִּשְׁפָּט are technical terminology for filing a lawsuit. The term יכח carries here the connotation of "arraignment in a court of law,"[253] while בּוֹא בַּמִּשְׁפָּט means literally "go to the place of judgment" with the idiomatic sense "enter litigation."[254] Job consistently exhibits a desire to file litigation against God in court to contend his case for innocence (Job 9:32; 13:15–19, 22–24; 19:7;

---

248. Dhorme, *Job*, 327; Gordis, *Job*, 245.

249. The term חפץ (or a cognate as here) appears eight times in Job, each occurrence (one possible exception is a homonym in 40:17) with a meaning of "delight, pleasure."

250. Duhm, *Hiob*, 114.

251. Driver and Gray, *Job*, 2:153; Gordis, *Job*, 245.

252. Gordis, *Job*, 245.

253. Boecker, *Redeformen des Rechtsleben*, 46.

254. Scholnick, "The Meaning of *mišpaṭ*," 524.

31:35–37).²⁵⁵ Eliphaz mocks the impropriety of these conceited claims for legal justice. Job's vain averments notwithstanding, God would never deign to enter a lawsuit with a mortal or be intimidated in any way by such pretentious allegations. He is transcendentally above such petty legal claims.

Verse 5

הֲלֹא רָעָתְךָ רַבָּה וְאֵין־קֵץ לַעֲוֹנֹתֶיךָ

Eliphaz unleashes his final insights as sage and counselor in a last-ditch effort to right Job's listing ship. If Job will admit to his sins and seek ritual purgation, hope remains that he may again find favor with the Almighty. To accomplish this Eliphaz attempts "shock therapy" to aid Job in realizing the full extent of his failure before the offended deity. The idiom אֵין־קֵץ signifies "without end, endless, limitless,"²⁵⁶ as a means of describing Job's gross wickedness. Eliphaz will now offer a ready-made sin list to assist Job through the process of ritual purgation.

Verse 6

כִּי־תַחְבֹּל אַחֶיךָ חִנָּם וּבִגְדֵי עֲרוּמִּים תַּפְשִׁיט

Habel notes that the crimes outlined in verses 6–8 pertain to those characteristic of an unrighteous leader and are prohibited not only in the Mosaic Law but also in the Hammurabi code, while the opposite virtue expected is exemplified by Dan'el and Keret in the Ugaritic epics.²⁵⁷ Some dispute remains over the term אַחֶיךָ, whether properly singular אָחִיךָ ("your brother"; so Targums) or plural אַחֶיךָ ("your brothers"; so LXX, Vulgate, Syriac, MT),²⁵⁸ but I tentatively have followed the latter due to the greater number of evidences. In the latter stages of the Babylonian *Theodicy*, the sagacious counselor likewise reproaches the grieving friend for his communal misdeeds:

> You have let your subtle mind go astray,
> [. . . . .] you have ousted wisdom,
> You despise property, you profane ordinances.²⁵⁹

---

255. Ibid., 524–25.
256. Dhorme, *Job*, 327.
257. Habel, *Job*, 339. Cf. Keret II.vi.30; Aqhat II.v.7–8.
258. Dhorme, *Job*, 328.
259. "Babylonian *Theodicy*," lines 212–14 (*BWL*, 83).

In both cases the sufferer's alleged failure of wisdom and lack of piety has incited his companion to reproach him for flagrant violations of the community's ethical norms.

Verse 7

לֹא־מַיִם עָיֵף תַּשְׁקֶה וּמֵרָעֵב תִּמְנַע־לָחֶם

The LXX takes עָיֵף and רָעֵב as collectives (διψῶντας and πεινώντων), but it is preferable to render the terms "faint" and "hungry" which can be construed as singular or plural in English.

Verse 8

וְאִישׁ זְרוֹעַ לוֹ הָאָרֶץ וּנְשׂוּא פָנִים יֵשֶׁב בָּהּ

Verse 8 is difficult and considered a gloss by some.[260] The construct phrase אִישׁ זְרוֹעַ (lit. "man of the arm") conveys the imagery of the physically strong (and rapacious).[261] The phrase נְשׂוּא פָנִים connotes "view favorably, hold in repute,"[262] and alludes to favoritism toward the *Vollbürger* ("full citizens") of the land.[263]

Verse 9

אַלְמָנוֹת שִׁלַּחְתָּ רֵיקָם וּזְרֹעוֹת יְתֹמִים יְדֻכָּא

Most versions render יְדֻכָּא (Pual yiqtol 3ms "is crushed") as if it were תְּדַכֵּא ("you crushed") (so LXX, Vulgate, Syriac, Targums),[264] but this may be explained as a preference for sense and style over literalness.

---

260. So Peake.
261. Dhorme, *Job*, 329.
262. Driver and Gray, *Job*, 2:153.
263. Duhm, *Hiob*, 115.
264. See Driver and Gray, *Job*, 2:153.

Verse 10

עַל־כֵּן סְבִיבוֹתֶיךָ פַחִים וִיבַהֶלְךָ פַּחַד פִּתְאֹם

Eliphaz achieves tremendous assonance in this couplet (n.b. the litany of *p* sounds as an onomatopoetic harbinger of the sudden eruption of disaster: פַחִים, פַּחַד, and פִּתְאֹם, together with other labial *b* and *m* phonemes). He explicates explosively and eloquently on the sure downfall of the evildoer.

Verse 11

אוֹ־חֹשֶׁךְ לֹא־תִרְאֶה וְשִׁפְעַת־מַיִם תְּכַסֶּךָּ

Eliphaz symbolizes the relentless despair that has engulfed Job through the imagery of turbulent, dark, and frigid waters (cf. Jon 2:6 [Eng 2:5]; Ps 69:2–3 [Eng 1–2]), imagery that is a foreshadowing of Sheol known elsewhere for its watery tumult and dismal darkness.[265]

Verse 12

הֲלֹא־אֱלוֹהַּ גֹּבַהּ שָׁמָיִם וּרְאֵה רֹאשׁ כּוֹכָבִים כִּי־רָמּוּ

From imagery of the dark and watery tomb of Sheol, Eliphaz shifts abruptly to a hymnic line exalting divine transcendence.[266] Most likely the next few verses are a response to Job's claim in 21:14–15 that the wicked pronounce to God, "Leave us alone! We have no desire to know your ways. Who is the Almighty that we should serve Him?" (NIV), as Eliphaz portrays Job as a card-carrying member of that class. The MT רְאֵה as imperatival is preferable to LXX "he sees" or Syriac "he has seen" as proved by the parallelism with Isaiah 40:26–27 where מרום "lift up your eyes on high" is parallel to וּרְאֵה as the imperative construction "and see."[267] Here Eliphaz is similar to the counselor of the Babylonian *Theodicy* (although the latter is partially obscured), who exhorts his friend:

> In your mind you have an urge to disregard the divine ordinances.

---

265. Johnston, "Underworld and the Dead," 416–17; Hartley, *Job*, 327.

266. Duhm argues that "the verse is a quoted poem that depicts the transcendence of God" ("Der Vers ist einem Gedicht entnommen, das die Erhabenheit Gottes schilderte") and thus doubts its originality (*Hiob*, 115). The redaction is unnecessary, however, as Eliphaz's eloquence here is hardly different from his lofty imagery elsewhere.

267. Dhorme, *Job*, 331.

> [.........] the sound rules of your goddess.
> The plans of the god [.......] like the centre of heaven,
> The decrees of the goddess are not [.......]²⁶⁸

The Mesopotamian counselor, like Eliphaz, emphasizes the transcendence and remoteness of the deity.

Eliphaz's Rebuke from Yahweh (42:7)

Finally in this section we consider Eliphaz's rebuke from Yahweh to investigate what further insight may be gained from our applied understanding of Eliphaz's role in the book of Job.

Translation

42:7 Now after Yahweh had spoken these words to Job, Yahweh said to Eliphaz the Temanite: "My anger burns against you and against your two friends because you have not spoken to me what is right as my servant Job has. 8 And now take for yourselves seven bulls and seven rams and go to my servant Job and offer a burnt offering for yourselves. Job my servant will pray for you, for I will regard his prayer not to deal with you in keeping with your folly, for you have not spoken to me what is right as my servant Job has."

Exegetical Notes

7 וַיְהִי אַחַר דִּבֶּר יְהוָה אֶת־הַדְּבָרִים הָאֵלֶּה אֶל־אִיּוֹב וַיֹּאמֶר יְהוָה אֶל־אֱלִיפַז הַתֵּימָנִי חָרָה אַפִּי בְךָ וּבִשְׁנֵי רֵעֶיךָ כִּי לֹא דִבַּרְתֶּם אֵלַי נְכוֹנָה כְּעַבְדִּי אִיּוֹב׃ 8וְעַתָּה קְחוּ־לָכֶם שִׁבְעָה־פָרִים וְשִׁבְעָה אֵילִים וּלְכוּ ׀ אֶל־עַבְדִּי אִיּוֹב וְהַעֲלִיתֶם עוֹלָה בַּעַדְכֶם וְאִיּוֹב עַבְדִּי יִתְפַּלֵּל עֲלֵיכֶם כִּי אִם־פָּנָיו אֶשָּׂא לְבִלְתִּי עֲשׂוֹת עִמָּכֶם נְבָלָה כִּי לֹא דִבַּרְתֶּם אֵלַי נְכוֹנָה כְּעַבְדִּי אִיּוֹב׃

Much discussion has centered upon the meaning of these verses, their relationship to the preceding human and divine speeches, the nature of the censure for Eliphaz and the other friends, and the verses' silence concerning

---

268. Babylonian *Theodicy*, lines 80–82 (*BWL*, 77).

Elihu.²⁶⁹ Key issues relate to the meaning of אֵלַי ("to me" vis-à-vis "about, concerning me") and the adverbial accusative נְכוֹנָה ("what is right; rightly") together with their significance contextually as a rebuke to Eliphaz and the other friends in light of the preceding dialogue. Although Yahweh proclaims that Eliphaz and the two friends have "not spoken rightly about/to me" as his servant Job had, still Job himself has been rebuked in the Yahweh speeches (38:2, "Who is this that darkens counsel by words without knowledge?" [cf. 40:2, 7–8] and Job's repentance in 42:1–6). The nagging question becomes the way in which Job has spoken rightly "about" God that the friends have not if Job likewise is rebuked? How is the content or form of Job's speeches superior to that of the friends, and what specifically are the friends reproved for? More precisely the pertinent issue lies in the nature of Eliphaz's censure and how this rebuke elucidates his role and purpose in the book, as well as what it says about his theological bent.

Most commentators traditionally have taken אֵלַי to signify עָלַי ("about / of / concerning me") in this phrase.²⁷⁰ König, for example, argues that the meaning is "of me," and he points to Genesis 20:2 as an example: "And Abraham said *of Sarah* (אֶל־שָׂרָה) his wife, 'She is my sister.'"²⁷¹ Dhorme in a similar way points to Jeremiah 40:16 as an illustration for the meaning of "speaking on the subject of" as in, "You are telling a lie *about* Ishmael" (אֶל־יִשְׁמָעֵאל) (NIV).²⁷² With this interpretation Yahweh rebukes Eliphaz and the other friends primarily for the *content* of their speeches—they have not spoken rightly *about* Yahweh because their theological orientation is completely mistaken and their approach to Job entirely injurious.

Recent discussion by Timmer, however, has countered persuasively that the meaning "to me" for אֵלַי best suits the context for several reasons and that therefore the rebuke pertains more so not to what the friends *have said* but rather to what they *have not yet said*.²⁷³ First, the preposition אֶל is used three times after the speaking verb דבר in the immediate context of

269. See especially Nam, "Job 42:7–9 and the Nature of God," esp. 7–8. Cf. Kottsieper, "«Thema verfehlt!»," 775–85; Timmer, "God's Speeches," 286–305.

270. As Kottsieper observes: "The overwhelming majority of contemporary interpretation is herein agreed, that אלי, analogous to עלי, and נכונה should be read in the sense of 'correctly, properly'" ("Die überwiegende Mehrzahl der heutigen Auslegen ist sich darin einig, daß אלי analog zu עלי und נכונה im Sinne 'Korrektes, Richtiges' aufzufassen sei") ("Zur Kritik Gottes an den drei Freunden," 775). Cf. Duhm, *Hiob*, 204; Dhorme, *Job*, 648; König, *Das Buch Hiob*, 452; Gordis, *Job*, 494.

271. König, *Hiob*, 452.

272. Dhorme, *Job*, 648.

273 Timmer interacts pervasively with Manfred Oeming, building upon the latter's work. Cf. Oeming, "'Ihr habt nicht recht von mir geredet wie mein Knecht Hiob,'" 103–16.

42:7–8, and the first occurrence is determinative for the subsequent uses. Verse 7 begins with the narrative setting "Now after Yahweh had spoken these words *to* Job" (אֶל־אִיּוֹב). The meaning of אֶל in this first phrase is clearly "to" (Yahweh has said little or nothing *about* Job in the preceding but he has directed his speeches *to* him; so also NIV, NASB, ESV, NET, RSV, NRSV, KJV, NKJV, NEB, ASV). As the immediate context this usage is determinative for the two subsequent occurrences in verses 7b–8. Yahweh is reproving Eliphaz and the other friends for not speaking rightly *to* him since Job *has spoken rightly to him* by repenting of his rash pronouncements.

Second, the versions support or at the very least do not contravene the meaning of "to" for אֵלַי in the verse, pointing away from a meaning of "concerning." For example, LXX renders as ἐνώπιόν μου in 42:7 and leaves untranslated in verse 8. The Vulgate renders *coram me* in verse 7 and *ad me* in verse 8.

Third, a study of the occurrences of אֶל + דבר in Job demonstrate that the dative of indirect object is indeed in view each time rather than a meaning of "concerning."[274] Timmer argues further that such is the case pervasively with this construction throughout the Hebrew Scriptures.[275]

Fourth, an important clue to the meaning of אֵלַי is found in the relation of this statement to the critique of Job found in the divine speeches of chapters 38–41. Yahweh has already dealt with and reproved Job's words in his two extended, confrontational discourses (see esp. 38:2–3; 40:2, 7–8). This fact has two implications for the meaning of 42:7–8. (1) Yahweh's reference here to what Job has said correctly vis-à-vis what the three friends have said likely does not refer back to what Job has uttered in the dialogue portions as that would be anachronistic and inconsistent. Yahweh already has addressed the content of those speeches in his earlier ripostes so he is more likely referring to the immediately preceding utterance, viz., Job's extended statement of repentance in 42:1–6. (2) Since Yahweh rebukes Job earlier for the content of his speeches, it is very unlikely that he now indicates *approval* of their content as compared with the content of the friends' speeches. These factors point in the direction of finding a solution in the more immediate context of Job's repentance in 42:1–6.

---

274. Of the five times דבר + אֶל appears in Job (excluding direct quotation framing [so-and-so said to so-and-so "thus-and-thus"] and the two uses under discussion in 42:7b, 8) none requires a meaning of "concerning" but rather each has the locative sense "to" (Job 2:13; 4:2; 13:3; 42:7a; 42:9).

275. Timmer contends: "Of the 465 or so occurrences of the collocation אל + דבר (with three or fewer words intervening) in the Hebrew Bible, only one requires the nuance 'regarding' (2 Sam 7:19; see the debatable cases in 1 Sam 3:12; Jer 30:4; 33:14; 51:12, where 'against' or 'to' is probably satisfactory)" ("God's Speeches," 302n63).

Fifth, the meaning of נְכוֹנָה (Niphal participle fem sing כון, "be established") likewise supports the view that Job's penitent statement in 42:1–6 is in view. The Niphal participle נָכוֹן with a term of speaking is used in only a handful of cases and refers unequivocally to what is certain, settled, established, trustworthy.[276] In Gen 41:32 the term refers to a word or matter that is made certain by God. Deuteronomy 13:15 and 17:4 make mention of a word or statement that is trustworthy and certain, therefore binding in a legal case. Psalm 5:10 speaks of the evildoer in which no truth (i.e., nothing trustworthy or certain) is found in his mouth. The opposite to נְכוֹנָה in this context is נְבָלָה ("folly"). The latter term is used twice in Job, once of Job's wife who is behaving the part of the foolish women in 2:10 and as a reference to those בְּנֵי־נָבָל ("senseless brood"; cf. "fools" [NIV]) who mock Job's misfortune in 30:8. Eliphaz and the other friends, as Timmer acknowledges, "are not described as having said what is foolish; rather, their folly is not having spoken truth, as Job did."[277]

So then, if Job has been rebuked earlier by Yahweh for the content of his dialogical speeches as we have argued, what then is the trustworthy, certain statement that Job has made? It can refer to nothing else than his extended statement of repentance in 42:1–6. The friends are charged with not speaking certain and trustworthy words to Yahweh because they have not humbled themselves to repent at the sight of the theophany as Job already has and have not yet been rebuked for the hubris with which they have approached Job and arrogated to themselves the role of divine spokesmen.

Thus, the indictment which Yahweh levels at Eliphaz has to do with his haughtiness in failing to humble himself before Yahweh in repentance. As the counselor seeking to bring Job to penitence and ritual purgation, he now himself is in need of these because he has not humbled himself before God in the midst of his verbal onslaught. Thus, we would argue that Yahweh's rebuke does not deal with the *content* of Eliphaz's speeches *per se*, but rather with the characteristic arrogance with which Eliphaz has asserted himself. This is not to say, of course, that Yahweh agrees with what Eliphaz has said. To suggest this would be reading too much into the context. We propose rather that while Yahweh is silent about the content of Eliphaz's speeches, he is very much displeased with the strident posture adopted by Eliphaz as one who arrogates to himself to speak unequivocally and unassailably as God's spokesman.

Glimpses of the genius of this book break forth. The ANE ritualistically purgative counselor abruptly has the tables turned on him. He must

---

276. *HALOT*, 464.
277. "God's Speeches," 303.

now seek humbling reconciliation with the offended deity under the auspices of Job.

Summary and Conclusion

The preceding analysis of salient portions of Eliphaz's speeches has sought to underscore the nature of his role as ANE counselor by forging links between his counsel and the counsel which would be expected of a ritualistically purgative counselor of the ANE as demonstrated in comparable ancient writings of theodicy. The survey has fortified our understanding of Eliphaz as one firmly fixed within the milieu of the ANE counselor motif. This insight provides a clearer understanding of Eliphaz's role and purpose within the book of Job as the counselor who is to bring Job to repentance and ritual cleansing and who ultimately fails to do so. This tension sets the stage for the stunning outcome when Job repudiates the counsel of his erstwhile peers. Yahweh steps in to adjudicate, signaling the futility of human wisdom to answer satisfactorily such questions of ultimate significance.

6

Conclusion

THE PRECEDING ANALYSIS HAS offered a fresh, albeit admittedly limited, re-assessment of the chief interlocutor to Job in the dialogue cycles of the book of Job. The study began by offering a new appraisal of the interpretive history of Eliphaz, arriving at several conclusions concerning the interpretive trajectory a reader of Job is likely to take with Eliphaz. This trajectory depends in large measure upon his or her predisposition toward Eliphaz's retributive doctrine, particularly the archetypal paradigm for his system of retribution as outlined in 4:7–11. In the ancient context this was not viewed with as much disdain as it would come to be in subsequent centuries, which has accounted for the interpretative polarity which would characterize later efforts to understand Eliphaz.

Next, I surveyed the ANE wisdom perspective of Eliphaz as an Edomite sage who was familiar with the role of ritualistically purgative counselor as a chief elder of his clan. This approach observed how Eliphaz was rooted in his hallowed theological and sapiential traditions, which were pervasive throughout the ancient world. Finally, I offered an exegetical analysis of the salient portions of Eliphaz's speeches. This analysis fortified the remarkable link with the content of counsel provided by "friends" and "counselors" in other ANE works of theodicy. This link underscores that Eliphaz is not to be treated as a flat, one-dimensional character in Job but rather is to be viewed as a sophisticated counselor who has at his disposal the best of human wisdom and insight. In spite of this, however, Eliphaz fails as a counselor because in his hubris he has not acknowledged the true source of wisdom—which lies not in shadowy dreams, the traditions of the ancients, or the customary cleansing rituals of the ANE religious milieu—but in Yahweh himself. As the Yahweh speeches demonstrate, God alone is the source of transcendent wisdom capable of resolving the ultimate questions prompted by human finitude.

As a Christian reader I must close the loop to acknowledge that centuries later this divine wisdom would come to fruition in the Savior born to redeem lost humanity, a humanity whose best insights are but foolishness to God (1 Cor 1:20). This Savior would be hailed as the one "whom God made our wisdom and our righteousness and sanctification and redemption" (1 Cor 1:30) and "in whom are hidden all the treasures of wisdom and knowledge" (Col 2:3). Eliphaz founders, but Jesus Christ consummates. Jesus Christ is the perfect merging of divine and human wisdom, the antidote for Job's suffering, the answer to his and all of humanity's greatest need. Christ is indeed the "Wounderful Counselor" to whom every person must give heed.

Appendix

I HAVE ARGUED IN this study that the canonical book of Job was composed during a period in which didactic theodicy was flourishing in the ANE, as the portrayal of competing claims to wisdom would suggest. An extensive collection of the so-called ANE wisdom literature of this sort originated as early as the Third Dynasty of Ur onward into the Cassite era, 2000–1500 BC, a period in which the development and spread of Babylonian literature were most prevalent.[1] Although tangential to the main assertions of this thesis, such a provenance aligns with a sixteenthth- to fifteenth-century BC authorship of Job by Elihu. Writing perhaps toward the end of his life, Elihu authors the book of Job—I would suggest—to reflect further on the events and theological perspectives of the incident in his youth. If so, Elihu is exhibiting under the inspiration of the Holy Spirit (cf. "the breath of the Almighty"; Job 32:8) the sovereign freedom and wisdom of Yahweh vis-à-vis other theological wisdom perspectives of the ANE.

In his essay arguing for Elihuan authorship of Job, Shimon Bakon concludes likewise that "it would be a gratifying guess that it is Elihu . . . who is the enigmatic author of Job."[2] That Elihu is the most probable author Bakon adduces from several factors. First, Elihu is the only character in the book called by his full name, "Elihu the son of Barachel the Buzite, of the family of Ram" (Job 32:2). Second, the speeches of Elihu tie together the different and seeming disparate parts of the book—often collectively a source of puzzlement for scholars—into an organic entity. Third, following Maimonides, Bakon contends that Elihu represents the only authentic Jewish theodicy in the book so that rather than being dismissed as spurious his speeches are to be viewed as integral to the intended message of the book. Fourth,

---

1. *Babylonian Wisdom Literature*, 10–11. Foster, "Dialogue Between a Man and His God," 485; Nougayrol, "Une Version Ancienne du 'Juste Souffrant,'" 240.
2. "The Enigma of Elihu," 228.

Elihu alone fully develops and provides distinct expression to one of the major themes of the book, *Läuterungsleiden*, which Bakon defines as "God's disciplinary measure to prevent man from falling into deeper sin."[3]

J. Weinberg takes up where Bakon leaves off to offer several additional clues in support of Elihuan authorship. First, historical-culturological comparisons of Job with other ANE wisdom literature reveal a similar practice of "embedded authorship" in which clues to authorship are comprised within the work, while not explicitly stated, serving both as an "intellectual game" meant to challenge and stimulate the audience intellectually and as a means of underscoring that what is being said is more important than who in particular is saying it. Second, biblical tradition itself was wont to obscure authorship of biblical writings to the point that the writer disappears into the tradition of the work—although for some genres such as prophecy, and to a far lesser extent such as wisdom, this was impossible. Third, while the three friends are introduced with the standard formula name + toponym with article and *nisbe* formation, which suggests provenance from other peoples and places (i.e., foreigners from the perspective of the writer), Elihu alone is introduced with "the full, ceremonial and honorable three- or four-member formula: personal name + patronymic + name of the *bêt 'āb* or *bêt 'ābôt* + name of the clan or tribe." Together the aggregation of these names hints strongly for Elihu's Hebrew orientation as distinct from the friends and therefore as the one with greater insight, suggestive of authorship. Fourth, Weinberg notes the extensive self-presentation of Elihu, another clue to the "purposefully individualized and vivid portray of a concrete man with convictions and ambitions of his own." He is presented vividly in a way that the other characters are not, an indication that his perspective is intended to be taken seriously. In addition, the spirit of the book of Job reflects this reality and bears the imprimatur of the youthful Elihu who is the most likely candidate for authorship. Finally, Weinberg includes a statistical analysis intended to bolster the claim of Elihu authorship by demonstrating that key terms in the book are found predominantly in the speeches of Elihu as well as in the speeches of Job. These thematic key-terms appear to solidify the significance of the Elihu speeches as integral to the fabric of the book, a likely sign of authorship.[4] In addition to these arguments, another may be adduced. Elihu is the only individual in the book of Job for whom inner thoughts are indicated in narrative style (as compared with the mere record of words spoken). In 32:2–3 the author of the book reveals reasons for which Elihu became angry: "Elihu . . . burned with anger. He burned

---

3. Ibid., 220–28.
4. "Was Elihu, the Son of Barachel, the Author of the Book of Job?" 154–64.

with anger at Job because he justified himself rather than God. He burned with anger also at Job's three friends because they had found no answer, although they had declared Job to be in the wrong." This intimacy with Elihu's thought process suggests access to his inner reflection, which although not proving authorship certainly tantalizes the reader toward this possibility.

Others are reluctant to posit Elihuan authorship of Job, however. Robert McCabe has adduced several compelling arguments against the foregoing hypothesis, and his views merit discussion. McCabe contends that Elihu serves a preparatory role by which he summarizes the content of the friends' speeches and prepares for the reader for the ensuing Yahweh speeches.[5] To support this trajectory for the book and more specifically for Elihu's function, McCabe adduces several keys in which Elihu's theological emphases differ from those of Joban author.[6] First, McCabe posits that the Joban author presents Job as man of "great religious integrity."[7] In particular, the divine assessment of Job's integrity underscores that Job's suffering was not a consequence of his sin. Elihu, on the other hand, presumes in several places that Job's suffering *was* the result of his previous sin (34:37; 36:9–10), a view inconsistent with the larger emphasis of the book. Second, McCabe posits that the Joban author emphasizes that Elihu is angry at Job for his self-righteous attitude and at the other friends for their failure to refute Job adequately. The author explicitly mentions Elihu's anger several times (32:2 [twice], 3, 5). In his speeches, however, Elihu presents himself as patient, cool-headed, and moved by the breath of the Almighty (32:6–22), a self-promotional staging which sets Elihu at odds with the perspective of the Joban author.

Third, McCabe suggests that Elihu's verdict of Job runs counter to Yahweh's assessment in the climax of the book.[8] Elihu condemns Job for speaking in ignorance and for rebelling wickedly against Yahweh. Thus, Elihu believes Job's basic position is wrong.[9] God's evaluation of Job, on the other hand, is that while Job has occasionally spoken in ignorance, the basic tenor of his understanding of God's justice and providence has been correct. In fact, Yahweh commends Job for speaking "what is right" about him (42:7, 8). In this way the Joban author "appears to be using Elihu's evaluation as

---

5. McCabe, "Elihu's Contribution," 79–80.

6. Ibid., 64–72.

7. Ibid., 65.

8. McCabe acknowledges, however, that Elihu's verdict of the three friends is correct (ibid., 67–68).

9. Ibid., 68.

a 'theological foil' for God."[10] Fourth, Elihu's understanding of suffering as having a disciplinary purpose (33:19–24; 36:8–11), rather than as the friends assert solely a penal objective, contravenes the message of the book concerning the mysterious nature of suffering. That is, as the book provides no final resolution to the secret divine purposes for suffering, Elihu's view goes contrary to the larger message of Job. Thus, "Elihu's disciplinary view of suffering is in conflict . . . since he provides an explanation for what God has kept shrouded in his secret will."[11] Again in this way the Joban author positions Elihu as a foil to illustrate finally the inadequacies of human wisdom so that Elihu's perspective, rather than being normative, serves as another demonstration of the limits of human sapience.

McCabe has contributed significantly to studies of Elihu through his careful and thorough analysis. Several of his insights are helpful in assessing the trajectory of the Elihu speeches. As I believe however that the foregoing arguments by Bakon and Weinberg in support of Elihuan authorship of Job bear weight, I will offer a few comments in response. First, the hypothesis that Elihu is author of Job does not necessarily suggest that his views are normative. As I illustrate below, I would offer that Elihu is looking back on his youthful experience and reflecting upon it. Much time elapses between the conclusion of the speeches and the end of Job's life as asserted in the epilogue, where the author records that "after this Job lived 140 years, and saw his sons, and his sons' sons, four generations. And Job died, an old man, and full of days" (Job 42:16–17). Certainly Elihu's perspective may have changed after the encounter with Yahweh, as the others' did, and the Yahweh speeches—rather than the Elihu speeches—are intended as the climax for the book. Second, Elihu's assessment of Job on the whole appears to have much validity as Job himself admits that he has sinned during the course of his speeches when he confesses that "I have uttered what I did not understand, things too wonderful for me, which I did not know . . . therefore I despise myself, and repent in dust and ashes" (42:3, 6). Thus, Elihu's assertion that Job "adds rebellion to his sin" (34:37) should be taken at face value. Earlier I argued that Job's speaking rightly about Yahweh from Yahweh's perspective has to do with Job's repentance rather than the content of his speeches. Third, I would suggest that in being largely correct in the tenor of his perspective, Elihu does offer further emphasis on the inadequacies of human wisdom. That is, in his youthful enthusiasm Elihu turns the tables on conventional wisdom by underscoring the reality that wisdom does not reside solely with the aged. In the ancient context such an

10. Ibid., 69.
11. Ibid., 70.

assertion would be analogous to a plot twist in which conventional thinking is turned on its head. Fourth, Elihu's perspective on suffering, while not entirely adequate, adds a fuller understanding of a significant purpose of suffering for the faithful devotee of Yahweh. This emphasis led Maimonides, as demonstrated earlier, to argue that Elihu offers the only truly Jewish perspective in the book. Elihu has not uttered the final word—the task which remains for Yahweh—but he has rounded out the picture by offering a fuller understanding of the nature of suffering.

Thus, I would offer that the content of the Elihu speeches do not preclude him necessarily from being author of the book of Job. Working from the inference of Elihuan authorship of Job, the following page illustrates a generalized chronology to the events in the book of Job in the form of a proposed genealogical chart.

Figure 1: Proposed Chronology of Eliphaz the Temanite[12]

Jacob (2006–1859 B.C.) (Gen 25:26)   Esau (2006–???) (Gen 25:25)

↓   ↓

Judah (Gen 29:35)   Eliphaz (Gen 36:4)

↓   ↓

Perez (Gen 38:29)   Teman (Gen 36:15)
                        (Edomite chieftans
↓   ↓   Gen 36:15–16)

Hezron (Gen 46:12; Ruth 4:18)   ????
    (Jacob's family goes down
     to Egypt 1876 B.C.)
↓   ↓

Ram (Ruth 4:19; 1 Chron 2:9)   **Eliphaz the Temanite** (Job 15:10)

    (*Elihu, the son of Barakel*
    of the family of Ram [Job 32:2]) ————→ (Job's trial)
Amminadab (Ruth 4:19; 1 Chron 2:10)   (Job speeches)

↓   (Job dies [42:17])
                        (Edomite kings
    (Israelites enslaved in Egypt 1580 B.C.)   Gen 36:15–16)
Nahshon (Ruth 4:20; 1 Chron 2:10)   (*Elihu authors Job*)
    (Exodus 1446 B.C.)
↓

Salmon (Ruth 4:20; 1 Chron 2:11)
    (Conquest 1406 B.C.)
↓

Boaz (Ruth 4:21)

---

12. Data reconstructed from biblical genealogies with the assistance of John H. Walton, *Chronological and Background Charts of the Old Testament*, 15–16, 28.

Bibliography

Abbot, George. *The Whole Booke of Job Paraphrased, or, Made Easier for Any to Understand*. London: Edward Griffin, 1640.
Ahituv, Shmuel. "An Edomite Ostracon." In *Michael: Historical, Epigraphical, and Biblical Studies in Honor of Prof. Michael Heltzer*, edited by Y. Avishur and R. Deutsch, 33-37. Tel Aviv–Jaffa, Israel: Archaeological Center Publications, 1999.
Albertson, R. G. "Job and Ancient Near Eastern Wisdom Literature." In *Scripture in Context II*, edited by W. Hallo, J. Moyer, and L. Perdue, 213-30. Winona Lake, IN: Eisenbrauns, 1983.
Albertz, Rainer. "The Sage and Pious Wisdom in the Book of Job: The Friends' Perspective." Translated by L. Perdue. In *The Sage in Israel and the Ancient Near East*, edited by J. Gammie and L. Perdue, 243-61. Winona Lake, IN: Eisenbrauns, 1990.
———. "Der sozialgeschtliche Hintergrund des Hiobbuches und der 'Babylonischen Theodizee.'" In *Die Botschaft und die Boten: Festschrift für Hans W. Wolff*, edited by J. Jeremias and L. Perlitt, 349-72. Neukirchen-Vluyn, Germany: Neukirchener Verlag, 1981.
———. *Weltschopfung und Menschenschopfung untersucht bei Deuterojesaja, Hiob und in den Psalmen*. Stüttgart: Calwer, 1974.
Alden, Robert L. *Job*. NAC. Nashville: Broadman and Holman, 1993.
Al-Fayyumi, Saadiah ben Joseph. *The Book of Theodicy: Translation and Commentary on the Book of Job*, translated by L. E. Goodman. New Haven, CT: Yale University Press, 1988.
Allison, Dale C. "Job in the 'Testament of Abraham.'" *JSP* 12, no. 2 (October 2001) 131-47.
Alonso-Schöckel, Luis A. "God's Answer to Job." In *Job and the Silence of God*, edited by C. Duquoc and C. Floristán, 45-51. New York: Seabury, 1983.
———. "Toward a Dramatic Reading of Job," translated by Robert Polzin. *Semeia* 7 (1977) 45-61.
——— and J. L. Sicre-Diaz. *Job: Comentario teológico y literario*. Madrid: Cristiandad, 1983.
Alt, Albrecht. "Zur Vorgeschichte des Buches Hiob." *ZAW* 55 (1937) 265-68.
Ambrose. "On the Prayer of Holy Job." In *The Fathers of the Church: A New Translation*, translated by M. P. McHugh. Vol. 65. Washington, D.C.: Catholic University Press, 1972.

Andersen, Francis I. *Job*. TOTC. Downers Grove, IL: InterVarsity, 1976.

Anonymi in Iob Commentarius. Edited by Kenneth B. Steinhauser. Vienna, Austria: Verlag der österreichischen Akademie der Wissenschaften, 2006.

Aquinas, Thomas. *The Literal Exposition on Job: A Scriptural Commentary Concerning Providence*, translated by Anthony Damico. Atlanta: Scholars Press, 1989.

Archer, Gleason L., Jr. *The Book of Job: God's Answer to the Problem of Undeserved Suffering*. Grand Rapids: Baker, 1982.

———. *A Survey of Old Testament Introduction*. 2nd ed. Chicago: Moody, 1994.

Asensio, Nieto F. "La vision de Elifaz y su proyyección sapiencial." *EstBib* 35 (1976) 145–63.

Astell, Ann W. *Job, Boethius, and Epic Truth*. Ithaca, NY: Cornell, 1994.

Atkinson, David J. *The Message of Job*. The Bible Speaks Today. Downers Grove, IL: InterVarsity, 1991.

Baab, O. J. "The Book of Job." *Int* 5, no. 3 (July 1951) 329–43.

Baker, Wesley C. *More than a Man Can Take: A Study of Job*. Philadelphia: Westminster, 1966.

Balentine, Samuel E. "Ask the Animals and They Will Teach You." In *'And God Saw that It Was Good': Essays on Creation and God in Honor of Terence Fretheim*, edited by F. Gaiser and M. Throntveit, 3–11. Word and World Supplement Series 5. St. Paul, MN: Luther Seminary, 2006.

———. *Job*. Smith and Helwys Bible Commentary. Macon, GA: Smith and Helwys, 2006.

———. "Job's 'Struggle for the Last Truth about God.'" *RevExp* 99, no. 4 (Fall 2002) 579–80.

———. "My Servant Job Shall Pray for You." *ThTo* 58, no. 4 (January 2002) 502–18.

———. "Who Will Be Job's Redeemer?" *PRSt* 26, no. 3 (Fall 1999) 269–89.

Ball, C. J. *The Book of Job*. Oxford: Clarendon Press, 1922.

Bardtke, H. "Prophetische Züge im Buche Hiob." In *Das Ferne und Nahe Wort: Festschrift für Leonhard Rost*, 1–10. Berlin: A. Töpelmann, 1967.

Barr, James. "The Book of Job and Its Modern Interpreters." *BJRL* 54 (Autumn 1971) 28–46.

Barrick, William. "Messianic Implications in Elihu's 'Mediator Speech' (Job 33:23–28)." Unpublished paper. National Meetings of the Evangelical Theological Society, 2003.

Bartlett, John R. *Edom and the Edomites*. Sheffield: JSOT Press, 1989.

———. "Edom and the Fall of Jerusalem." *PEQ* 114 (January–June 1982) 13–24.

———. "Edom in the Nonprophetical Corpus." In *You Shall Not Abhor an Edomite for He Is Your Brother: Edom and Seir in History and Tradition*, edited by D. Edelman, 13–21. Atlanta: Scholars Press, 1995.

———. "From Edomites to Nabataeans: A Study in Continuity." *PEQ* 111 (January–June 1979) 53–66.

———. "The Land of Seir and the Brotherhood of Edom." *JTS* 20, no. 1 (April 1969) 1–20.

———. "The Rise and Fall of the Kingdom of Edom." *PEQ* 104 (January–June 1972) 26–37.

Baskin, Judith. *Pharaoh's Counsellors: Job, Jethro, and Balaam in Rabbinic and Patristic Traditions*. BJS 47. Chico, CA: Scholars, 1983.

———. "Rabbinic Interpretations of Job." In *The Voice from the Whirlwind: Interpreting the Book of Job*, edited by L. Perdue and W. Gilpin, 101–10. Nashville: Abingdon, 1992.

Beit-Arieh, Itzhaq. "The Edomites in Cisjordan." In *You Shall Not Abhor an Edomite for He Is Your Brother: Edom and Seir in History and Tradition*, edited by D. Edelman, 33–38. Atlanta: Scholars Press, 1995.

Bennett, Crystal M. "An Archaeological Survey of Biblical Edom." *Perspective* 12 (Spring 1971) 35–44.

Bennett, T. Miles. *When Human Wisdom Fails: An Exposition of the Book of Job*. Grand Rapids: Baker, 1971.

Bergant, Dianne. *Job, Ecclesiastes*. Wilmington, DE: Michael Glazier, 1982.

Berrigan, Daniel. *Job and Death No Dominion*. Lanham, MD: Rowman and Littlefield, 2000.

Berry, Donald K. *An Introduction to Wisdom and Poetry of the Old Testament*. Nashville: Broadman and Holman, 1995.

Besserman, Lawrence L. *The Legend of Job in the Middle Ages*. Cambridge, MA: Harvard University Press, 1979.

Beuken, Willem A. M. "Job's Imprecation as the Cradle of a New Religious Discourse: The Perplexing Impact of the Semantic Correspondences Between Job 3, Job 4–5, and Job 6–7." In *The Book of Job*, edited by W. A. M. Beuken, 41–78. Leuven: University Press, 1994.

Bienkowski, Piotr. "The Archaeological Evidence from Transjordan." In *You Shall Not Abhor an Edomite for He Is Your Brother: Edom and Seir in History and Tradition*, edited by D. Edelman, 41–62. Atlanta: Scholars Press, 1995.

———. "The Beginning of the Iron Age in Edom: A Reply to Finkelstein." *Levant* 24 (1992) 167–69.

———. *Early Edom and Moab: The Beginning of the Iron Age in Southern Jordan*. Sheffield: J. R. Collis, 1992.

———. "Iron Age Settlement in Edom: A Revised Framework." In *The World of the Arameans II, Studies in History and Archaeology in Honor of Paul-Eugène Dion*, edited by P. M. Davian, J. Weavers, and M. Weigl, 257–69. Sheffield: JSOT Press, 2001.

Blair, J. Allen. *Job: Devotional Studies on Living Patiently*. Neptune, NJ: Loizeaux Brothers, 1966.

Blenkinsopp, Joseph. *A History of Prophecy in Israel*. Revised ed. Louisville: Westminster John Knox, 1996.

———. *Sage, Priest, Prophet: Religious and Intellectual Leadership in Ancient Israel*. Louisville: Westminster John Knox, 1995.

———. *Wisdom and Law in the Old Testament*. Oxford: Oxford University Press, 1983.

Blommerde, Anton C. *Northwest Semitic Grammar and Job*. Rome: Pontifical Biblical Institute, 1969.

Brändle, Werner. "Hiob—ein tragischer Held? Überlegungen zur Theodizeethematik der Hiobdichtung." *KD* 39 (1993) 282–92.

Bräumer, Hansjörg. *Das Buch Hiob, Band 1: Kapitel 1–19*. Wuppertaler Studienbibel. Brockhaus: Wuppertal, 1992.

Breakstone, Raymond. *Job: A Case Study*. New York: Bookman Associates, 1964.

Brenner, Althalya. "God's Answer to Job." *VT* 31, no. 2 (April 1981) 129–37.

———. "Job the Pious? The Characterization of Job in the Narrative Framework of the Book." *JSOT* 43 (February 1989) 37–52.
Bricker, Daniel P. "The Doctrine of the 'Two Ways' in Proverbs." *JETS* 38, no. 4 (December 1995) 501–17.
———. "Innocent Suffering in Mesopotamia." *TynBul* 51, no. 2 (2000) 193–214.
Bruce, F. F. *1 and 2 Corinthians*. NCB. London: Marshall, Morgan, and Scott, 1971.
Brueggemann, Walter. *In Man We Trust: The Neglected Side of Biblical Faith*. Atlanta: John Knox, 1972.
———. "Theodicy in a Social Dimension." *JSOT* 33 (October 1985) 3–25.
Budde, D. Karl. *Das Buch Hiob: übersetzt und erklärt*. Göttingen: Vandenhoek and Ruprecht, 1896.
Bullinger, E. W. *The Book of Job*. Reprint ed.; Grand Rapids: Kregel, 1990.
Bullock, C. Hassell. *An Introduction to the Old Testament Poetic Books*. Revised ed. Chicago: Moody, 1988.
Burden, J. J. "Decision by Debate: Examples of Popular Proverb Performance in the Book of Job." *OTE* 4 (1991) 37–65.
Burns, John B. "The Chastening of the Just in Job 5:17–23: Four Strikes of Erra." *Proceedings of the Eastern Great Lakes and Midwest Biblical Societies* 10 (1990) 18–30.
Burrell, David B. *Deconstructing Theodicy: Why Job Has Nothing to Say to the Puzzle of Suffering*. Grand Rapids: Baker, 2008.
Buttenweiser, Moses. *The Book of Job*. New York: MacMillan, 1922.
Caesar, Lael O. "Job: Another New Thesis." *VT* 49, no. 4 (October 1999) 435–47.
———. "Job as a Paradigm for the Eschaton." *JATS* 11 (Spring–Autumn 2000) 148–62.
Calvin, John. *Sermons on Job*. Translated by Arthur Golding. Reprint of 1574 ed. Carlisle, PA: Banner of Truth, 1993.
Carson, Donald A. "Job: Mystery and Faith." *Southern Baptist Journal of Theology* 4, no. 2 (Summer 2000) 38–55.
Caryl, Joseph. *An Exposition of Job*. Reprint ed.; Evansville, IN: Sovereign Grace Publishers, 1959.
Cheney, Michael. *Dust, Wind, and Agony: Character, Speech, and Genre in Job*. ConBOT 36. Stockholm: Almqvist and Wiksell International, 1994.
Chieregatti, A. *Giobbe: Lettura Spirituale*. Bologna: Dehoniane, 1995.
Christiansen, Bent. "Text, Trope, and Translation: Complex Polysemy and Rhetorical Strategy in the Elihu Speeches of Job 32:1—36:33." Th.M. thesis, The Master's Seminary, 2008.
Christo, Gordon. "The Battle Between God and Satan in the Book of Job." *JATS* 11 (2000) 282–86.
Chrysostom, John. "Resisting the Temptation of the Devil: Homily III." In *Nicene and Post-Nicene Fathers*, edited by P. Schaff. 14 vols. Reprint of 1889 ed.; Peabody, MA: Hendrickson, 1994.
Chung, Jae Hyun. "A Theological Reflection on Human Suffering: Beyond Causal Malediction and Teleological Imposition toward Correlational Solidarity." *AJT* 20, no. 1 (April 2006) 3–16.
Clements, Roland E. "Wisdom, Virtue, and the Human Condition." In *The Bible in Human Society*, edited by M. D. Carroll R., D. J. A. Clines, and P. R. Davies, 139–57. JSOT Supplements 200. Sheffield, England: Sheffield Academic, 1995.

Clines, David J. A. "The Argument of Job's Three Friends." In *Art and Meaning: Rhetoric in Biblical Literature*, edited by D. J. A. Clines, D. Gunn, and A. Hauser, 199-214. JSOT Supplements 19. Sheffield, England: Sheffield Academic Press, 1982.

———. "Deconstructing the Book of Job." In *What Does Eve Do to Help? And Other Readerly Questions to the Old Testament*. Sheffield, England: JSOT Press, 1990.

———. "False Naivety in the Prologue to Job." *HAR* 9 (1985) 127-36.

———. *Job 1-20*. WBC. Nashville: Nelson, 1989.

———. "Job 5,1-8: A New Exegesis." *Bib* 62 (1981) 185-94.

———. *Job 21-37*. WBC. Nashville: Nelson, 2006.

———. *Job 38-42*. WBC. Nashville: Nelson, 2011.

———. "On the Poetic Achievement of Job." In *Palabra, Prodigio, Poesía*. Edited by V. Bertomeu. Rome: Pontifical Biblical Institute, 2003.

———. "The Shape and Argument of the Book of Job." In *Sitting with Job: Selected Studies on the Book of Job*, edited by R. Zuck, 125-40. Grand Rapids: Baker, 1992.

———. "Verb Modality and the Interpretation of Job IV 20-21." *VT* 30, no. 3 (July 1980) 354-57.

———. "Why Is There a Book of Job and What Does It Do to You if You Read It?" In *The Book of Job*, edited by W. A. M. Beuken, 1-20. Leuven: Leuven University Press, 1994.

Coggins, Richard J. "Prophecy—True and False." In *Of Prophets' Visions and the Wisdom of Sages*, edited by H. McKay and D. J. A. Clines, 80-94. Sheffield, England: Sheffield Academic Press, 1993.

Cohen, M. "Fauves et songe nocturne dans le premier discours d'Eliphaz." *Graphé* 6 (1997) 35-58.

Conzelmann, Hans. *1 Corinthians*. Translated by J. W. Leitch. Hermeneia. Philadelphia: Fortress, 1975.

Cooper, Alan. "Reading and Misreading the Prologue to Job." *JSOT* 46 (Fall 1990) 67-79.

Cornelius, Izak. "Job." In *Zondervan Illustrated Bible Backgrounds Commentary: Old Testament*, edited by John H. Walton. Grand Rapids: Zondervan, 2009.

Cotter, David W. *A Study of Job 4-5 in the Light of Contemporary Literary Theory*. SBLDS 124. Atlanta: Scholars Press, 1992.

Cotton, Bill. *Will You Torment a Windblown Leaf? A Commentary on Job*. Ross-shire, Scotland: Christian Focus, 2001.

Course, John E. *Speech and Response: A Rhetorical Analysis of the Introductions to the Speeches of the Book of Job (Chapters 4-24)*. Washington, D. C.: Catholic Biblical Association of America, 1994.

Cox, Dermot. *The Triumph of Impotence: Job and the Tradition of the Absurd*. Rome: Gregorian University, 1978.

Cox, Samuel A. *A Commentary on the Book of Job*. London: C. Kegan Paul and Company, 1880.

Craigie, Peter C. "Job and Ugaritic Studies." In *Studies in the Book of Job*, edited by Walter E. Aufrecht, 1-27. Waterloo, ON: Wilfrid Laurier University Press, 1985.

Crenshaw, James L. "Job, Book of." In *ABD* 3:858-68.

———. *Old Testament Wisdom*. Revised ed. Louisville: Westminster John Knox, 1998.

———. "Wisdom and Authority: Sapiential Rhetoric and Its Warrants." In *Congress Volume, Vienna 1980*, edited by J. A. Emerton, 10-29. Leiden: E. J. Brill, 1981.

Cresson, B. "The Condemnation of Edom in Post-Exilic Judaism." In *The Use of the Old Testament in the New and Other Essays*, edited by J. M. Efird, 125–48. Durham, NC: Stinespring, 1972.

Curtis, John B. "On Job's Response to Yahweh." *JBL* 98 (1979) 497–511.

Cuthbertson, Dave. "Job's Friends Give Wrong Answers." *Christian Standard*, June 14, 1998.

Dahood, Mitchell. "Eblaite and Biblical Hebrew." *CBQ* 44, no. 1 (January 1982) 1–24.

———. "ŚʿRT 'Storm' in Job 4,15." *Bib* 48 (1967) 544–45.

———. "Some Northwest-Semitic Words in Job." *Bib* 38 (1957) 312–14.

Dailey, Thomas F. *The Repentant Job: A Ricoeurian Icon for Biblical Theology*. Lanham, MD: University Press of America, 1994.

———. "The Wisdom of Irreverence: Job as an Icon for Postmodern Spirituality." *Int* 53, no. 3 (July 1999) 276–89.

Davidson, A. B. *The Book of Job*. Cambridge Bible. Cambridge: University Press, 1889.

Davies, David. *The Book of Job I–XIV*. London: Simpkin Marshall, Hamilton, Kent, and Co., 1909.

Day, Peggy L. *An Adversary in Heaven: Satan in the Hebrew Bible*. HSM 43. Atlanta: Scholars Press, 1988.

De León, Luis P. *Exposición del libro de Job*. 2 vols. Estudio, edición, y notas de J. San Jose Léra. Salamanca: University of Salamanca, 1992.

Dearman, J. Andrew. "Edomite Religion: A Survey and an Examination of Some Recent Contributions." In *You Shall Not Abhor an Edomite for He Is Your Brother: Edom and Seir in History and Tradition*, edited by D. Edelman, 119–36. Atlanta: Scholars Press, 1995.

Delitzsch, Franz. *Biblical Commentary on the Book of Job*. Translated by Francis Bolton. Reprint of 1872 ed.; Grand Rapids: Eerdmans, 1956.

Dell, Katharine J. *The Book of Job as Sceptical Literature*. BZAW 197. Berlin: Walter de Gruyter, 1991.

Dhorme, Édouard. *A Commentary on the Book of Job*. Translated by H. Knight. Reprint of 1967 ed.; Nashville: Thomas Nelson, 1984.

Dicou, A. "Geen wijsheid meer in Edom: Jeremia 49.7 en Obadja 7–8." *ACEBT* 9 (1988) 90–96.

Dicou, Bert. *Edom, Israel's Brother and Antagonist: The Role of Edom in Biblical Prophecy and Story*. JSOT Supplements 169. Sheffield, England: JSOT Press, 1994.

Donner, Herbert. "Der 'Freund des Königs.'" *ZAW* 73, no. 3 (1961) 269–76.

Doran, Robert. "Jewish Hellenistic Historians Before Josephus." In *Aufstieg und Niedergang der römischen Welt*, edited by H. Temporini and W. Haase, 246–97. Berlin: Walter de Gruyter, 1987.

Dornisch, Loretta. "The Book of Job and Ricoeur's Hermeneutics." *Semeia* 19 (1981): 3–21.

Dorsey, David A. *The Literary Structure of the Old Testament: A Commentary on Genesis–Malachi*. Grand Rapids: Baker, 1999.

Downing, F. L. "Voices from the Whirlwind: Contemporary Criticism and the Book of Job." *PRSt* 26, no. 4 (Winter 1999) 389–404.

Driver, Samuel R. and George B. Gray. *A Critical and Exegetical Commentary on the Book of Job*. ICC. Edinburgh: T. and T. Clark, 1921.

Duhm, D. Bernard. *Das Buch Hiob*. Freiburg, Germany: J. C. B. Mohr, 1897.

Dumbrell, William J. "The Purpose of the Book of Job." In *The Way of Wisdom: Essays in Honor of Bruce K. Waltke*, edited by J. I. Packer and S. Soderlund, 91–105. Grand Rapids: Zondervan, 2000.

Eaton, J. H. *Job*. Sheffield, England: JSOT Press, 1985.

Ebach, Jürgen. *Streiten mit Gott*. Neukirchen-Vluyn, Germany: Neukirchener Verlag, 1996.

Edelman, Diana V. "Edom: A Historical Geography." In *You Shall Not Abhor an Edomite for He Is Your Brother: Edom and Seir in History and Tradition*, edited by D. Edelman, 1–11. Atlanta: Scholars Press, 1995.

Ehrlich, Bernard. "The Book of Job as a Book of Morality." *JBQ* 34, no. 1 (January–March 2006) 30–38.

Ehrlich, Ernst L. *Der Traum im Alten Testament*. BZAW 73. Berlin: Alfred Topelmann, 1953.

Eichhorst, William R. "The Issue of Biblical Inerrancy in Definition and Defense." *Grace Journal* 10 (Winter 1969) 3–15.

Eisen, Robert. *The Book of Job in Medieval Jewish Philosophy*. Oxford: Oxford University Press, 2004.

Eitan, Israel. "Biblical Studies." *HUCA* 14 (1939) 1–22.

Ellison, H. L. *A Study of Job: From Tragedy to Triumph*. 1958. Reprint; Grand Rapids: Zondervan, 1971.

Emerton, John A. "New Light on Israelite Religion: The Implications of the Inscriptions from Kuntillet 'Ajrud." *ZAW* 94, no. 1 (1982) 2–20.

Estes, Daniel J. *Handbook on the Wisdom Books and Psalms*. Grand Rapids: Baker, 2005.

Evans, Craig A. *Noncanonical Writings and New Testament Interpretation*. Peabody, MA: Hendrickson, 1992.

Ewald, Georg H. A. von. *Commentary on the Book of Job*. Translated by J. Frederick Smith. Edinburgh: Williams and Norgate, 1882.

Ewald, Heinrich. *Das Buch Ijob*. Göttingen: Vandenhoek and Ruprecht, 1854.

Feinberg, Charles L. "The Book of Job." *BSac* 91 (January–March 1934) 78–86.

———. "Job and the Nation Israel Second Study: At the Mercy of the Critics." *BSac* 97 (January–March 1940) 27–33.

Feinberg, John S. *The Many Faces of Evil: Theological Systems and the Problem of Evil*. Wheaton, IL: Crossway, 2004.

Fine, Hillel. "The Tradition of a Patient Job." *JBL* 74, no. 1 (March 1955) 28–32.

Finkelstein, Israel. "Edom in the Iron I." *Levant* 24 (1992) 159–66.

Fishbane, Michael. "The Book of Job and Inner-Biblical Discourse." In *The Voice from the Whirlwind: Interpreting the Book of Job*, edited by Leo Perdue and W. Clark Gilpin, 86–98. Nashville: Abingdon, 1992.

Fohrer, Georg. *Das Buch Hiob*. KAT. Gütersloh, Germany: Gütersloh Verlaghaus Gerd Mohn, 1963.

———. *Studien zum Buche Hiob*. Gütersloh, Germany: Gütersloh Verlag Gerd Mohn, 1963.

Fokkelman, J. P. *Major Poems of the Hebrew Bible*. 3 vols. Assen, Netherlands: Van Gorcum, 2000.

Fontaine, Carole R. "The Sage in Family and Tribe." In *The Sage in Israel and the Ancient Near East*, edited by J. Gammie and L. Perdue, 155–64. Winona Lake, IN: Eisenbrauns, 1990.

Forrest, R. W. E. "The Two Faces of Job: Imagery and Integrity in the Prologue." In *Ascribe to the Lord: Biblical and Other Essays in Memory of Peter C. Craigie*, edited by L. Eslinger and C. Taylor, 385-98. Sheffield, England: JSOT Press, 1988.

Foster, Frank H. "Is the Book of Job a Translation from an Arabic Original?" *AJSL* 49 (1932) 21-45.

Fox, Michael V. "Job the Pious." *ZAW* 117, no. 3 (2005) 351-66.

Frame, Tom. "Sacred Violence." *St. Mark's Review* 187 (2001) 2-27.

Freedman, David N. "Between God and Man: Prophets in Ancient Israel." In *Prophecy and Prophets*, edited by Y. Gitay, 57-87. Atlanta: Scholar's Press, 1997.

———. "The Book of Job." In *The Hebrew Bible and Its Interpreters*. Edited by W. H. Popp, B. Halpern, and D. N. Freedman, 33-51. Winona Lake, IN: Eisenbrauns, 1990.

Freehof, Solomon B. *The Book of Job*. New York: Union of American Hebrew Congregations, 1958.

Fuchs, Gisela. "Die Klage des Propheten: Beobachtungen zu den Konfesionen Jeremias in Vergleich mit den Klagen Hiobs." *BZ* 41, no. 2 (1997) 212-28.

Fullerton, Kemper. "Double Entendre in the First Speech of Eliphaz." *JBL* 49, no. 4 (1930) 320-74.

Fyall, Robert S. *How Does God Treat His Friends? Lessons from the Book of Job*. Ross-shire, Scotland: Christian Focus, 1995.

———. *Now My Eyes Have Seen You: Images of Creation and Evil in the Book of Job*. Downers Grove, IL: InterVarsity, 2002.

Gailey, James. *Jerome's Latin Version of Job from the Greek: Chapters 1-26, Its Text, Character, and Provenance*. Princeton, NJ: Princeton Seminary Pamphlet Series, 1948.

Gard, Donald H. *The Exegetical Method of the Greek Translator of the Book of Job*. SBLMS 8. Philadelphia: Society of Biblical Literature, 1952.

Garland, D. David. *Job*. Bible Study Commentary. Grand Rapids: Zondervan, 1971.

Gaspar, Joseph W. *Social Ideas in the Wisdom Literature of the Old Testament*. Catholic University of America Studies in Sacred Theology. Washington, D. C.: Catholic University of America Press, 1947.

Gehman, H. S. "The Theological Approach of the Greek Translator of Job 1-15." *JBL* 68, no. 3 (September 1949) 231-40.

Gerleman, Gillis. "The Book of Job." In *Studies in the Septuagint I*. Lund: Gleerup, 1946.

Gese, Hermut. "Die Frage nach dem Lebenssinn: Hiob und die Folgen." *ZTK* 79, no. 2 (1982) 161-79.

Gibson, Edgar C. S. *The Book of Job*. WC. London: Methuen and Co., 1919.

Gibson, John C. L. "The Book of Job and the Cure of Souls." *SJT* 42, no. 3 (1989) 303-17.

———. *Davidson's Introductory Hebrew Grammar*. Edinburgh: T. and T. Clark, 1994.

———. "Eliphaz the Temanite: Portrait of a Hebrew Philosopher." *SJT* 28, no. 3 (1975) 259-72.

———. *Job*. The Daily Study Bible Series. Philadelphia: Westminster, 1985.

Girard, René. "'The Ancient Trail Trodden by the Wicked': Job as Scapegoat," translated by A. McKenna. *Semeia* 33 (1985): 13-41.

———. *Job: The Victim of His People*, translated by Y. Freccero. Stanford, CA: Stanford University Press, 1987.

———. "Job as Failed Scapegoat." In *The Voice from the Whirlwind*, edited by L. Perdue and W. Gilpin, 185-207. Nashville: Abingdon, 1992.

Glatzer, Nahum N. "The Book of Job and Its Interpreters." In *Biblical Motifs: Origins and Transformations*, edited by A. Altmann and P. Lain, 197–220. Cambridge, MA: Harvard University Press, 1966.

———. "Introduction: A Study of Job." In *The Dimensions of Job: A Study of Selected Readings*, edited by N. Glatzer, 1–48. New York: Schocken, 1969.

Glatzer, Nahum N., ed. *The Dimensions of Job: A Study and Selected Readings*. New York: Schocken Books, 1969.

Glazier-MacDonald, Beth. "Edom in the Prophetical Corpus." In *You Shall Not Abhor an Edomite for He Is Your Brother: Edom and Seir in History and Tradition*, edited by D. Edelman, 23–32. Atlanta: Scholars Press, 1995.

Glueck, Nelson. "The Boundaries of Edom." *HUCA* 11 (1936) 141–57.

———. "The Civilization of the Edomites." *BA* 10, no. 4 (December 1947) 77–84.

———. "Iron II Kenite and Edomite Pottery." *Perspective* 12 (Spring 1971) 45–56.

Good, Edwin M. *In Turns of Tempest: A Reading of Job*. Stanford: Stanford University Press, 1990.

———. "Job." In *Harper's Bible Commentary*. San Francisco: Harper & Row, 1988.

———. "Job and the Literary Task." *Sound* 56, no. 4 (Winter 1973) 470–84.

———. "The Problem of Evil in the Book of Job." In *The Voice from the Whirlwind*, edited by L. Perdue and W. Gilpin, 50–69. Nashville: Abingdon, 1992.

Gordis, Robert. *The Book of God and Man: A Study of Job*. Chicago: University of Chicago Press, 1965.

———. *The Book of Job: Commentary, New Translation, and Special Studies*. New York: The Jewish Theological Seminary of America, 1978.

———. *Poets, Prophets, and Sages: Essays in Biblical Interpretation*. Bloomington, IN: Indiana University Press, 1971.

———. "The Temptation of Job: Tradition versus Experience in Religion." *Judaism* 4, no. 3 (Summer 1955) 195–208.

———. "The Temptation of Job—Tradition versus Experience in Religion." In *Dimensions of Job*, edited by N. Glatzer, 74–85. New York: Schocken, 1969.

Gorg, Manfred. "Ijob aus dem Lande Us: Ein Beitrag zur 'theologischen Geographie.'" *BN* 12 (1980) 7–12.

Gorringe, Timothy J. "Job and the Pharisees." *Int* 40, no. 1 (January 1986) 17–28.

Grabbe, Lester L. *Comparative Philology and the Text of Job: A Study in Methodology*. Missoula, MT: Scholars Press, 1977.

Gradl, Felix. *Das Buch Ijob*. Stüttgart, Germany: Verlag Katholisches Bibelwerk, 2001.

Gray, John. "The Book of Job in the Context of Near Eastern Literature." *ZAW* 82, no. 2 (1970) 251–69.

Grayson, A. Kirk. "Mesopotamia, History of (Babylonia)." In *ABD* 4:755–77.

Green, William H. *The Argument of the Book of Job Unfolded*. New York: Hurst, 1891.

Greenberg, Moshe. "Reflections on Job's Theology." In *The Book of Job*. Philadelphia: The Jewish Publication Society of America, 1980.

Greenstein, Edward L. "A Forensic Understanding of the Speech from the Whirlwind." In *Texts, Temples, and Traditions: A Tribute to Menahem Haran*, edited by M. Fox, V. Hurowitz, A. Hurvitz, et al., 241–58. Winona Lake, IN: Eisenbrauns, 1990.

———. "The Language of Job and Its Poetic Function." *JBL* 122, no. 4 (Winter 2003) 651–66.

Gregory the Great. *Morals on Job*. 3 vols. Oxford, UK: John Henry Parker, 1844.

Gruber, Martin. "Human and Divine Wisdom in the Book of Job." In *Boundaries of the Ancient Near Eastern World*, edited by M. Lubetski, C. Gottlieb, and S. Keller, 88–102. Sheffield, England: JSOT Supplements, 1998.

———. "Tur-Sinai's Job in the Jewish Liturgy." *Review of Rabbinic Judaism* 6, no. 1 (February 2003) 87–100.

Grundy, Peter. "Why Do We Suffer? Job's Dialogue with Eliphaz." *St. Mark's Review* 187 (2001) 6–11.

Guillaume, A. *Studies in the Book of Job*. Leiden: Brill, 1968.

Gutiérrez, Gustavo. *On Job: God-Talk and the Suffering of the Innocent*, translated by M. O'Connell. Maryknoll, NY: Orbis, 1987.

Habel, Norman C. *The Book of Job*. OTL. Philadelphia: Westminster, 1985.

———. *Job*. Cambridge, England: Cambridge University Press, 1975.

———. "In Defense of God the Sage." In *The Voice from the Whirlwind*, edited by L. Perdue and W. Gilpin, 21–38. Nashville: Abingdon, 1992.

———. "'Naked I Came . . .': Humanness in the Book of Job." In *Die Botschaft und die Boten: Festschrift für Hans W. Wolff*, edited by J. Jeremias and L. Perlitt, 373–92. Neukirchen-Vluyn, Germany: Neukirchener Verlag, 1981.

———. "The Role of Elihu in the Design of the Book of Job." In *In the Shelter of Elyon: Essays on Ancient Palestinian Life and Literature in Honor of G. W. Ahlström*, edited by W. Barrick and J. Spencer. JSOT Supplements 31. Sheffield, England: JSOT Press, 1984.

———. "Of Things Beyond Me: Wisdom in the Book of Job." *CurrTM* 10, no. 3 (June 1983) 142–54.

———. "'Only the Jackal Is My Friend': On Friends and Redeemers in Job." *Interpretation* 31, no. 3 (July 1977): 227–36.

Habtu, Tewoldemedhin. "Job." In *Africa Bible Commentary*, edited by T. Adeyemo. Grand Rapids: Zondervan, 2006.

Hallermayer, Michaela. *Text und Überlieferung des Buches Tobit*. Berlin: Walter de Gruyter, 2008.

Hanson, A. T. B. and Miriam Hanson. *The Book of Job*. London: SCM Press, 1962.

Harding, James E. "A Spirit of Deception in Job 4:15? Interpretive Indeterminacy and Eliphaz's Vision." *BibInt* 13, no. 2 (2005) 137–66.

Harris, R. Laird. "The Book of Job and Its Doctrine of God." *Grace Journal* 13 (Fall 1972) 3–33.

Hart, Stephen. "Some Preliminary Thoughts on Settlement in Southern Edom." *Levant* 18 (1986) 51–58.

Hartley, John E. *The Book of Job*. NICOT. Grand Rapids: Eerdmans, 1988.

———. "From Lament to Oath: A Study of Progression in the Speeches of Job." In *The Book of Job*, edited by W. A. M. Beuken. Leuven: Leuven University Press, 1994.

———. "Job 2: Ancient Near Eastern Background." In *Dictionary of the Old Testament: Wisdom, Poetry, & Writings*, edited by T. Longman III and P. Enns, 346–61. Downers Grove, IL: InterVarsity, 2008.

———. "Job: Theology of." In *NIDOTTE* 4:780–96.

Hawthorne, Ralph R. "Jobine Theology." *BSac* 102 (1945) 37–54.

———. "Jobine Theology: Part 1." *BSac* 101 (1944) 64–75.

———. "Jobine Theology: Part 2." *BSac* 101 (1944) 173–86.

———. "Jobine Theology: Part 3." *BSac* 101 (1944) 290–303.

———. "Jobine Theology: Part 4." *BSac* 101 (1944) 417–33.

Hesse, Franz. *Hiob*. Zürich: Theologischer Verlag, 1978.
Hill, Andrew E., and John Walton. *A Survey of the Old Testament*. 3rd ed. Grand Rapids: Zondervan, 2009.
Hitzig, Ferdinand. *Das Buch Hiob*. Leipzig, Germany: C.F. Winter, 1874.
Hoffer, Victoria. "Illusion, Allusion, and Literary Artifice in the Frame Narrative of Job." In *The Whirlwind: Essays on Job, Hermeneutics, and Theology in Memory of Jane Morse*, edited by S. Cook, C. Patton, and J. Watts. JSOT Supplements 336. London: Sheffield Academic, 2001.
Hoffman, Yair. *A Blemished Perfection: The Book of Job in Context*. Sheffield, England: Sheffield Academic Press, 1996.
———. "The Relation Between the Prologue and the Speech-Cycles in Job." *VT* 31 (1981) 160–70.
———. "The Use of Equivocal Words in the First Speech of Eliphaz." *VT* 30 (1980) 114–19.
Holbert, John C. "Eliphaz." In *ABD* 2:471.
———. *Preaching Job*. St. Louis: Chalice Press, 1999.
Holladay, William L. "Indications of Segmented Sleep in the Bible." *CBQ* 69, no. 2 (April 2007) 215–21.
Holland, Glenn. "Paul's Use of Irony as a Rhetorical Technique." In *The Rhetorical Analysis of Scripture: Essays from the 1995 London Conference*, edited by S. Porter and T. Olbricht, 234–48. JSNT Supplement Series 146. Sheffield, England: Sheffield Academic Press, 1997.
———. "Speak Like a Fool: Irony in 2 Corinthians 10–13." In *Rhetoric and the New Testament*, edited by S. Porter and T. Olbricht, 250–64. JSNT Supplement Series 90. Sheffield, England: Sheffield Academic Press, 1993.
Hone, Ralph E., ed. *The Voice Out of the Whirlwind: The Book of Job*. San Francisco: Chandler, 1960.
Horst, Friedrich. *Hiob 1–19*. Biblische Kommentar, Altes Testament. Neukirchen-Vluyn, Germany: Neukirchener, 1974.
Hölscher, Gustav. *Das Buch Hiob*. 2nd ed. HAT. Tübingen, Germany: J. C. B. Mohr, 1952.
House, Paul R. *Old Testament Theology*. Downers Grove, IL: InterVarsity, 1998.
Hübner, Hans. *Biblische Theologie des Neuen Testaments*. 3 vols. Göttingen, Germany: Vandenhoeck und Ruprecht, 1990–1995.
Irwin, Walter A. "An Examination of the Progress of Thought in the Dialogue of Job." *JR* 13 (1933) 150–64.
Irwin, William H. "Conflicting Parallelism in Job 5,13; Isa 30,28; Isa 32,7." *Bib* 76 (1995) 72–74.
Jacobs, Sidney J. "The Comfort of Eliphaz." *Reconstructionist* 32 (March 1966): 21–28.
Jacobson, Richard. "Satanic Semiotics, Joban Jursiprudence." *Semeia* 19 (1981): 63–71.
Janzen, Gerald. *Job*. Interpretation. Atlanta: John Knox, 1985.
Jastrow, Morris, Jr. *The Book of Job*. Philadelphia: J. P. Lippincott, 1920.
Jepsen, Alfred. *Das Buch Hiob und seine Deutung*. Stüttgart, Germany: Calwer, 1965.
Johnson, L. D. *Out of the Whirlwind: The Major Message of the Book of Job*. Nashville: Broadman, 1971.
Kaiser, Otto. *Introduction to the Old Testament*. Translated by J. Sturdy. Minneapolis: Augsburg, 1975.

Kallen, H. M. *The Book of Job as a Greek Tragedy*. New York: Moffat, Yard, and Co., 1918.

Kaufmann, H. E. *Die Anwendung des Buchs Hiob in der Rabbinischen Agadah*. Frankfurt am Main: Slobotsky, 1983.

Kaufmann, Walter. *The Faith of a Heretic*. Garden City, NY: Doubleday, 1961.

Kautzsch, Karl. *Das sogenannte Volksbuch von Hiob*. Tübingen: J. C. B. Mohr, 1900.

Keel, Othmar. *Jahwes Entgegnung an Ijob: Eine Deutung Von Ijob 38–41 vor dem Hintergrund der Zeitgenössischen Bildkunst*. FRLANT 121. Göttingen, Germany: Vandenhoeck and Ruprecht, 1978.

Kelley, Page H. "The Speeches of the Three Friends." *RevExp* 68 (1971) 479–85.

Kent, H. Harold. *Job, Our Contemporary*. Grand Rapids: Eerdmans, 1967.

Kidner, Derek. *The Wisdom of Proverbs, Job, and Ecclesiastes*. Downers Grove, IL: InterVarsity, 1985.

Kimhi, Moses. *Commentary on the Book of Job*. Edited by H. Basser and B. Walfish. Atlanta: Scholars Press, 1992. (Hebrew) Kissane, Edward J. *The Book of Job*. Dublin: Browne and Nolan, 1939.

Knauf, Ernst A. "Teman." In *ABD* 6:347–48.

Knight, Harold. "Job (Considered as a Contribution to Hebrew Theology)." *SJT* 9 (1956) 63–76.

Koch, Klaus. "Gibt es ein Vergeltungsdogma im Alten Testament?" *ZTK* 52 (1955) 1–42.

Köhlmoos, Melanie. *Das Auge Gottes: Textstrategie im Hiobbuch*. Tübingen, Germany: Mohr Siebeck, 1999.

Konkel, August H. *Job*. Cornerstone Biblical Commentary. Carol Stream, IL: Tyndale House, 2006.

Kopf, Lothar. "Arabische Etymologien und Parallelen zum Bibelwörterbuch." *VT* 9 (1959) 247–87.

Kottsieper, Ingo. "«Thema verfehlt!» Zur Kritik Gottes an den drei Freunden in Hi 42,7–9." In *Gott und Mensch im Dialog: Festschrift für Otto Kaiser zum 80. Geburtstag*, edited by M. Witte, 775–85. BZAW 345. Berlin: Walter de Gruyter, 2004.

Kraeling, Emil. *The Book of the Ways of God*. New York: Scribner's, 1939.

Kraft, Robert, ed. *The Testament of Job According to the SV Text*. Pseudepigrapha Series 4. Missoula, MT: Scholars Press, 1974.

Kramer, Samuel N. "The Sage in Sumerian Literature: A Composite Portrait." In *The Sage in Israel and the Ancient Near East*, edited by J. Gammie and L. Perdue, 31–44. Winona Lake, IN: Eisenbrauns, 1990.

Kroeze, Jan H. *Het boek Job verklaard*. COut. Kampen, Netherlands: J. H. Kok, 1961.

Kuhn, Hanni. "Why Are Job's Opponents Still Made to Eat Broom-Root?" *BT* 40, no. 3 (July 1989) 332–36.

La Sor, William, David A. Hubbard, and Frederic W. Bush. *Old Testament Survey: The Message, Form and Background of the Old Testament*. Grand Rapids: Eerdmans, 1982.

Lambert, Wilfred G. *Babylonian Wisdom Literature*. Oxford, England: Clarendon, 1960.

———. "Some New Babylonian Wisdom Literature." In *Wisdom in Ancient Israel*, edited by J. Day, R. Gordon, and H. G. M. Williamson, 30–42. Cambridge, England: Cambridge University Press, 1995.

Landersdorfer, Simon K. *Eine babylonische Quelle für das Buch Job? Eine literarische-geschichtliche Studie*. St. Louis, MO: Herder, 1911.

Langenhorst, Georg. *Hiob unser Zeitgenosse: Die literarische Hiob-Rezeption im 20. Jahrhundert als theologische Herausforderung.* Mainz, Germany: Matthias-Grünewald Verlag, 1994.

Langer, M. "Alte Weisheit für die junge Menschen: Gedanken zum Buch Hiob im Religionsunterricht der gymnasialen Oberstufe." In *Steht nicht geschrieben?*, edited by J. Frühwald-König, 457–80. Regensburg: Pustet, 2001.

Larcher, R. P. *Le livre du Job.* Paris: Les Éditions du Cerf, 1957.

Lasine, Stuart. "Bird's-Eye and Worm's-Eye Views of Justice in the Book of Job." *JSOT* 42 (October 1988) 29–53.

———. "Job and His Friends in the Modern World: Kafka's *The Trial*." In *The Voice from the Whirlwind*, edited by L. Perdue and W. Gilpin, 144–56. Nashville: Abingdon, 1992.

Laurin, Robert. "The Theological Structure of Job." *ZAW* 84 (1972) 86–89.

Lawrie, Douglas G. "How Critical Is It to Be Historically Critical? The Case of the Composition of the Book of Job." *JNSL* 27 (2001) 121–46.

Lawson, Steven J. *Job.* Holman Old Testament Commentary 10. Nashville: Broadman & Holman, 2004.

———. *When All Hell Breaks Loose, You May Be Doing Something Right: Surprising Insights from the Life of Job.* Colorado Springs: NavPress, 1993.

Lévêque, Jean. *Job et son Dieu.* 2 vols. Paris: Gabalda, 1970.

———. "Tradition and Betrayal in the Speeches of the Friends." In *Job and the Silence of God*, edited by C. Duquoc and C. Floristán, 39–44. New York: Seabury, 1983.

Limburg, James. "The Root ריב and the Prophetic Lawsuit Speeches." *JBL* 88, no. 3 (September 1969) 291–304.

Lindblom, J. *Prophecy in Ancient Israel.* Philadelphia: Fortress, 1962.

Lindsay, J. "The Babylonian Kings and Edom." *PEQ* 108 (January–June 1976) 23–39.

Liu, Kwang-Chi. "Religions of Israel's Transjordanian Neighbors during the Iron Age II Period: A Comparative Study of the Religions of Edom, Moab, and Ammon." PhD diss., The Southern Baptist Theological Seminary, 2007.

Long, Burke O. "Reports of Visions Among the Prophets." *JBL* 95 (1976) 353–65.

Longman, Tremper, and Raymond B. Dillard. *An Introduction to the Old Testament.* 2nd ed. Grand Rapids: Zondervan, 2006.

Lowth, Robert. "Lectures on the Sacred Poetry of the Hebrews." Translated and edited by G. Gregory. Reprinted in *The Voice Out of the Whirlwind: The Book of Job*, edited by R. Hone. San Francisco: Chandler, 1960.

Luc, Alex. "Storm and the Message of Job." *JSOT* 87 (March 2000) 111–23.

Lugt, Pieter van der. *Rhetorical Criticism and the Poetry of the Book of Job.* New York: E. J. Brill, 1995.

———. "Speech Cycles in the Book of Job: A Response to James E. Patrick." *VT* 56, no. 4 (October 2006) 554–57.

———. "Stanza-Structure and Word Repetition in Job 3–14." *JSOT* 40 (February 1988) 3–38.

Lust, Johan. "A Gentle Breeze or a Roaring Thunderous Sound?" *VT* 25, no. 1 (January 1975) 110–15.

Lust, Johan, Erik Eynikel, and Katrin Hauspie. *Greek-English Lexicon of the Septuagint.* Revised ed. Stuttgart: Deutsche Bibelgesellschaft, 2003.

Maag, Viktor. *Hiob: Wandlung Und Verarbeitung Des Problems in Novelle, Dialogdichtung Und Spätfassungen.* FRLANT 128. Göttingen, Germany: Vandenhoeck & Ruprecht, 1982.

MacDonald, Burton. "Early Edom: The Relation Between the Literary and Archaeological Evidence." In *Scripture and Other Artifacts: Essays on the Bible and Archaeology in Honor of Philip J. King,* edited by M. Coogan, J. Exum, and L. Stager, 230–46. Louisville: Westminster, 1994.

MacKenzie, R. A. F. "Job." In *Jerome Biblical Commentary,* edited by R. Brown, J. Fitzmyer, and R. Murphy. Englewood Cliffs, NJ: Prentice Hall, 1968.

———. "The Cultural and Religious Background of the Book of Job." In *Job and the Silence of God,* edited by C. Duquoc and C. Floristán, 3–7. New York: Seabury, 1983.

Mack-Fisher, Loren R. "The Scribe (and Sage) in the Royal Court at Ugarit." In *The Sage in Israel and the Ancient Near East,* edited by J. Gammie and L. Perdue, 109–15. Winona Lake, IN: Eisenbrauns, 1990.

Macnicoll, Patricia. "Questioning the Character of God: A Study of Subversion in the Book of Job." PhD diss., Union Theological Seminary, 2002.

Manzanedo, M. "La antropología filosófica en el comentario tomaista al libro de Job." *Ang* 62 (1985) 419–71.

Mattingly, Gerald L. "The Pious Sufferer in Mesopotamia's Traditional Theodicy and Job's Counselors." In *The Bible in Light of Cuneiform Literature: Scripture in Context III,* edited by W. Hallo, B. Jones, and G. Mattingly, 305–48. Lewiston, ME: Edwin Mellen, 1990.

McCabe, Robert V. "Elihu's Contribution to the Thought of the Book of Job." *DBSJ* 2 (Fall 1997) 47–80.

———. "The Significance of the Elihu Speeches in the Context of the Book of Job." ThD diss., Grace Theological Seminary, 1985.

———. "Were Old Testament Believers Indwelt by the Holy Spirit?" *DBSJ* 9 (2004) 215–64.

McKeating, Henry. "The Central Issue of the Book of Job." *ExpTim* 82, no. 8 (May 1971) 244–47.

McKechnie, James. *Job: Moral Hero, Religious Egoist, and Mystic.* Greenock, UK: James McElvie and Sons, 1925.

McKenna, David. *Job.* Communicator's Commentary. Waco, TX: Word, 1986.

Mende, Theresia. *Durch Leiden zur Vollendung: Die Elihureden im Buch Ijob (Ijob 32–37).* Trier: Paulinus-Verlag, 1990.

Merrill, Eugene H. *Everlasting Dominion: A Theology of the Old Testament.* Nashville: Broadman & Holman, 2006.

Methodius. "Fragments on Job." In *Ante-Nicene Fathers,* edited by A. Roberts and J. Donaldson. 10 vols. Reprint ed. Peabody, MA: Hendrickson, 1994.

Michel, Walter L. *Job in the Light of Northwest Semitic.* Rome: Biblical Institute Press, 1987.

Mickel, Tobias. *Seelsorgerliche Aspekte im Hiobbuch: Ein Beitrag zur Biblischen Dimension der Poimenik.* Theologische Arbeiten 48. Berlin: Evangelische Verlagsanstalt, 1990.

Miles, John J., Jr. "Gagging on Job, or The Comedy of Religious Exhaustion." *Semeia* 7 (1977) 71–126.

Miller, James E. "The Vision of Eliphaz as Foreshadowing in the Book of Job." *Proceedings of the Eastern Great Lakes and Midwest Biblical Society* 9 (1989) 98–112.

Mitchell, Stephen. *The Book of Job*. San Francisco: Harper Collins, 1992.

Moore, Carey A. *Tobit: A New Translation with Introduction and Commentary*. AB. New York: Doubleday, 1996.

Moore, Rick D. "The Integrity of Job." *CBQ* 45, no. 1 (January 1983) 17–31.

Moore, T. M. "When Orthodoxy Is Not Enough: Calvin on Job's Interlocutors." *Reformation and Revival* 12 (Winter 2003) 11–21.

Moster, Julius B. "The Punishment of Job's Friends." *JBQ* 25, no. 4 (October–December 1997) 211–19.

Murphy, Roland E. *The Book of Job*. New York: Paulist Press, 1999.

———. *The Tree of Life: An Exploration of Biblical Wisdom Literature*. 3rd ed. Grand Rapids: Eerdmans, 2002.

———. *Wisdom Literature: Job, Proverbs, Ruth, Canticles, Ecclesiastes, and Esther*. FOTL 13. Grand Rapids: Eerdmans, 1981 Na'aman, N. "Sources and Composition in the Biblical History of Edom." In *Sefer Moshe: The Moshe Weinfeld Jubilee Volume*, edited by C. Cohen, A. Hurvitz, and S. Paul, 313–20. Winona Lake, IN: Eisenbrauns, 2004.

Naylor, Peter. *1 Corinthians*. EP Study Commentary. Darlington, UK: Evangelical Press, 2004.

Neiman, David. *The Book of Job*. Jerusalem: Massada, 1972.

Nemo, Philippe. *Job and the Excess of Evil*, translated by M. Kigel. Pittsburgh: Duquesne University, 1998.

Newell, B. Lynne. "Job: Repentant or Rebellious?" *WTJ* 46 (1984) 298–316 Newsom, Carol A. *The Book of Job: A Contest of Moral Imaginations*. New York: Oxford University Press, 2003.

———. "The Book of Job: Introduction, Commentary, and Reflections." In *NIB* 4:317–637.

———. "Considering Job." *CurBS* 1 (1993) 87–118.

———. "Job." In *The Women's Bible Commentary*. Edited by C. Newsom and S. Ringe. Expanded edition. Louisville: Westminster John Knox, 1998.

———. "Job and His Friends: A Conflict of Moral Imaginations." *Int* 53 (July 1999) 239–53.

———. "Reconsidering Job." *Currents in Biblical Research* 5, no. 2 (Fall 2007) 155–82.

Nicholson, E. W. "The Limits of Theodicy as a Theme in the Book of Job." In *Wisdom in Ancient Israel*, edited by J. Day, R. Gordon, and H. G. M. Williamson, 71–82. Cambridge, England: Cambridge University Press, 1995.

Oblath, Michael D. "Job's Advocate: A Tempting Suggestion." *BBR* 9 (1999) 189–201.

Oeming, Manfred. "'Ihr habt nicht recht von mir geredet wie mein Knecht Hiob': Gottes Schlusswort als Schlüssel zur Interpretation des Hiobsbuch und als kritische Anfrage an die moderne Theologie." *EvT* 60 (2000) 103–16.

Olson, Alan M. "The Silence of Job as the Key to the Text." *Semeia* 19 (1981) 113–19.

Oorschot, Jürgen Van. "Gottes Gerechtigkeit und Hiobs Lied." *TBei* 30 (1999) 202–13.

Orlinsky, Harry M. *Israel Exploration Journal Reader*. New York: KTAV, 1981.

———. "Studies in the Septuagint of the Book of Job." *HUCA* 29 (1958) 229–71.

Oswalt, John N. *The Bible among the Myths: Unique Revelation or Just Ancient Literature?* Grand Rapids: Zondervan, 2009.

Otzen, Benedikt. *Tobit and Judith*. London: Sheffield Academic Press, 2002.

Paine, Stephen W. "The Christian Man and the Bible." *Bulletin of the Evangelical Theological Society* 11 (Winter 1968) 13–26.

Parsons, Gregory W. "Guidelines for Understanding and Proclaiming the Book of Job." *BSac* 151 (October–December 1994) 393–413.

———. "Job, Theology of." In *Evangelical Dictionary of Biblical Theology*, edited by W. Elwell, 415–19. Grand Rapids: Baker, 1996 ———. "Literary Features of the Book of Job." *BSac* 138 (July–September 1981) 213–22.

———. "The Structure and Purpose of the Book of Job." *BSac* 138 (April–June 1981) 139–57.

Paterson, John. *The Wisdom of Israel: Job and Proverbs*. Bible Guides. Nashville: Abingdon, 1961.

Patrick, James E. "The Fourfold Structure of Job: Variations on a Theme." *VT* 55, no. 2 (April 2005) 185–206.

Patrick, Dale. "Job's Address of God." *ZAW* 91 (1979) 268–82.

Patterson, Richard D. "The Widow, the Orphan, and the Poor in the Old Testament and the Extra-Biblical Literature." *BSac* 130 (July–September 1973) 223–34.

Paul, Shalom M. "Job 4:15—A Hair Raising Encounter." *ZAW* 95, no. 1 (1983) 119–21.

———. "Unrecognized Biblical Legal Idioms in the Light of Comparative Akkadian Expressions." *RB* 86, no. 2 (April 1979) 235–36.

Peake, Arthur S. *Job*. NCB. Edinburgh: T. C. and E. C. Jack, 1904.

———. "Job: The Problem of the Book." In *Theodicy in the Old Testament*, edited by J. Crenshaw. Philadelphia: Fortress, 1983.

———. *The Problem of Suffering in the Old Testament*. London: Epworth, 1904.

Penchansky, David. *The Betrayal of God: Ideological Conflict in Job*. Louisville: Westminster John Knox, 1990.

Perdue, Leo G. *Wisdom and Creation: The Theology of Wisdom Literature*. Nashville: Abingdon, 1994.

———. *Wisdom in Revolt: Metaphorical Theology in the Book of Job*. Sheffield: Almond, 1991.

———. *Wisdom Literature: A Theological History*. Louisville: Westminster John Knox, 2007.

Pfeiffer, Robert H. "The Dual Origin of Hebrew Monotheism." *JBL* 46 (1927) 193–206.

———. "Edomite Wisdom." *ZAW* 44 (1926) 113–25.

Pickett, Raymond. *The Cross in Corinth: The Social Significance of the Death of Jesus*. Sheffield, England: Sheffield Academic Press, 1997.

Pinker, Aron. "Job's Perspectives on Death." *JBQ* 35, no. 2 (April–June 2007) 73–84.

Pixley, J. V. *El libro de Job*. San Jose, CR: Seminario Biblico Latinoamerica, 1982.

Pogoloff, Stephen. *Logos and Sophia: The Rhetorical Situation of 1 Corinthians*. Atlanta: Scholars Press, 1992.

Polzin, Robert, and David Robertson, eds. *Studies in the Book of Job*. Semeia 7. Missoula, MT: Society of Biblical Literature, 1977.

Pope, Marvin H. *Job*. AB. Garden City, NY: Doubleday, 1973.

Porter, Stanley E. "Job: A Practical Commentary." *JETS* 29 (1986) 471–72 ———. "The Message of the Book of Job: Job 42:7b as Key to Interpretation?" *EvQ* 63 (October 1991) 291–304.

Potter, R. "Job." In *A New Catholic Commentary on the Holy Scripture*. Edited by R. Fuller. New York: Thomas Nelson, 1969.

Preuss, Horst D. *Old Testament Theology*. 2 vols. Translated by L. Perdue. Lousiville: Westminster John Knox, 1996.
Priaulx, Carteret. *The Book of Job*. London: Wertheim, Macintosh, and Hunt, 1858.
Pritchard, James B. *Ancient Near Eastern Texts Relating to the Old Testament*. Princeton: Princeton University Press, 1950.
———. *The Ancient Near East*. Vol. 1. Princeton: Princeton University Press, 1958.
Pury, Roland de. *Hiob, Der Mensch Im Aufruhr*. BibS(N) 15. Neukirchen-Vluyn, Germany: Neukirchener Verlag, 1957.
Pyeon, Yohan. *You Have Not Spoken What Is Right about Me: Intertextuality and the Book of Job*. New York: Peter Lang, 2003.
Quell, Gottfried. *Wahre und Falsche Propheten: Beitrage zur Forderung Christlicher Theologie*. Gütersloh, Germany: Bertelsmann, 1952.
Rad, Gerhard von. *Old Testament Theology*. 2 vols. Translated by D. G. M. Stalker. New York: Harper & Row, 1962.
———. *Wisdom in Israel*. Translated by J. Martin. London: SCM Press, 1972.
Rankin, O. S. *Israel's Wisdom Literature: Its Bearing on Theology and History*. Reprint ed. Edinburgh: T. and T. Clark, 1954.
Reddy, Mummadi P. "Book of Job: A Reconstruction." *ZAW* 90, no. 1 (1978) 59–94.
Reichert, Victor E. *Job*. London: The Soncino Press, 1946.
Reichert, Victor E., and A. J. Rosenberg. *Job: Hebrew Text and English Translation with an Introduction and Commentary*, edited by A. Cohen. London: The Soncino Press, 1993.
Reiss, Moshe. "The Fall and Rise of Job the Dissenter." *JBQ* 33, no. 4 (October–December 2005) 257–66.
Reitman, James. *Unlocking Wisdom: Forming Agents of God in the House of Mourning: A Canonical-Linguistic Exposition of the Books of Job and Ecclesiastes*. Springfield, MO: 21st Century, 2008.
Reyburn, William. *A Handbook on the Book of Job*. New York: United Bible Societies, 1992.
Richter, Heinz. *Studien zu Hiob*. Berlin: Evangelische Verlagsanstalt, 1959.
Ridout, Samuel. *The Book of Job*. Neptune, NJ: Loizeaux Brothers, 1919.
Rimbach, James A. "Crushed Before the Moth (Job 4:19)." *JBL* 100 (June 1981) 244–46.
Robertson, David A. *Linguistic Evidence in Dating Early Hebrew Poetry*. Missoula, MT: Society of Biblical Literature, 1972.
Robinson, H. Wheeler. "The Council of Yahweh." *JTS* 45 (1944) 151–57.
———. *The Cross of Job*. London: SCM Press, 1938.
Robinson, T. H. *Job and His Friends*. London: SCM Press, 1954.
Rodd, Cyril S. *The Book of Job*. Narrative Commentaries. Philadelphia: Trinity Press International, 1990.
Rose, Martin. "Yahweh in Israel—Qaus in Edom?" *JSOT* 4 (October 1977) 28–34.
Rowley, H. H. *The Book of Job*. NCB. Grand Rapids: Eerdmans, 1980.
———. "The Book of Job and Its Meaning." *BJRL* 41 (1958) 167–207.
Ruprecht, Eberhard. "Leiden und Gerechtigkeit bei Hiob." *ZTK* 73, no. 4 (1976) 424–45.
Sacks, Robert. *The Book of Job with Commentary: A Translation for Our Time*. Atlanta: Scholars Press, 1999.
Sandelin, Karl-Gustav. *Wisdom as Nourisher: A Study of an Old Testament Theme, Its Development within Early Judaism, and Its Impact on Early Christianity*. Abo: Abo Akademi, 1986.

Sanders, Paul S., ed. *Twentieth-Century Interpretations of the Book of Job*. Englewood Cliffs, NJ: Prentice-Hall, 1968.

Sarna, Nahum M. "The Book of Job: General Introduction." In *The Book of Job*. Philadelphia: Jewish Publication Society of America, 1980.

———. "Notes on the Use of the Definite Article in the Poetry of Job." In *Texts, Temples, and Traditions: A Tribute to Menahem Haran*, edited by M. Fox, V. Hurowitz, A. Hurvitz, et al., 279–84. Winona Lake, IN: Eisenbrauns, 1990.

Sarrazin, B. "Du rire dans la Bible? La théophanie de Job comme parodie." *RSR* 76, no. 1 (January–March 1988) 39–56.

Sasson, Jack M. "Gilgamesh Epic." In *ABD* 2:1024–27.

Sasson, Victor. "An Edomite Joban Text: With a Biblical Joban Parallel." *ZAW* 117, no. 4 (2005) 606–15.

———. "The Literary and Theological Function of Job's Wife in the Book of Job." *Bib* 79, no. 1 (1998) 86–90.

Sauer, J. "Ammon, Moab, and Edom." In *Biblical Archaeology Today*, edited by J. Amitai, 206–14. Jerusalem: Israel Exploration Society, 1985.

Savran, George. "Seeing Is Believing: On the Relative Priority of Visual and Verbal Perception of the Divine." *BibInt* 17 (2009) 320–61.

Schaller, Berndt. "Zur Komposition und Konzeption des Testaments Hiobs." In *Studies on the Testament of Job*, edited by M. Knibb and P. van der Horst, 46–92. Cambridge, England: Cambridge University Press, 1989.

Scheindlin, Raymond P. *The Book of Job*. New York: W. W. Norton, 1998.

Scherer, Paul. "The Book of Job: Exposition." In *The Interpreter's Bible*. 12 vols. Edited by G. Buttrick. New York: Abingdon, 1954.

Scholnick, Sylvia H. "Lawsuit Drama in the Book of Job." PhD diss., Brandeis University, 1976.

———. "Poetry in the Courtroom: Job 38–41." In *Directions in Hebrew Poetry*, edited by E. Follis, 185–204. JSOT Supplement Series 40. Sheffield, England: JSOT Press, 1987.

Schreiner, Susan E. *Where Shall Wisdom Be Found? Calvin's Exegesis of Job from Medieval and Modern Perspectives*. Chicago: University of Chicago Press, 1994.

Schultz, Carl. "Job." In *Evangelical Commentary on the Bible*. Edited by W. Elwell. Grand Rapids: Baker, 1995.

Schunk, M. and P. Guillame. "Job's Intercession: Antidote to Divine Folly." *Bib* 88 (2007) 257–72.

Scott, R. B. Y. *The Way of Wisdom in the Old Testament*. New York: Macmillan, 1971.

Sell, Alan P. F. "The Rise and Reception of Modern Biblical Criticism." *EvQ* 42, no. 3 (July–September 1980) 132–48.

Selms, A. van. *Job: A Practical Commentary*. Translated by J. Vriend. Grand Rapids: Eerdmans, 1985.

Seow, C. L. *Job 1–21: Interpretation and Commentary*. Illuminations. Grand Rapids: Eerdmans, 2013.

Sheehan, Jonathan. "The Poetics and Politics of Theodicy." *Proof* 27, no. 2 (Spring 2007) 211–32.

Shupak, Nili. "Learning Methods in Ancient Israel." *VT* 53, no. 3 (July 2003) 416–26.

Siebald, Manfred. "Job's Comforters." In *A Dictionary of Biblical Tradition in English Literature*. Grand Rapids: Eerdmans, 1992.

———. "Job's Comforters." In *The Book of Job: Why Do the Innocent Suffer?*, edited by L. Boadt. New York: St. Martin's Griffin, 1997.
Simonetti, Manlio, and Marco Conti, eds. *Job*. ACCS. Edited by T. Oden. Downers Grove, IL: InterVarsity, 2006.
Simundson, Daniel J. *The Message of Job: A Theological Commentary*. Augsburg Old Testament Studies. Minneapolis: Augsburg, 1986.
Singer, Richard E. *Job's Encounter*. New York: Bookman, 1963.
Sitaramayya, K. B. *The Marvel and Mystery of Pain: A New Interpretation of the Book of Job*. Bangalore: P. C. C. Publications, 2001.
Skehan, Patrick W. "Job's Final Plea (Job 29–31) and the Lord's Reply (Job 38–41)." *Bib* 45, no. 1 (1964) 51–62.
Smalley, Beryl. *Medieval Exegesis of Wisdom Literature*. Edited by R. Murphy. Atlanta: Scholars, 1986.
Smick, Elmer B. "Another Look at the Mythological Elements in the Book of Job." *WTJ* 40 (Spring 1978) 213–28.
———. "Architectonics, Structured Poems, and Rhetorical Devices in the Book of Job." In *Tribute to Gleason Archer*, edited by W. Kaiser and R. Youngblood, 87–104. Chicago: Moody, 1986.
———. *Job*. Vol. 4 of *The Expositor's Bible Commentary*, edited by F. Gaebelein. Grand Rapids: Zondervan, 1988.
———. "Mythology and the Book of Job." *JETS* 13 (Spring 1970) 101–8.
———. "Semeiological Interpretation of the Book of Job." *WTJ* 48 (Spring 1986) 135–49.
Smith, Gary V. "Job IV 12–21: Is It Eliphaz's Vision?" *VT* 40 (1990) 453–63.
———. "Is There a Place for Job's Wisdom in Old Testament Theology?" *TrinJ* 13 (Spring 1992) 3–20.
Smith, Mark S. "The Divine Family at Ugarit and Israelite Monotheism." In *The Whirlwind: Essays on Job, Hermeneutics, and Theology in Memory of Jane Morse*, edited by S. Cook, C. Patton, and J. Watts. JSOT Supplements 336. London: Sheffield Academic, 2001.
Snaith, Norman H. *The Book of Job: Its Origin and Purpose*. SBT. Second Series 11. London: SCM Press, 1968.
Soden, Wolfram von. *The Ancient Orient: An Introduction to the Study of the Ancient Near East*. Grand Rapids: Eerdmans, 1994.
———. "'Weisheitstexte' in Akkadischer Sprache." In *Weisheitstexte I: Texte aus der Umwelt des Alten Testament*, edited by W. Römer and W. von Soden. Gütersloh, Germany: Gütersloher Verlagshaus, 1982.
Spicer, Tobias. "Remarks on the Vision of Eliphaz." *Methodist Review* 7 (1824): 453–55.
Spittler, Russell P. "The Testament of Job: A History of Research and Interpretation." In *Studies on the Testament of Job*, edited by M. Knibb and P. van der Horst, 7–32. Cambridge, England: Cambridge University Press, 1989.
Stanley, Christopher D. *Arguing with Scripture: The Rhetoric of Quotations in the Letters of Paul*. New York: T&T Clark, 2004.
Stedman, Ray C. *Expository Studies in Job: Behind Suffering*. Waco, TX: Waco Books, 1981.
Steinmann, Andrew E. "The Graded Numerical Sayings in Job." In *Fortunate the Eyes That See: Essays in Honor of David Noel Freedman in Honor of His Seventieth Birthday*, edited by A. Beck, A. Bartlett, P. Raabe, and C. Franke, 288–97. Grand Rapids: Eerdmans, 1995.

———. "The Structure and Message of the Book of Job." *VT* 46, no. 1 (January 1996) 85–100.

Steveson, Pete. "Misconceptions of Job's 'Friends.'" *BV* 21 (November 1987) 9–15.

Stone, Michael E. "Ideal Figures and Social Context: Priest and Sage in the Early Second Temple Age." In *Ancient Israel Religion: Essays in Honor of Frank Moore Cross*, edited by P. Miller, P. Hanson, and S. McBride, 575–86.

Stordalen, T. "Dialogue and Dialogism in the Book of Job." *SJOT* 20, no. 1 (June 2006) 18–37.

Surburg, Raymond F. "The Influence of the Two Delitzsches on Biblical and Near Eastern Studies." *CTQ* 47, no. 3 (July 1983) 225–40.

Sweet, Ronald F. G. "The Sage in Akkadian Literature: A Philological Study." In *The Sage in Israel and the Ancient Near East*, edited by J. Gammie and L. Perdue, 45–65. Winona Lake, IN: Eisenbrauns, 1990.

———. "The Sage in Mesopotamian Palaces and Royal Courts." In *The Sage in Israel and the Ancient Near East*, edited by J. Gammie and L. Perdue, 99–107. Winona Lake, IN: Eisenbrauns, 1990.

Syring, Wolf-Dieter. *Hiob und sein Anwalt: Die Prosatexte des Hiobbuches und ihre Rolle in seiner Redaktions- und Rezeptionsgeschichte*. BZAW 336. Berlin: Walter de Gruyter, 2004.

Tebes, Juan M. "'You Shall Not Abhor an Edomite for He Is Your Brother': The Tradition of Esau and the Edomite Genealogies from an Anthropological Perspective." *JHS* 6 (2006) 2–30.

Terrien, Samuel. "The Book of Job: Introduction and Exegesis." *The Interpreter's Bible*, edited by G. Buttrick. 12 vols. New York: Abingdon, 1954.

———. *Job: Poet of Existence*. Indianapolis: Bobbs-Merrill Company, 1957.

The Babylonian Talmud: Seder Nezikin. Translated by I. Epstein. London: The Socino Press, 1935.

The Book of Tobit: The Text in Aramaic, Hebrew, and Old Latin with English Translations. Edited by A. Neubauer. Reprint of 1878 ed. Eugene, OR: Wipf and Stock, 2005.

The Targum of Job. Translated by C. Mongan. Collegeville, MN: The Liturgical Press, 1991.

Thomas, David. *Book of Job: Expository and Homiletical Commentary*. 1878. Reprint ed; Grand Rapids: Kregel, 1982.

Thomas, Derek. *Calvin's Teaching on Job: Proclaiming the Incomprehensible God*. Rossshire, Scotland: Christian Focus, 2004.

———. *The Storm Breaks: Job Simply Explained*. Welwyn Commentaries. Darlington, England: Evangelical Press, 2003.

Ticciati, Susannah. "Does Job Fear God for Naught?" *Modern Theology* 21, no. 3 (July 2005) 353–66.

———. *Job and the Disruption of Identity: Reading Beyond Barth*. New York: T&T Clark, 2005.

Timmer, Daniel. "God's Speeches, Job's Responses, and the Problem of Coherence in the Book of Job." *CBQ* 71, no. 2 (April 2009) 286–305.

Torrey, Charles C. "The Edomites in Southern Judah." *JBL* 17, no. 1 (1898) 16–20.

Tov, Emanuel. *Textual Criticism of the Hebrew Bible*. 3rd revised and expanded ed. Minneapolis: Fortress, 2012.

Tsevat, Matitiahu. "The Meaning of the Book of Job." *HUCA* 37 (1966) 73–106.

———. *The Meaning of the Book of Job and Other Biblical Studies.* New York: KTAV, 1980.
Tsoi, Jonathan T. P. "The Vision of Eliphaz (Job 4:12–21)—An Irony of Human Life." *Theology and Life* 25 (2002) 155–82.
Tur-Sinai, N. H. *The Book of Job: A New Commentary.* Reprint ed. Jerusalem: Kiryat Sepher, 1967.
Vanderhooft, David S. "The Edomite Dialect and Script: A Review of the Evidence." In *You Shall Not Abhor an Edomite for He Is Your Brother: Edom and Seir in History and Tradition*, edited by D. Edelman, 137–57. Atlanta: Scholars Press, 1995.
Vaux, Roland de. "Téman, ville ou region d'Edom?" *RB* 76, no. 3 (July 1969) 379–85.
Vermeylen, J. *Job, Ses Amis et Son Dieu: La Légende de Job et Ses Relectures Postexiliques.* StudBib 2. Leiden: Brill, 1986.
———. "Le méchant dans les discours des amis de Job." In *The Book of Job*, edited by W. A. M. Beuken, 101–27. Leuven: Leuven University Press, 1994.
Viberg, Åke. "Job." In *NDBT* 200–203.
Vicchio, Stephen J. *Job in the Ancient World, the Image of the Biblical Job: A History.* Vol. 1. Eugene, OR: Wipf and Stock, 2006.
———. *Job in the Medieval World, the Image of the Biblical Job: A History.* Vol. 2. Eugene, OR: Wipf and Stock, 2006.
———. *Job in the Modern World, the Image of the Biblical Job: A History.* Vol. 3. Eugene, OR: Wipf and Stock, 2006.
Vischer, William. "God's Truth and Man's Lie: A Study of the Message of the Book of Job." Translated by D. Miller. *Int* 15, no. 2 (April 1961) 131–46.
Volz, Paul. *Hiob und Weisheit.* 2nd ed. Göttingen: Vandenhoek and Ruprecht, 1921.
Voorst, Bruce van. "Dust and Ashes." *ChrCent*, August 26, 2008.
Vriezen, T. C. "The Edomite Deity Qaus." *OtSt* 14 (1965) 330–53.
Walton, John H. *Ancient Israelite Wisdom in Its Cultural Context: A Survey of Parallels Between Biblical and Ancient Near Eastern Texts.* Grand Rapids: Zondervan, 1989.
———. "Job 1: Book of." In *Dictionary of the Old Testament: Wisdom, Poetry, & Writings*, edited by T. Longman III and P. Enns, 333–46. Downers Grove, IL: InterVarsity, 2008.
Waltke, Bruce K. *An Old Testament Theology: An Exegetical, Canonical, and Thematic Approach.* Grand Rapids: Zondervan, 2007.
Ward, William B. *Out of the Whirlwind: A Study in the Book of Job.* Richmond: John Knox, 1958.
Waters, Larry J. "Elihu's Categories of Suffering from Job 32–37." *BSac* 166 (October–December 2009) 405–20.
———. "Elihu's Theology and His View of Suffering." *BSac* 156 (April–June 1999) 143–59.
———. "Elihu's View of Suffering in Job 32–37." PhD diss., Dallas Theological Seminary, 1998.
———. "Reflections on Suffering from the Book of Job." *BSac* 154 (October–December 1997) 436–51.
Watson, Robert A. *The Book of Job.* The Expositor's Bible. New York: A. C. Armstrong and Son, 1892.
Watson, Wilfred G. E. *Classical Hebrew Poetry: A Guide to Its Techniques.* Sheffield: JSOT Press, 1984.

Watts, James W. "The Unreliable Narrator of Job." In *The Whirlwind: Essays on Job, Hermeneutics, and Theology in Memory of Jane Morse*, edited by S. Cook, C. Patton, and J. Watts, 168-80. JSOT Supplements 336. London: Sheffield Academic, 2001.

Webster, Edwin C. "Strophic Patterns in Job 3-28." *JSOT* 26 (June 1983) 33-60.

Weeks, Stuart. "The Context and Meaning of Proverbs 8:30a." *JBL* 125, no. 3 (2006) 433-42.

Weiser, Artur. *Das Buch Hiob*. Göttingen: Vandenhoek and Ruprecht, 1963.

Westermann, Claus. *Der Aufbau des Buches Hiob*. Calwer theologische Monographien. Stuttgart: Calwer Verlag, 1977.

———. *Basic Forms of Prophetic Speech*. Translated by H. White. Louisville: Westminster John Knox, 1991.

———. "The Two Faces of Job." In *Job and the Silence of God*, edited by C. Duquoc and C. Floristán, 15-22. New York: Seabury, 1983.

Whedbee, William. "The Comedy of Job." *Semeia* 7 (1977): 1-39.

Whitted, Qiana. "In My Flesh I Shall See God: Ritual Violence and Racial Redemption in 'The Black Christ.'" *African American Review* 38, no. 3 (Fall 2004): 379-93.

Whybray, Roger N. *Job*. Sheffield, England: Sheffield Academic Press, 1998.

———. *The Intellectual Tradition in the Old Testament*. Berlin: De Gruyter, 1974.

———. *Two Jewish Theologies: Job and Ecclesiastes*. Hull, England: University of Hull, 1980.

Wilcox, John T. *The Bitterness of Job: A Philosophical Reading*. Ann Arbor, MI: University of Michigan Press, 1994.

Wilde, A. de. *Das Buch Hiob*. Leiden: E. J. Brill, 1981.

Williams, James G. "Comedy, Irony, Intercession: A Few Notes in Response." *Semeia* 7 (1977) 135-45.

———. "Deciphering the Unspoken: The Theophany of Job." *HUCA* 49 (1978) 59-72.

Williams, H. H. Drake. *The Wisdom of the Wise: The Presence and Function of Scripture Within 1 Cor. 1:18—13:23*. Leiden: Brill, 2001.

Williams, Ronald J. "Current Trends in the Book of Job." In *Studies in the Book of Job*, edited by W. Aufrecht, 1-27. Waterloo, ON: Wilfrid Laurier University Press, 1985.

———. *Hebrew Syntax: An Outline*. 2nd ed. Toronto: University of Toronto Press, 1976.

———. "Theodicy in the Ancient Near East." *CJT* 2 (January 1956) 14-26.

Wilson, Gerald H. *Job*. NIBCOT. Peabody, MA: Hendrickson, 2007.

Wilson, Lindsay. "The Book of Job and the Fear of God." *TynBul* 46, no. 1 (1995) 61-79.

———. "Job 38-39 and Biblical Theology." *RTR* 62, no. 3 (2003) 121-38.

———. "Protest and Faith in the Book of Job: An Holistic Reading." ThM thesis, Australian College of Theology, 1991.

———. "Realistic Hope or Imaginative Exploration? The Identity of Job's Arbiter." *Pacifica* 9, no. 3 (October 1996) 243-52.

———. "The Role of the Elihu Speeches in the Book of Job." *RTR* 55, no. 2 (1996) 81-94.

Wilson, Robert R. *Prophecy and Society in Ancient Israel*. Philadelphia: Fortress, 1980.

Wolde, Ellen J. van, ed. *Job's God*. London: SCM Press, 2004.

Wolfers, David. *Deep Things Out of Darkness: The Book of Job, Essays and a New Translation*. Kampen, The Netherlands: Kok Pharos Publishing, 1995.

———. "The Speech Cycles in the Book of Job." *VT* 43, no. 3 (July 1993) 385-402.

Woudstra, Martin H. "Edom and Israel in Ezekiel." *CTJ* 3, no. 1 (April 1968) 21-35.

Yaffe, M. D., ed. *Thomas Aquinas's Literal Exposition on Job*. Atlanta: Scholars Press, 1989.

Yates, Kyle M., Jr. "Understanding the Book of Job." *RevExp* 68, no. 4 (Fall 1971) 443–56.

Young, William W., III. "The Patience of Job: Between Providence and Disaster." *HeyJ* 48, no. 4 (July 2007) 593–613.

Zenger, Erich. "Die späte Weisheit und das Gesetz." In *Literatur und Religion des Frühjudentums*, edited by J. Maier and J. Schreiner. Würzburg, Germany: Gütersloher Verlagshaus Gerd Mohn, 1973.

Zerafa, Peter P. *The Wisdom of God in the Book of Job*. Rome: Herder, 1978.

Ziegler, Joseph. *Iob*. Septuaginta Vetus Testamentum Graecum, Auctoritate Academiae Scientarium Gottingensis. Göttingen: Vandenhoek and Ruprecht, 1982.

Zimmerli, Walther. "The Place and Limit of Wisdom in the Framework of Old Testament Theology." *SJT* 17, no. 2 (June 1964) 146–58.

Zuck, Roy B. *Job*. Everyman's Bible Commentary. Chicago: Moody, 1978.

———. "Job." In *The Bible Knowledge Commentary*. 2 vols. Wheaton, IL: Victor Books, 1985.

———. "A Theology of the Wisdom Books and the Song of Songs." In *A Biblical Theology of the Old Testament*, edited by R. Zuck, 207–56. Chicago: Moody, 1991.

Zuckerman, Bruce. *Job the Silent: A Study in Historical Counterpoint*. New York: Oxford University Press, 1991.

General Index

Abbott, George, 67–68
act-outcome connection, 7, 163, 178, 183, 213
Ahituv, Shmuel, 8, 130
Akkadian, 117, 127, 142, 145, 146, 147, 189, 198
Albertz, Rainer, 9, 16, 137, 140, 141, 142, 143, 188
Albertson, R. G., 9
Albright, William F., 124, 125, 198, 203
Alden, Robert, 185
Alter, Robert, 1
Ammon, Ammonite, 130, 135
Ancient Near East.
 wisdom of, 144–45, 173, 235
 wisdom literature of, 91, 142, 146, 173, 235–36
Andersen, Francis I., 8, 118, 143, 188, 192
angels, 118, 138, 171–72, 188, 189, 191–92
Antiochene interpretation, 44–45
Aquila, 19, 34, 52, 189, 206
Aquinas. *See* Thomas Aquinas.
Arabian peninsula, 18, 120, 123, 126, 127, 128
Arabic, 52, 57, 116–17, 134, 136, 184, 193, 206, 207, 214, 217
Aristeas, 28–29
Assyria, Assyrian, 26–27, 126, 134, 179, 181, 182–83
Atkinson, David, 2

Baal, 198, 203
Babylonia, 55, 122, 126, 128, 142, 146, 149, 159, 162, 173, 179, 181, 235
Babylonian *Theodicy*, 106, 114, 142, 143, 153, 164, 171, 179, 183, 192–93, 214, 215, 216, 217–18, 224, 226–27
Baker, John, 1
Bakon, Shimon, 235–36, 238
Balaam, 116, 125, 188
Balentine, Samuel, 10, 118
Ball, C. J., 3, 92
Barr, James, 4, 10, 141
Baruch, 122
Behemoth, 24, 100
Bildad, 1, 3, 19, 31, 59, 63, 99
Blenkinsopp, Joseph, 8, 123, 159
Blommerde, Anton C., 188, 191
Brenner, Athalya, 5, 103
Brueggemann, Walter, 112, 113
Buccellati, Giorgio, 146, 151, 161, 170
Budde, D. Karl, 7, 74–76, 88, 183, 204
Buttenwieser, Moses, 3, 81, 83–85, 89, 92, 184

Caesar, Lael, 97–100, 137, 157, 180
Calvin, John, 3, 63–66, 88
Carlyle, Thomas, 1
Carter, T. L., 38–39, 41
Cassite period, 126, 128, 153, 173, 235
Ceresko, Anthony, 145, 153–56
Childs, Brevard, 13, 141
Chrysostom, John. *See* John Chrysostom.

Clement of Rome, 42–43, 88
Clements, Ronald, 153
Clines, David J. A., 8, 114, 115, 116, 141, 144, 157, 169, 180, 186, 188, 189, 191, 192, 195, 200, 201, 202, 203, 207, 210, 214, 222
contextual approach, 11–13
Cotter, David, 109–111, 179
Cox, Claude E., 19, 20

Dahood, Mitchell, 188, 194
Davidson, A. B., 3, 78–79, 88
Dearman, J. Andrew, 8, 121, 124, 133, 134
Delitzsch, Franz, 73–74, 181
Dell, Katharine J., 4, 9, 20, 103
Denning-Bolle, Sara, 145, 146, 147, 151, 164, 165, 170
Deuteronomy, 83, 119, 121, 134, 135, 148, 154, 230,
Dhorme, Édouard, 179, 181, 186, 188, 189, 191, 192, 194, 195, 199, 200, 202, 204, 205, 206, 207, 210, 211, 212, 213, 214, 215, 217, 218, 219, 222, 223, 224, 225, 226, 228
Dicou, Bert, 8, 121, 131, 134, 135, 158
DINGIR.ŠA.DIB.BA incantation, 147, 166–67, 168
Driver, Samuel R., 5, 141, 178, 184, 186, 202, 207, 211, 214, 219, 223, 225
Duhm, Bernard, 180, 181, 203, 204, 210, 212, 221, 223, 225, 226, 228

Ebach, Jürgen, 178, 186–87, 197, 209, 210, 211, 212, 213, 214, 218, 220
Ebla, Eblaite, 116, 126, 203
Ecclesiastes. *See* Qohelet.
Edelman, Diana V., 8, 120, 144
Edom.
   commerce of, 127–28, 144
   inscriptions, 8, 123, 129–30, 136
   monarchy of, 144
   religion of, 133–40
   wisdom of, 8, 128–29, 131, 208
Elihu, 31, 32, 62, 82, 129, 173, 190, 218, 222, 235–39
Eliphaz.
   anger of, 32, 84

   bluntness of, 3, 82
   coldness of, 74, 78, 80, 84
   comic figure, as, 103–4, 112
   covenant with stones of field, 202, 204–5
   criteria for evaluating, 15–16
   Deuteronomic theology, and, 9, 83, 92, 93, 134, 135, 161
   disputation speech, 208
   divine appeasement, 7, 14, 118, 160, 176, 180, 208, 220
   divine council, 211–12
   Edomite provenance of, 8, 80, 115, 118–24, 140, 143, 144, 158, 163, 208
   effective counsel of, 6, 7, 114
   elder of city/village, 157–58, 232
   eloquence of, 3, 23, 32, 41, 43, 46, 48, 50, 56, 71, 72, 78, 79, 87, 95, 96, 107, 114, 163, 177, 183, 197, 199
   enumerated list, 199–202
   evil eye, 214
   fictitious character, as, 58, 72
   first speech, 175–208
   flat or wooden characterization, 5, 78, 84, 232
   genealogy of, 115–16
   Gentile, as, 49, 158–59
   grief counselor, as, 114
   ineffective counsel of, 10
   interpretative ambiguity of, 1–4
   Hurrian provenance of, 116
   incantations, use of, 168–69
   kindness of, 6, 31, 32, 64, 72, 78, 82, 87. 94, 113
   king of the Temanites, 3, 19, 25, 29, 30–31, 49, 52, 53, 69, 116
   lacunae in previous scholarship on, 8
   Mesopotamian wisdom, and, 9, 144–45, 159, 160–73, 227
   name, meaning of, 115–19
   oldest friend, 2, 68, 73, 74, 77, 78
   pastoral wisdom of, 6–7, 9, 157
   Paul's citation of, 35–42, 55
   primary interlocutor, ix, 2, 7, 9, 10, 16, 21, 48, 72, 88, 118, 180, 232

primordial man, 210–11
Rabbinic interpretation of, 49–51
rebuke by Yahweh, 3, 16–17, 33, 35, 40–41, 42, 49, 55, 59, 62, 66, 68, 73, 80, 81, 83, 85, 227–31
reception history of, 8, 15–89
rehabilitation in interpretative history, 4, 5, 106
remedial suffering, 16, 82
retributive doctrine, 16, 47, 59, 65, 67, 72, 79, 87. 93, 112, 138, 139, 163–64, 176–84, 198, 232
revelatory experience, 16, 70, 72. 95, 98–99, 137–38, 172–73, 184–95, 213
ritual purgation, 16, 215, 224, 230, 231, 232
Satan, as exploiting, 3, 50, 51, 70, 100–102, 112
second speech, 208–220
sin list, 16, 224
Temanite, 8, 115, 119–23, 144, 158, 227
theological sophistication of, 5, 7, 24, 79, 95, 96, 111, 177, 180, 232
third speech, 220–27
tone of, 15, 26, 29, 32, 44, 46, 49, 51, 53, 56, 59, 63, 66, 68, 71, 72, 73, 74, 76, 77, 78, 79, 80, 81, 85, 88, 94, 98, 100, 102, 105, 109, 177, 180, 213
traditional wisdom theology of, 2, 83, 102, 104, 219
transcendence of God, 226–27
villainous characterization of, 2–3, 4, 88. 92
Emerton, John A., 8, 120, 121
Erra, 162, 182
Eršahunga prayer, 147, 167, 168
Eusebius of Caesarea, 19, 28, 29
Ewald, Heinrich, 71–73, 89, 92
exodus (from Egypt), 37, 121, 124, 239
Exodus (book of), 83, 116, 117, 119, 129, 137, 148, 185, 188, 198, 223

Fohrer, Georg, 2, 141, 176, 178, 205, 214
Fullerton, Kemper, 3, 15, 16, 82, 85–88, 100, 112
Fyall, Robert, 3, 24, 100–102

Gard, Donald H., 3, 4, 9, 20
Genesis, 18, 19, 37, 48, 50, 115–16, 118, 119, 120, 121, 123, 124, 132, 137, 178, 185, 186–87, 198, 210, 211, 222, 228, 230, 239
Gentry, Peter J., 19, 20, 21
Gerleman, Gillis, 3
Gerstenberger, Erhard, 151
Gibson, John C. L., 1, 2, 94–97
Gilgamesh Epic, 128
Glueck, Nelson, 120, 124, 126, 131
Good, E. M., 1, 4, 141
Gordis, Robert, 2, 9, 23, 143, 158, 178, 185, 186, 188, 189, 191, 192, 193, 194, 195, 200, 204, 205, 210, 211, 212–13, 214, 216, 217, 219, 220, 222, 223, 228
Grabbe, Lester, 145, 170
graded numerical sayings, 199–200
Gradl, Felix, 183, 213
Gray, George B, 5, 141, 178, 184, 186, 202, 207, 211, 214, 219, 223, 225
Gray, John, 9, 19
Green, William Henry, 76–77, 89
Gregory the Great, 53–56, 60, 63, 88, 89, 116
Gruber, Mayer, 158–59

Habel, Norman C., 16, 92, 141, 179, 180, 191, 192, 193, 195, 197, 198, 200, 202–3, 205, 207, 208, 210, 212, 213, 216, 218, 222, 224
Hallo, William, 11–12
Harding, James E., 2, 4, 109, 137–38
Harrison, Roland, 124
Hartley, John, 141, 143, 146, 176, 180, 182, 183, 189, 191, 195, 197, 198, 199, 200, 201, 202, 205, 206, 207, 210, 212, 214, 216, 217, 219, 221, 226
Heater, Homer, 18, 20, 23
Hoffman, Yair, 4, 109, 141

Horst, Friedrich, 8, 118, 180, 182, 197, 199, 206, 207, 208, 214, 219
Horvat Uzza, 130, 136
Hutcheon, Linda, 38, 39, 42

Isaiah (book of), 23, 101, 106, 119, 134, 137, 148, 158, 184, 194, 195, 205, 206, 213, 226
Israel.
   prophets of, 49, 158
   religion of, 121, 129, 134–35
   rivalry with Edom, 127–28, 131
   wisdom tradition of, 1, 91, 148–56
Jastrow, Morris, 3, 9, 81, 82–83, 88
Jerome, 19, 38, 44, 51–53, 89, 206
Job, book of.
   ANE parallels, 9
   author of, 4, 6, 10, 78, 80, 85, 86, 94, 97, 99, 100, 104, 105, 109–110, 112, 114, 141, 143, 159–60, 173, 187, 200, 235–39
   Hebrew of, 19
   Jewish provenance of, 158–60
   LXX version of, 17–26, 27, 34, 52
   social setting of, 140–43
Job, character of.
   intercession for friends, 32
   Jobab, as, 18–19, 29, 30, 118
   king of Edom, 30
   piety of, 178
   resistance to Eliphaz's counsel, 7
   righteousness of, 27, 42, 61
   sin of, 217
   wife of, 27, 29, 30, 31, 32, 45, 54, 230
   wisdom of, 157–58, 212
Jobes, Karen, and Moises Silva, 17
John Chrysostom, 2, 21, 44–49, 88

Kassite. *See* Cassite period.
Keret. *See* Kirta epic.
King's Highway, 126, 127, 144
Kirta epic, 203, 224
Kitchen, Kenneth A., 11, 12
Köhlmoos, Melanie, 2
Kos. *See* Qos.
Kottsieper, Ingo, 228
Kuntillet 'Ajrud, 121, 130, 135
Kutz, Karl V., 17, 19, 26

Lambert, Wilfrid, 145, 146, 149, 153, 162, 166, 168, 183
Latin Vulgate, 26, 28, 51–53, 55, 60, 69, 224, 225, 229
León, Luis de, 68–71
Leviathan, 24, 100–101
lion, 182–84
Lipšur litanies, 147, 167
Louw, Johannes, 17, 22
Ludlul bēl nēmeqi, 146–47, 153, 170, 171, 172, 173, 217
Lust, Johann, 55, 189

Macintosh, A. A., 116–17
Maimonides, 17, 56–59, 61, 88, 113, 235, 239
Marshall, J. T., 80–81
Marduk, 9, 145, 146, 170–71
Mattingly, Gerald, 9, 11, 105
McCabe, Robert V., 237–39
McKane, William, 152
Mesopotamia.
   commerce of, 126–27
   divination rituals of, 169–72
   incantations of, 128, 164–68, 227
   retributive doctrine of, 161–63
   scribal culture of, 147
   wisdom of, 9, 145–47, 149, 150, 159, 160–73
   wisdom literature of, 144, 146, 153
Methodius, 44, 89
Michel, Walter, 116, 185, 186, 188, 191, 192, 194
Moab, Moabite, 19, 124, 130, 135, 137
Moor, Johannes C. de, 141, 143, 153
Moralia in Iob, 53–54, 116
Moses, 14, 51, 83, 113, 116, 119, 121, 129, 154, 224
Moses Maimonides. *See* Maimonides.
Newsom, Carol, 5, 105–9, 140, 141, 159, 180
Numbers (book of), 34, 116, 119, 124, 126, 137, 144, 154, 188, 190, 198

Oeming, Manfred, 5–6, 228
Origen, 19, 44, 52
Orlinsky, Harry M., 3, 18, 19, 20
Qohelet, 10, 76, 98, 142, 144, 149, 150, 156, 188

Qos, 130, 133, 134, 135, 136–37

Paul, apostle, 4, 21, 33–42, 43, 55, 88, 105
Peake, Arthur S., 2, 79–80, 88, 94, 225
Perdue, Leo, 90–94, 142, 161
Pfeiffer, Robert, 129, 130, 131–33, 138, 141
Phoenicia, Phoenician, 130, 188
Pope, Marvin, 94, 118, 189, 192, 194, 195, 205, 214
Preuss, Horst D., 185
Proverbs, 49, 76, 83, 113, 129, 130, 132, 142, 149, 151–52, 153, 184, 197, 198, 210
Psalms, 34, 35, 48, 49, 74, 110, 117, 129, 132, 144, 148, 179, 183, 184, 191, 197, 198, 210, 211, 220, 230
Pyeon, Yohan, 9, 105, 141

Rad, Gerhard von, 91, 148, 150
Rahab, 101
Ramses II, 124, 134
Ramses III, 125
Resheph, 24, 50, 100, 203
Reyburn, William, 184, 190, 191, 193
Rowley, H. H., 14, 185, 188, 191, 194
Rubio, Gonzalo, 126–27

Sandmel, Samuel, 9, 11
Sasson, Jack M., 128
Sasson, Victor, 8, 130, 131, 136
Satan, 3, 29, 31, 50, 51, 55, 76, 100, 101, 102, 112
Seir, Mount, 120, 121, 125, 134, 135, 158
Selms, A. van, 7, 8, 105, 118
Septuagint (LXX) Job.
  additions to Masoretic text, 18
  eloquence of Eliphaz in, 23, 25
  literary qualities, 25
  paraphrastic translation, 19
  shorter length than Masoretic text, 3, 18, 19
  softening of Eliphaz's tone, 3, 21–22, 43
  theological shaping in translation, 23–25
  translation technique, 17, 18, 20, 25, 26
Schaff, Philip, 44, 45, 53, 54
Shaddai, 22, 25, 198, 223
Shamash, 114, 162
Sirach, 34, 38, 151, 179, 186, 190, 200, 212
Smith, Gary V., 10, 99
Sorlin, Henri, 44–45, 46, 47
Stanley, Christopher D., 35, 36–38, 39, 40
Steinmann, Andrew E., 16, 200–202, 204
Šurpu incantation, 147, 164, 165
Symmachus, 19, 34, 52, 189
Syriac, 19, 42, 52, 214, 224, 225, 226

Tanis, 124–25
Tannin, 101
Targum, 188, 191, 194, 204, 207, 213, 224, 225
Theodotion, 18, 19, 34, 52, 119
Thomas Aquinas, 60–63, 179
Teman, 8, 19, 115, 119–23, 135, 144, 157
Terrien, Samuel, 6, 8, 115, 133, 178
Testament of Job, 29–33, 40, 88, 113
theodicy, 4, 5, 7, 9, 13, 104, 143, 173, 231, 232, 235
Timmer, Daniel C., 228–30
Tobit, book of, 26–28
Tobit, character of, 27
Toorn, Karel van der, 142, 145, 160, 161, 163, 169
Tur-Sinai, N. H., 200, 214

Ugarit, Ugaritic, 24, 117, 141, 143, 153, 159, 184, 188, 198, 203, 224
Uz, 8, 115

Vanderhooft, David S., 8
Vicchio, Stephen J., 3, 19, 23, 24, 26, 28, 51, 52
Vulgate. *See* Latin Vulgate.

Walton, John, 9, 11, 12–13, 127, 159–60, 161, 239
Weeks, Stuart, 152

Weinberg, J., 1, 236, 238
Westermann, Claus, 150, 152, 188
Whedbee, William, 103–5
Whybray, R. Norman, 140, 141, 142, 143, 148, 149, 150, 151, 156, 157, 158, 190, 192, 194
Williams, Ronald J., 189, 190, 191, 193
Wolfers, David, 190

Yam, 101, 203

Zalcman, Lawrence, 136–37
Zophar, 1, 3, 59, 63, 128
Zuckerman, Bruce, 5, 103, 104

www.ingramcontent.com/pod-product-compliance
Lightning Source LLC
Chambersburg PA
CBHW071242230426
43668CB00011B/1548